THE HEALTH CARE SYSTEM

WHO BENEFITS?

ISSN 1543-2556

THE HEALTH CARE SYSTEM

WHO BENEFITS?

Barbara Wexler

INFORMATION PLUS® REFERENCE SERIES
Formerly published by Information Plus, Wylie, Texas

GALE®

THOMSON
™
GALE

Detroit • New York • San Diego • San Francisco • Cleveland • New Haven, Conn. • Waterville, Maine • London • Munich

The Health Care System: Who Benefits?

Barbara Wexler

Project Editors
Kathleen J. Edgar and Ellice Engdahl

Editorial
Paula Cutcher-Jackson, Debra Kirby, Prindle
LaBarge, Elizabeth Manar, Charles B. Montney,
Heather Price

Permissions
Shalice Shah-Caldwell

Product Design
Cynthia Baldwin

Composition and Electronic Prepress
Evi Seoud

Manufacturing
Keith Helmling

LIBRARY OF CONGRESS CATALOGING-IN-PUBLICATION DATA

ISBN 0-7876-5103-6 (set)
ISBN 0-7876-6616-5
ISSN 1543-2556

TABLE OF CONTENTS

The health of the nation depends on access to and availability of health care. This chapter describes the components of the health care system in the United States and the characteristics of both people who receive regular medical care and those who do not have access to it.

Modern health care treatment requires that its practitioners have a great deal of training and skill. This chapter examines the training, working conditions, and earnings of health care practitioners, along with physician-patient communication.

Many different types of health care institutions exist in the United States, including hospitals, hospices, nursing homes, home health care, and mental health facilities; each is profiled here. Among the issues discussed are the plight of public hospitals and the rapid rise of home health care agencies.

There are a variety of measures of health care quality; and the professional, government, and voluntary organizations and agencies charged with evaluating quality are described in this chapter. Included are examples and descriptions of the fraud, abuse, and mistakes that compromise quality care. Also considered are efforts to standardize and regulate the quality of medical care, including medical practice guidelines, professional licensure, institutional accreditation, and peer review.

Americans are spending an increasing amount of money on health care, with the money coming from both private and public funds. This chapter explores the types of services that Americans pay for, the rea-sons for cost increases, and what can be done about controlling sky-rocketing costs. Programs such as Medicare, Medicaid, and long-term health care are also discussed.

Many factors affect the availability of health insurance, including employment, income, and age. Sources of health insurance—for those who can afford it or are eligible to receive it—are private insurance, Medicare, and Medicaid. Although many Americans, including millions of children, are uninsured, government programs and legislation have been designed to reverse this strain on American society.

This chapter begins with a comparison of expenditures for health care. It contains a comparison of key health care quality indicators and concludes with overviews of the health care systems in the United States, Germany, Canada, United Kingdom, France, and Japan.

The delivery of health care services has changed dramatically since the 1950s. The Internet and advancing technology have produced new methods of health care delivery such as telemedicine and online pharmaceutical services. This chapter describes challenges faced by the U.S. health care system, recent innovations, and efforts to improve quality in health service delivery.

Consumer satisfaction or dissatisfaction with health care has an impact on utilization, reimbursement, and even health outcomes—how well patients fare after treatment. This chapter looks at how consumers assess quality and the evaluative measures that providers and payers use to monitor consumer satisfaction with care and treatment.

PREFACE

The Health Care System: Who Benefits? is one of the latest volumes in the Information Plus Reference Series. Previously published by the Information Plus company of Wylie, Texas, the Information Plus Reference Series (and its companion set, the Information Plus Compact Series) became a Gale Group product when Gale and Information Plus merged in early 2000. Those of you familiar with the series as published by Information Plus will notice a few changes. Gale has adopted a new layout and style that we hope you will find easy to use. Other improvements include greatly expanded indexes in each book, and more descriptive tables of contents.

While some changes have been made to the design, the purpose of the Information Plus Reference Series remains the same. Each volume of the series presents the latest facts on a topic of pressing concern in modern American life. These topics include today's most controversial and most studied social issues: abortion, capital punishment, care for the elderly, crime, health care, the environment, immigration, minorities, social welfare, women, youth, and many more. Although written especially for the high school and undergraduate student, this series is an excellent resource for anyone in need of factual information on current affairs.

By presenting the facts, it is Gale's intention to provide its readers with everything they need to reach an informed opinion on current issues. To that end, there is a particular emphasis in this series on the presentation of scientific studies, surveys, and statistics. These data are generally presented in the form of tables, charts, and other graphics placed within the text of each book. Every graphic is directly referred to and carefully explained in the text. The source of each graphic is presented within the graphic itself. The data used in these graphics are drawn from the most reputable and reliable sources, in particular from the various branches of the U.S. government and from major independent polling organizations. Every effort has been made to secure the most recent information available. The reader should bear in mind that many major studies take years to conduct, and that additional years often pass before the data from these studies are made available to the public. Therefore, in many cases the most recent information available in 2003 dated from 2000 or 2001. Older statistics are sometimes presented as well, if they are of particular interest and no more recent information exists.

Although statistics are a major focus of the Information Plus Reference Series, they are by no means its only content. Each book also presents the widely held positions and important ideas that shape how the book's subject is discussed in the United States. These positions are explained in detail and, where possible, in the words of their proponents. Some of the other material to be found in these books includes: historical background; descriptions of major events related to the subject; relevant laws and court cases; and examples of how these issues play out in American life. Some books also feature primary documents, or have pro and con debate sections giving the words and opinions of prominent Americans on both sides of a controversial topic. All material is presented in an even-handed and unbiased manner; the reader will never be encouraged to accept one view of an issue over another.

HOW TO USE THIS BOOK

The U.S. health care system is a multi-faceted establishment consisting of health care providers, patients, and treatment facilities, just to name a few components. This book examines the state of the nation's health care system, the education and training of health care providers, and the various types of health care institutions. The ever-increasing cost of health care, prevalence of insurance, and a comparison of health care throughout the world are also covered.

The Health Care System: Who Benefits? consists of nine chapters and three appendices. Each of the chapters is devoted to a particular aspect of the health care system in the United States. For a summary of the information covered in each chapter, please see the synopses provided in the Table of Contents at the front of the book. Chapters generally begin with an overview of the basic facts and background information on the chapter's topic, then proceed to examine sub-topics of particular interest. For example, Chapter 3: Health Care Institutions begins with a brief history of hospitals in the United States and describes the different types of hospitals and the patients they serve. Explored next are other health care facilities commonly utilized, including surgical centers and urgent care facilities; long-term care facilities such as nursing homes; mental health facilities; home health care; and hospice. The chapter concludes with a discussion of managed care organizations, highlighting health maintenance organizations (HMOs) and preferred provider organizations (PPOs). Readers can find their way through a chapter by looking for the section and sub-section headings, which are clearly set off from the text. Or, they can refer to the book's extensive index if they already know what they are looking for.

Statistical Information

The tables and figures featured throughout *The Health Care System: Who Benefits?* will be of particular use to the reader in learning about this issue. These tables and figures represent an extensive collection of the most recent and important statistics on the health care system, as well as related issues—for example, graphics in the book cover the rate of home health care usage; number of emergency department visits; national health expenditure amounts; percent of people without health insurance; and public opinion on the state of the health care system. Gale believes that making this information available to the reader is the most important way in which we fulfill the goal of this book: to help readers understand the issues and controversies surrounding the health care system in the United States and reach their own conclusions.

Each table or figure has a unique identifier appearing above it, for ease of identification and reference. Titles for the tables and figures explain their purpose. At the end of each table or figure, the original source of the data is provided.

In order to help readers understand these often complicated statistics, all tables and figures are explained in the text. References in the text direct the reader to the relevant statistics. Furthermore, the contents of all tables and figures are fully indexed. Please see the opening section of the index at the back of this volume for a description of how to find tables and figures within it.

Appendices

In addition to the main body text and images, *The Health Care System: Who Benefits?* has three appendices. The first is the Important Names and Addresses directory. Here the reader will find contact information for a number of government and private organizations that can provide further information on aspects of the health care system. The second appendix is the Resources section, which can also assist the reader in conducting his or her own research. In this section, the author and editors of *The Health Care System: Who Benefits?* describe some of the sources that were most useful during the compilation of this book. The final appendix is the index. It has been greatly expanded from previous editions, and should make it even easier to find specific topics in this book.

ADVISORY BOARD CONTRIBUTIONS

The staff of Information Plus would like to extend their heartfelt appreciation to the Information Plus Advisory Board. This dedicated group of media professionals provides feedback on the series on an ongoing basis. Their comments allow the editorial staff who work on the project to make the series better and more user-friendly. Our top priorities are to produce the highest-quality and most useful books possible, and the Advisory Board's contributions to this process are invaluable.

The members of the Information Plus Advisory Board are:

• Kathleen R. Bonn, Librarian, Newbury Park High School, Newbury Park, California

• Madelyn Garner, Librarian, San Jacinto College— North Campus, Houston, Texas

• Anne Oxenrider, Media Specialist, Dundee High School, Dundee, Michigan

• Charles R. Rodgers, Director of Libraries, Pasco-Hernando Community College, Dade City, Florida

• James N. Zitzelsberger, Library Media Department Chairman, Oshkosh West High School, Oshkosh, Wisconsin

COMMENTS AND SUGGESTIONS

The editors of the Information Plus Reference Series welcome your feedback on *The Health Care System: Who Benefits?* Please direct all correspondence to:

Editors
Information Plus Reference Series
27500 Drake Rd.
Farmington Hills, MI 48331-3535

ACKNOWLEDGMENTS

The editors wish to thank the copyright holders of material included in this volume and the permissions managers of many book and magazine publishing companies for assisting us in securing reproduction rights. We are also grateful to the staffs of the Detroit Public Library, the Library of Congress, the University of Detroit Mercy Library, Wayne State University Purdy/Kresge Library Complex, and the University of Michigan Libraries for making their resources available to us.

Following is a list of the copyright holders who have granted us permission to reproduce material in The Health Care System: Who Benefits? *Every effort has been made to trace copyright, but if omissions have been made, please let us know.*

For more detailed source citations, please see the sources listed under each individual table and figure.

Agency for Healthcare Research and Quality: Figure 4.1, Figure 4.2

Centers for Disease Control and Prevention: Figure 1.1, Figure 1.2, Figure 1.3, Figure 1.4, Figure 1.5, Figure 1.6, Figure 1.7, Table 1.1, Table 1.2, Table 1.3, Table 1.4, Table 1.5, Table 1.6, Table 2.1, Table 2.2, Table 2.3, Table 2.4, Table 2.5, Table 2.6, Table 2.7, Table 2.9, Table 2.10, Figure 3.2, Table 3.1, Table 3.2, Table 3.3, Table 3.4, Table 3.5, Table 3.6, Table 3.7, Table 3.8, Table 3.9, Table 3.10, Table 3.11, Table 3.12, Table 3.14, Figure 4.4, Table 5.1, Table 5.3, Table 5.8, Table 5.9, Table 5.10, Table 6.3, Table 6.4, Table 6.5, Table 6.6, Table 8.1

Centers for Medicare & Medicaid Services: Figure 5.1, Figure 5.2, Table 5.2, Table 5.4, Table 5.5, Table 5.6, Table 5.7

Families USA Foundation. Reproduced by permission.: Table 5.11

Harris Interactive. Reproduced by permission.: Table 9.1, Table 9.2, Table 9.7, Table 9.8

Henry J. Kaiser Family Foundation. Reproduced by permission.: Figure 8.1, Figure 8.2, Figure 8.3, Figure 9.6, Figure 9.7, Figure 9.8, Table 9.3, Table 9.4, Table 9.9

Henry J. Kaiser Family Foundation, Commonwealth Fund, and Tufts New England Medical Center. Reproduced by permission.: Figure 5.3, Figure 5.4, Figure 5.5

Henry J. Kaiser Family Foundation and Health Research and Education Trust. Reproduced by permission.: Figure 9.5

National Public Radio/Henry J. Kaiser Family Foundation/Kennedy School of Government. Reproduced by permission.: Figure 9.1, Figure 9.2, Figure 9.3, Figure 9.4, Table 9.5, Table 9.6

Oregon Basic Health Services Program: Figure 5.6

Organisation for Economic Co-operation and Development (OECD). Reproduced by permission.: Table 7.1, Table 7.2, Table 7.3, Table 7.4, Table 7.5, Table 7.6, Table 7.8, Table 7.9, Table 7.10, Table 7.11, Table 7.12, Table 7.13

U.S. Census Bureau: Figure 1.8, Figure 6.1, Figure 6.2, Figure 6.3, Figure 6.4, Figure 6.5, Table 6.1, Table 6.2

U.S. Department of Commerce: Table 2.8

U.S. Department of Health and Human Services: Figure 4.3, Figure 4.5, Figure 4.6, Table 4.1

U.S. General Accounting Office: Figure 3.1, Table 3.13

CHAPTER 1
THE NATION'S HEALTH CARE SYSTEM

When asked to describe the U.S. health care system, most Americans would probably offer a description of just a single facet of a huge, complex interaction of people, institutions, and technology. Like snapshots, each account offers an image, frozen in time, of one of the many health care providers and the settings in which medical care is delivered. Examples of these are:

• Physician offices: For many Americans health care may be described as the interaction between a primary care physician and patient to address minor and urgent medical problems such as colds, flu, or back pain. A primary care physician (usually a general practitioner, family practitioner, internist, or pediatrician) is the "frontline" caregiver—the first practitioner to evaluate and treat the patient. Routine physical examinations, prevention such as immunization and health screening to detect disease, and treatment of acute and chronic diseases commonly take place in physicians' offices.

• Medical clinics: These settings provide primary care services comparable to those provided in physicians' offices and may be organized to deliver specialized support such as prenatal care for expectant mothers, well-baby care for infants, or treatment for specific medical conditions such as hypertension (high blood pressure), diabetes, or asthma.

• Hospitals: These institutions contain laboratories, imaging centers (also known as radiology departments where x-rays and other imaging studies are performed) and other equipment for diagnosis and treatment as well as emergency departments, operating rooms, and highly trained personnel.

Medical care is provided through many other avenues, including outpatient surgical centers, school health programs, pharmacies, worksite clinics, and voluntary health agencies such as Planned Parenthood, the American Red Cross, and the American Lung Association.

IS THE U.S. HEALTH CARE SYSTEM AILING?

While medical care in the United States is often considered the best available, some observers feel the system that delivers it is fragmented and in complete disarray. Dr. John Geyman, a retired physician and professor emeritus at the University of Washington in Seattle believes that U.S. health care does not compare favorably with services provided in other industrialized Western nations. In *Health Care in America: Can Our Ailing System Be Healed?* (Butterworth-Heinemann, Boston, Massachusetts, 2002), Dr. Geyman contends that escalating costs and wide variations in access and quality are symptoms of our diseased health care delivery system.

Dr. Geyman cited the nearly 43 million uninsured Americans (15 percent of the total 288 million people estimated by the U.S. Census Bureau to be living in the United States in 2002) and the fact that the United States has the highest health care expenditures of any of the world's other 28 industrialized countries as indicators of serious systemic problems. He noted that for 11 key indicators of health care quality (including measures of life expectancy at different ages) the United States earned 10th place or lower when ranked among 13 industrialized nations. Dr. Geyman also observed that among comparable Western industrialized countries, the U.S. population is the only one without universal health insurance.

Dr. Geyman contends that the traditional approaches to solving health care delivery problems have been ineffective because they are incremental—shortsighted and piecemeal—rather than broad changes intended to provide optimal health care services to the greatest number of people. Global reform of health care financing is one solution Dr. Geyman offers to improve the present health care system. He advocates a single-payer system for universal coverage and federal government intervention to improve access, affordability, and quality of health care services.

THE COMPONENTS OF THE HEALTH CARE SYSTEM

The health care system consists of all personal medical care services—prevention, diagnosis, treatment, and rehabilitation (services to restore function and independence)—plus the institutions and personnel that provide these services and the government, public, and private organizations and agencies that finance service delivery.

The health care system may be viewed as a complex made up of three interrelated components: people in need of health care services, called health care consumers; people who deliver health care services—the professionals and practitioners called health care providers; and the systematic arrangements for delivering health care—the public and private agencies that organize, plan, regulate, finance, and coordinate services—called the institutions or organizations of the health care system. The institutional component includes hospitals, clinics, and home health agencies, as well as the insurance companies and programs that pay for services like Blue Cross, Blue Shield, managed care plans such as health maintenance organizations (HMOs), and entitlement programs like Medicare and Medicaid (federal and state government public assistance programs). Other institutions are the professional schools that train students for careers in medical, public health, dental, and allied health professions, such as nursing. Also included are agencies and associations that research and monitor the quality of health care services; license and accreditation providers and institutions; local, state, and national professional societies; and the companies that produce medical technology, equipment, and pharmaceuticals.

Much of the interaction among the three components of the health care system occurs directly between individual health care consumers and providers. Other interactions are indirect and impersonal such as immunization programs or screening to detect disease, performed by public health agencies for whole populations. All health care delivery does, however, depend on interactions among all three components. The ability to benefit from health care depends on an individual's or group's ability to gain entry to the health care system. The process of gaining entry to the health care system is referred to as access, and many factors can affect access to health care. This chapter provides an overview of how Americans access the health care system.

ACCESS TO THE HEALTH CARE SYSTEM

Today, access to health care services is a key measure of the overall health and prosperity of a nation or a population, but access and availability were not always linked to health status. In fact many medical historians assert that until the beginning of the twentieth century, a visit with a physician was as likely to be harmful as it was to be help-ful. It is only relatively recently—during the past 100 years—that medical care has been considered to have a positive influence on health and longevity.

There are three aspects of accessibility: consumer access, comprehensive availability of services, and supply of services adequate to meet community demand. Quality health care services must be accessible to health care consumers when and where they are needed. The health care provider must have access to a full range of facilities, equipment, drugs, and services provided by other practitioners. The institutional component of health care delivery—the hospitals, clinics, and payers—must have access to information to enable them to plan an adequate supply of appropriate services for their communities.

Consumer Access to Care

Access to health care services is influenced by a variety of factors. Characteristics of health care consumers strongly affect when, where, and how they access services. Differences in age, educational level achieved, economic status, race, ethnicity, cultural heritage, and geographic location determine when consumers seek health care services, where they go to receive them, their expectations of care and treatment, and the extent to which they wish to participate in decisions about their own medical care.

People have different reasons for seeking access to health care services. Their personal beliefs about health and illness, motivations to obtain care, expectations of the care they will receive, and knowledge about how and where to receive care vary. For an individual to have access to quality care, there must be appropriately defined points of entry into the health care system. For many consumers a primary care physician is the portal to the health care system. In addition to evaluating the patient's presenting problem (health care need), the primary care physician also directs the consumer to other providers of care such as physician specialists or mental health professionals.

Some consumers access the health care system by seeking care from a clinic or hospital outpatient department where teams of health professionals are available at one location. Others gain entry via a public health nurse, school nurse, social worker, pharmacist, or member of the clergy who can refer them to an appropriate source, site, or health care practitioner.

Comprehensive Availability of Health Care Services

Historically, the physician was the exclusive provider of all medical services. Until the twentieth century, the family doctor served as physician, surgeon, pharmacist, therapist, advisor, and dentist. He carried all of the tools of his trade in a small bag and could easily offer state-of-the-art medical care in his patient's home, since hospitals had little more to offer in the way of equipment or facilities. Today it is neither practical nor desirable to ask one practitioner to serve in all of these roles. It would be impossible for one professional to perform the full range of health care services, from primary prevention of disease and diagnosis to treatment and rehabilitation. Modern physicians and other health care practitioners must have access to a comprehensive array of trained personnel, facilities, and equipment so that they can, in turn, make them accessible to their patients.

While many medical problems are effectively treated in a single office visit with a physician, even simple diagnosis and treatment relies on a variety of ancillary (supplementary) services and personnel. To make the diagnosis, the physician may order an imaging study such as an x-ray that is performed by a radiology technician and interpreted by a radiologist (physician specialist in imaging techniques). Laboratory tests may be performed by technicians and analyzed by pathologists (physicians who specialize in microscopic analysis and diagnosis). More complicated medical problems involve teams of surgeons and high-tech surgical suites equipped with robotic assistants, and rehabilitation programs where highly trained physical and occupational therapists skillfully assist patients to regain function and independence.

Some health care services are more effectively, efficiently, and economically provided to groups rather than individuals. Immunization to prevent communicable diseases and screening to detect diseases in their earliest and most treatable stages are examples of preventive services best performed as cooperative efforts of voluntary health organizations, medical and other professional societies, hospitals, and public health departments.

Access Requires Enough Health Care Services to Meet Community Needs

For all members of a community to have access to the full range of health care services, careful planning is required to ensure both the adequate supply and distribution of needed services. To evaluate community needs and effectively allocate health care resources, communities must gather demographic data and information about social and economic characteristics of the population. They also must monitor the spread of disease and the frequency of specific medical conditions over time. All these population data must be considered in relation to available resources, including health care personnel, the distribution of facilities, equipment, and human resources (manpower), and advances in medicine and technology.

For example, a predicted shortage of nurses may prompt increased spending on nursing education; reviews of nurses' salary, benefits, and working conditions; and the cultivation of non-nursing personnel to perform specific responsibilities previously assigned to nurses. Similarly, when ongoing surveillance anticipates an especially

virulent influenza (flu) season, public health officials, agencies, and practitioners intensify efforts to provide timely immunization to vulnerable populations such as older adults. Government agencies such as the Centers for Disease Control and Prevention (CDC), National Institutes of Health (NIH), state and local health departments, professional societies, voluntary health agencies, and universities work together to research, analyze, and forecast health care needs. Their recommendations allow health care planners, policymakers, and legislators to allocate resources so that supply keeps pace with demand and to ensure that new services and strategies are developed to address existing and emerging health care concerns.

A REGULAR SOURCE OF HEALTH CARE IMPROVES ACCESS

According to the CDC, the determination of whether an individual has a regular source—a regular provider or site—of health care is a powerful predictor of access to health care services. Generally persons without regular sources have less access or access to fewer services, including key preventive medicine services such as prenatal care, routine immunization, and health screening. Many factors have been found to contribute to keeping individuals from having regular sources of medical care, with income level being the best predictor of unmet medical needs or problems gaining access to health care services.

Each year, the CDC conducts the Behavioral Risk Factor Surveillance System (BRFSS) survey, a state-based random-digit-dialed telephone survey conducted by the 50 states, the District of Columbia, Puerto Rico, Guam, and the Virgin Islands. Though there are federal guidelines for questions asked, states may add other questions. In 1995 BRFSS asked "Is there one particular clinic, health center, doctor's office or other place you usually go if you are sick or need advice about your health?" The survey found that people ages 18–29 were least likely to have a regular source of care, but the likelihood of having a regular source of medical care increased with age in all states. In most of the states, more white and black adults than Hispanics reported a regular source for care.

Not surprisingly, persons without health insurance coverage were less likely to have a regular source for care, and in nearly all the states included in the survey, persons with household incomes of less than $15,000 per year were less likely to have a regular source for health care than those with household incomes of $50,000 or more. Table 1.1 shows that uninsured persons were about three times as likely as insured persons to go without regular sources of medical care. (CDC data include confidence intervals, which are statistical measures of uncertainty. A confidence interval is a range of values that attempts to measure the degree to which the data are certain. A narrow confidence interval suggests high precision—specific

TABLE 1.1

Percentage of persons without a regular source of medical care, by selected state and health insurance status, 1995

	Insured		Uninsured		Total	
State	%	(95% CI*)	%	(95% CI)	%	(95% CI)
Alaska	14.1	(11.0%–17.2%)	39.5	(30.3%–48.7%)	18.0	(14.9%–21.1%)
Arizona	14.1	(11.6%–16.6%)	55.4	(47.2%–63.6%)	20.4	(17.9%–22.9%)
Illinois	12.2	(10.0%–14.4%)	38.3	(28.0%–48.6%)	15.0	(12.7%–17.3%)
Kansas	11.4	(9.7%–13.4%)	33.2	(25.8%–40.6%)	13.9	(12.9%–15.7%)
Louisiana	11.8	(9.9%–13.7%)	24.7	(19.1%–30.3%)	14.5	(12.5%–16.5%)
Mississippi	12.2	(10.2%–14.2%)	25.9	(18.6%–33.2%)	14.2	(12.2%–16.2%)
New Jersey	9.5	(7.2%–11.5%)	33.5	(22.7%–44.3%)	11.4	(9.4%–13.4%)
North Carolina	8.6	(6.2%–10.4%)	35.2	(26.3%–44.1%)	11.8	(9.8%–13.6%)
Oklahoma	6.6	(5.1%–8.1%)	35.4	(28.6%–42.2%)	10.9	(9.2%–12.6%)
Virginia	14.8	(12.8%–16.8%)	34.1	(26.7%–41.5%)	17.1	(15.1%–19.1%)
Median	12.0		34.7		14.3	

*Confidence interval.

SOURCE: "Table 2. Percentage of persons without a regular source of medical care, by state and health insurance status—selected states, Behavioral Risk Factor Surveillance System, 1995," in "Demographic Characteristics of Persons Without a Regular Source of Medical Care—Selected States, 1995," *Morbidity and Mortality Weekly Report,* vol. 47, no. 14, April 17, 1998

values are accurate within a tiny range—whereas a wide range implies a lack of precision. In general, when a confidence interval is very wide, it is an indication of an inadequate sample size.)

The CDC also determined that persons without a regular source of care were most likely to be young, male, Hispanic, and without health insurance and with low household incomes. Along with these findings, the CDC learned that most persons without a regular source for care did not feel they needed a regular source for medical care (*Morbidity and Mortality Weekly Report,* vol. 47, no. 14, April 17, 1998, from the CDC.)

When BRFSS participants were asked during 2000 whether the cost of medical care prevented them from seeing a doctor during the 12 months prior to the survey, nearly 10 percent said cost kept them from seeking care. (See Figure 1.1 for 1999 data and Figure 1.2 for 2000 data.)

The National Health Interview Survey (NHIS) is an ongoing annual household poll conducted by the National Center for Health Statistics (NCHS), Centers for Disease Control and Prevention (CDC) that tracks the health behaviors and actions of American civilians. It is important to recognize that findings from the NHIS, a national representative survey intended to be generalized to apply to the entire U.S. population, often are not comparable to findings from smaller or selected populations such as the BRFSS. The U.S. Census Bureau collects the data through personal household interviews. In 2001, 38,633 households were surveyed. Within those households participating in the NHIS, 86 percent of adults had a usual place to go for medical care—a higher percentage than in previous years and up from 83.8 percent in 1999. This number dropped slightly in the first few months of 2002.

(See Figure 1.3.) The NHIS reported an increasing trend from 1998 through 2001 in the percent of persons who cited financial barriers as the reason they failed to obtain medical care during the 12 months prior to the survey. In 1998, 4.2 percent of respondents said they had not sought care because of financial barriers and by 2001 4.6 percent failed to obtain needed care. (See Figure 1.4.)

The NHIS found that during the first three months of 2002 people ages 18–64 were the least able to obtain needed care due to financial barriers, and in this age group more women than men lacked access to care. (See Figure 1.5.) During the same three-month period, black and Hispanic persons were more likely than white non-Hispanics to have problems accessing medical care because of financial concerns. (See Figure 1.6.)

Race and Ethnicity Continue to Affect Access to Health Care

The U.S. Public Health Service's Agency for Healthcare Research and Quality (AHRQ) looks at ways to identify, address, and ultimately eliminate differences in access, availability, and the quality of health care services. Working with the National Institutes of Health (NIH) and national and local foundations, AHRQ seeks to develop plans and strategies to reduce and overcome disparities. One example of this collaborative effort is a program to improve access and quality of care for African Americans suffering from chronic illnesses who primarily receive care from inner-city and rural health care providers. Another project aims to expand access to preventive medicine services among low-income, Medicaid-eligible populations. (Medicaid is a program run by state and federal governments to provide health insurance for persons younger than age 65 who cannot afford to pay for private health insurance.)

FIGURE 1.1

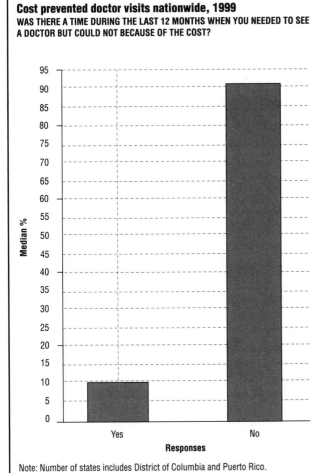

Cost prevented doctor visits nationwide, 1999
WAS THERE A TIME DURING THE LAST 12 MONTHS WHEN YOU NEEDED TO SEE A DOCTOR BUT COULD NOT BECAUSE OF THE COST?

Note: Number of states includes District of Columbia and Puerto Rico.

SOURCE: "Cost Prevented Doctor Visit Nationwide—1999," in *Behavioral Risk Factor Surveillance System Prevalence Data,* U.S. Department of Health and Human Services, Centers for Disease Control and Prevention, National Center for Chronic Disease Prevention and Health Promotion, Division of Adult and Community Health, Atlanta, GA, April 1, 2002 [Online] http://apps.nccd.cdc.gov/brfss/display.asp?cat=HC&yr=1999 &qkey=2977&state=US [accessed August 1, 2002]

FIGURE 1.2

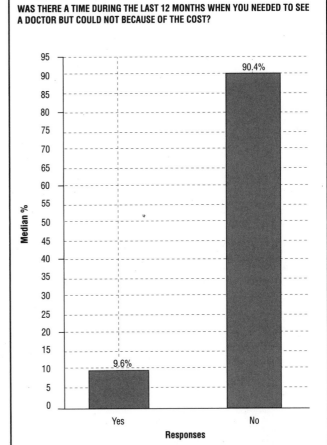

Cost prevented doctor visits nationwide, 2000
WAS THERE A TIME DURING THE LAST 12 MONTHS WHEN YOU NEEDED TO SEE A DOCTOR BUT COULD NOT BECAUSE OF THE COST?

SOURCE: "Cost Prevented Doctor Visit Nationwide—2000," in *Behavioral Risk Factor Surveillance System Prevalence Data,* U.S. Department of Health and Human Services, Centers for Disease Control and Prevention, National Center for Chronic Disease Prevention and Health Promotion, Division of Adult and Community Health, Atlanta, GA, April 1, 2002 [Online] http://apps.nccd.cdc.gov/brfss/display.asp?yr=2000&cat=HC &state=US&qkey=2977&grp=0&SUBMIT3=Go [accessed August 1, 2002]

The AHRQ observes that income level and lack of health insurance are not the only barriers to access faced by members of racial or ethnic minority populations. The AHRQ asserts that having health insurance does not guarantee access and that even entering a health care provider's office does not ensure receipt of appropriate or quality health care services. AHRQ researchers described asthma care as an example of consistent variation in access to and use of medical care. Among children with asthma enrolled in Medicaid, black children were 70 percent more likely to visit an emergency department and 52 percent less likely to be cared for in an office visit with a health care practitioner. Black children were similarly less likely to obtain routine well-child visits (check-ups) and prescriptions for medication.

The 2001 NHIS found that Hispanic adults and children continued to be less likely to have a regular source for medical care than white non-Hispanic and black non-

Hispanic children. Health educators speculate that this gap may in part be caused by language barriers as well as lack of insurance coverage or information about the availability of health care services.

Researchers think that many factors contribute to differences in access, including cultural perceptions and beliefs about health and illness, patient preferences, availability of services, and provider bias. They recommend special efforts to inform and educate minority health care consumers and increased understanding and sensitivity among practitioners and other providers of care. In addition to factual information, minority consumers must overcome the belief that they are at a disadvantage because of their race or ethnicity. Along with action to dispel barriers to access, educating practitioners, policymakers, and consumers can help to reduce the perception of disadvantage.

FIGURE 1.3

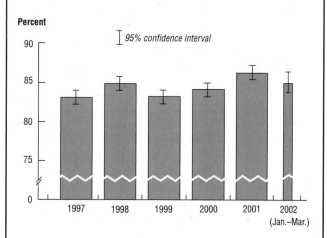

Percent of adults aged 18 years and over with a usual place to go for medical care, 1997–quarter one 2002

Note: The usual place to go for medical care does not include a hospital emergency room. The analysis excluded persons with unknown usual place to go for medical care (about 0.6% of respondents).

SOURCE: "Figure 2.1 Percent of adults aged 18 years and over with a usual place to go for medical care: United States, 1997–quarter one 2002," in *National Health Interview Survey,* U.S. Department of Health and Human Services, Centers for Disease Control and Prevention, National Center for Health Statistics, Division of Data Services, Hyattsville, MD, September 20, 2002 [Online] http://www.cdc.gov/nchs/about/major/nhis/released200209/figure02_1.htm [accessed October 1, 2002]

FIGURE 1.4

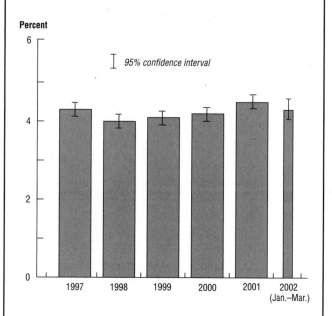

Percent of persons who failed to obtain needed medical care during the past 12 months due to financial barriers, 1997–quarter one 2002

Note: The analysis excluded persons with unknown success in obtaining needed medical care (about 0.5% of respondents). The estimate for 2002 was based on data collected from January through March.

SOURCE: "Figure 3.1. Percent of persons who failed to obtain needed medical care during the past 12 months due to financial barriers: United States, 1997–quarter one 2002," in *National Health Interview Survey,* U.S. Department of Health and Human Services, Centers for Disease Control and Prevention, National Center for Health Statistics, Division of Data Services, Hyattsville, MD, September 20, 2002 [Online] http://www.cdc.gov/nchs/about/major/nhis/released200209/figure03_1.htm [accessed October 1, 2002]

Children Need Better Access to Health Care Too

Data from the more than 38,000 households included in the 1998 NHIS were analyzed to look at selected health measures, including children's access to care, and compiled in the report *Summary Health Statistics for U.S. Children in 2002.* Among other factors, the analysis focuses on the unmet health care needs of children 17 years of age and under, poverty status, insurance coverage, usual place of medical care, and whether children's health needs were being met. The data from the NHIS show the association between family income and not having a usual source of medical care as well as having unmet medical needs. The likelihood of lacking a regular source of care or having unmet needs was higher among poor and near poor families of all races and ethnic groups. Having health insurance and the type of health insurance also predicted whether a child had a regular source of care and whether all the child's medical needs were met.

About 2 percent of children in the United States had at least one unmet health care need in 1998. Table 1.2 shows that children with unmet medical needs were most likely to be uninsured, with 8.8 percent of all those uninsured having unmet needs. They were also more likely to have family incomes of less than $20,000 (4 percent). Unmet needs were not only for direct medical care but also for prescription medications, glasses, mental health services, and dental care.

The uninsured and those with low incomes were also more likely to have no usual source of care and to delay care due to cost. Almost 6 percent of all children had no usual source of medical care in 1998. Those without any insurance (25.3 percent) and those in families earning less than $20,000 (almost 10 percent) were most likely not to have a usual source of care. Slightly more than 6 percent of children whose family income was less than $20,000 and 14.5 percent of children who were uninsured had delayed care due to cost.

Data from the regular NHIS survey conducted from 1999–2000 estimated that 6.8 percent of children had no regular source of medical care. Table 1.3 shows that while nearly 30 percent of uninsured children lacked a usual source for care, the proportion dropped to 5.2 percent among those with public insurance and 3.8 percent of children with private insurance. Almost 37 percent of children who were both poor and uninsured had no usual source of care.

NHIS data revealed an increase in the percentage of children with a regular source for medical care from 93 per-

FIGURE 1.5

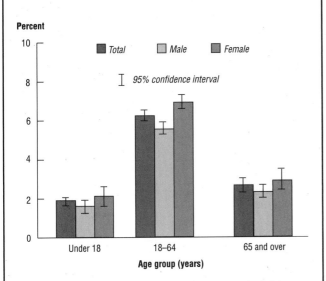

Percent of persons who failed to obtain needed medical care during the past 12 months due to financial barriers, by age group and sex, quarter one 2002

Note: The analysis excluded 117 persons with unknown success in obtaining needed medical care.

SOURCE: "Figure 3.2. Percent of persons who failed to obtain needed medical care during the past 12 months due to financial barriers, by age group and sex: United States, quarter one 2002," in *National Health Interview Survey,* U.S. Department of Health and Human Services, Centers for Disease Control and Prevention, National Center for Health Statistics, Division of Data Services, Hyattsville, MD, September 20, 2002 [Online] http://www.cdc.gov/nchs/about/major/nhis/released200209/figure03_2.htm [accessed October 1, 2002]

FIGURE 1.6

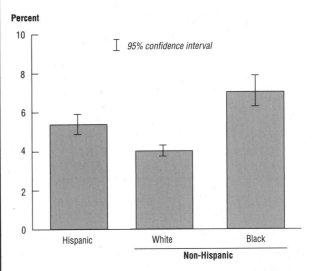

Age-sex-adjusted percent of persons who failed to obtain needed medical care during the past 12 months due to financial barriers, by race/ethnicity, quarter one 2002

Note: The analysis excluded 117 persons with unknown success in obtaining needed medical care. Estimates are age-sex-adjusted to the projected year 2000 standard population using three age groups: less than 18 years, 18–64 years, and 65 years and over.

SOURCE: "Figure 3.3. Age-sex-adjusted percent of persons who failed to obtain needed medical care during the past 12 months due to financial barriers, by race/ethnicity for: United States, quarter one 2002," in *National Health Interview Survey,* U.S. Department of Health and Human Services, Centers for Disease Control and Prevention, National Center for Health Statistics, Division of Data Services, Hyattsville, MD, September 20, 2002 [Online] http://www.cdc.gov/nchs/about/major/nhis/released200209/figure03_3.htm [accessed October 1, 2002]

cent in 2000 to 94.2 percent in 2001. (See Figure 1.7.) Children were more likely than adults under age 65 to have a regular place to go for care and those least likely to have a usual place for care were the youngest adults, those between 18 and 24 years old. Still, poverty continues to limit children's access to medical care. Figure 1.8 shows how the proportion of children (persons less than 18 years old) living in poverty has been greater than poverty in older age groups since the early 1970s. The NHIS report estimated that between 1999 and 2000, almost 13.1 percent of children had not been to a medical office or clinic in the previous 12 months. (See Table 1.4.) This percent went as high as 36.1 percent of poor and uninsured children.

The *2000 National Survey of Early Childhood Health* (2002) records statistics on children from 4–35 months of age. According to the NSECH, almost 30 percent of young children ages 4–35 months whose parents or guardians reported they had missed (14 percent) or delayed (15 percent) seeking care lacked health insurance. (See Table 1.5.) Some or great difficulty paying for children's health and medical care expenses was reported by almost 40 percent of those responsible for young children who had no insur-

ance. (See Table 1.6.) In contrast, nearly 90 percent of persons with either public or private health insurance reported no trouble paying for their children's health expenses. Health professionals are especially concerned about delayed or missed medical visits for children in this age group because well-child visits are not only opportunities for early detection of developmental problems and timely treatment of illnesses but also ensure that children receive the recommended schedule of immunizations.

HOW TO REDUCE DISPARITIES IN ACCESS TO CARE. For decades, health care researchers have documented sharp differences in the ability of ethnic and racial groups to access medical services. The U.S. government has repeatedly called for an end to these disparities. Although some observers feel that universal health insurance coverage is an important first step in eliminating disparities, there is widespread concern that the challenge is more complicated and calls for additional analysis and action.

In an article in the June 2000 issue of the *Journal of General Internal Medicine* (vol. 17, no. 6), Harvard Medical

TABLE 1.2

Percents (with standard errors) of selected health care risk factors, for children 17 years of age and under, by selected characteristics, 1998

Selected characteristic	Uninsured for health care	Unmet medical need	Delayed care due to cost	No usual source of care	Two or more visits to the emergency room in the past year
	Percent (standard error)[2]				
Total	12.2 (0.36)	2.1 (0.14)	3.8 (0.19)	5.9 (0.25)	6.9 (0.28)
Sex					
Male	12.0 (0.43)	2.0 (0.19)	3.6 (0.25)	5.6 (0.31)	7.5 (0.42)
Female	12.4 (0.52)	2.2 (0.21)	4.0 (0.29)	6.1 (0.34)	6.2 (0.34)
Age					
0–4 years	10.8 (0.52)	1.5 (0.20)	3.2 (0.31)	3.3 (0.30)	9.8 (0.62)
5–17 years	12.7 (0.45)	2.3 (0.17)	4.0 (0.24)	6.8 (0.32)	5.8 (0.29)
5–11 years	12.5 (0.59)	2.1 (0.23)	3.5 (0.31)	5.6 (0.39)	5.5 (0.39)
12–17 years	13.1 (0.57)	2.5 (0.27)	4.6 (0.35)	8.3 (0.48)	6.2 (0.41)
Race/ethnicity[3]					
Non-Hispanic white	8.6 (0.41)	1.7 (0.16)	3.6 (0.24)	3.6 (0.25)	6.2 (0.36)
Non-Hispanic black	12.3 (0.86)	2.7 (0.38)	4.2 (0.48)	7.9 (0.70)	9.9 (0.82)
Non-Hispanic other	15.9 (2.51)	2.7 (0.81)	2.7 (0.76)	8.6 (1.38)	6.7 (1.39)
Hispanic	26.1 (0.90)	3.0 (0.39)	4.5 (0.48)	12.6 (0.67)	6.9 (0.49)
Mexican American	31.7 (1.32)	3.7 (0.63)	5.0 (0.76)	15.5 (1.04)	5.8 (0.55)
Family structure[4]					
Mother and father	11.4 (0.41)	1.5 (0.14)	3.3 (0.22)	5.0 (0.27)	5.8 (0.31)
Mother, no father	13.7 (0.69)	3.6 (0.38)	5.6 (0.47)	6.9 (0.54)	10.5 (0.69)
Father, no mother	15.7 (1.83)	4.8 (1.21)	5.5 (1.20)	10.5 (1.68)	6.0 (1.55)
Neither mother nor father	18.9 (2.06)	*1.9 (0.75)	*2.5 (0.75)	14.3 (2.02)	8.7 (1.64)
Parent's education[5]					
Less than high school diploma	29.0 (1.25)	3.4 (0.47)	4.4 (0.53)	14.7 (0.95)	10.5 (0.96)
High school diploma or GED[6]	14.7 (0.79)	2.1 (0.28)	4.7 (0.45)	6.4 (0.54)	8.6 (0.64)
More than high school	7.1 (0.37)	1.8 (0.18)	3.4 (0.24)	3.4 (0.23)	5.3 (0.29)
Family income[7]					
Less than $20,000	21.6 (0.85)	3.8 (0.39)	6.1 (0.52)	9.6 (0.61)	11.5 (0.74)
$20,000 or more	9.3 (0.38)	1.6 (0.14)	3.1 (0.20)	4.6 (0.24)	5.7 (0.28)
$20,000–$34,999	21.5 (1.08)	3.0 (0.40)	5.8 (0.60)	9.0 (0.66)	8.4 (0.75)
$35,000–$54,999	9.1 (0.75)	2.0 (0.35)	3.7 (0.50)	4.9 (0.48)	5.9 (0.55)
$55,000–$74,999	3.7 (0.66)	*0.8 (0.28)	2.1 (0.45)	2.7 (0.50)	4.2 (0.54)
$75,000 or more	2.0 (0.32)	*0.1 (0.09)	0.8 (0.22)	1.8 (0.33)	3.9 (0.48)
Poverty status[8]					
Poor	21.0 (1.08)	3.6 (0.47)	5.7 (0.63)	10.1 (0.76)	11.8 (0.94)
Near poor	22.9 (1.04)	3.8 (0.46)	6.9 (0.63)	8.8 (0.68)	8.9 (0.74)
Not poor	4.9 (0.31)	0.9 (0.13)	2.1 (0.21)	3.2 (0.24)	4.7 (0.29)
Health insurance coverage[9]					
Private	...	0.9 (0.12)	2.1 (0.17)	2.7 (0.20)	5.2 (0.28)
Medicaid/other public	...	2.1 (0.36)	2.9 (0.39)	4.7 (0.50)	13.3 (0.85)
Other	...	*2.0 (0.78)	3.4 (1.00)	3.9 (1.11)	9.1 (1.70)
Uninsured	100.0 (0.00)	8.8 (0.81)	14.5 (1.06)	25.3 (1.34)	7.0 (0.71)
Place of residence					
Large MSA[10]	12.3 (0.50)	2.2 (0.22)	3.8 (0.28)	6.2 (0.37)	6.2 (0.34)
Small MSA[10]	10.4 (0.59)	2.1 (0.22)	4.1 (0.34)	6.0 (0.45)	7.0 (0.56)
Not in MSA[10]	14.6 (0.92)	1.8 (0.28)	3.3 (0.41)	4.9 (0.50)	8.2 (0.70)
Region					
Northeast	7.3 (0.59)	1.5 (0.22)	3.0 (0.30)	2.2 (0.41)	5.7 (0.55)
Midwest	7.7 (0.61)	1.7 (0.28)	3.5 (0.39)	3.5 (0.38)	7.0 (0.58)
South	15.6 (0.73)	2.4 (0.25)	4.3 (0.37)	7.6 (0.49)	8.0 (0.58)
West	16.4 (0.74)	2.6 (0.31)	4.1 (0.40)	9.2 (0.59)	5.9 (0.39)

School physician Dr. JudyAnn Bigby asserts that "Eliminating racial disparities ... requires an understanding of the ecology of health, the interconnectedness of biologic, behavioral, physical, and socio-environmental factors that determine health." Dr. Bigby believes that a multifaceted approach must be used to address the many issues involved in access, including improving the physical environment, overcoming economic and social barriers, ensuring the availability of effective health services, and acting to reduce personal behavioral risk factors such as smoking, obesity, poor nutrition, substance abuse, and physical inactivity. Developing strategies to promote personal, institutional, and community change simultaneously may stimulate the sweeping reforms needed to reduce and ultimately eliminate disparities.

TABLE 1.2

Percents (with standard errors) of selected health care risk factors, for children 17 years of age and under, by selected characteristics, 1998 [CONTINUED]

Selected characteristic	Selected health care risk factors[1]				
	Uninsured for health care	Unmet medical need	Delayed care due to cost	No usual source of care	Two or more visits to the emergency room in the past year
Current health status			Percent (standard error)[2]		
Excellent/very good/good	12.2 (0.36)	2.0 (0.13)	3.7 (0.19)	5.9 (0.25)	6.5 (0.28)
Fair/poor	12.3 (1.95)	7.5 (1.70)	8.2 (1.70)	6.6 (1.61)	27.6 (2.86)
Sex and age					
Male:					
0–4 years	11.3 (0.79)	1.6 (0.30)	3.3 (0.43)	3.3 (0.41)	11.0 (0.89)
5–17 years	12.3 (0.55)	2.2 (0.23)	3.7 (0.31)	6.5 (0.40)	6.2 (0.44)
5–11 years	12.2 (0.73)	2.0 (0.32)	3.1 (0.38)	5.0 (0.46)	6.3 (0.58)
12–17 years	12.3 (0.73)	2.3 (0.35)	4.5 (0.48)	8.3 (0.62)	6.2 (0.59)
Female:					
0–4 years	10.2 (0.69)	1.4 (0.28)	3.1 (0.47)	3.3 (0.44)	8.5 (0.77)
5–17 years	13.2 (0.65)	2.5 (0.26)	4.3 (0.36)	7.2 (0.46)	5.3 (0.39)
5–11 years	12.7 (0.83)	2.3 (0.35)	4.0 (0.49)	6.2 (0.61)	4.6 (0.50)
12–17 years	13.8 (0.89)	2.8 (0.40)	4.7 (0.52)	8.4 (0.68)	6.2 (0.61)

* Figure does not meet standard of reliability or precision.
. . . Category not applicable.
0.0 Quantity more than zero but less than 0.05.
[1]The data in this table are based on the following questions: "{Are you/Is anyone} covered by health insurance or some other kind of health care plan?"; "During the past 12 months, was there any time when {you/someone in the family} needed medical care, but did not get it because {you/the family} couldn't afford it?"; "During the past 12 months, {have/has {you/anyone in the family} delayed seeking medical care because of worry about the cost?"; "Is there a place that {child's name} usually goes when {he/she} is sick or you need advice about {his/her} health?"; "During the past 12 months, how many times has {child's name} gone to a hospital emergency room about {his/her} health? (This includes emergency room visits that resulted in a hospital admission.)"
[2]Unknowns for the variable of interest are not included in the denominators when calculating percents.
[3]"Non-Hispanic other" includes non-Hispanic children whose race was identified as American Indian, Alaska Native, Asian, or Pacific Islander. Children of Hispanic origin may be of any race.
[4]Mother and father can include biological, adoptive, step, in-law, or foster relationships. Legal guardians are classified in "Neither mother nor father."
[5]Parent's education is the education level of the parent with the higher level of education, regardless of that parent's age.
[6]GED is General Educational Development high school equivalency diploma.
[7]"Less than $20,000" and "$20,000 or more" include both respondents reporting specific dollar amounts and respondents reporting that their incomes were within those categories. The indented categories include only those respondents who reported specific dollar amounts. Children with unknown family income are not shown.
[8]Poverty status is based on family income and family size using the U.S. Census Bureau's poverty thresholds. "Poor" children in families defined as below the poverty threshold. "Near poor" children are in families with incomes of 100% to less than 200% of the poverty threshold. "Not poor" children are in families with incomes that are 200% of the poverty threshold or greater.
[9]Private health insurance may be obtained through the workplace or purchased directly. Among children under 18 years of age, "Medicaid/other public" includes those with Medicaid or other public health insurance coverage (e.g., most State-sponsored coverage). "Other coverage" includes Medicare, military health insurance coverage, and/or another form of government-sponsored health insurance coverage. Children with only Indian Health Service coverage are considered uninsured.
[10]"MSA" is metropolitan statistical area. Large MSAs have a population size of 1,000,000 or more; small MSAs have a population size of less than 1,000,000. "Not in MSA" consists of persons not living in a metropolitan statistical area.

SOURCE: "Table 16. Percents (with standard errors) of selected health care risk factors, for children 17 years of age and under, by selected characteristics: United States, 1998," in *Summary Health Statistics for U.S. Children: National Health Interview Survey, 1998,* Centers for Disease Control and Prevention, National Center for Health Statistics, Hyattsville, MD, 2002

IS ACCESS A RIGHT OR A PRIVILEGE?

The AHRQ and other health care researchers and policymakers have observed that having health insurance does not necessarily ensure access to medical care. They contend that many other factors, including cost-containment measures put in place by private and public payers have reduced access to care. Nonetheless, reduced access affects vulnerable populations—the poor, persons with disabilities and other special health care needs, and immigrants—more than others. These groups are disproportionately affected.

Health care is a resource that is rationed. In the United States and other countries without universal or national programs of health insurance, persons with greater incomes and assets are more likely than low-income families to have health insurance and as a result have greater access to health care services. In the United States in 2000, of 288 million Americans, more than 38 million people, including 8.5 million children, had no health insurance and either experienced sharply reduced access to the health care system or were excluded altogether.

A wide range of groups and organizations support the idea that health care is a fundamental human right, not a privilege. These organizations include Physicians for a National Health Program, American Association of Retired Persons, National Health Care for the Homeless, Inc., and the Friends Committee on National Legislation, a Quaker public interest lobby. The American Medical Association's "Patient Bill of Rights" includes the "right to essential health care."

TABLE 1.3

No usual source of health care among children under 18 years of age, according to selected characteristics, average annual 1993–94, 1997–98, and 1999–2000

[Data are based on household interviews of a sample of the civilian noninstitutionalized population]

Characteristic	Under 18 years of age			Under 6 years of age			6-17 years of age		
	1993–94	1997–98[1]	1999–2000[1]	1993–94	1997–98[1]	1999–2000[1]	1993–94	1997–98[1]	1999–2000[1]
	Percent of children without a usual source of health care[2]								
All children[3]	7.7	6.7	6.8	5.2	4.5	4.6	9.0	7.8	7.9
Race[4]									
White only	7.0	5.8	6.2	4.7	4.1	4.4	8.3	6.7	7.1
Black or African American only	10.3	8.9	7.7	7.6	5.6	4.4	11.9	10.4	9.2
American Indian and Alaska Native only	*9.3	*10.8	*9.3	*	*	*	*8.7	*	*9.3
Asian only	9.7	10.7	9.9	*3.4	*	*5.9	13.5	14.4	12.1
Native Hawaiian and Other Pacific Islander only	*	*	*	*	*	*	*	*	*
2 or more races	- - -	- - -	*5.0	- - -	- - -	*	- - -	- - -	*7.2
Hispanic origin and race[4]									
Hispanic or Latino	14.3	13.2	14.1	9.3	7.6	9.0	17.7	16.7	17.2
Not Hispanic or Latino	#	#	5.4	#	#	3.6	#	#	6.3
White only	5.7	4.5	4.7	3.7	3.4	3.3	6.7	5.0	5.4
Black or African American only	10.2	8.8	7.6	7.7	5.4	4.5	11.6	10.4	9.0
Poverty status[5]									
Poor	13.9	12.4	12.8	9.4	8.2	7.9	16.8	15.0	15.6
Near poor	9.8	10.1	10.6	6.7	6.5	8.0	11.6	12.0	12.0
Nonpoor	3.7	3.5	3.7	1.8	2.0	2.5	4.6	4.2	4.2
Hispanic origin and race and poverty status[4,5]									
Hispanic or Latino:									
Poor	19.6	17.0	18.3	12.7	8.4	11.8	24.8	22.7	22.8
Near poor	15.3	16.0	17.5	9.9	10.2	12.2	18.9	19.9	20.6
Nonpoor	5.0	5.7	6.3	*2.7	*3.1	*4.3	6.5	7.3	7.2
Not Hispanic or Latino:									
White only:									
Poor	10.2	11.4	11.3	6.5	10.7	*6.9	12.7	12.0	13.6
Near poor	8.7	6.6	7.9	6.3	4.5	6.3	10.1	7.7	8.6
Nonpoor	3.4	2.8	3.2	1.6	1.6	2.3	4.2	3.3	3.6
Black or African American only:									
Poor	13.7	9.1	8.9	10.9	*5.4	*4.3	15.5	11.2	11.0
Near poor	9.1	12.5	9.2	*6.0	*7.2	*6.6	10.8	15.0	10.5
Nonpoor	4.6	6.4	4.2	*	*4.0	*	5.8	7.4	4.7
Health insurance status[6]									
Insured	5.0	3.6	3.8	3.3	2.6	2.6	5.9	4.2	4.5
Private	3.8	3.1	3.4	2.0	2.0	2.2	4.6	3.6	3.9
Medicaid	8.5	5.4	5.2	6.0	3.9	3.3	10.8	6.6	6.4
Uninsured	23.5	27.8	29.1	18.0	19.0	20.8	26.0	31.6	32.8
Poverty status and health insurance status[5]									
Poor:									
Insured	9.1	6.2	6.4	6.0	4.8	3.2	11.5	7.2	8.3
Uninsured	29.4	35.5	36.7	25.0	26.5	28.5	31.5	39.2	40.4
Near poor:									
Insured	6.0	5.1	5.6	4.0	3.4	4.7	7.2	6.1	6.2
Uninsured	22.9	27.1	28.8	18.0	18.4	21.5	25.3	30.9	32.2
Nonpoor:									
Insured	2.9	2.5	2.8	1.5	1.6	1.9	3.6	3.0	3.2
Uninsured	14.5	19.7	19.9	6.4	*10.6	14.4	18.1	23.4	22.3

TABLE 1.3

No usual source of health care among children under 18 years of age, according to selected characteristics, average annual 1993–94, 1997–98, and 1999–2000 [CONTINUED]

[Data are based on household interviews of a sample of the civilian noninstitutionalized population]

Characteristic	Under 18 years of age			Under 6 years of age			6-17 years of age		
	1993–94	1997–98[1]	1999–2000[1]	1993–94	1997–98[1]	1999–2000[1]	1993–94	1997–98[1]	1999–2000[1]
Geographic region	Percent of children without a usual source of health care[2]								
Northeast	4.1	3.1	2.8	2.9	*2.5	2.3	4.8	3.5	3.0
Midwest	5.2	4.6	5.2	4.1	4.0	3.7	5.9	4.9	5.9
South	10.9	8.4	8.5	7.3	5.3	5.8	12.7	9.9	9.8
West	8.6	9.8	9.6	5.3	5.5	5.6	10.6	12.0	11.6
Location of residence									
Within MSA[7]	7.7	6.8	6.7	5.0	4.4	4.7	9.2	8.0	7.8
Outside MSA[7]	7.8	6.4	7.3	6.0	4.7	4.2	8.7	7.2	8.7

* Estimates are considered unreliable. Data preceded by an asterisk have a relative standard error of 20–30 percent. Data not shown have a relative standard error of greater than 30 percent.

- - - Data not available.

\# Estimates calculated upon request.

[1]Data starting in 1997 are not strictly comparable with data for earlier years due to the 1997 questionnaire redesign.

[2]Persons who report the emergency department as the place of their usual source of care are defined as having no usual source of care.

[3]Includes all other races not shown separately, unknown poverty status, and unknown health insurance status.

[4]Starting with data year 1999–2000, estimates by race and Hispanic origin are tabulated using the 1997 Standards for federal data on race and ethnicity; prior to data year 1999–2000 the 1977 Standards are used. Estimates for specific race groups are shown when they meet requirements for statistical reliability and confidentiality. Starting with data year 1999–2000, the categories "White only," "Black or African American only," "American Indian and Alaska Native (AI/AN) only," "Asian only," and" Native Hawaiian and Other Pacific Islander only" include persons who reported only one racial group; and the category "2 or more races" includes persons who reported more than one of the five racial groups in the 1997 Standards or one of the five racial groups and "Some other race". Prior to data year 1999–2000, estimates for the race categories shown include persons who reported one race or who reported more than one race and identified one race as best representing their race; and the category "Asian only" includes Native Hawaiian and Other Pacific Islander. Because of the differences between the two Standards, race-specific estimates starting with data year 1999–2000 are not strictly comparable with estimates for earlier years. To estimate change between 1997–98 and 1999–2000, race-specific estimates for 1999–2000 based on the 1977 Standards can be used. In comparison with the 1999–2000 estimates based on the 1997 Standards, estimates of the percent of children under 18 years of age with no usual source of care based on the 1977 Standards are: identical for white children; 0.1 percentage points lower for black children; 0.6 percentage points lower for AI/AN children; and 1.0 percentage points lower for Asian and Pacific Islander children.

[5]Prior to 1997 poverty status is based on family income and family size using Bureau of the Census poverty thresholds. Beginning in 1997 poverty status is based on family income, family size, number of children in the family, and for families with two or fewer adults the age of the adults in the family. Poor persons are defined as below the poverty threshold. Near poor persons have incomes of 100 percent to less than 200 percent of the poverty threshold. Nonpoor persons have incomes of 200 percent or greater than the poverty threshold. Missing family income data were imputed for 14 percent of children in 1993–96. Poverty status was unknown for 17 percent of children in the sample in 1997, 21 percent in 1998, 24 percent in 1999, and 23 percent in 2000.

[6]Health insurance categories are mutually exclusive. Persons who reported both Medicaid and private coverage are classified as having Medicaid coverage. Medicaid includes other public assistance through 1996. Starting in 1997 Medicaid includes state-sponsored health plans and Child Health Insurance Program (CHIP). In 1993–96 health insurance status was unknown for 8–9 percent of children in the sample. In 1997–2000 health insurance status was unknown for 1 percent of children in the sample.

[7]MSA is metropolitan statistical area.

SOURCE: "Table 76. No usual source of health care among children under 18 years of age, according to selected characteristics: United States, average annual 1993–94, 1997–98, and 1999–2000," in *Health, United States, 2002,* Centers for Disease Control and Prevention, National Center for Health Statistics, Hyattsville, MD, 2002

FIGURE 1.7

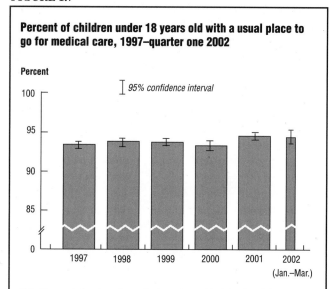

Percent of children under 18 years old with a usual place to go for medical care, 1997–quarter one 2002

Note: The usual place to go for medical care does not include a hospital emergency room. The analysis excluded children with unknown usual place to go for medical care (about 0.4% of respondents).

SOURCE: "Figure 2.2. Percent of children under 18 years old with a usual place to go for medical care: United States, 1997–quarter one 2002," in *National Health Interview Survey*, U.S. Department of Health and Human Services, Centers for Disease Control and Prevention, National Center for Health Statistics, Division of Data Services, Hyattsville, MD, September 20, 2002 [Online] http://www.cdc.gov/nchs/about/major/nhis/released200209/figure02_2.htm [accessed October 1, 2002]

FIGURE 1.8

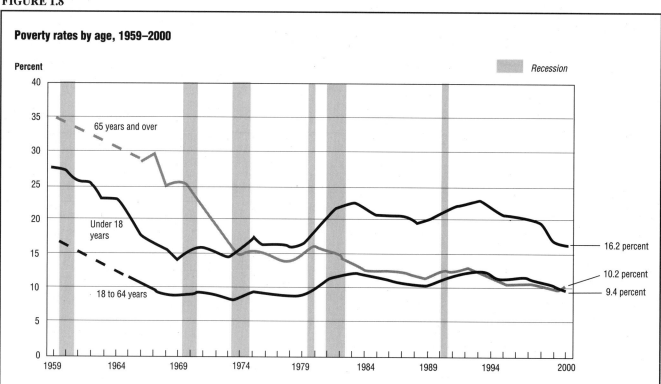

Poverty rates by age, 1959–2000

Note: The data points represent the midpoints of the respective years. The latest recession began in July 1990 and ended in March 1991. Data for people 18 to 64 and 65 and older are not available from 1960 to 1965.

SOURCE: Joseph Dalaker, "Figure 2. Poverty Rates by Age: 1959 to 2000," in *Poverty in the United States: 2000,* Current Population Reports P60-214, U.S. Census Bureau, Washington, DC, September 2001

TABLE 1.4

No health care visits to an office or clinic within the past 12 months among children under 18 years of age, according to selected characteristics, average annual 1997–98 and 1999–2000

[Data are based on household interviews of a sample of the civilian noninstitutionalized population]

Characteristic	Under 18 years of age		Under 6 years of age		6-17 years of age	
	1997–98	1999–2000	1997–98	1999–2000	1997–98	1999–2000
	Percent of children without a health care visit[1]					
All children[2]	12.8	13.1	5.7	6.7	16.3	16.1
Race[3]						
White only	12.2	12.3	5.5	6.5	15.5	15.1
Black or African American only	14.3	15.0	6.5	7.0	18.1	18.6
American Indian and Alaska Native only	13.8	20.4	*	*	*17.6	22.2
Asian only	16.3	16.5	*5.6	*8.5	22.1	20.9
Native Hawaiian and Other Pacific Islander only	*	*	*	*	*	*
2 or more races	- - -	10.6	- - -	*	- - -	16.6
Hispanic origin and race[3]						
Hispanic or Latino	19.3	20.1	9.7	10.2	25.3	26.1
Not Hispanic or Latino	#	11.7	#	5.9	#	14.4
White only	10.7	10.7	4.3	5.5	13.7	13.0
Black or African American only	14.5	14.7	6.5	7.1	18.3	18.0
Poverty status[4]						
Poor	17.7	18.3	8.1	11.3	23.8	22.2
Near poor	16.1	17.8	7.0	9.6	20.8	22.2
Nonpoor	9.7	9.7	3.9	4.2	12.5	12.3
Hispanic origin and race and poverty status[3,4]						
Hispanic or Latino:						
Poor	23.4	24.2	11.8	15.3	31.2	30.2
Near poor	20.1	23.1	9.3	12.0	27.3	29.8
Nonpoor	12.9	13.7	7.1	*4.5	16.2	18.5
Not Hispanic or Latino:						
White only:						
Poor	13.7	15.5	*5.4	*9.1	19.3	18.8
Near poor	14.0	14.8	6.0	8.0	18.1	18.2
Nonpoor	9.1	8.8	3.4	4.1	11.6	11.0
Black or African American only:						
Poor	16.1	15.3	*7.5	*8.9	21.0	18.2
Near poor	16.6	18.6	*7.0	*10.8	21.1	22.3
Nonpoor	12.2	11.7	*4.0	*3.8	15.6	14.8
Health insurance status[5]						
Insured	10.4	10.7	4.5	5.2	13.4	13.4
Private	10.4	10.6	4.3	4.7	13.2	13.2
Medicaid	9.9	11.0	4.9	6.4	13.9	14.2
Uninsured	28.8	30.4	14.6	19.1	34.9	35.4
Poverty status and health insurance status[4]						
Poor:						
Insured	13.2	13.5	5.7	7.8	18.4	16.9
Uninsured	34.5	36.1	19.6	27.1	40.6	40.0
Near poor:						
Insured	12.5	13.9	4.4	7.0	16.9	17.7
Uninsured	27.9	32.2	16.9	20.3	32.7	37.8
Nonpoor:						
Insured	8.9	9.0	3.6	3.8	11.4	11.5
Uninsured	23.0	22.7	*8.8	13.1	28.6	26.9

TABLE 1.4

No health care visits to an office or clinic within the past 12 months among children under 18 years of age, according to selected characteristics, average annual 1997–98 and 1999–2000 [CONTINUED]

[Data are based on household interviews of a sample of the civilian noninstitutionalized population]

Characteristic	Under 18 years of age		Under 6 years of age		6-17 years of age	
	1997–98	1999–2000	1997–98	1999–2000	1997–98	1999–2000
Geographic region	Percent of children without a health care visit[1]					
Northeast	7.0	6.6	3.1	4.8	8.9	7.6
Midwest	12.2	11.0	5.9	5.4	15.3	13.5
South	14.3	15.4	5.6	7.8	18.5	19.1
West.	6.3	17.1	7.9	8.2	20.7	21.7
Location of residence						
Within MSA[6]	12.3	12.6	5.4	6.3	15.9	15.8
Outside MSA[6]	14.6	14.7	6.9	8.5	17.9	17.3

* Estimates are considered unreliable. Data preceded by an asterisk have a relative standard error of 20–30 percent. Data not shown have a relative standard error of greater than 30 percent.

- - - Data not available.

#Estimates calculated upon request.

[1]Respondents were asked how many times a doctor or other health care professional was seen in the past 12 months at a doctor's office, clinic, or some other place. Excluded are visits to emergency rooms, hospitalizations, home visits, and telephone calls. Beginning in 2000 dental visits were also excluded. This table presents the percent of children with no visits in the past 12 months.

[2]Includes all other races not shown separately, unknown poverty status, and unknown health insurance status.

[3]Starting with data years 1999–2000, estimates by race and Hispanic origin are tabulated using the 1997 Standards for federal data on race and ethnicity; prior to data years 1999–2000 the 1977 Standards are used. Estimates for specific race groups are shown when they meet requirements for statistical reliability and confidentiality. Starting with data years 1999–2000, the categories "White only," "Black or African American only," "American Indian and Alaska Native (AI/AN) only," "Asian only," and "Native Hawaiian and Other Pacific Islander only" include persons who reported only one racial group; and the category "2 or more races" includes persons who reported more than one of the five racial groups in the 1997 Standards or one of the five racial groups and "Some other race." Prior to data years 1999–2000, estimates for the race categories shown include persons who reported one race or who reported more than one race and identified one race as best representing their race; and the category "Asian only" includes Native Hawaiian and Other Pacific Islander. Because of the differences between the two Standards, race-specific estimates starting with data years 1999–2000 are not strictly comparable with estimates for earlier years. To estimate change between 1997–98 and 1999–2000, race-specific estimates for 1999–2000 based on the 1977 Standards can be used. In comparison with the 1999–2000 estimates based on the 1997 Standards, estimates of the percent of children under 18 years of age with no health care visits based on the 1977 Standards are: 0.1 percentage points higher for white children; 0.3 percentage points lower for black children; 1.0 percentage points lower for AI/AN children; and 1.2 percentage points lower for Asian and Pacific Islander children.

[4]Poverty status is based on family income, family size, number of children in the family, and for families with two or fewer adults the age of the adults in the family, using Bureau of the Census poverty thresholds. Poor persons are defined as below the poverty threshold. Near poor persons have incomes of 100 percent to less than 200 percent of the poverty threshold. Nonpoor persons have incomes of 200 percent or greater than the poverty threshold. Poverty status was unknown for 17 percent of children in the sample in 1997, 21 percent in 1998, 24 percent in 1999, and 23 percent in 2000.

[5]Health insurance categories are mutually exclusive. Persons who reported both Medicaid and private coverage are classified as having Medicaid coverage. Starting in 1997 Medicaid includes state-sponsored health plans and Child Health Insurance Program (CHIP).

[6]MSA is metropolitan statistical area.

SOURCE: "Table 75. No health care visits to an office or clinic within the past 12 months among children under 18 years of age, according to selected characteristics: United States, average annual 1997–98 and 1999–2000," in *Health, United States, 2002*, Centers for Disease Control and Prevention, National Center for Health Statistics, Hyattsville, MD, 2002

TABLE 1.5

Percent of young children (4–35 months of age) who missed or delayed medical care by child's type of health insurance, 2000

Missed or delayed medical care during the past 12 months	Child's type of health insurance				All young children
	Private only	Public only	Other insured	Uninsured	
	Percent of young children				
Child needed medical care and did not get it	4	4	6	14	5
Child got medical care later than parent/guardian would have liked	10	10	15	15	11
	Standard error of percent				
Child needed medical care and did not get it	0.9	0.8	1.7	3.5	0.6
Child got medical care later than parent/guardian would have liked	1.3	1.4	2.6	3.6	0.9

SOURCE: "Table 26. Percent of young children (4–35 months of age) who missed or delayed medical care by child's type of health insurance: United States, 2000," in *Summary Statistics From the National Survey of Childhood Health, 2000,* Centers for Disease Control and Prevention, National Center for Health Statistics, Hyattsville, MD, 2002

TABLE 1.6

Percent of young children (4–35 months of age) by extent of difficulty paying for selected health services for the child and by child's type of health insurance, 2000

Extent of difficulty paying for selected services	Child's type of health insurance				All young children
	Private only	Public only	Other insured	Uninsured	
	Percent of young children				
Prenatal care during pregnancy?					
No trouble at all	94	92	92	80	92
Some trouble or a lot of trouble	6	8	8	20	8
Medical expenses for child's birth?					
No trouble at all	87	92	92	76	88
Some trouble or a lot of trouble	13	8	8	24	12
Child's health and medical expenses?					
No trouble at all	89	89	91	61	87
Some trouble or a lot of trouble	11	11	9	39	13
	Standard error of percent				
Prenatal care during pregnancy?					
No trouble at all	1.0	1.5	2.1	0.5	0.8
Some trouble or a lot of trouble	1.0	1.5	2.1	0.5	0.8
Medical expenses for child's birth?					
No trouble at all	1.6	1.7	1.8	4.8	1.1
Some trouble or a lot of trouble	1.6	1.7	1.8	4.8	1.1
Child's health and medical expenses?					
No trouble at all	1.5	1.8	2.1	5.6	1.1
Some trouble or a lot of trouble	1.5	1.8	2.1	5.6	1.1

SOURCE: "Table 27. Percent of young children (4–35 months of age) by extent of difficulty paying for selected health services for the child and by child's type of health insurance: United States, 2000," in *Summary Statistics From the National Survey of Childhood Health, 2000,* Centers for Disease Control and Prevention, National Center for Health Statistics, Hyattsville, MD, 2002

CHAPTER 2

PHYSICIANS, NURSES, DENTISTS, AND OTHER HEALTH CARE PRACTITIONERS

The art of medicine consists of amusing the patient while nature cures the disease.
—Voltaire (1694–1778)

One of the first duties of the physician is to educate the masses not to take medicine.
—William Osler (1849–1919)

PHYSICIANS

Physicians routinely perform medical examinations, provide preventive medicine services, diagnose illness, treat patients suffering from injury or disease, and offer counsel about how to achieve and maintain good health. There are two types of physicians trained in traditional Western medicine: the MD (Doctor of Medicine) is schooled in allopathic medicine and the DO (Doctor of Osteopathy) learns osteopathy. Allopathy is the philosophy and system of curing disease by producing conditions that are incompatible with disease, such as prescribing antibiotics to combat bacterial infection. The philosophy of osteopathy is different; it is based on recognition of the body's capacity for self-healing and it emphasizes structural and manipulative therapies such as postural education, manual treatment of the musculoskeletal system (osteopathic physicians are trained in hands-on diagnosis and treatment), and preventive medicine. Osteopathy is also considered a "holistic" practice because it considers the whole person, rather than simply the diseased organ or system.

In modern medical practice, the philosophical differences may not be obvious to most health care consumers since MDs and DOs use many comparable methods of treatment, including prescribing medication and performing surgery. In fact, the American Osteopathic Association (AOA), the national medical professional society that represents about 47,000 DOs, admits that many people who seek care from osteopathic physicians may be entirely unaware of their physicians' training, which emphasizes holistic interventions or special skills such as manipula-

tive techniques. Like MDs, DOs complete four years of medical school and postgraduate residency training; may specialize in areas such as surgery, psychiatry, or obstetrics; and must pass state licensing examinations in order to practice.

Medical School, Postgraduate Training and Qualifications

Modern medicine requires considerable skill and extensive training. The road to gaining admission to medical school and becoming a physician is long, difficult, and intensely competitive. Applicants to medical school must earn excellent college grades while acquiring their undergraduate degrees, achieve high scores on entrance exams, and demonstrate emotional maturity and motivation to be admitted to medical school. Once admitted to medical school, students spend the first two years primarily in laboratories and classrooms learning basic medical sciences such as anatomy (detailed understanding of body structure), physiology (biological processes and vital functions), and biochemistry. They also learn how to take medical histories, perform complete physical examinations, and recognize symptoms of diseases. During their third and fourth years, the medical students work under supervision at teaching hospitals and clinics where they learn acute, chronic, preventive, and rehabilitative patient care. By completing "clerkships"—spending time in different specialties such as internal medicine, obstetrics and gynecology, pediatrics, psychiatry, and surgery—they acquire the necessary skills and gain experience to diagnose and treat a wide variety of illnesses.

Following medical school, new physicians must complete a year of internship, also referred to as "postgraduate year 1 (PGY1)" emphasizing either general medical practice or one of the specialties and providing clinical experience in various hospital services—inpatient care, outpatient clinics, emergency rooms, and operating rooms. In the past, many physicians entered practice after this first year of postgraduate training. In the present era of specialization, most physicians choose to continue in residency training, which lasts an additional three to six years, depending on the specialty. Those who choose a subspecialty such as cardiology, infectious diseases, oncology, or plastic surgery must spend additional years in residency and may then chose to complete fellowship training. Immediately after residency, they are eligible to take an examination to earn board certification in their chosen specialty. Fellowship training involves a year or two of laboratory and clinical research work as well as opportunities to gain additional clinical and patient care expertise.

Conventional and Newer Medical Specialties

Rapid advances in science and medicine along with changing needs have resulted in a variety of new medical and surgical specialties, subspecialties, and concentrations. For example, geriatrics, the medical subspecialty concerned with the prevention and treatment of diseases in the elderly, has developed in response to the growing population of older adults in need of medical care. In 1909 Dr. Ignatz L. Nascher coined the term geriatrics from the Greek "geras" (old age) and "iatrikos" (physician). Geriatricians are physicians trained in internal medicine or family practice who obtain additional training and certification in the diagnosis and treatment of older adults. According to the American Geriatrics Society, the United States currently needs at least 20,000 geriatricians to care for its 36 million older adults. In 2002 board-certified geriatricians numbered only 9,500—still less than half of the estimated need.

Another relatively new medical specialty has resulted in "intensivists." Intensivists, as the name indicates, are trained to staff hospital intensive care units (ICUs, sometimes known as critical care units or CCUs), where the most critically ill patients are cared for using a comprehensive array of state-of-the-art technology and equipment. This specialty arose in response to both the increasing complexity of care provided in ICUs and the demonstrated benefits of immediate availability of highly trained physicians to care for critically ill patients.

More traditional medical specialties include:

- Anesthesiologist—administers anesthesia (partial or complete loss of sensation) and monitors patients in surgery

- Cardiologist—diagnoses and treats diseases of the heart and blood vessels

- Dermatologist—trained to diagnose and treat diseases of the skin, hair, and nails

- Family Practitioner—delivers primary care to persons of all ages and, when necessary, refers patients to other physician specialists

- Gastroenterologist—specializes in digestive system disorders

- Internist—provides diagnosis and nonsurgical treatment of a broad array of illnesses affecting adults

- Neurologist—specializes in the nervous system—diagnosis and treatment of brain, spinal cord, and nerve disorders

- Obstetrician-gynecologist—provides health care for women and their reproductive systems, as well as care for mother and baby before, during, and immediately following delivery

- Oncologist—dedicated to the diagnosis and treatment of cancer

- Otolaryngologist—skilled in the medical and surgical treatment of ear, nose, and throat disorders and related structures of the face, head, and neck

- Pathologist—uses skills in microscopic chemical analysis and diagnostics to direct detection of disease in the laboratory

- Psychiatrist—specializes in the prevention, diagnosis, and treatment of mental health and emotional disorders

- Pulmonologist—specializes in diseases of the lungs and respiratory system

- Urologist—provides diagnosis as well as medical and surgical treatment of the urinary tract in both men and women as well as male reproductive health services.

HIGH COSTS, LONG HOURS, AND LOW WAGES. Historically, medical training has been difficult and involved long hours. Residents typically worked 24- to 36-hour shifts and more than 80 hours a week. Lack of sleep and low wages are a way of life for most medical students and residents, although the 36-hour shift has come under criticism as an unnecessary, and possibly dangerous, practice. In 1995 the state of New York limited most residents to 24-hour shifts and 80-hour weeks. The regulations were the first of their kind in the country. New York has almost 150 teaching hospitals and trains 16 percent of the nation's doctors.

In 2001 the Committee of Interns and Residents and the American Medical Student Association, which represents more than 30,000 physicians-in-training, were two of several groups to petition the U.S. Department of Labor's Occupational Safety and Health Administration (OSHA) to limit the number of hours medical residents must work. The petition observed that sleep deprivation among physicians in training, who may work as many as 130 hours a week with only one day off, increases their risk of automobile accidents, depression, and other ailments, and poses risks to the patients they treat. The petition sought a limit of 80 hours per week, with a maximum of 24 hours in one shift and with 10 hours between shifts.

For emergency medicine residents, the maximum allowable hours of work per day would be 12.

By 2002, several states and many professional associations including the AOA approved an 80-hour workweek for all interns and residents. The AOA ruled that interns and residents may not work more than 24 consecutive hours. To reduce the possibility of diagnostic and treatment errors, residents are forbidden to assume responsibility for new patients after they have worked 24 hours. The AOA mandated that its training programs comply with this measure by November 1, 2002, in order to retain their accreditation. On July 20, 2002, in a published statement, Dr. James Zini, the 2001–2002 president of the AOA, said: "Patient safety is our number one priority, and that is the main reason the osteopathic profession will implement these changes this fall."

For the 2001–2002 school year, median annual medical school costs ranged from about $11,000 for in-state residents at public schools, to $27,000 for nonresidents; private school tuition and fees were as much as $30,000 per year. Still, tuition and fees do not even completely cover the cost of educating prospective physicians—tuition is subsidized by other university teaching hospital activities as well as grants and endowments. Graduating in 2000, the average medical school student had incurred debt comparable to a home mortgage—about $100,000. Medical school debt has increased a staggering 60 percent since 1993, when students owed an average of $60,000 at graduation. Although physicians' earning power is considerable, and many students are able to repay their debts during their first years of practice, some observers believe that the extent of their indebtedness may unduly influence medical students' career choices. They may train for higher paying specialties and subspecialties rather than following their natural interests or opting to practice in underrepresented specialties or under-served geographic areas. The high cost of medical education also is believed to limit the number of minority applicants.

Applying to Medical School

The average premedical student applies to 12 medical schools. There is an average of 2.6 applicants for every available opening. The ratio, however, jumps as high as 70 to 1 for small, selective schools such as the Mayo Medical School in Rochester, Minnesota, or the Yale College of Medicine in New Haven, Connecticut. After a drop in the 1980s, medical school applications increased steadily throughout the 1990s until 1996, after which applications began to decrease again. The Association of American Medical Colleges (AAMC) reported 34,859 medical school applications in 2001, a drop of 6 percent from the previous year, and steeply down (almost 26 percent) from an all-time high of 46,965 in 1996. These applicants were vying for 16,500 available places.

There are several explanations for the decline in medical school applications. With the exponential growth in the cost of medical school, some prospective students may no longer be willing or able to incur such significant debt. Another factor may be physician concern about the growing health care system bureaucracy and unavoidable paperwork, including requirements to seek approval from insurers for many diagnostic tests, surgical procedures, and admission of patients to hospitals. Intrusion into medical practice from government and private payers, fear of malpractice suits, and increasing consumer demand for greater equality in physician–patient relationships, may have combined to diminish some of the professional satisfaction, prestige, and status associated with the medical practice.

Still, despite mounting costs for medical education and growing constraints on physicians' practices, a medical degree still offers continuing employment, economic security, and a measurable way to help people. Many potential physicians consider medicine a rewarding and relatively "recession-proof" way to earn a living.

APPLICANTS AND STUDENTS BECOMING OLDER AND MORE DIVERSE. Classes in American medical schools more closely resemble the American population in gender and ethnic background than they did two decades ago. However, minority enrollment has declined in recent years from its peak in the early and mid-1990s. For the 1999–2000 school year, about 43.3 percent of those enrolled in medical school (allopathic and osteopathic programs) classes were female. About 18.9 percent were Asian, about 7.1 percent were black, and about 6.1 percent were Hispanic. (See Table 2.1.) Medical students are also older than they used to be. In the past, almost all students entered medical school directly from undergraduate college. While the majority of students in the late 1990s were still fresh from college, 20 percent were between the ages of 24 and 27 upon application to medical school, and nearly 10 percent were between the ages of 28 and 31, and many medical schools have come to value the maturity and experience of older students.

Number of Physicians Increasing

In 2000 an estimated 772,296 physicians practiced medicine in the United States, about 36 percent more than the 567,610 practicing in 1990. (See Table 2.2.) The overwhelming majority (94.2 percent) were MDs; the remaining 5.8 percent were osteopathic physicians (DOs). The proportion of physicians increased dramatically in the 1980s and 1990s—from 189.8 per 100,000 in 1980, to 230.2 in 1990, to 277.8 in 2000.

Table 2.3 reveals that in 2000, New England and the Middle Atlantic states had the highest ratio (30.4 and 28.9 per 10,000, respectively) of physicians practicing in patient care (as opposed to researchers, educators, or retired) to population. Idaho and Oklahoma were the

TABLE 2.1

Total enrollment of minorities in schools for selected health occupations, according to detailed race and Hispanic origin, academic years 1970–71, 1980–81, 1990–91, and 1998–99

[Data are based on reporting by health professions associations]

Occupation, detailed race, and Hispanic origin	1970–71[1]	1980–81	1990–91	1999–2000[2]	1970–71[1]	1980–81	1990–91	1999–2000[2]
	Number of students				Percent distribution of students			
Dentistry[3]								
All races	19,187	22,842	15,951	17,242	100.0	100.0	100.0	100.0
White, non-Hispanic[4]	17,531	20,208	11,185	11,106	91.4	88.5	70.1	64.4
Black, non-Hispanic	872	1,022	940	808	4.5	4.5	5.9	4.7
Hispanic	185	519	1,254	912	1.0	2.3	7.9	5.3
American Indian	28	53	53	99	0.1	0.2	0.3	0.6
Asian	490	1,040	2,519	4,317	2.6	4.6	15.8	25.0
Medicine (Allopathic)								
All races[4]	40,238	65,189	65,163	66,444	100.0	100.0	100.0	100.0
White, non-Hispanic	37,944	55,434	47,893	42,589	94.3	85.0	73.5	64.1
Black, non-Hispanic	1,509	3,708	4,241	5,051	3.8	5.7	6.5	7.6
Hispanic	196	2,761	3,538	4,322	0.5	4.2	5.4	6.5
Mexican	–	951	1,109	1,746	–	1.5	1.7	2.6
Mainland Puerto Rican	–	329	457	482	–	0.5	0.7	0.7
Other Hispanic[5]	–	1,481	1,972	2,094	–	2.3	3.0	3.2
American Indian	18	221	277	574	0.0	0.3	0.4	0.9
Asian	571	1,924	8,436	12,950	1.4	3.0	12.9	19.5
Medicine (Osteopathic)								
All races	2,304	4,940	6,792	10,388	100.0	100.0	100.0	100.0
White, non-Hispanic[4]	2,241	4,688	5,680	8,019	97.3	94.9	83.6	77.2
Black, non-Hispanic	27	94	217	399	1.2	1.9	3.2	3.8
Hispanic	19	52	277	370	0.8	1.1	4.1	3.6
American Indian	6	19	36	65	0.3	0.4	0.5	0.6
Asian	11	87	582	1,535	0.5	1.8	8.6	14.8
Nursing, registered[3,6]								
All races	211,239	230,966	221,170	238,244	–	–	100.0	100.0
White, non-Hispanic[4]	–	–	183,102	193,061	–	–	82.8	81.0
Black, non-Hispanic	–	–	23,094	23,611	–	–	10.4	9.9
Hispanic	–	–	6,580	9,227	–	–	3.0	3.9
American Indian	–	–	1,803	1,816	–	–	0.8	0.8
Asian	–	–	6,591	10,529	–	–	3.0	4.4
Optometry[3,5]								
All races	3,094	4,540	4,650	5,313	100.0	100.0	100.0	100.0
White, non-Hispanic[4]	2,913	4,148	3,706	3,619	94.1	91.4	79.7	68.1
Black, non-Hispanic	32	57	134	108	1.0	1.3	2.9	2.0
Hispanic	30	80	186	269	1.0	1.8	4.0	5.1
American Indian	2	12	21	30	0.1	0.3	0.5	0.6
Asian	117	243	603	1,287	3.8	5.4	13.0	24.2
Pharmacy[7]								
All races	17,909	21,628	22,764	32,537	100.0	100.0	100.0	100.0
White, non-Hispanic[4]	16,222	19,153	18,325	22,184	90.6	88.6	80.5	68.2
Black, non-Hispanic	659	945	1,301	2,697	3.7	4.4	5.7	8.3
Hispanic	254	459	945	1,086	1.4	2.1	4.2	3.3
American Indian	29	36	63	156	0.2	0.2	0.3	0.5
Asian	672	1,035	2,130	6,414	3.8	4.8	9.4	19.7

states with the fewest physicians active in patient care (14.4 and 14.8 per 10,000) and the Mountain region—including Montana, Idaho, Wyoming, Colorado, New Mexico, Arizona, Utah, and Nevada—was the region with the fewest practicing physicians (18.1 per 10,000).

Many Specialists

Most doctors are specialists rather than primary care generalists. Primary care physicians are the "frontline" of the health care system—the first health professionals most people see for medical problems or routine care. Family practitioners, internists, pediatricians, and general practitioners are considered to be primary care practitioners.

Primary care physicians tend to see the same patients regularly and develop relationships with patients over time as they offer preventive services, scheduled visits, follow-up, and urgent medical care. When necessary, they refer patients for consultation with, and care from, physician specialists. In 2000 only 12 percent of professionally active physicians were in general and family practice, 13.9 percent were in internal medicine, and 7 percent were in pediatrics. (See Table 2.4.) These doctors are considered primary care physicians and together account for almost 33 percent of active physicians. The rest were physician specialists. The most common specialists are general surgeons, obstetricians and gynecologists, anes-

TABLE 2.1

Total enrollment of minorities in schools for selected health occupations, according to detailed race and Hispanic origin, academic years 1970–71, 1980–81, 1990–91, and 1998–99 [CONTINUED]

[Data are based on reporting by health professions associations]

Occupation, detailed race, and Hispanic origin	1970–71[1]	1980–81	1990–91	1999–2000[2]	1970–71[1]	1980–81	1990–91	1999–2000[2]
	Number of students				Percent distribution of students			
Podiatry								
All races	1,268	2,577	2,226	2,258	100.0	100.0	100.0	100.0
White, non-Hispanic[4]	1,228	2,353	1,671	1,576	96.8	91.3	75.1	69.8
Black, non-Hispanic	27	110	237	192	2.1	4.3	10.6	8.5
Hispanic	5	39	148	122	0.4	1.5	6.6	5.4
American Indian	1	6	7	10	0.1	0.2	0.3	0.4
Asian	7	69	163	358	0.6	2.7	7.3	15.9

—Data not available.

[1]Data for osteopathic medicine, podiatry, and optometry are for 1971–72. Data for pharmacy and registered nurses are for 1972–73.
[2]Data for podiatry exclude New York College of Podiatric Medicine. Data for registered nurses are for 1996–97 and optometry are for 1998–99.
[3]Excludes Puerto Rican schools.
[4]Includes race and ethnicity unspecified.
[5]Includes Puerto Rican Commonwealth students.
[6]In 1990 the National League for Nursing developed a new system for analyzing minority data. In evaluating the former system, much underreporting was noted. Therefore, race-specific data before 1990 would not be comparable and are not shown. Additional changes in the minority data question were introduced for academic years 1992–93 and 1993–94 resulting in a discontinuity in the trend.
[7]Prior to 1992–93 pharmacy total enrollment data are for students in the final 3 years of pharmacy education. Beginning in 1992–93 pharmacy data are for all students.
Note: Total enrollment data are collected at the beginning of the academic year. Data for chiropractic students and occupational, physical, and speech therapy students were not available for this table.

SOURCE: "Table 105. Total enrollment of minorities in schools for selected health occupations, according to detailed race and Hispanic origin: United States, academic years 1970–71, 1980–81, 1990–91, and 1998–2000," in *Health, United States, 2002,* Centers for Disease Control and Prevention, National Center for Health Statistics, Hyattsville, MD, 2002

thesiologists, and psychiatrists. In 1999 about 73 percent (473,241) of all nonfederal doctors were in office-based rather than hospital-based practices.

Working Conditions

Many physicians work long, irregular hours. The American Medical Association (AMA) reported that in 2000 the average physician worked about 60 hours a week performing patient care and administrative duties such as office management. Physicians in salaried positions, such as those employed by health maintenance organizations (HMOs), usually have shorter and more regular hours and enjoy more flexible work schedules than those in private practice. Instead of working as solo practitioners, growing numbers of physicians work in clinics, or are partners in group practices or other integrated health care systems. Medical group practices allow physicians to have more flexible schedules, realize purchasing economies of scale, pool their money to finance expensive medical equipment, and can be better able to adapt to changes in the health care environment.

During the late 1990s the typical physician spent about 50 hours per week on patient care. More than half (54 percent) of it was spent in the office, while about 18 percent was spent making hospital rounds, and 13 percent was in surgery. Naturally, physicians' hours varied somewhat depending on their specialties. General and family practitioners and pediatricians spent far more time conducting office visits, while surgeons, obstetricians, and gynecologists spent more time at the hospital performing

procedures. According to the AMA, the average physician saw a total (hospital and office visits) of 118.4 patients per week. General and family practitioners examined and treated 144.4 patients per week; pediatricians, 133.5; obstetricians and gynecologists, 112.2; internists, 110.7; and surgeons, 106.9.

The average physician had 79.2 office visits per week. These ranged from 111.6 office visits for general and family practitioners, 104.4 for pediatricians, 86.6 for obstetricians and gynecologists, 75.4 for surgeons, and 64.3 for internists (physicians who specialize in internal medicine).

Physicians' Earnings and Opportunities

Physicians' earnings are among the highest of any profession. According to the AMA, the median (half were higher and half were lower) net income (after expenses and taxes) for all physicians in 1999 was $160,000. The range of salaries varies widely and is often based on a physician's specialty, the number of years in practice, hours worked, and geographic location. Cardiovascular surgeons and neurosurgeons were top earners with incomes in excess of $300,000, while pediatricians earned the least, $126,000 a year.

Although the costs of running a medical practice have increased as a result of additional administrative requirements such as complicated billing and reimbursement formulas, the prospects for physicians' employment and earnings continue to be excellent. Demand for physicians' services keeps pace with the growing and aging U.S.

TABLE 2.2

Active health personnel according to occupation, 1980–2000

[Data are compiled by the Bureau of Health Professions]

Occupation	1980	1985[1]	1990	1995	1999	2000[2]
			Number of active health personnel			
Chiropractors	25,600	—	41,500	47,200	—	—
Dentists[3]	121,900	133,500	147,500	158,600	164,700	168,000
Nurses, registered	1,272,900	1,538,100	1,789,600	2,115,800	2,271,300	—
Associate and diploma	908,300	1,024,500	1,107,300	1,235,100	1,290,400	—
Baccalaureate	297,300	419,900	549,000	673,200	739,000	—
Masters and doctorate	67,300	93,700	133,300	207,500	241,900	—
Nutritionists/Dieticians	32,000	—	67,000	—	—	97,000
Occupational therapists	25,000	—	34,000	—	—	55,000
Optometrists	22,330	23,900	26,000	28,900	—	29,500
Pharmacists	142,780	159,200	161,900	182,300	—	208,000
Physical therapists	50,000	—	92,000	—	—	144,000
Physicians	427,122	542,653	567,610	672,859	753,176	772,296
Federal	17,642	23,305	20,784	21,153	17,338	19,228
Doctors of medicine[4]	16,585	21,938	19,166	19,830	17,224	19,110
Doctors of osteopathy	1,057	1,367	1,618	1,323	114	118
Non-Federal	409,480	519,348	546,826	651,706	735,838	753,068
Doctors of medicine[4]	393,407	497,473	520,450	617,362	693,345	708,463
Doctors of osteopathy	16,073	21,875	26,376	34,344	42,493	44,605
Podiatrists[5]	7,000	9,700	10,600	10,300	—	—
Speech therapists	50,000	—	65,000	—	—	97,000
			Number per 100,000 population			
Chiropractors	11.2	—	16.5	17.8	—	—
Dentists[3]	54.0	56.5	59.5	60.7	60.7	60.4
Nurses, registered	560.0	641.4	713.7	797.6	832.9	—
Associate and diploma	399.9	425.8	441.6	465.5	473.2	—
Baccalaureate	130.9	175.6	218.9	253.8	271.0	—
Masters and doctorate	29.6	39.9	53.2	78.2	88.7	—
Nutritionists/Dieticians	14.0	—	26.7	—	—	35.2
Occupational therapists	10.9	—	13.5	—	—	20.0
Optometrists	9.8	9.9	10.4	10.9	—	11.1
Pharmacists	62.5	66.3	64.4	68.9	—	75.6
Physical therapists	21.8	—	36.6	—	—	52.3
Physicians	189.8	221.3	230.2	255.9	277.4	277.8
Federal	7.8	9.5	8.4	8.0	6.4	6.9
Doctors of medicine[4]	7.4	8.9	7.7	7.5	6.3	6.9
Doctors of osteopathy	0.5	0.6	0.7	0.5	0.1	0.0
Non-Federal	182.0	211.8	221.8	247.9	271.0	270.9
Doctors of medicine[4]	174.9	202.9	211.1	234.8	255.4	254.9
Doctors of osteopathy	7.1	8.9	10.7	13.1	15.7	16.0
Podiatrists[5]	3.0	4.2	4.2	3.9	—	—
Speech therapists	21.8	—	25.9	—	—	36.4

—Data not available.

[1]Osteopath data are for 1986 and podiatric data are for 1984.

[2]Data for optometrists and speech therapists are for 1996.

[3]Excludes dentists in military service, U.S. Public Health Service, and Department of Veterans Affairs.

[4]Excludes physicians with unknown addresses and those who do not practice or practice less than 20 hours per week.

[5]Podiatrists in patient care.

Note: Some numbers in this table for dentists have been revised and differ from previous editions of *Health, United States*. Ratios for physicians and dentists are based on civilian population; ratios for all other health occupations are based on resident population. From 1989 to 1994 data for doctors of medicine are as of January 1; in other years these data are as of December 31.

SOURCE: "Table 103. Active health personnel according to occupation: United States, 1980–2000," *Health, United States, 2002*, Centers for Disease Control and Prevention, National Center for Health Statistics, Hyattsville, MD, 2002

population and rapidly evolving biotechnological advances promise to enable physicians to do more, for more people. According to the U.S. Bureau of Labor Statistics, future opportunities for physicians will be plentiful, especially in rural and low-income communities.

Physician Office Visits

In 2000 Americans made more than 823 million office visits to physicians, an average of about 3 visits per year. (See Table 2.5.) Women visited physicians (3.5 times) more often than men (2.6 times) and as expected, persons over 65 years of age saw doctors more than twice as often as most younger persons. Men age 75 and older made the most office visits—about 6.7 per year. Blacks of all ages made fewer physician office visits than whites, and black children under age 18 visited physicians about 1.7 times per year while white children made 2.4 visits per year.

People also visited physicians in other settings including hospital emergency departments and home visits, making the total of all ambulatory care visits to physi-

TABLE 2.3

Active non-federal physicians and doctors of medicine in patient care, according to geographic division and state, 1975, 1985, 1995, and 2000

[Data are based on reporting by physicians]

Geographic division and state	Total physicians[1]				Doctors of medicine in patient care[2]			
	1975	1985	1995[3]	2000[4]	1975	1985	1995	2000
	Number per 10,000 civilian population							
United States	15.3	20.7	24.2	25.8	13.5	18.0	21.3	22.7
New England	19.1	26.7	32.5	34.3	16.9	22.9	28.8	30.4
Maine	12.8	18.7	22.3	26.8	10.7	15.6	18.2	21.7
New Hampshire	14.3	18.1	21.5	23.8	13.1	16.7	19.8	21.7
Vermont	18.2	23.8	26.9	32.0	15.5	20.3	24.2	28.8
Massachusetts	20.8	30.2	37.5	38.6	18.3	25.4	33.2	34.4
Rhode Island	17.8	23.3	30.4	32.5	16.1	20.2	26.7	28.8
Connecticut	19.8	27.6	32.8	33.7	17.7	24.3	29.5	30.3
Middle Atlantic	19.5	26.1	32.4	33.7	17.0	22.2	28.0	28.9
New York	22.7	29.0	35.3	36.2	20.2	25.2	31.6	32.3
New Jersey	16.2	23.4	29.3	31.1	14.0	19.8	24.9	26.2
Pennsylvania	16.6	23.6	30.1	31.6	13.9	19.2	24.6	25.4
East North Central	13.9	19.3	23.3	24.8	12.0	16.4	19.8	21.1
Ohio	14.1	19.9	23.8	25.4	12.2	16.8	20.0	21.3
Indiana	10.6	14.7	18.4	20.0	9.6	13.2	16.6	18.0
Illinois	14.5	20.5	24.8	26.1	13.1	18.2	22.1	23.1
Michigan	15.4	20.8	24.8	26.3	12.0	16.0	19.0	20.2
Wisconsin	12.5	17.7	21.5	23.1	11.4	15.9	19.6	20.9
West North Central	13.3	18.3	21.8	23.0	11.4	15.6	18.9	19.9
Minnesota	14.9	20.5	23.4	24.9	13.7	18.5	21.5	23.0
Iowa	11.4	15.6	19.2	19.8	9.4	12.4	15.1	15.5
Missouri	15.0	20.5	23.9	24.7	11.6	16.3	19.7	20.2
North Dakota	9.7	15.8	20.5	21.5	9.2	14.9	18.9	19.8
South Dakota	8.2	13.4	16.7	19.2	7.7	12.3	15.7	17.7
Nebraska	12.1	15.7	19.8	21.7	10.9	14.4	18.3	20.1
Kansas	12.8	17.3	20.8	21.8	11.2	15.1	18.0	18.8
South Atlantic	14.0	19.7	23.4	24.5	12.6	17.6	21.0	22.0
Delaware	14.3	19.7	23.4	24.7	12.7	17.1	19.7	21.0
Maryland	18.6	30.4	34.1	35.4	16.5	24.9	29.9	31.1
District of Columbia	39.6	55.3	63.6	62.5	34.6	45.6	53.6	54.5
Virginia	12.9	19.5	22.5	23.9	11.9	17.8	20.8	22.0
West Virginia	11.0	16.3	21.0	23.5	10.0	14.6	17.9	19.5
North Carolina	11.7	16.9	21.1	22.3	10.6	15.0	19.4	20.5
South Carolina	10.0	14.7	18.9	21.0	9.3	13.6	17.6	19.4
Georgia	11.5	16.2	19.7	20.4	10.6	14.7	18.0	18.6
Florida	15.2	20.2	22.9	24.1	13.4	17.8	20.3	21.2
East South Central	10.5	15.0	19.2	20.7	9.7	14.0	17.8	19.1
Kentucky	10.9	15.1	19.2	20.6	10.1	13.9	18.0	19.1
Tennessee	12.4	17.7	22.5	23.6	11.3	16.2	20.8	21.8
Alabama	9.2	14.2	18.4	19.8	8.6	13.1	17.0	18.2
Mississippi	8.4	11.8	13.9	16.6	8.0	11.1	13.0	15.2
West South Central	11.9	16.4	19.5	20.6	10.5	14.5	17.3	18.2
Arkansas	9.1	13.8	17.3	18.8	8.5	12.8	16.0	17.3
Louisiana	11.4	17.3	21.7	23.8	10.5	16.1	20.3	22.4
Oklahoma	11.6	16.1	18.8	19.4	9.4	12.9	14.7	14.8
Texas	12.5	16.8	19.4	20.3	11.0	14.7	17.3	17.9
Mountain	14.3	17.8	20.2	20.7	12.6	15.7	17.8	18.1
Montana	10.6	14.0	18.4	20.4	10.1	13.2	17.1	18.8
Idaho	9.5	12.1	13.9	15.8	8.9	11.4	13.1	14.4
Wyoming	9.5	12.9	15.3	17.3	8.9	12.0	13.9	15.7
Colorado	17.3	20.7	23.7	24.0	15.0	17.7	20.6	20.9
New Mexico	12.2	17.0	20.2	20.9	10.1	14.7	18.0	18.5
Arizona	16.7	20.2	21.4	20.9	14.1	17.1	18.2	17.6
Utah	14.1	17.2	19.2	19.6	13.0	15.5	17.6	17.8
Nevada	11.9	16.0	16.7	18.0	10.9	14.5	14.6	15.9

cian offices, hospital outpatient, and emergency departments more than 1 billion for the first time, and the average number of visits for each American 3.7 in 2000. Understandably, persons who considered their health to be "fair or poor" made more visits than those who considered their health "good to excellent." In 2000 just 10.6 percent of respondents in good health made 10 or more

health care visits compared to almost 42 percent of persons who rated their health as fair or poor. (See Table 2.6.)

Poor and near poor persons of all races were more likely to report more than 10 health care visits during 2000 than the nonpoor, however, more poor and near poor whites (20.1 and 16.9 percent, respectively) made at least

TABLE 2.3

Active non-federal physicians and doctors of medicine in patient care, according to geographic division and state, 1975, 1985, 1995, and 2000 [CONTINUED]

[Data are based on reporting by physicians]

Geographic division and state	Total physicians[1]				Doctors of medicine in patient care[2]			
	1975	1985	1995[3]	2000[4]	1975	1985	1995	2000
	Number per 10,000 civilian population							
Pacific	17.9	22.5	23.3	23.7	16.3	20.5	21.2	21.5
Washington	15.3	20.2	22.5	23.7	13.6	17.9	20.2	21.2
Oregon	15.6	19.7	21.6	22.9	13.8	17.6	19.5	20.5
California	18.8	23.7	23.7	23.8	17.3	21.5	21.7	21.6
Alaska	8.4	13.0	15.7	18.5	7.8	12.1	14.2	16.3
Hawaii	16.2	21.5	24.8	26.4	14.7	19.8	22.8	24.0

[1]Includes active non-federal doctors of medicine and active doctors of osteopathy.
[2]Excludes doctors of osteopathy (DO's); States with more than 2,500 active DO's are Pennsylvania, Michigan, Ohio, Florida, Texas, New York, and New Jersey. States with fewer than 100 active DO's are Wyoming, Vermont, North Dakota, South Dakota, Nebraska, Montana, Alaska, Louisiana, and District of Columbia. Excludes doctors of medicine in medical teaching, administration, research, and other nonpatient care activities.
[3]Data for doctors of osteopathy are as of July 1996.
[4]Data for doctors of osteopathy are as of January 2001.
Note: Data for doctors of medicine are as of December 31.

SOURCE: "Table 100. Active non-Federal physicians and doctors of medicine in patient care, according to geographic division and State: United States, 1975, 1985, 1995, and 2000," in *Health, United States, 2002*, Centers for Disease Control and Prevention, National Center for Health Statistics, Hyattsville, MD, 2002

TABLE 2.4

Primary care doctors of medicine, according to specialty, U.S. and outlying areas, selected years, 1949–2000

[Data are based on reporting by physicians]

Specialty	1949[1]	1960[1]	1970	1980	1990	1995	1997	1998	1999	2000
	Number									
Total[2]	201,277	260,484	334,028	467,679	615,421	720,325	756,710	777,859	797,634	813,770
Active doctors of medicine[3]	191,577	247,257	310,845	414,916	547,310	625,443	664,556	667,000	669,949	692,368
Primary care generalists	113,222	125,359	115,822	146,093	183,294	207,810	216,598	218,421	221,206	227,992
General/family practice	95,980	88,023	57,948	60,049	70,480	75,976	78,258	79,769	81,487	83,165
Internal medicine	12,453	26,209	39,924	58,462	76,295	88,240	93,797	93,227	92,976	96,469
Pediatrics	4,789	11,127	17,950	27,582	36,519	43,594	44,543	45,425	46,743	48,358
Primary care specialists	—	—	2,817	14,949	27,434	35,290	32,918	34,299	37,424	40,675
Internal medicine	—	—	1,948	13,069	22,054	26,928	24,582	25,365	27,140	29,382
Pediatrics	—	—	869	1,880	5,380	8,362	8,336	8,934	10,284	11,293
	Percent of active doctors of medicine									
Primary care generalists	59.1	50.7	37.3	35.2	33.5	33.2	32.6	32.7	33.0	32.9
General/family practice	50.1	35.6	18.6	14.5	12.9	12.1	11.8	12.0	12.2	12.0
Internal medicine	6.5	10.6	12.8	14.1	13.9	14.1	14.1	14.0	13.9	13.9
Pediatrics	2.5	4.5	5.8	6.6	6.7	7.0	6.7	6.8	7.0	7.0
Primary care specialists	—	—	0.9	3.6	5.0	5.6	5.0	5.1	5.6	5.9
Internal medicine	—	—	0.6	3.1	4.0	4.3	3.7	3.8	4.1	4.2
Pediatrics	—	—	0.3	0.5	1.0	1.3	1.3	1.3	1.5	1.6

— Data not available.
[1]Estimated by the Bureau of Health Professions, Health Resources Administration. Active doctors of medicine (M.D.'s) include those with address unknown and primary specialty not classified.
[2]Includes M.D.'s engaged in federal and non-federal patient care (office-based or hospital-based) and other professional activities.
[3]Beginning in 1970, M.D.'s who are inactive, have unknown address, or primary specialty not classified are excluded.
Note: Data are as of December 31 except for 1990–94 data, which are as of January 1, and 1949 data, which are as of midyear. Outlying areas include Puerto Rico, Virgin Islands, and the Pacific islands of Canton, Caroline, Guam, Mariana, Marshall, American Samoa, and Wake.

SOURCE: "Table 102. Primary care doctors of medicine, according to specialty: United States and outlying U.S. areas, selected years, 1949–2000," in *Health, United States, 2002*, Centers for Disease Control and Prevention, National Center for Health Statistics, Hyattsville, MD, 2002

10 visits during the year than poor and near poor blacks (16.8 and 14.2 percent, respectively) and Hispanics (16.1 and 11.6 percent, respectively). (See Table 2.6.) Hispanics at all income levels were most likely to report no health care visits during 2000, possibly reflecting cultural or language barriers to access.

There also was considerable geographic variation in utilization and numbers of health visits. In 2000, persons living in the West made fewer health care visits than those in other parts of the country—20 percent of persons living in the West made no health care visits during the year, compared to 12.4 percent in the Northeast. (See Table 2.6.)

TABLE 2.5

Ambulatory care visits to physician offices and all other places by selected patient characteristics, selected years 1995–2000

[Data are based on reporting by a sample of office-based physicians and hospital outpatient and emergency departments]

Age, sex, and race	All places[1]				Physician offices			
	1995	1998	1999	2000	1995	1998	1999	2000
	Number of visits in thousands							
Total	860,858	1,005,078	944,122	1,014,848	697,082	829,280	756,734	823,542
Under 18 years	194,643	213,486	183,072	212,165	150,351	168,520	135,627	163,459
18–44 years	285,184	328,475	300,051	315,774	219,065	260,379	227,005	243,011
45–64 years	188,319	237,700	240,688	255,894	159,531	203,296	201,911	216,783
45–54 years	104,891	132,146	130,824	142,233	88,266	112,316	108,597	119,474
55–64 years	83,429	105,555	109,864	113,661	71,264	90,979	93,315	97,309
65 years and over	192,712	225,416	220,311	231,014	168,135	197,085	192,190	200,289
65–74 years	102,605	115,526	106,066	116,505	90,544	102,306	92,642	102,447
75 years and over	90,106	109,890	114,245	114,510	77,591	94,779	99,548	97,842
	Number of visits per 100 persons							
Total, age adjusted[2]	334	377	352	374	271	312	283	304
Total, crude	329	373	347	370	266	308	279	300
Under 18 years	275	297	254	293	213	235	188	226
18–44 years	264	303	277	291	203	240	209	224
45–64 years	364	419	410	423	309	358	344	358
45–54 years	339	384	368	385	286	327	305	324
55–64 years	401	473	477	481	343	407	405	412
65 years and over	612	697	679	706	534	609	592	613
65–74 years	560	643	596	656	494	569	521	577
75 years and over	683	764	779	766	588	659	679	654
Sex and age								
Male, age adjusted[2]	290	321	309	325	232	261	246	261
Male, crude	277	310	297	314	220	251	235	251
Under 18 years	274	303	255	302	209	239	189	231
18–44 years	190	202	206	203	139	149	150	148
45–54 years	275	302	300	316	229	251	247	260
55–64 years	351	435	427	428	300	379	361	367
65–74 years	508	608	580	614	445	538	510	539
75 years and over	711	739	758	771	616	640	663	670
Female, age adjusted[2]	377	431	393	420	309	360	317	345
Female, crude	378	433	396	424	310	362	320	348
Under 18 years	277	291	252	285	217	231	187	221
18–44 years	336	401	345	377	265	328	267	298
45–54 years	400	462	432	451	339	399	361	384
55–64 years	446	506	522	529	382	433	445	453
65–74 years	603	672	610	692	534	595	530	609
75 years and over	666	780	792	763	571	671	689	645
Race and age[3]								
White, age adjusted[2]	339	376	356	380	282	316	292	315
White, crude	338	376	357	381	281	317	293	316
Under 18 years	295	293	258	306	238	235	197	243
18–44 years	267	305	284	301	211	248	222	239
45–54 years	334	380	368	386	286	328	312	330
55–64 years	397	462	474	480	345	406	410	416
65–74 years	557	639	597	641	496	572	526	568
75 years and over	689	768	781	764	598	669	687	658
Black or African American, age adjusted[2]	309	400	355	353	204	281	239	239
Black or African American, crude	281	373	322	324	178	259	211	214
Under 18 years	193	315	237	264	100	217	144	167
18–44 years	260	317	267	257	158	207	155	149
45–54 years	387	426	398	383	281	310	277	269
55–64 years	414	561	543	495	294	411	404	373
65–74 years	553	660	611	656	429	511	485	512
75 years and over	534	725	780	745	395	537	608	568

* Estimates are considered unreliable. Data preceded by an asterisk have a relative standard error of 20–30 percent.
[1]All places includes visits to physician offices and hospital outpatient and emergency departments.
[2]Estimates are age adjusted to the year 2000 standard population using six age groups: under 18 years, 18–44 years, 45–54 years, 55–64 years, 65–74 years, and 75 years and over.
[3]Beginning in 1999 the instruction for the race item on the Patient Record Form was changed so that more than one race could be recorded. In previous years only one racial category could be checked. Estimates for racial groups presented in this table are for visits where only one race was recorded. Estimates for visits where multiple races were checked were unreliable and are not presented in this table.
Note: Rates are based on the civilian noninstitutionalized population as of July 1 adjusted for net underenumeration using the 1990 National Population Adjustment Matrix from the U.S. Bureau of the Census. Rates will be overestimated to the extent that visits by institutionalized persons are counted in the numerator (for example, hospital emergency department visits by nursing home residents) and institutionalized persons are omitted from the denominator.

SOURCE: Adapted from "Table 83. Ambulatory care visits to physician offices and hospital outpatient and emergency departments by selected patient characteristics: United States, selected years 1995–2000," in *Health, United States, 2002,* Centers for Disease Control and Prevention, National Center for Health Statistics, Hyattsville, MD, 2002

TABLE 2.6

Health care visits to doctor's offices, emergency departments, and home visits within the past 12 months, according to selected characteristics, 1997–2000

[Data are based on household interviews of a sample of the civilian noninstitutionalized population]

	Number of health care visits[1]											
	None			1–3 visits			4–9 visits			10 or more visits		
Characteristic	1997	1999	2000	1997	1999	2000	1997	1999	2000	1997	1999	2000
	Percent distribution											
All persons[2,3]	16.5	17.5	16.6	46.2	45.8	45.4	23.6	23.3	24.7	13.7	13.4	13.3
Age												
Under 18 years	11.8	12.4	12.2	54.1	54.4	53.7	25.2	25.0	26.4	8.9	8.2	7.7
Under 6 years	5.0	5.9	6.3	44.9	45.9	44.3	37.0	36.8	38.3	13.0	11.3	11.2
6–17 years	15.3	15.5	15.1	58.7	58.5	58.2	19.3	19.4	20.7	6.8	6.7	6.0
18–44 years	21.7	24.2	23.2	46.7	45.8	45.3	19.0	17.8	19.2	12.6	12.3	12.2
18–24 years	22.0	24.8	24.3	46.8	46.1	45.6	20.0	17.8	18.8	11.2	11.4	11.2
25–44 years	21.6	24.0	22.9	46.7	45.7	45.2	18.7	17.8	19.3	13.0	12.6	12.6
45–64 years	16.9	16.9	15.0	42.9	42.4	43.4	24.7	25.0	25.7	15.5	15.7	15.8
45–54 years	17.9	18.4	16.4	43.9	43.2	45.3	23.4	22.8	23.7	14.8	15.7	14.6
55–64 years	15.3	14.7	12.8	41.3	41.1	40.6	26.7	28.4	28.8	16.7	15.8	17.8
65 years and over	8.9	7.9	7.6	34.7	34.3	32.1	32.5	34.1	36.6	23.8	23.7	23.7
65–74 years	9.8	8.6	9.0	36.9	36.9	34.5	31.6	33.2	34.4	21.6	21.3	22.1
75 years and over	7.7	7.2	5.8	31.8	31.1	29.3	33.8	35.1	39.3	26.6	26.6	25.6
Sex[3]												
Male	21.3	23.1	21.5	47.1	45.5	46.0	20.6	20.6	22.4	11.0	10.8	10.1
Female	11.8	12.0	11.9	45.4	46.1	44.8	26.5	25.9	27.0	16.3	15.9	16.4
Race[3,4]												
White only	16.0	16.9	16.0	46.1	45.7	45.1	23.9	23.8	25.3	14.0	13.6	13.7
Black or African American only	16.8	18.4	17.3	46.1	46.2	46.7	23.2	21.9	23.4	13.9	13.5	12.6
American Indian and Alaska Native only	17.1	20.6	21.2	38.0	34.3	42.9	24.2	27.8	20.0	20.7	17.2	15.8
Asian only	22.8	23.1	20.2	49.1	47.3	49.2	19.7	19.4	20.9	8.3	10.2	9.7
Native Hawaiian and Other Pacific Islander only	*	*	*	*	*	*	*	*	*	*	*	*
2 or more races[3,4]	—	15.2	12.1	—	40.8	41.6	—	22.2	28.3	—	21.8	17.9
Hispanic origin and race[3,4]												
Hispanic or Latino	24.9	26.2	26.5	42.3	44.3	41.8	20.3	19.2	20.0	12.5	10.3	11.7
Mexican	28.9	30.2	30.7	40.8	43.0	40.9	18.5	18.2	18.0	11.8	8.7	10.4
Not Hispanic or Latino	#	16.2	15.2	#	46.0	45.8	#	23.9	25.3	#	13.9	13.6
White only	14.7	15.5	14.5	46.6	46.0	45.4	24.4	24.5	26.0	14.3	14.1	14.1
Black or African American only	16.9	18.4	17.2	46.1	46.2	46.9	23.1	21.9	23.4	13.8	13.5	12.6
Respondent-assessed health status[3]												
Fair or poor	7.8	9.8	8.8	23.3	25.9	21.9	29.0	24.3	27.4	39.9	40.1	41.9
Good to excellent	17.2	18.1	17.2	48.4	47.7	47.6	23.3	23.2	24.6	11.1	11.0	10.6
Poverty status[3,5]												
Poor	20.3	21.5	21.9	37.1	39.2	36.9	22.7	21.3	23.3	19.9	18.1	17.9
Near poor	19.9	22.2	21.4	42.8	41.5	41.9	21.8	21.6	22.1	15.5	14.7	14.7
Nonpoor	14.0	14.9	13.7	48.0	47.0	46.6	25.0	25.0	26.3	13.0	13.1	13.3

REGISTERED NURSES

Registered nurses (RNs) are licensed by the state to care for the sick and to promote health. RNs supervise hospital care, administer medication and treatment as prescribed by physicians, monitor the progress of patients, and provide health education. Nurses work in a variety of settings, including hospitals, nursing homes, physicians' offices, clinics, and schools.

Education for Nurses

There are three types of education for registered nurses. These include associate degrees (two-year community college programs), baccalaureate programs (four years of college), and postgraduate (master's degree and doctorate) programs. The baccalaureate degree provides more knowledge of community health services, as well as the psychological and social aspects of caring for patients, than does the associate degree. Those who complete the four-year baccalaureate degree and the other advanced degrees are generally better prepared to attain administrative or management positions eventually and may have greater opportunities for upward mobility in related disciplines such as research, teaching, and public health.

Between 1980 and 1999, the number of registered nurses grew from 1.3 million to 2.3 million. (See Table 2.2.) Over the same period, the proportion of nurses per

TABLE 2.6

Health care visits to doctor's offices, emergency departments, and home visits within the past 12 months, according to selected characteristics, 1997–2000 [CONTINUED]

[Data are based on household interviews of a sample of the civilian noninstitutionalized population]

	Number of health care visits[1]											
	None			1–3 visits			4–9 visits			10 or more visits		
Characteristic	1997	1999	2000	1997	1999	2000	1997	1999	2000	1997	1999	2000
	Percent distribution											
Hispanic origin and race and poverty status[3,4,5]												
Hispanic or Latino:												
Poor	30.6	31.2	32.0	33.8	38.2	33.1	20.0	18.7	18.9	15.6	11.8	16.1
Near poor	29.1	30.2	30.1	39.0	42.1	40.8	20.9	17.5	17.6	11.0	10.1	11.6
Nonpoor	18.7	21.0	20.9	48.6	46.8	45.1	20.3	21.9	23.3	12.3	10.2	10.7
Not Hispanic or Latino:												
White only:												
Poor	16.3	17.2	18.5	37.7	38.9	36.0	24.0	23.3	25.4	22.1	20.7	20.1
Near poor	17.1	19.8	18.5	43.7	40.8	40.4	22.3	23.3	24.1	17.0	16.1	16.9
Nonpoor	13.2	14.0	12.7	47.6	46.9	46.3	25.7	25.5	27.0	13.4	13.6	14.0
Black or African American only:												
Poor	17.8	18.0	18.2	37.4	39.9	40.3	23.3	23.1	24.6	21.5	19.0	16.8
Near poor	18.9	19.9	20.4	43.0	44.0	44.6	23.4	20.5	20.8	14.7	15.6	14.2
Nonpoor	15.6	16.3	14.3	50.5	48.2	49.9	23.3	23.7	24.8	10.6	11.8	11.0
Health insurance status[6,7]												
Under 65 years of age:												
Insured	14.3	15.4	14.1	49.0	48.6	48.5	23.6	23.2	24.7	13.1	12.7	12.7
Private	14.8	15.9	14.4	50.8	50.1	50.2	23.0	22.9	24.3	11.4	11.1	11.0
Medicaid	9.7	10.5	10.4	35.0	35.4	33.0	27.1	26.1	26.7	28.2	28.0	29.9
Uninsured	33.7	37.3	36.6	42.8	41.6	42.2	15.3	13.2	13.9	8.2	7.9	7.3
65 years of age and over:												
Private	7.4	6.5	6.1	36.0	34.8	32.5	33.7	35.0	38.4	22.9	23.7	23.0
Medicaid	10.2	*7.0	6.7	21.0	23.9	19.3	28.1	32.7	32.1	40.7	36.4	41.9
Medicare only	13.0	10.7	9.9	35.0	35.3	35.9	31.0	32.8	34.6	21.1	21.1	19.6
Poverty status and health insurance status[5,6,7]												
Under 65 years of age:												
Poor:												
Insured	13.7	14.6	15.3	38.8	41.4	38.9	24.5	23.2	25.8	22.9	20.7	20.1
Uninsured	36.7	39.8	37.9	38.8	39.3	39.3	14.9	12.6	13.1	9.5	8.3	9.6
Near poor:												
Insured	15.6	17.0	15.8	45.5	44.9	45.0	22.3	22.6	23.0	16.6	15.5	16.2
Uninsured	34.5	38.0	38.6	41.8	40.2	40.6	15.6	13.4	13.7	8.1	8.4	7.1
Nonpoor:												
Insured	13.4	14.7	13.1	50.3	49.1	49.0	24.2	24.2	25.7	12.1	12.0	12.1
Uninsured	29.1	32.9	32.0	45.4	43.7	44.9	17.0	14.6	15.7	8.4	8.8	7.3

100,000 population rose from 560 per 100,000 to 832.9 per 100,000. The largest percentage increases occurred among those holding baccalaureate, master's, and doctorate degrees.

NEED FOR NURSES EXCEEDS SUPPLY. Although the number of registered nurses holding baccalaureate degrees increased sharply during the 1990s, there is still a shortage of nurses and it is predicted to persist until 2020. Some health care experts believe that the shortage is intensifying because more lucrative fields are now open to women, the traditional nursing population. Nursing school enrollment has declined. In an article in the *Journal of Nursing Administration* (vol. 32, no. 2, February 2002), Marilyn Kettering Murray, MN, RN, reported that the nursing shortage has already sharply compromised hospital operations. Research conducted in 2001 found that the nursing shortage has caused more than 25 percent of hospitals surveyed to redirect patients to alternative facilities for emergency treatment, reduce their available number of beds (28 percent), and cancel scheduled surgeries (15 percent).

Industry observers feel the shortage results from a combination of factors including an aging population, a sicker population of hospitalized patients requiring more labor-intensive care, and public perception that nursing is a thankless, unglamorous job involving grueling physical labor, long hours, and low pay. A 2001 survey found that nursing was rated the 137th most desirable job out of 250 professions. They also note that the public, particularly high school students considering careers in health care, are unaware of the many new opportunities in nursing such as advance practice nursing which offers additional independence and increased earning potential and the technology-driven field of applied informatics (computer management of information).

TABLE 2.6

Health care visits to doctor's offices, emergency departments, and home visits within the past 12 months, according to selected characteristics, 1997–2000 [CONTINUED]

[Data are based on household interviews of a sample of the civilian noninstitutionalized population]

	Number of health care visits[1]											
	None			1–3 visits			4–9 visits			10 or more visits		
Characteristic	1997	1999	2000	1997	1999	2000	1997	1999	2000	1997	1999	2000
	Percent distribution											
Geographic region[3]												
Northeast	13.2	12.8	12.4	45.9	46.4	46.2	26.0	25.6	27.3	14.9	15.2	14.0
Midwest	15.9	16.2	14.4	47.7	46.7	46.2	22.8	23.8	25.6	13.6	13.3	13.9
South	17.2	18.9	18.4	46.1	45.5	44.7	23.3	22.5	24.1	13.5	13.2	12.9
West	19.1	20.9	20.0	44.8	44.8	44.9	22.8	21.9	22.2	13.3	12.4	12.8
Location of residence[3]												
Within MSA[8]	16.2	17.4	16.5	46.4	45.9	45.8	23.7	23.4	24.5	13.7	13.2	13.1
Outside MSA[8]	17.3	17.7	16.7	45.4	45.1	43.5	23.3	22.9	25.5	13.9	14.4	14.2

* Estimates are considered unreliable. Data preceded by an asterisk have a relative standard error of 20–30 percent. Data not shown have a relative standard error of greater than 30 percent.
—Data not available.
Estimates calculated upon request.
[1]This table presents a summary measure of ambulatory and home health care visits during a 12-month period based on the following questions: "During the past 12 months, how many times have you gone to a hospital emergency room about your own health?"; "During the past 12 months, did you receive care at home from a nurse or other health care professional? What was the total number of home visits received?"; "During the past 12 months, how many times have you seen a doctor or other health care professional about your own health at a doctor's office, a clinic, or some other place? Do not include times you were hospitalized overnight, visits to hospital emergency rooms, home visits, or telephone calls." Beginning in 2000 dental visits were also excluded. For each question respondents were shown a flashcard with response categories of: 0, 1, 2–3, 4–9, 10–12, or 13 or more visits in 1997–99. Beginning in 2000 response categories were expanded to: 0, 1, 2–3, 4–5, 6–7, 8–9, 10–12, 13–15, 16 or more. For tabulation of the 1997–99 data responses of 2–3 were recoded to 2 and responses of 4–9 were recoded to 6. Beginning in 2000 tabulation of responses of 2–3 were recoded to 2 and other responses were recoded to the midpoint of the range. The summary measure was constructed by adding recoded responses for these questions and categorizing the sum as: none, 1–3, 4–9, or 10 or more health care visits in the past 12 months.
[2]Includes all other races not shown separately, unknown poverty status, and unknown health insurance status.
[3]Estimates are age adjusted to the year 2000 standard population using six age groups: Under 18 years, 18–44 years, 45–54 years, 55–64 years, 65–74 years, and 75 years and over.
[4]Starting with data year 1999, estimates by race and Hispanic origin are tabulated using the 1997 Standards for federal data on race and ethnicity; prior to data year 1999 the 1977 Standards are used. Estimates for specific race groups are shown when they meet requirements for statistical reliability and confidentiality. Starting with data year 1999, the categories "White only," "Black or African American only," "American Indian and Alaska Native (AI/AN) only," "Asian only," and "Native Hawaiian and Other Pacific Islander only" include persons who reported only one racial group; and the category "2 or more races" includes persons who reported more than one of the five racial groups in the 1997 Standards or one of the five racial groups and "Some other race." Prior to data year 1999, estimates for the race categories shown include persons who reported one race or who reported more than one race and identified one race as best representing their race; and the category "Asian only" includes Native Hawaiian and Other Pacific Islander. Because of the differences between the two Standards, race-specific estimates starting with data year 1999 are not strictly comparable with estimates for earlier years. To estimate change between 1997 and 1999, race-specific estimates for 1999 based on the 1977 Standards can be used. In comparison with the 1999 estimates based on the 1997 Standards, the age-adjusted percent of persons with a specified number of health care visits based on the 1977 Standards are: (no visits) identical for white and black persons; 0.1 percentage points higher for AI/AN persons; 0.4 percentage points lower for Asian and Pacific Islander persons; (1–3 visits) identical for white persons; 0.1 percentage points lower for black persons; 1.3 percentage points higher for AI/AN persons; 0.1 percentage points lower for Asian and Pacific Islander persons; (4–9 visits) identical for white persons; 0.2 percentage points higher for black persons; 2.2 percentage points lower for AI/AN persons; 0.4 percentage points higher for Asian and Pacific Islander persons; (10 or more visits) identical for white and black persons; 0.9 percentage points higher for AI/AN persons; and 0.1 percentage points higher for Asian and Pacific Islander persons.
[5]Poverty status is based on family income, family size, number of children in the family, and for families with two or fewer adults the age of the adults in the family using Bureau of the Census poverty thresholds. Poor persons are defined as below the poverty threshold. Near poor persons have incomes of 100 percent to less than 200 percent of poverty threshold. Nonpoor persons have incomes of 200 percent or greater than the poverty threshold. Poverty status was unknown for 20 percent of persons in the sample in 1997, 25 percent in 1998, 28 percent in 1999, and 27 percent in 2000.
[6]Estimates for persons under 65 years of age are age adjusted to the year 2000 standard using four age groups: Under 18 years, 18–44 years, 45–54 years, and 55–64 years of age. Estimates for persons 65 years of age and over are age adjusted to the year 2000 standard using two age groups: 65–74 years and 75 years and over.
[7]Health insurance categories are mutually exclusive. Persons who reported both Medicaid and private coverage are classified as having Medicaid coverage. Starting in 1997 Medicaid includes state-sponsored health plans and Child Health Insurance Program (CHIP).
[8]MSA is metropolitan statistical area.

SOURCE: "Table 72. Health care visits to doctor's offices, emergency departments, and home visits within the past 12 months, according to selected characteristics: United States, 1997–2000," in *Health, United States, 2002*, Centers for Disease Control and Prevention, National Center for Health Statistics, Hyattsville, MD, 2002

ADVANCE PRACTICE NURSES AND PHYSICIAN ASSISTANTS

Much of the preventive medical care and treatment usually delivered by physicians may also be provided by mid-level practitioners—health professionals with less formal education and training than physicians. Advance practice nurses, a group that includes certified nurse midwives (CNMs), nurse practitioners (NPs), as well as physician assistants (PAs) are mid-level practitioners who work under the auspices, supervision, or direction of physicians. They perform physical examinations, order and interpret laboratory and radiological studies, and prescribe medication. They even do procedures—flexible sigmoidoscopy, biopsy, suturing, casting, and administering anesthesia—once performed exclusively by physicians.

The origins of each profession are key to understanding the differences between them. Nursing has the longer history, and nurses are recognized members of the health care team. For this reason, NPs—registered nurses with advanced academic and clinical experience—initially were easily integrated into many practice settings.

Physician assistant is the newer of the two disciplines. PAs have been practicing in the United States for about 30 years. The career originated as civilian employment for returning Vietnam War veterans who had worked as medics. The veterans needed immediate employment and few had the educational prerequisites, time, or resources to pursue the training necessary to become physicians. At the same time, the United States was projecting a dire shortage of primary care physicians, especially in rural and inner city practices. The use of PAs and NPs was seen as an ideal rapid response to the demand for additional medical services. They could be deployed quickly to serve remote communities or underserved populations for a fraction of the costs associated with physicians.

The numbers of physician assistants and nurse practitioners have increased dramatically since the beginning of the 1990s. In the United States, there were more than 70,000 advanced practice nurses and almost 43,000 practicing physician assistants in 2002. Together, mid-level practitioners are expected to outnumber primary care physicians by 2005. According to the American Academy of Physician Assistants (AAPA), at the start of the 2002 school year there were almost 10,000 students enrolled in PA programs.

Training, Certification, and Practice

Advance practice nurses usually have considerable clinical nursing experience before completing certificate or master's degree nurse practitioner programs. Key components of NP programs are instruction in nursing theory and practice as well as preceptorship under direct supervision of a physician or nurse practitioner. The American College of Nurse Practitioners states that NPs are prepared to practice "either independently or as part of a health care team," but NP scope of practice varies by state.

PA training programs are accredited by the Commission on Accreditation of Allied Health Education Programs. According to the AAPA, most students have an undergraduate degree and about 45 months of health care experience before they enter a two-year PA training program. Graduates sit for a national certifying examination and once certified must earn 100 hours of continuing medical education every two years and pass a recertification exam every six years.

PA practice is always delegated by the physician and conducted with physician supervision. The extent and nature of physician supervision varies from state to state. For example, Connecticut permits a physician to supervise up to six PAs while California limits a supervising physician to two. Although PAs work interdependently with MDs, supervision is not necessarily direct and onsite; some PAs working in remote communities are supervised primarily by telephone.

PATIENTS ARE SATISFIED WITH CARE FROM MID-LEVEL PRACTITIONERS. Health care consumers bonded with NPs almost overnight. Their presence in neonatal and well-baby clinics, physicians' offices, school health, and busy pediatrics practices immediately improved access to, and availability of, primary health care services. Their focus on patient education, counseling, and preventive medicine generated measurable improvements in patient satisfaction.

Consumers seem receptive to care from advance practice nurses in a variety of settings. Researchers measured patient satisfaction with emergency services delivered by a family nurse practitioner in a rural hospital. They found "Patients' perceptions of care provided by the NP were favorable." Physician response was equally approving— the physician group managing emergency services was so impressed with the competence of the first NP, they hired additional NPs to staff the department.

During 2000, studies published in the *Journal of the American Medical Association* (JAMA) and *British Medical Journal* (BMJ) reported that patient satisfaction with NPs and clinical outcomes (the results of the care delivered) were indistinguishable from those achieved under physician care. Mary Mundinger, DrPH, RN, FAAN, and her colleagues conducted the first large-scale, randomized clinical trial of NPs and MDs in similar New York City practices. They found that physicians and NPs used comparable hospital and other services, and their patients, largely non-English speaking and medically underserved, fared equally well in terms of health outcomes.

An editorial in the same issue of JAMA, written by a physician, was critical of Dr. Mundinger's research methods and conclusions. Harold Sox, MD, felt that the one-year follow-up was not long enough to assess outcomes or practitioner competence accurately. Dr. Sox argued that Dr. Mundinger's claim of comparable care was "far from convincing."

The BMJ study speculated that increased patient satisfaction with care from mid-level practitioners might be attributable to greater accessibility to NPs, such as the relative ease in obtaining same-day appointments and the extra time—in this study, an average of two additional minutes per visit—NPs spent with patients.

DENTISTS

Dentists diagnose and treat problems of the teeth, gums, and the mouth, take X rays, apply protective plastic sealant to children's teeth, fill cavities, straighten teeth, and treat gum disease. In 2000 there were 223,155 practicing dentists in the United States, almost twice as many as were practicing 30 years earlier. The United States boasts the highest concentration of dentists of any country in the world.

Fluoridation of community water supplies and improved dental hygiene have dramatically improved the dental health of Americans. Dental caries (cavities) among all age groups have declined significantly. As a result, many dental services are shifting focus from young people to adults. Many adults today are choosing to have orthodontic services, such as straightening their teeth. In addition, the older adult population generally requires more complex dental procedures, such as endodontic (root canal) services, bridges, and dentures.

Most Dentists Have Their Own Practices

The overwhelming majority of dentists own solo dental practices, where only one dentist operates in each office. According to the American Dental Association (ADA), about two-thirds (66 percent) of the nation's private dentists were working in solo practices during the late 1990s, while 33 percent were working in group dental practices. Dentists work an average of 37.3 hours per week, supervise 2 full-time and 2 part-time staffers, such as dental technicians and hygienists, and schedule about 84 office visits per week. (Some of these patients are only seen by the hygienist.) According to the U.S. Bureau of Labor Statistics, self-employed dentists in general practice had an average net income (after taxes and expenses) of $158,080 and dental specialists netted about $240,580. In 2000 salaried dentists median earnings were $129,030.

Dental Specialists

In 2000 about 20 percent of all dentists practiced in one of the eight specialty areas recognized by the ADA. Orthodontists, who straighten teeth, make up the largest group of specialists. The next largest group, oral and maxillofacial surgeons, operate on the mouth and jaws. The rest of the specialists concentrate in pediatric dentistry (dentistry for children), periodontics (treating the gums), prosthodontics (making dentures and artificial teeth), endodontics (root canals), public health dentistry (community dental health), and oral pathology (diseases of the mouth). Cosmetic dentistry, including tooth whitening and restoration, is one of the newest and fastest-growing specialties.

Training to Become a Dentist

Entry into dental schools requires two to four years of college-level pre-dental education—most dental students have earned excellent grades and have at least a bachelor's degree when they enter dental school. Dental school usually lasts four academic years. A student begins by studying the basic sciences, including anatomy, microbiology, biochemistry, and physiology. During the last two years, students receive practical experience by treating patients, usually in dental clinics supervised by licensed dentists.

In 2001 more than 4,000 students graduated from the nation's 55 dental schools. Men outnumbered women graduates by almost two to one. Of the graduates, more than two-thirds were white and less than 10 percent were black. Other minorities made up about 25 percent.

Visiting the Dentist

In 2000 about two-thirds (66.2 percent) of Americans over 2 years of age had visited their dentists at least once in the past year. (See Table 2.7.) Children ages 2 to 17 (74.1 percent) were more likely to have visited the dentist than any other age group, and women of all ages were somewhat more likely to see the dentist than men (69 percent). The proportion of non-Hispanic whites visiting dentists (70.2 percent) was considerably higher than the proportions of non-Hispanic blacks (57.5 percent) and Hispanics (51.4 percent). As anticipated, persons who were poor or near poor were much less likely to visit the dentist annually than those who were not poor.

ALLIED HEALTH CARE PROVIDERS

Many health care services are provided by an interdisciplinary team of health professionals. The complete health care team may include physicians, nurses, mid-level practitioners, and dentists; physical and occupational therapists; audiologists and speech-language pathologists; licensed practical nurses, nurses' aides, and home health aides; pharmacists, optometrists, podiatrists, dental hygienists, social workers, registered dieticians, and others. Table 2.8 describes some of these allied heath professions. Specific health care teams are assembled to meet the varying needs of patients. For example, the team involved in stroke rehabilitation might include a physician, nurse, physical and occupational therapists, a speech-language pathologist, and a social worker.

Physical and Occupational Therapists

Physical therapists (PTs) are licensed practitioners who work with patients to preserve and restore function, improve capabilities and mobility, and regain independence following illness or injury. They also aim to prevent or limit disability, and slow the progress of debilitating diseases. Treatment involves exercise to improve range of motion, balance, coordination, flexibility, strength, and endurance. PTs may also use electrical stimulation to promote healing, hot and cold packs to relieve pain and inflammation (swelling), and therapeutic massage.

According to the U.S. Bureau of Labor Statistics, PTs worked at 132,000 jobs in 2000, but 1 in 4 were part-time jobs and some PTs held two or more jobs at the same time. Two-thirds of practicing PTs worked in hospitals and the remaining PTs were employed in physicians' offices, outpatient rehabilitation clinics, nursing homes, and home health agencies. Though most work in rehabilitation, PTs may spe-

TABLE 2.7

Dental visits in the past year according to selected patient characteristics, 1997–2000

[Data are based on household interviews of a sample of the civilian noninstitutionalized population]

Characteristic	2 years of age and over[1]			2–17 years of age			18–64 years of age			65 years of age and over[2]		
	1997	1999	2000	1997	1999	2000	1997	1999	2000	1997	1999	2000
	Percent of persons with a dental visit in the past year[3]											
Total[4]	64.9	65.2	66.2	72.7	72.6	74.1	64.1	64.6	65.3	54.8	55.0	56.4
Sex												
Male	62.6	62.5	63.3	72.3	72.3	73.7	60.4	60.4	61.0	55.4	54.7	55.9
Female	67.2	67.8	69.0	73.0	72.8	74.6	67.7	68.5	69.5	54.4	55.2	56.9
Race[5]												
White only	66.5	67.2	68.1	74.0	74.5	75.8	65.7	66.6	67.4	56.8	56.8	58.4
Black or African American only	56.5	56.2	57.4	68.8	67.6	70.0	57.0	55.8	57.1	35.4	39.7	38.1
American Indian and Alaska Native only	51.5	56.2	54.6	66.8	58.2	71.5	49.9	55.2	55.0	*	*50.6	*
Asian only	61.8	63.6	66.3	69.9	69.6	72.6	60.3	63.1	65.6	53.9	53.2	60.6
Native Hawaiian and Other Pacific Islander only	*	*	*	*	*	*	*	*	*	*	*	*
2 or more races	—	58.6	62.7	—	73.0	71.2	—	57.8	60.6	—	*35.1	58.0
Black or African American; White	—	63.7	58.5	—	68.7	65.5	—	58.8	60.3	—	*	*
American Indian and Alaska Native; White	—	55.8	60.1	—	70.3	63.3	—	53.5	61.8	—	*	*
Hispanic origin and race[5]												
Hispanic or Latino	52.9	52.3	51.4	61.0	59.3	60.4	50.8	50.6	49.1	47.8	44.0	44.4
Not Hispanic or Latino	#	66.9	68.3	#	74.9	76.7	#	66.3	67.4	#	55.6	57.2
White only	68.2	68.9	70.2	76.4	77.0	78.7	67.5	68.3	69.4	57.2	57.3	59.1
Black or African American only	56.5	56.1	57.5	68.8	67.7	70.0	56.9	55.7	57.2	35.3	39.6	37.9
Poverty status[6]												
Poor	47.2	46.2	47.6	62.0	57.8	61.8	46.4	46.0	46.7	30.3	31.9	30.3
Near poor	48.9	48.5	50.0	61.6	61.6	65.2	46.4	46.1	46.8	39.6	38.9	40.9
Nonpoor	72.3	72.0	73.1	79.7	79.9	80.1	71.1	70.8	72.0	66.3	64.4	66.7
Hispanic origin and race and poverty status[5,6]												
Hispanic or Latino:												
Poor	41.9	41.5	41.3	56.8	49.6	53.9	39.0	39.7	38.1	33.0	32.1	31.4
Near poor	46.2	43.8	44.6	54.1	54.0	56.0	42.6	41.0	40.0	49.2	34.8	45.8
Nonpoor	65.1	63.8	62.5	74.8	72.0	69.1	62.5	62.0	61.3	56.5	58.9	54.3
Not Hispanic or Latino:												
White only:												
Poor	49.9	49.8	52.0	63.3	62.6	63.0	50.3	50.6	52.1	31.1	31.9	34.4
Near poor	51.0	50.2	52.3	64.8	63.2	69.0	48.2	48.0	49.2	41.2	39.6	40.5
Nonpoor	73.6	73.6	75.0	80.7	81.8	82.5	72.5	72.4	73.8	67.6	65.4	68.3
Black or African American only:												
Poor	46.7	44.9	46.0	66.7	61.0	67.5	44.5	42.1	45.3	26.2	33.5	17.3
Near poor	44.9	47.6	48.5	60.1	66.3	66.3	44.7	45.2	45.7	23.6	30.9	36.0
Nonpoor	65.4	64.2	66.0	75.5	72.7	73.9	66.2	64.7	65.4	48.9	51.5	55.1

cialize in areas such as sports medicine, pediatrics, or neurology. PTs often work as members of a health care team and may supervise physical therapy assistants or aides.

Occupational therapists (OTs) focus on helping people relearn and improve their abilities to perform the "activities of daily living," the tasks they perform during the course of their work and home lives. Examples of activities of daily living that OTs help patients to regain are dressing, bathing themselves, and meal preparation. For persons with long-term or permanent disabilities, OTs may assist them to find new ways to accomplish their responsibilities on the job, sometimes using adaptive equipment or by asking employers to accommodate workers with special needs such as persons in wheelchairs. OTs use computer programs and simulations to help patients restore fine motor skills, and practice reasoning, decision making, and problem solving.

The U.S. Bureau of Labor Statistics reported that OTs filled 78,000 jobs in 2000 with 1 in 6 holding more than one job at a time. The demand for OTs and PTs is expected to exceed the available supply through 2010. In addition to hospital and rehabilitation center jobs, it is anticipated that PTs and OTs will increasingly be involved in school program efforts to meet the needs of disabled and special education students.

Pharmacists Provide Valuable Patient Care Services

Today pharmacists are involved in many more aspects of patient care than simply compounding and dispensing medication from behind the drugstore counter. According to the American Pharmaceutical Association (APhA), its more than 50,000 members (including practicing pharmacists, pharmaceutical scientists, students, and technicians) provide pharmaceutical care that not only improves patient adherence to prescribed drug treatment but also

TABLE 2.7

Dental visits in the past year according to selected patient characteristics, 1997–2000 [CONTINUED]

[Data are based on household interviews of a sample of the civilian noninstitutionalized population]

Characteristic	2 years of age and over[1]			2–17 years of age			18–64 years of age			65 years of age and over[2]		
	1997	1999	2000	1997	1999	2000	1997	1999	2000	1997	1999	2000
	Percent of persons with a dental visit in the past year[3]											
Geographic region												
Northeast	69.6	70.9	72.4	77.5	78.5	81.1	69.6	71.5	72.2	55.5	54.3	58.0
Midwest	68.3	68.1	69.8	76.4	76.8	77.2	67.4	67.6	69.3	57.6	54.3	58.7
South	60.0	60.6	61.0	68.0	68.0	69.6	59.4	59.4	59.9	49.0	52.4	50.6
West	64.9	64.7	65.4	71.5	69.9	72.1	62.9	63.3	63.4	61.9	61.9	62.8
Location of residence												
Within MSA[7]	66.5	67.1	67.5	73.6	73.1	74.4	65.7	66.8	66.8	57.6	58.1	58.8
Outside MSA[7]	59.1	58.3	61.6	69.3	70.7	73.2	58.0	56.2	59.8	46.1	45.0	49.3

* Estimates are considered unreliable. Data preceded by an asterisk have a relative standard error of 20–30 percent. Data not shown have a relative standard error greater than 30 percent.
—Data not available.
Estimates calculated upon request.
[1]Estimates are age adjusted to the year 2000 standard using six age groups: 2–17 years, 18–44 years, 45–54 years, 55–64 years, 65–74 years, and 75 years and over.
[2]Estimates for the elderly are the percent of persons 65 years of age and over with a dental visit in the past year. Data from the 1997–2000 National Health Interview Survey estimate that 29–30 percent of persons 65 years of age and over were edentulous (having lost all their natural teeth). In 1997–2000 about 70 percent of elderly dentate persons compared with 17–20 percent of elderly edentate persons had a dental visit in the past year.
[3]Respondents were asked "About how long has it been since you last saw or talked to a dentist? Include all types of dentists, such as orthodontists, oral surgeons, and all other dental specialists as well as dental hygienists." This table presents the percent of persons with a visit in the past one year or less.
[4]Includes all other races not shown separately and unknown poverty status.
[5]Starting with data year 1999, estimates by race and Hispanic origin are tabulated using the 1997 Standards for federal data on race and ethnicity; prior to data year 1999 the 1977 Standards are used. Estimates for specific race groups are shown when they meet requirements for statistical reliability and confidentiality. Starting with data year 1999, the categories "White only," "Black or African American only," "American Indian and Alaska Native (AI/AN) only," "Asian only," and "Native Hawaiian and Other Pacific Islander only" include persons who reported only one racial group; and the category "2 or more races" includes persons who reported more than one of the five racial groups in the 1997 Standards or one of the five racial groups and "Some other race." Prior to data year 1999, estimates for the race categories shown include persons who reported one race or who reported more than one race and identified one race as best representing their race; and the category "Asian only" includes Native Hawaiian and Other Pacific Islander. Because of the differences between the two Standards, race-specific estimates starting with data year 1999 are not strictly comparable with estimates for earlier years. To estimate change between 1998 and 1999, race-specific estimates for 1999 based on the 1977 Standards can be used. In comparison with the 1999 estimates based on the 1997 Standards, age-adjusted estimates of the percent of persons with a recent dental visit based on the 1977 Standards are: 0.1 percentage points lower for white and black persons; identical for AI/AN persons; and 0.2 percentage points lower for Asian and Pacific Islander persons.
[6]Poverty status is based on family income, family size, number of children in the family, and for families with two or fewer adults the age of the adults in the family, using Bureau of the Census poverty thresholds. Poor persons are defined as below the poverty threshold. Near poor persons have incomes of 100 percent to less than 200 percent of the poverty threshold. Nonpoor persons have incomes of 200 percent or greater than the poverty threshold. Poverty status was unknown for 20 percent of persons in the sample in 1997, 25 percent in 1998, 28 percent in 1999, and 27 percent in 2000.
[7]MSA is metropolitan statistical area.
Note: In 1997 the National Health Interview Survey questionnaire was redesigned. Data for additional years are available.

SOURCE: "Table 80. Dental visits in the past year according to selected patient characteristics: United States, 1997–2000," in *Health, United States, 2002*, Centers for Disease Control and Prevention, National Center for Health Statistics, Hyattsville, MD, 2002

reduces the frequency of drug therapy mishaps, which can have serious and even life-threatening consequences.

Studies citing the value of pharmacists in patient care describe pharmacists improving rates of immunization against disease (pharmacists can provide immunization in 27 states), assisting patients to better control chronic diseases such as asthma and diabetes, reducing the frequency and severity of drug interactions and adverse reactions, and helping patients effectively manage pain and symptoms of disease, especially at the end of life. Pharmacists also offer public health education programs about prescription medication safety, prevention of poisoning, appropriate use of nonprescription (over-the-counter) drugs, and medical self-care.

INCREASE IN HEALTH CARE EMPLOYMENT

In 2001 almost 12 million persons worked in the health care services, a 51.9 percent increase since 1985, when 7.9 million worked in the health field. (See Table 2.9.) Workers in health care professions accounted for 8.8 percent of all employed Americans (excluding military personnel). In 1970 only 5.5 percent of employed civilians worked in health care services.

Since 1970 the proportion of health care workers employed in hospitals has dropped dramatically. More than 6 in 10 (63.4 percent) of health services personnel worked in hospitals in 1970. By 1990 that number had dropped to 49.6 percent employed in hospitals, and by 2001 that number fell again, to 43.4 percent. While hospitals still employ a larger proportion of health workers than any other service locations, more patients are now able to receive treatment in physicians' offices, clinics, and other outpatient settings. In addition, insurers are less willing to pay for lengthy hospitalizations than they were in the past.

Why Is Health Care Booming?

Three major factors appear to have influenced the escalation in health care employment: advances in

TABLE 2.8

Allied health care providers

Dental hygienists provide services for maintaining oral health. Their primary duty is to clean teeth.

Emergency Medical Technicians (EMTs) provide immediate care to critically ill or injured people in emergency situations.

Home health aides provide nursing, household, and personal care services to patients who are homebound or disabled.

Licensed practical nurses (LPNs) are trained and licensed to provide basic nursing care under the supervision of registered nurses and doctors.

Medical records personnel analyze patient records and keep them up-to-date, complete, accurate, and confidential.

Medical technologists perform laboratory tests to help diagnose diseases and to aid in identifying their causes and extent.

Nurses' Aides, Orderlies, and Attendants help nurses in hospitals, nursing homes and other facilities.

Occupational therapists help disabled persons adapt to their disabilities. This may include helping a patient relearn basic living skills or modifying the environment.

Optometrists measure vision for corrective lenses and prescribe glasses.

Pharmacists are trained and licensed to make up and dispense drugs in accordance with a physician's prescription.

Physician assistants (PAs) work under a doctor's supervision. Their duties include performing routine physical exams, prescribing certain drugs, and providing medical counseling.

Physical therapists work with disabled patients to help restore function, strength and mobility. PTs use exercise, heat, cold, water, and electricity to relieve pain and restore function.

Podiatrists diagnose and treat diseases, injuries, and abnormalities of the feet. They may use drugs and surgery to treat foot problems.

Psychologists are trained in human behavior and provide counseling and testing services related to mental health.

Radiation technicians take and develop x-ray photographs for medical purposes.

Registered dietitians (RDs) are licensed to use dietary principles to maintain health and treat disease.

Respiratory therapists treat breathing problems under a doctor's supervision and help in respiratory rehabilitation.

Social workers help patients to handle social problems such as finances, housing, and social and family problems that arise out of illness or disability

Speech pathologists diagnose and treat disorders of speech and communication.

SOURCE: U.S. Department of Commerce, Washington, DC

TABLE 2.9

Persons employed in health service sites, selected years 1970–2001

[Data are based on household interviews of a sample of the civilian noninstitutionalized population]

Site	1970[1]	1980[1]	1990[1]	1995	1996	1997	1998	1999	2000	2001
	Number of persons in thousands									
All employed civilians	76,805	99,303	117,914	124,900	126,708	129,558	131,463	133,488	135,208	135,073
All health service sites	4,246	7,339	9,447	10,928	11,199	11,525	11,504	11,646	11,597	11,947
Offices and clinics of physicians	477	777	1,098	1,512	1,501	1,559	1,581	1,624	1,671	1,774
Offices and clinics of dentists	222	415	580	644	614	662	666	694	669	698
Offices and clinics of chiropractors[2]	19	40	90	99	99	118	127	142	124	118
Hospitals	2,690	4,036	4,690	4,961	5,041	5,130	5,116	5,117	5,028	5,189
Nursing and personal care facilities	509	1,199	1,543	1,718	1,765	1,755	1,801	1,786	1,716	1,745
Other health service sites	330	872	1,446	1,995	2,178	2,301	2,213	2,283	2,389	2,423
	Percent of employed civilians									
All health service sites	5.5	7.4	8.0	8.7	8.8	8.9	8.8	8.7	8.6	8.8
	Percent distribution									
All health service sites	100.0	100.0	100.0	100.0	100.0	100.0	100.0	100.0	100.0	100.0
Offices and clinics of physicians	11.2	10.6	11.6	13.8	13.4	13.5	13.7	13.9	14.4	14.8
Offices and clinics of dentists	5.2	5.7	6.1	5.9	5.5	5.7	5.8	6.0	5.8	5.8
Offices and clinics of chiropractors[2]	0.4	0.5	1.0	0.9	0.9	1.0	1.1	1.2	1.1	1.0
Hospitals	63.4	55.0	49.6	45.4	45.0	44.5	44.5	43.9	43.4	43.4
Nursing and personal care facilities	12.0	16.3	16.3	15.7	15.8	15.2	15.7	15.3	14.8	14.6
Other health service sites	7.8	11.9	15.3	18.3	19.4	20.0	19.2	19.6	20.6	20.3

[1]Data for years prior to 1995 are not strictly comparable with data from 1995 onwards due to a redesign of the Current Population Survey.
[2]Data for 1980 are from the American Chiropractic Association; data for all other years are from the U.S. Bureau of Labor Statistics.
Note: Employment is full- or part-time work. Totals exclude persons in health-related occupations who are working in nonhealth industries, as classified by the U.S. Bureau of the Census, such as pharmacists employed in drugstores, school nurses, and nurses working in private households. Totals include Federal, State, and county health workers. In 1970–82, employed persons were classified according to the industry groups used in the 1970 Census of Population. In 1983–91, persons were classified according to the system used in the 1980 Census of Population. Beginning in 1992 persons were classified according to the system used in the 1990 Census of Population.

SOURCE: "Table 99. Persons employed in health service sites: United States, selected years 1970–2001," in *Health, United States, 2002,* Centers for Disease Control and Prevention, National Center for Health Statistics, Hyattsville, MD, 2002

technology, the increasing amounts of money spent on health care, and the aging of the nation's population. In other sectors of the economy, technology often replaces humans in the labor force. But health care technology has increased the demand for highly trained specialists to operate the sophisticated equipment. Because of technological advances, patients are likely to undergo more tests and diagnostic procedures, take more drugs, see more specialists, and be subjected to more aggressive treatments than ever before.

The second factor in the increase in health care employment involves the amount of money the nation spends on keeping its citizens in good health. Americans spent $1.3 trillion on health care in 2000. For each year that the amount of money spent on health care continues to grow, employment in the field grows as well. Some believe that government and private financing for the health care industry, unlike most other fields, is virtually unlimited.

The third factor contributing to the rise in the number of health care workers is the aging of the nation's population. There are greater numbers of older adults in the United States than ever before, and they are living longer. According to the U.S. Bureau of the Census estimates, by 2005 there will be 4.9 million Americans age 85 or older; and by 2030, 18.2 million people will be over the age of 85.

The increase in the number of older people is expected to boost the demand for home health care services, assisted living, and nursing home care. Many nursing homes now offer special care for stroke patients, persons with Alzheimer's disease (progressive cognitive impairment), and persons who need a respirator to breathe. To care for such patients, nursing homes need more physical therapists, nurses' aides, and respiratory therapists—three of the fastest-growing occupations. The U.S. Bureau of Labor Statistics estimated that by 2006 the number of physical therapists would increase 70.8 percent, to 196,000, and the number of respiratory therapists would grow 45.8 percent, to 119,000.

COMPLEMENTARY AND ALTERNATIVE MEDICINE

The National Center for Complementary and Alternative Medicine (NCCAM), an institute of the National Institutes of Health (NIH) defines alternative medicine as "a group of diverse medical and health care systems, practices, and products that are not presently considered to be part of conventional medicine." Though there is some overlap between them, the NCCAM further distinguishes between "complementary," "alternative," and "integrative" medicine" in the following manner:

- Alternative medicine is therapy or treatment that is used instead of conventional medical treatment.

- Complementary medicine is nonstandard therapy or treatment that is used along with conventional medicine, not in place of it. Complementary medicine appears to offer health benefits but there is generally no scientific evidence to support its utility.

- Integrative medicine is the combination of conventional medical treatment and complementary and alternative medicine (CAM) therapies that have been scientifically researched and have demonstrated evidence that they are both safe and effective.

Generally alternative therapies are untested and unproven, while complementary and integrative practices that are used in conjunction with mainstream medicine often have substantial scientific basis of demonstrated safety and efficacy.

Growing Popularity of Complementary and Alternative Medicine

In the United States, there is increasing enthusiasm for and use of complementary and alternative medicine (CAM) approaches and practices. Surveys conducted in 1991 and 1997 by Harvard Medical School researcher Dr. David Eisenberg and his colleagues about the use of alternative medicine in the United States found that more than 4 in 10 Americans had used at least one alternative therapy (including the services of nutritionists, Pilates and tai' chi instructors, and chiropractors among others). The earlier survey published in the *New England Journal of Medicine* in 1993 found that:

- In 1990 about one third of Americans regularly used alternative medicine therapies and treatment.

- Americans made more office visits to alternative medical practitioners than to traditional primary care physicians.

- About $14 billion per year was spent on alternative medicine.

The November 1998 *Journal of the American Medical Association* survey revealed that:

- Americans' use of alternative medicine had skyrocketed since the prior survey from 34 percent to 42 percent.

- Total visits to alternative medicine practitioners rose by 47 percent.

- About $27 billion was spent out-of-pocket (not paid by insurance) for alternative medicine, nearly twice as much as was spent in seven years earlier and about as much as Americans paid out-of-pocket for conventional treatments from physicians in the same year.

- The highest rates of CAM use were among college graduates living in the Western United States, ages 35–49, with incomes greater than $50,000 per year.

TABLE 2.10

Number and percent of office visits, by therapeutic and preventive services provided and patient's sex, 2000

Therapeutic and preventive services ordered or provided	Number of visits in thousands[1]	Standard error in thousands	Percent of visits	Standard error of percent	Patient's sex			
					Female[2]		Male[3]	
					Percent of visits	Standard error of percent	Percent of visits	Standard error of percent
All visits	823,542	34,820	—	—	—	—	—	—
None	515,550	23,198	62.6	1.2	61.6	1.3	64.0	1.5
Counseling/education								
Diet	126,988	9,441	15.4	0.9	15.4	0.9	15.5	1.0
Exercise	80,839	7,250	9.8	0.7	9.8	0.7	9.8	0.9
Injury prevention	24,610	3,193	3.0	0.4	2.5	0.3	3.6	0.5
Growth/development	21,460	2,657	2.6	0.3	2.2	0.3	3.2	0.4
Stress management	18,403	2,768	2.2	0.3	2.5	0.4	1.8	0.3
Prenatal instructions	18,396	2,117	2.2	0.2	3.8	0.4	*	—
Mental health	18,221	3,109	2.2	0.4	2.2	0.4	2.2	0.4
Tobacco use/exposure	18,213	2,265	2.2	0.3	2.0	0.3	2.5	0.3
Breast self-examination	17,827	3,052	2.2	0.4	3.6	0.6	*	—
Skin cancer prevention	14,311	2,486	1.7	0.3	1.4	0.2	2.2	0.4
Family planning/contraception	9,564	1,155	1.2	0.1	1.9	0.2	*	—
HIV/STD transmission [4,5]	5,190	716	0.6	0.1	0.9	0.1	0.3	0.1
Other therapy								
Complementary and alternative medicine	31,589	3,481	3.8	0.4	3.8	0.4	3.9	0.4
Physiotherapy	22,273	2,221	2.7	0.2	2.5	0.3	2.9	0.3
Psycho-pharmacotherapy	19,947	2,828	2.4	0.3	2.3	0.3	2.6	0.4
Psychotherapy	18,669	2,992	2.3	0.4	2.2	0.4	2.4	0.4
Other	36,839	3,569	4.5	0.4	4.3	0.4	4.7	0.4
Blank	21,356	3,146	2.6	0.4	2.3	0.3	3.0	0.5

—Category not applicable.
* Figure does not meet standard of reliability or precision.
[1]Total exceeds "All visits" because more than one service may be reported per visit.
[2]Based on 488,199,000 visits made by females.
[3]Based on 335,343,000 visits made by males.
[4]HIV is human immunodeficiency virus.
[5]STD is sexually transmitted disease.

SOURCE: Donald K. Cherry and David A.Woodwell, "Table 16. Number and percent of office visits with corresponding standard errors, by therapeutic and preventive services ordered or provided and patient's sex: United States, 2000," in *National Ambulatory Medical Care Survey: 2000 Summary*, Advance Data From Vital and Health Statistics, No. 328, Centers for Disease Control and Prevention, National Center for Health Statistics, Hyattsville, MD, June 5, 2002

Although most CAM services are provided by alternative medical practitioners, CAM is also delivered by some traditionally trained physicians. In the *National Ambulatory Medical Care Survey: 2000 Summary* the CDC reported that CAM therapies were ordered or provided at nearly 32 million physician office visits, or about 4 percent of all physician office visits. (See Table 2.10.)

ALTERNATIVE MEDICINE SYSTEMS AND PRACTITIONERS

This section considers two alternative medicine systems that originated in Western culture—homeopathy and naturopathic medicine—and two alternative medicine systems that developed in non-Western cultures—acupuncture and traditional Chinese medicine. It also describes some of the CAM practitioners who are providing care for Americans.

Homeopathic Medicine

Homeopathic medicine (also called homeopathy) is based on the belief that "like cures like" and uses very diluted amounts of natural substances to encourage the body's own self-healing mechanisms. Homeopathy was developed by a German physician, Dr. Samuel Hahnemann, in the 1790s. Dr. Hahnemann found that he could produce symptoms of particular diseases by injecting small doses of various herbal substances. This discovery inspired him to administer to sick people extremely diluted formulations of substances that would produce the same symptoms they suffered from in an effort to stimulate natural recovery and regeneration.

According to Dr. Kenneth Pelletier, a clinical professor of medicine at Stanford University School of Medicine and director of the NIH-funded Complementary and Alternative Medicine Program at Stanford, homeopathy has demonstrated effectiveness for a variety of ailments. In his book *The Best of Alternative Medicine: What Works? What Does Not?* (Simon & Schuster, New York, 2000), Dr. Pelletier reports that clinical trials of homeopathy found it effective for the treatment of disorders such as seasonal allergies, asthma, childhood diarrhea, fibromyalgia, influenza, and rheumatoid arthritis.

Naturopathic Medicine

As its name suggests, naturopathic medicine (also called naturopathy) uses naturally occurring substances to prevent, diagnose, and treat disease. Although it is now considered an alternative medicine system, it is one of the oldest medicine systems and has its origins in Native American culture and also draws from Greek, Chinese, and East Indian ideas about health and illness.

The guiding principles of modern naturopathic medicine are "first, do no harm" and "nature has the power to heal." Naturopathy seeks to treat the whole person since disease is seen as arising from many causes rather than a single cause. Naturopathic physicians are taught that "prevention is as important as cure" and to view creating and maintaining health as equally important as curing disease. They are instructed to identify and treat the causes of diseases rather than acting only to relieve symptoms.

Naturopathic treatment methods include nutritional counseling. Methods also include the use of dietary supplements, herbs, and vitamins; hydrotherapy (water-based therapies, usually involving whirlpool or other baths); exercise; manipulation; massage; heat therapy; and electrical stimulation. Since naturopathy draws on Chinese and Indian medical techniques, naturopathic physicians often use Chinese herbs, acupuncture, and East Indian medicines to treat disease.

Dr. Pelletier's research found studies demonstrating that naturopathy was effective for conditions such as asthma, atherosclerosis, back pain, some cancers, depression, diabetes, eczema (a skin condition), middle ear infections, migraine headaches, natural childbirth, and osteoarthritis. Further, Dr. Pelletier asserted that licensed naturopathic physicians are among the best trained CAM practitioners and he predicted that research would continue to confirm the benefits and efficacy of the safe, inexpensive, and low-risk therapies they can provide.

Traditional Chinese Medicine

Traditional Chinese medicine (TCM) uses nutrition, acupuncture, massage, herbal medicine, and Qi Gong (exercises to improve the flow of vital energy through the body) to help people achieve balance and unity of their minds, bodies, and spirits. Practiced for more than 3,000 years by about one quarter of the world's population, TCM has been adopted by naturopathic physicians, chiropractors, and other CAM practitioners in the United States.

TCM views balancing qi (pronounced "chee"), the vital life force that flows over the surface of the body and through internal organs, as central to health, wellness, disease prevention, and treatment. This vital force or energy is thought to flow through the human body in meridians, or channels. The Chinese believe that pain and disease develop when there is any sort of disturbance in the natural flow. TCM also seeks to balance the feminine and masculine qualities of yin and yang using other techniques such as moxibustion, which is the stimulation of acupuncture points with heat, and cupping, in which the practitioner increases circulation by putting a heated jar on the skin of a body part.

Herbal medicine is the most commonly prescribed treatment, and herbal preparations may be consumed as teas made from boiled fresh herbs or dried powders, or in combined formulations known as patent medicines. More than 200 herbal preparations are used in TCM, and several (such as ginseng, ma huang, and ginger) have become popular in the United States. Ginseng is supposed to improve immunity and prevent illness; ma huang is a stimulant used to promote weight loss and relieve lung congestion; and ginger is prescribed to aid digestion, relieve nausea, reduce arthritic knee pain, and improve circulation. Many modern pharmaceutical drugs are derived from TCM herbal medicines. For example, ma huang components are used to make ephedrine and pseudoephedrine; GBE made from ginko biloba is used to treat cerebral insufficiency (lack of blood flow to the brain); and during 2000 ginko biloba was shown to improve memory and slow the progression of dementia in some patients.

Acupuncture

Acupuncture is a Chinese practice that dates back more than 5,000 years. Chinese medicine describes acupuncture—the insertion of extremely thin, sterile needles to any of 360 specific points on the body—as a way to balance qi. After a diagnosis of an imbalance in the flow of energy, the acupuncturist inserts needles at specific points along the meridians. Each point controls a different part of the body. Once the needles are in place, they are rotated gently or are briefly charged with a small electric current.

Traditional Western medicine explains the acknowledged effectiveness of acupuncture as the result of triggering the release of pain-relieving substances called endorphins that occur naturally in the body, as well as neurotransmitters and neuropeptides that influence brain chemistry. In addition to providing lasting pain relief, acupuncture has demonstrated success in helping people with substance abuse problems, relieving nausea, heightening immunity by increasing total white blood cells and T-cell production, and assisting patients to recover from stroke and other neurological impairments. Imaging techniques have confirmed that acupuncture acts to alter brain chemistry and function.

Chiropractic Physicians

Doctors of chiropractic (also known as chiropractors or DCs) treat patients whose health problems are associated mainly with the body's structural and neurological systems, especially the spine. These practitioners believe that interference with these systems can impair normal functions and lower resistance to disease. Chiropractors think that misalignment or compression of the spinal nerves, for example, can alter many important body functions. According to the American Chiropractic Association (ACA), they "consider man as an integrated being and give special attention to the physiological and biochemical aspects including structural, spinal, musculoskeletal, neurological, vascular, nutritional, emotional, and environmental relationships." Doctors of chiropractic medicine do not use or prescribe pharmaceutical drugs or perform surgery. Instead, they rely on adjustment and manipulation of the musculoskeletal system, particularly the spinal column.

Many chiropractors use nutritional therapy and prescribe dietary supplements; some employ a technique known as applied kinesiology to diagnose and treat disease. Applied kinesiology is based on the belief that every organ problem is associated with weakness of a specific muscle. Chiropractors who use this technique claim they can accurately identify organ system dysfunction without any laboratory or other diagnostic tests.

In addition to manipulation, chiropractors also use a variety of other therapies to support healing and relax muscles before they make manual adjustments. These treatments include:

- heat and cold therapy to relieve pain, speed healing, and reduce swelling

- hydrotherapy to relax muscles and stimulate blood circulation

- immobilization such as casts, wraps, traction, and splints to protect injured areas

- electrotherapy to deliver deep tissue massage and boost circulation

- ultrasound to relieve muscle spasms and reduce swelling

According to the ACA, chiropractic is the third-largest group of health care professionals after medicine and dentistry. The ACA predicts that there will be nearly twice as many practicing doctors of chiropractic by 2010 as there were in 1999 when approximately 50 million patients sought care from slightly more than 70,000 chiropractors. Visits to chiropractors are most often for treatment of low back pain, neck pain, and headaches.

Critics of chiropractic are concerned about injuries resulting from powerful manual adjustments, and some physicians question chiropractors' abilities to establish medical diagnoses. Others worry that persons seeking chi-

ropractic care instead of traditional allopathic medical care may be forgoing lifesaving diagnoses and treatment.

Alternative Medicine Is More Than a Fad

Researchers from the Harvard Medical School looked at long-term trends in the use of CAM therapies in the United States and published their findings in the August 21, 2001 issue of the *Annals of Internal Medicine*. The researchers conducted more than 2000 surveys and traced patterns of CAM utilization since the 1960s. They questioned survey respondents about 20 different CAM practices such as acupuncture, aromatherapy, biofeedback, energy healing, massage, and yoga.

The study found that over the past 40 years nearly all of the 20 CAM therapies had increased in popularity, though interest surged during the 1960s and 1970s. The researchers observed that specific CAM therapies gained acceptance during each decade. In the 1960s Americans discovered diet programs, vitamins, and self-help support groups and in the 1970s they turned to herbal medicine, biofeedback, and energy healing. The 1980s saw growing popularity of massage and naturopathy and during the 1990s the appeal of massage increased along with interest in aromatherapy, energy healing, herbal medicine, and yoga.

Unlike the earlier studies that found CAM users to be mostly educated adults living in Western states, the Harvard researchers found the use of alternative therapies was unrelated to education, gender, or ethnicity. They observed that the increases in acceptance and use of CAM during the past 50 years suggest that demand for CAM therapies will continue in the future.

CRITICS SAY ALTERNATIVE MEDICINE IS A WASTE OF MONEY. Although complementary and alternative medicine practices are gaining in popularity throughout the United States and Europe, many allopathic physicians and scientists regard them with skepticism because they have not been rigorously tested or proven to be effective. In the May 15, 2002 issue of *Time* magazine, columnist Leon Jaroff asserts that the NCCAM budget of about $105 million per year is being misspent and that NCCAM is staffed with CAM practitioners and professionals who are biased in favor of CAM practices and unable to access objectively their value to the American people.

Jaroff also contends that NCCAM monies are repeatedly given to the same alternative practitioners and researchers and that few of the results of NCCAM studies have been published. The *Time* columnist says NCCAM is always positive about CAM practices and he would like to see NCCAM publish at least one report that is critical or refutes the claims of CAM practitioners. Jaroff asserts that scientific repudiation of many CAM treatments would convince Americans that they are spending increasing sums of money on essentially worthless remedies and therapies.

CHAPTER 3

HEALTH CARE INSTITUTIONS

A hospital is no place to be sick.
—Samuel Goldwyn (1882–1974)

HOSPITALS

The first hospitals in the United States were established more than two hundred years ago. No records of hospitals in the early colonies exist, but almshouses, which sheltered the poor, also cared for those who were ill. The first almshouse opened in 1662 in the Massachusetts Bay Colony. In 1756 the Pennsylvania Hospital in Philadelphia became the first American institution devoted entirely to care of the sick.

Until the late 1800s, American hospitals had a bad reputation. The upper classes viewed hospitals as places for the poor who could not afford home care, and the poor saw hospitalization as a humiliating consequence of personal economic failure. People from all walks of life thought hospitals were places to go to die.

TYPES OF HOSPITALS

There are more than 6,500 hospitals in the United States that are described as short-stay or long-term, depending on the length of time a patient spends before discharge. Short-stay facilities include community, teaching, and public hospitals. Sometimes short-stay hospitals are referred to as acute care facilities because the services provided aim to help resolve pressing problems or medical conditions such as a heart attack rather than long-term chronic conditions such as the need for rehabilitation following a head injury. Long-term hospitals are usually rehabilitation and psychiatric hospitals or facilities for the treatment of tuberculosis or other pulmonary (respiratory) diseases.

Hospitals also are distinguished by their ownership, scope of services, and whether they are teaching hospitals with academic affiliations. Hospitals may be operated as proprietary (for-profit) businesses, owned either by corpo-

rations or individuals such as the physicians on staff, or they may be voluntary—owned by not-for-profit corporations, religious organizations, or operated by federal, state, or city governments. Voluntary, not-for-profit hospitals are usually governed by a board of trustees, selected from among community business and civic leaders, who serve without pay to oversee hospital operations.

Most community hospitals offer emergency services as well as a range of inpatient and outpatient medical and surgical services. The nation's more than 1,000 tertiary hospitals provide highly specialized services such as neonatal intensive care units (for care of sick newborns), trauma services, or cardiovascular surgery programs. The majority of tertiary hospitals serve as teaching hospitals.

Teaching hospitals are those community and tertiary hospitals affiliated with medical schools, nursing schools, or allied health professions training programs. Teaching hospitals are the primary sites for training new physicians where interns and residents work under the supervision of experienced physicians. Non-teaching hospitals also may maintain affiliations with medical schools and some also serve as sites for nursing and allied health professions students as well as physicians-in-training.

Community Hospitals

The most common type of hospital in the United States is the community, or general, hospital. Community hospitals, where most people receive care, are typically small, with 50 to 500 beds. These hospitals normally provide quality care for routine medical and surgical problems. In the 1990s many smaller hospitals closed because they were no longer profitable. The larger ones, usually located in cities and adjacent suburbs, are often equipped with a full complement of medical and surgical personnel and state-of-the-art equipment.

Some community hospitals are nonprofit corporations, supported by local funding. These include hospitals supported by religious, cooperative, or osteopathic organizations. During the 1990s, increasing numbers of not-for-profit community hospitals have converted their ownership status, becoming proprietary hospitals that are owned and operated on a for-profit basis by corporations. These hospitals have joined investor-owned corporations because they need additional financial resources to maintain their existence in an increasingly competitive industry. Investor-owned corporations acquire not-for-profit hospitals to build market share, expand their provider networks, and penetrate new health care markets.

Teaching Hospitals

Most teaching hospitals, which provide clinical training for medical students and other health care professionals, are affiliated with a medical school and may have several hundred beds. Many of the physicians on staff at the hospital also hold teaching positions at the university affiliated with the hospital, in addition to teaching physicians-in-training at the bedsides of the patients. Patients in teaching hospitals understand that they may be examined by medical students and residents in addition to their primary "attending" physicians.

One advantage of obtaining care at a teaching hospital is the opportunity to receive treatment from highly qualified physicians with access to the most advanced technology and equipment. A disadvantage is the inconvenience and invasion of privacy that may result from multiple examinations performed by residents and students. When compared with smaller community hospitals, some teaching hospitals have reputations for being very impersonal; however, patients with complex, unusual, or difficult diagnoses usually benefit from the presence of acknowledged medical experts and more comprehensive resources available at these facilities.

Public Hospitals

Public hospitals are owned and operated by federal, state, or city governments. Many have a continuing tradition of caring for the poor. They are usually located in the inner cities and are often in precarious financial situations because many of their patients are unable to pay for services. These hospitals depend heavily on Medicaid payments supplied by local, state, and federal agencies or on grants from local governments. Medicaid is an entitlement program run by both the state and federal government for the provision of health care insurance to persons younger than 65 years of age who cannot afford to pay for private health insurance. The federal government matches the states' contribution to provide a certain minimal level of available coverage, and the states may offer additional services at their own expense.

Well-known public hospitals include Bellevue Hospital Center (New York City), Parkland Memorial Hospital Center (Dallas, Texas), Truman Medical Center (Kansas City, Missouri), University of Southern California Medical Center (Los Angeles, California), and Temple University Hospital (Philadelphia, Pennsylvania). Many public hospitals are also teaching hospitals.

TREATING SOCIETY'S MOST VULNERABLE MEMBERS. Increasingly, public hospitals must bear the burden of the weaknesses in the nation's health care system. The major problems in U.S. society are readily apparent in the emergency rooms and corridors of public hospitals—poverty, drug and alcohol abuse, crime-related and domestic violence, and infectious diseases such as acquired immunodeficiency syndrome (AIDS) and tuberculosis.

LOSING MONEY. The typical public hospital provides millions of dollars in health care for which it is not reimbursed by private insurance, Medicare (an entitlement program run by the federal government through which persons age 65 and older receive health care insurance), or Medicaid. The National Association of Public Hospitals (NAPH) estimated that nearly half of all public hospital charges are not ultimately paid. This figure has grown sharply as the number of uninsured Americans has grown. State and local governments provide subsidies to help offset these expenses. However, even with the subsidies, the unpaid costs incurred by the nation's public hospitals add up to billions of dollars' worth of care each year.

PROVIDING NEEDED SERVICES. The NAPH believes that the mission of public hospitals is to respond to the needs of their communities. As a result, most provide a broad spectrum of services. Although the need for trauma care exists across all socioeconomic levels, the American Hospital Association reported that NAPH members are twice as likely to have trauma centers as other community hospitals.

Almost half of NAPH-member hospitals provide prison services, and some hospitals have dedicated beds for prisoners. County and city revenues provide most, if not all, of the funds available for prison services. Many of the NAPH-member hospitals are also major academic centers, training medical and dental residents as well as nursing and allied health professionals.

MORE THAN THEY CAN HANDLE . For many Americans, the public hospital emergency room has replaced the physician's office as the place to seek health care services. With no insurance and little money, many people go to the only place that will take them without question. Insurance companies and health care planners estimate that more than half of all emergency room visits are for non-emergency treatment.

Poor or near poor children up to 18 years of age of all races were more likely to visit emergency rooms (25.9 and 23.7 percent, respectively) in 2000 than those who were nonpoor (18.8 percent). (See Table 3.1.) About 29.1 percent of children on Medicaid visited emergency rooms at least once in 2000, as opposed to 18.2 percent of children who were privately insured and 17.3 percent of uninsured chil-

TABLE 3.1

Emergency department visits within the past 12 months among children under 18 years of age, by selected characteristics, 1997–2000

[Data are based on household interviews of a sample of the civilian noninstitutionalized population]

Characteristic	Under 18 years of age			Under 6 years of age			6–17 years of age		
	1997	1999	2000	1997	1999	2000	1997	1999	2000
	Percent of children with 1 or more emergency department visits								
All children[1]	19.9	17.9	20.3	24.3	23.3	25.7	17.7	15.3	17.6
Race[2]									
White only	19.4	17.1	20.0	22.6	21.9	24.8	17.8	14.8	17.7
Black or African American only	24.0	22.5	22.6	33.1	32.3	30.8	19.4	18.2	18.9
American Indian and Alaska Native only	*24.1	33.3	38.1	*24.3	*29.5	*	*24.0	*36.2	*39.0
Asian only	12.6	9.4	12.4	20.8	*13.4	*16.7	8.6	*7.4	9.8
Native Hawaiian and Other Pacific Islander only	*	*	*	*	*	*	*	*	*
2 or more races	—	23.3	24.3	—	28.7	31.8	—	*19.7	18.3
Hispanic origin and race[2]									
Hispanic or Latino	21.1	15.9	18.7	25.7	21.4	23.9	18.1	12.6	15.6
Not Hispanic or Latino	#	18.3	20.6	#	23.8	26.1	#	15.7	18.0
White only	19.2	17.4	20.2	22.2	22.1	25.1	17.7	15.3	17.9
Black or African American only	23.6	22.5	22.6	32.7	32.5	30.9	19.2	18.2	18.9
Poverty status[4]									
Poor	25.4	24.4	25.9	29.9	31.6	32.3	22.5	20.6	22.3
Near poor	22.6	22.2	23.7	28.8	30.4	28.9	19.4	17.8	20.9
Nonpoor	17.4	15.4	18.8	21.0	19.0	23.8	15.8	13.8	16.5
Hispanic origin and race and poverty status[2,3]									
Hispanic or Latino:									
Poor	22.0	16.4	20.7	24.8	21.0	26.9	20.1	13.0	16.8
Near poor	20.8	15.2	18.9	28.9	21.7	20.5	15.6	11.6	18.0
Nonpoor	20.3	17.2	17.5	22.7	23.0	24.8	18.9	14.3	13.7
Not Hispanic or Latino:									
White only:									
Poor	26.3	26.3	27.1	28.0	34.9	37.1	25.1	22.4	20.9
Near poor	23.0	24.5	26.0	26.5	33.0	30.7	21.2	20.1	23.6
Nonpoor	17.4	15.1	19.0	20.6	18.1	23.0	15.9	13.8	17.2
Black or African American only:									
Poor	29.8	29.8	28.8	40.9	42.5	30.1	22.8	23.4	28.2
Near poor	23.6	23.5	21.9	33.6	33.7	39.1	19.1	18.7	13.8
Nonpoor	17.8	18.8	20.6	23.8	27.1	30.0	15.5	15.6	16.8
Health insurance status[4]									
Insured	19.8	18.1	20.7	24.4	23.1	25.8	17.5	15.7	18.2
Private	17.2	15.3	18.2	20.6	18.8	22.5	15.8	13.7	16.2
Medicaid	28.4	28.6	29.1	33.2	34.5	33.5	24.3	24.4	26.0
Uninsured	20.2	16.4	17.3	23.0	25.5	24.7	18.9	12.7	13.9
Poverty status and health insurance status[3]									
Poor:									
Insured	26.6	26.9	27.4	31.4	32.8	33.2	23.2	23.4	24.1
Uninsured	20.9	15.8	19.8	20.9	25.8	28.1	20.9	11.9	15.8
Near poor:									
Insured	22.7	23.3	25.1	29.2	31.2	29.3	19.2	18.7	22.8
Uninsured	22.2	18.3	18.6	27.3	26.6	26.9	20.1	14.8	14.2
Nonpoor:									
Insured	17.3	15.4	18.7	20.8	18.7	23.6	15.7	13.9	16.4
Uninsured	18.8	16.1	20.1	23.7	25.8	27.8	16.7	12.0	16.7
Geographic region									
Northeast	18.5	17.1	19.6	20.7	20.3	21.4	17.4	15.5	18.7
Midwest	19.5	18.4	20.3	26.0	24.1	25.6	16.4	15.8	17.8
South	21.8	19.2	22.0	25.6	25.7	28.7	19.9	16.1	18.7
West	18.5	15.9	18.1	23.5	21.4	24.7	15.9	13.1	14.7
Location of residence									
Within MSA[5]	19.7	16.7	19.9	23.9	22.0	24.5	17.4	14.0	17.6
Outside MSA[5]	20.8	22.4	21.9	26.2	29.1	31.3	18.6	19.7	17.8

dren. In the 18 and older age group, 30.2 percent of poor persons made one or more emergency department visits and 25.1 of the near poor made one or more visits. Of adults age 18–64, 17.5 percent of people who were privately insured made one or more emergency room visits during 2000, as opposed to 41.8 percent of those who had Medicaid and 19.6 percent of those who were uninsured. (See Table 3.2.)

Public hospitals are frequently underfunded and understaffed, and service can be exceedingly slow. All-day

TABLE 3.1

Emergency department visits within the past 12 months among children under 18 years of age, by selected characteristics, 1997–2000

[CONTINUED]

[Data are based on household interviews of a sample of the civilian noninstitutionalized population]

Characteristic	Under 18 years of age			Under 6 years of age			6–17 years of age		
	1997	1999	2000	1997	1999	2000	1997	1999	2000
	Percent of children with 2 or more emergency department visits								
All children[1]	7.1	5.5	7.0	9.6	8.7	9.9	5.8	4.0	5.5
Race[2]									
White only	6.6	4.7	6.4	8.4	7.3	8.7	5.7	3.4	5.3
Black or African American only	9.6	9.1	10.4	14.9	15.8	16.2	6.9	6.1	7.8
American Indian and Alaska Native only	*	*	*	*	*	*	*	*	*
Asian only	*5.7	*	*3.1	*12.9	*	*	*	*.	*
Native Hawaiian and Other Pacific Islander only	*	*	*	*	*	*	*	*	*
2 or more races	—	10.5	*8.6	—	*15.7	*14.1	—	*	*
Hispanic origin and race[3]									
Hispanic or Latino	8.9	5.2	7.0	11.8	7.9	9.4	7.0	3.6	5.6
Not Hispanic or Latino	#	5.5	7.0	#	8.8	10.0	#	4.0	5.5
White only	6.2	4.7	6.3	7.8	7.4	'8.6	5.5	3.4	5.2
Black or African American only	9.3	9.1	10.5	14.6	15.9	16.6	6.8	6.1	7.8
Poverty status[3]									
Poor	11.2	10.5	12.4	14.4	15.5	17.4	9.1	7.7	9.7
Near poor	8.6	7.6	8.5	12.7	12.4	12.9	6.4	5.0	6.1
Nonpoor	5.2	3.9	5.5	6.7	6.1	7.3	4.6	3.0	4.7
Hispanic origin and race and poverty status[2,3]									
Hispanic or Latino:									
Poor	10.6	5.7	8.7	13.9	*8.1	11.7	8.4	*	*6.7
Near poor	8.1	6.0	8.0	12.2	*9.9	9.4	*5.4	*	7.1
Nonpoor	7.4	5.5	5.7	8.2	*9.2	9.3	7.0	*3.6	*3.7
Not Hispanic or Latino:									
White only:									
Poor	11.0	10.8	13.3	12.4	18.5	18.8	10.1	*7.3	*9.9
Near poor	8.4	7.7	8.5	11.8	13.0	12.6	6.6	*5.0	6.4
Nonpoor	5.0	3.5	5.3	6.0	5.2	6.5	4.5	2.8	4.8
Black or African American only:									
Poor	12.9	14.6	14.9	19.6	22.2	19.7	*8.7	10.9	12.9
Near poor	9.5	9.5	9.2	*14.0	*15.7	19.8	*7.5	*	*4.1
Nonpoor	5.1	6.3	8.8	*8.1	*13.1	14.5	*4.0	*3.7	*6.5
Health insurance status[4]									
Insured	7.0	5.6	7.0	9.6	8.6	9.6	5.7	4.1	5.7
Private	5.0	3.6	5.1	6.6	5.4	6.8	4.4	2.8	4.3
Medicaid	13.2	12.8	13.3	16.2	17.0	16.0	10.6	9.7	11.4
Uninsured	7.7	4.9	6.7	9.8	9.0	11.3	6.8	*3.2	4.5
Poverty status and health insurance status[3]									
Poor:									
Insured	12.0	12.1	13.8	15.4	16.9	18.8	9.6	9.2	10.9
Uninsured	8.0	*4.8	*7.4	*8.7	*	*11.4	*7.7	*	*5.4
Near poor:									
Insured	8.6	8.3	8.7	12.7	13.4	12.4	6.4	5.4	6.8
Uninsured	8.3	*5.1	7.3	*12.2	*	*14.3	6.8	*	3.7
Nonpoor:									
Insured	5.1	3.9	5.4	6.4	5.9	7.1	4.5	3.0	4.6
Uninsured	7.1	*4.5	*7.0	*11.8	*	*	*5.0	*	*5.7

waits in the emergency room for initial treatment are not uncommon. A NAPH survey found that the average wait to get a hospital bed upon admission from the emergency room was 5.6 hours, although waits of three to four days were not unusual. Seriously ill patients could wait an average of 3.2 hours to be admitted into intensive care units.

PUBLIC HOSPITALS IN PERIL OF CLOSING. Many urban public hospitals are located in inner cities and are often the only resources for 24-hour standby emergency and trauma care. As a result, they care for a disproportion-

ate number of victims of violence. Between 1983 and 1999, 10 of the original 23 hospitals with designated trauma centers in Los Angeles, California, closed their trauma units, causing severe overcrowding in those that remained. During the 1992 Los Angeles riots, King Drew Medical Center treated 94 lacerations, 54 gunshot wounds, 87 assaults, and 19 stab wounds over the course of six days.

By August 2002 Los Angeles faced another public hospital crisis with the threatened closure of two more county hospitals, Harbor-UCLA Medical Center and

TABLE 3.1

Emergency department visits within the past 12 months among children under 18 years of age, by selected characteristics, 1997–2000

[CONTINUED]

[Data are based on household interviews of a sample of the civilian noninstitutionalized population]

Characteristic	Under 18 years of age			Under 6 years of age			6–17 years of age		
	1997	1999	2000	1997	1999	2000	1997	1999	2000
Geographic region	Percent of children with 2 or more emergency department visits								
Northeast	6.2	4.9	6.3	7.6	6.5	7.7	5.4	4.0	5.6
Midwest	6.6	5.8	6.6	10.4	9.8	9.0	4.8	4.0	5.5
South	8.0	6.1	8.5	10.1	9.8	12.5	6.9	4.3	6.6
West	7.1	4.7	5.4	10.0	7.6	8.5	5.6	3.3	3.9
Location of residence									
Within MSA[5]	7.2	5.0	6.6	9.6	8.0	8.8	5.9	3.4	5.5
Outside MSA[5]	6.8	7.4	8.6	9.7	11.3	14.9	5.6	5.8	5.8

*Estimates are considered unreliable. Data preceded by an asterisk have a relative standard error of 20–30 percent. Data not shown have a relative standard error of greater than 30 percent.
— Data not available.
#Estimates calculated upon request.
[1]Includes all other races not shown separately, unknown poverty status, and unknown health insurance status.
[2]Starting with data year 1999, estimates by race and Hispanic origin are tabulated using the 1997 Standards for federal data on race and ethnicity; prior to data year 1999 the 1977 Standards are used. Estimates for specific race groups are shown when they meet requirements for statistical reliability and confidentiality. Starting with data year 1999, the categories "White only," "Black or African American only," "American Indian and Alaska Native (AI/AN) only," "Asian only," and "Native Hawaiian and Other Pacific Islander only" include persons who reported only one racial group; and the category "2 or more races" includes persons who reported more than one of the five racial groups in the 1997 Standards or one of the racial groups and "Some other race." Prior to data year 1999, estimates for the race categories shown include persons who reported one race or who reported more than one race and identified one race as best representing their race; and the category "Asian only" includes Native Hawaiian and Other Pacific Islander. Because of the differences between the two Standards, race-specific estimates starting with data year 1999 are not strictly comparable with estimates for earlier years. To estimate change between 1998 and 1999, race-specific estimates for 1999 based on the 1977 Standards can be used. In comparison with the 1999 estimates based on the 1997 Standards, estimates of the percent of children under 18 years of age with 1 or more emergency department visits based on the 1977 Standards are: 0.1 percentage points higher for white children; 0.2 percentage points higher for black children; 2.0 percentage points higher for Asian and Pacific Islander children; and 2.1 percentage points lower for AI/AN children.
[3]Poverty status is based on family income, family size, number of children in the family, and for families with two or fewer adults the age of the adults in the family, using Bureau of the Census poverty thresholds. Poor persons are defined as below the poverty threshold. Near poor persons have incomes of 100 percent to less than 200 percent of the poverty threshold. Nonpoor persons have incomes of 200 percent or greater than the poverty threshold. Poverty status was unknown for 17 percent of children in the sample in 1997, 21 percent in 1998, 24 percent in 1999, and 23 percent in 2000.
[4]Health insurance categories are mutually exclusive. Persons who reported both Medicaid and private coverage are classified as having Medicaid coverage. Starting in 1997 Medicaid includes state-sponsored health plans and Child Health Insurance Program (CHIP).
[5]MSA is metropolitan statistical area.

SOURCE: "Table 77. Emergency department visits within the past 12 months among children under 18 years of age, according to selected characteristics: United States, 1997–2000," in *Health, United States, 2002,* Centers for Disease Control and Prevention, National Center for Health Statistics, Hyattsville, MD, 2002

Olive View-UCLA Medical Center, facilities that provide trauma and emergency care and are considered "lifelines" for the working poor. Three quarters of the Los Angeles county health system's patients are uninsured and some industry observers believe that the remaining three hospitals that form the core of the county health system would be unable to accommodate them.

REASONS FOR HOSPITALIZATION

In 2000 an estimated 31.7 million inpatients were discharged from short-stay nonfederal hospitals. These inpatients included an estimated 12.5 million males and 19.2 million females. The overall discharge rate for 2000 was 1,140.1 discharges per 10,000 civilian population and the average length of stay was 4.9 days. The discharge rate per 10,000 population for females was 1,350.5, well above the 920.2 discharge rate for males. (See Table 3.3.) The numbers were higher for females primarily because women are hospitalized for childbirth and pregnancy-related conditions. Older adults (age 65 and older) accounted for nearly 40 percent of all hospital discharges.

By Diagnosis

Heart disease is the number-one killer of Americans, and in 2000 diseases of the circulatory system, which include heart disease, ranked first among diagnoses for patients discharged from nonfederal short-stay hospitals, accounting for an estimated 6.3 million discharges. Table 3.4 shows that heart disease alone resulted in nearly 4.4 million discharges.

The leading specific diagnoses after heart disease were 3.7 million discharges for women delivering babies, 3.4 million for diseases of the respiratory system, and 3.1 million for diseases of the digestive system. Approximately 2.5 million were discharged for potentially preventable accidents such as injury and poisoning. For female patients 15 to 44 years of age, the most frequent diagnoses were deliveries. Mental disorders were the most frequent diagnoses for all patients 15 to 44 years of age. For patients age 45 to 64 years and 65 years and over, heart disease, malignant neoplasms, mental disorders, and pneumonia were common causes of hospitalization. (See Table 3.4.)

The average length of stay (LOS) was 4.9 days in 2000, down from 5.1 days in 1998. (See Table 3.5.)

TABLE 3.2

Emergency department visits within the past 12 months among adults 18 years of age and over by selected characteristics, 1997–2000

[Data are based on household interviews of a sample of the civilian noninstitutionalized population]

Characteristic	1 or more emergency department visits				2 or more emergency department visits			
	1997	1998	1999	2000	1997	1998	1999	2000
	Percent of adults with emergency department visit							
All adults 18 years of age and over[1,2]	19.6	19.7	17.2	20.2	6.7	6.7	5.2	6.9
Age								
18–44 years	20.7	20.4	17.7	20.6	6.8	7.0	5.6	7.0
18–24 years	26.3	24.7	21.7	25.9	9.1	8.3	7.3	8.9
25–44 years	19.0	19.1	16.5	18.9	6.2	6.6	5.0	6.4
45–64 years	16.2	17.1	14.6	17.6	5.6	5.7	4.3	5.6
45–54 years	15.7	17.0	14.3	17.9	5.5	6.0	4.3	5.8
55–64 years	16.9	17.2	15.1	17.0	5.7	5.2	4.3	5.3
65 years and over	22.0	21.9	19.9	23.7	8.1	7.3	5.6	8.6
65–74 years	20.3	20.0	17.3	21.6	7.1	6.8	4.7	7.4
75 years and over	24.3	24.3	23.1	26.2	9.3	8.0	6.7	10.1
Sex[2]								
Male	19.1	19.5	16.1	18.8	5.9	6.1	4.3	5.8
Female	20.2	19.9	18.2	21.6	7.5	7.3	6.0	8.0
Race[2,3]								
White only	19.0	19.1	16.6	19.4	6.2	6.1	4.7	6.4
Black or African American only	25.9	25.3	22.2	26.5	11.1	10.7	8.8	10.7
American Indian and Alaska Native only	24.8	28.6	29.2	30.5	13.1	12.4	*11.7	*12.8
Asian only	11.6	14.4	9.7	13.6	*2.9	5.8	*	*3.8
Native Hawaiian and Other Pacific Islander only	*	*	*	*	*	*	*	*
2 or more races	—	—	24.4	32.9	—	—	11.4	11.4
American Indian and Alaska Native; White	—	—	26.0	33.9	—	—	*13.9	*9.2
Hispanic origin and race[2,3]								
Hispanic or Latino	19.2	18.6	15.3	18.4	7.4	6.6	4.5	7.1
Mexican	17.8	16.3	14.4	17.4	6.4	5.7	4.1	7.1
Not Hispanic or Latino	#	#	17.5	20.6	#	#	5.3	6.9
White only	19.1	19.3	16.9	19.8	6.2	6.1	4.8	6.4
Black or African American only	25.9	25.2	22.2	26.5	11.0	10.6	8.8	10.7
Poverty status[2,4]								
Poor	29.2	28.1	27.6	30.2	13.7	13.4	11.7	14.3
Near poor	24.9	24.4	21.7	25.1	10.0	10.1	8.0	10.6
Nonpoor	17.5	18.0	15.4	18.6	5.0	5.2	4.1	5.3
Hispanic origin and race and poverty status[2,3,4]								
Hispanic or Latino:								
Poor	22.9	19.6	17.1	24.4	10.2	8.1	6.6	11.3
Near poor	19.2	20.4	15.9	19.4	8.4	6.9	5.0	7.6
Nonpoor	17.9	17.4	14.5	17.1	5.5	4.8	3.8	6.1
Not Hispanic or Latino:								
White only:								
Poor	30.8	30.1	29.4	30.6	14.1	13.9	11.7	14.3
Near poor	25.5	24.7	22.2	26.8	9.8	10.3	7.6	11.5
Nonpoor	17.2	17.8	15.5	18.2	4.8	4.9	4.1	5.0
Black or African American only:								
Poor	35.5	32.7	33.5	38.0	17.9	17.9	16.8	19.0
Near poor	30.8	29.7	27.8	29.9	12.9	13.5	13.0	13.1
Nonpoor	20.7	22.4	18.4	24.1	7.8	8.0	5.7	8.4
Health insurance status[5,6]								
18–64 years of age:								
Insured	18.8	18.9	16.1	19.5	6.1	6.1	4.7	6.4
Private	16.9	17.2	14.5	17.5	4.7	4.8	3.6	5.1
Medicaid	36.9	38.3	35.0	41.8	19.5	20.7	17.2	20.7
Uninsured	20.0	20.3	18.3	19.6	7.5	8.0	7.0	7.0
65 years of age and over:								
Private	21.4	21.3	19.2	23.2	6.7	6.6	5.3	7.8
Medicaid	32.3	33.2	29.1	35.9	18.0	13.9	11.6	18.1
Medicare only	20.9	20.4	19.5	21.7	8.8	7.1	4.9	7.7

Length of stay ranged from about 2.5 days for childbirth to 10.1 days for perinatal (around the time of birth) conditions. Other long stays included 8.6 days for malignant neoplasms of the large intestine and rectum, 8.1 days to treat episodes of psychoses, 8 days to treat septicemia (blood infections), and 7 days for the treatment of fractures in the spine or the femur (the long thighbone).

TABLE 3.2

Emergency department visits within the past 12 months among adults 18 years of age and over by selected characteristics, 1997–2000

[CONTINUED]

[Data are based on household interviews of a sample of the civilian noninstitutionalized population]

Characteristic	1 or more emergency department visits				2 or more emergency department visits			
	1997	1998	1999	2000	1997	1998	1999	2000
Poverty status and health insurance status[4,5]	Percent of adults with emergency department visit							
18–64 years of age:								
Poor:								
Insured	32.1	29.2	29.8	33.6	15.9	14.8	13.3	17.4
Uninsured	24.4	25.0	22.7	26.0	10.0	11.4	10.3	10.6
Near poor:								
Insured	26.6	26.8	23.1	27.3	10.3	11.2	8.7	11.6
Uninsured	21.3	18.9	18.6	20.1	9.1	7.9	7.5	7.7
Nonpoor:								
Insured	16.6	17.1	14.7	17.6	4.5	4.6	3.7	4.9
Uninsured	19.0	19.8	16.3	19.2	5.4	6.9	6.5	6.4
Geographic region[2]								
Northeast	19.5	19.6	16.9	20.0	6.9	6.2	5.1	6.2
Midwest	19.3	18.9	17.2	20.1	6.2	6.3	5.1	6.9
South	20.9	21.2	17.7	21.3	7.3	7.6	5.7	7.6
West	17.7	18.1	16.4	18.7	6.0	5.9	4.5	6.3
Location of residence[2]								
Within MSA[7]	19.1	19.0	16.6	19.6	6.4	6.4	4.9	6.6
Outside MSA[7]	21.5	22.3	19.5	22.5	7.8	7.7	6.4	7.8

*Data preceded by an asterisk have a relative standard error of 20–30 percent. Data not shown have a relative standard error of greater than 30 percent.

—Data not available.

Estimates calculated upon request.

[1]Includes all other races not shown separately, unknown poverty status, and unknown health insurance status.

[2]Estimates are for persons 18 years of age and over and are age adjusted to the year 2000 standard using five age groups: 18–44 years, 45–54 years, 55–64 years, 65–74 years, and 75 years and over.

[3]Starting with data year 1999, estimates by race and Hispanic origin are tabulated using the 1997 Standards for federal data on race and ethnicity; prior to data year 1999 the 1977 Standards are used. Estimates for specific race groups are shown separately when they meet requirements for statistical reliability and confidentiality. Starting with data year 1999, the categories "White only," "Black or African American only," "American Indian and Alaska Native (AI/AN) only," "Asian only," and "Native Hawaiian and Other Pacific Islander only" include persons who reported only one racial group; and the category "2 or more races" includes persons who reported more than one of the five racial groups in the 1997 Standards or one of the five racial groups and "Some other race." Prior to data year 1999, estimates for the race categories shown include persons who reported one race or who reported more than one race and identified one race as best representing their race; and the category "Asian only" includes Native Hawaiian and Other Pacific Islander. Because of the differences between the two Standards, race-specific estimates starting with data year 1999 are not strictly comparable with estimates for earlier years.0f estimate change between 1998 and 1999, race-specific estimates for 1999 based on the 1977 Standards can be used. In comparison with the 1999 estimates based on the 1997 Standards, age-adjusted estimates of the percent of adults with 1 or more emergency department visits based on the 1977 Standards are: 0.1 percentage points higher for white and black adults; 0.3 percentage points higher for Asian and Pacific Islander adults; and 2.0 percentage points lower for AI/AN adults.

[4]Poverty status is based on family income, family size, number of children in the family, and for families with two or fewer adults the age of the adults in the family, using Bureau of the Census poverty thresholds. Poor persons are defined as below the poverty threshold. Near poor persons have incomes of 100 percent to less than 200 percent of the poverty threshold. Nonpoor persons have incomes of 200 percent or greater than the poverty threshold. Poverty status was unknown for 22 percent of adults in the sample in 1997, 27 percent in 1998, and 29 percent in 1999 and 2000.

[5]Estimates for persons 18–64 years of age are age adjusted to the year 2000 Standard using three age groups: 18–44 years, 45–54 years, and 55–64 years of age. Estimates for persons 65 years of age and over are age adjusted to the year 2000 Standard using two age groups: 65–74 years and 75 years and over.

[6]Health insurance categories are mutually exclusive. Persons who reported both Medicaid and private coverage are classified as having Medicaid coverage. Starting in 1997 Medicaid includes state-sponsored health plans and Child Health Insurance Program (CHIP).

[7]MSA is metropolitan statistical area.

SOURCE: "Table 79. Emergency department visits within the past 12 months among adults 18 years of age and over, according to selected characteristics: United States, 1997–2000," in *Health, United States, 2002*, Centers for Disease Control and Prevention, National Center for Health Statistics, Hyattsville, MD, 2002

By Procedures

In 2000, nearly 40 million surgical and nonsurgical procedures were performed on patients discharged from short-stay hospitals. (See Table 3.6.) More than 81 percent (32.6 million) of all procedures fell into just five categories: obstetrical procedures (more than 6.2 million); operations on the digestive system (5.1 million); operations on the cardiovascular system (5.9 million); operations on the musculoskeletal system (3.2 million); and miscellaneous diagnostic and therapeutic procedures (12.2 million), which had the greatest number of hospital discharges. This category included computerized tomography (usually referred to as CT scan), arteriography and

angiocardiography, diagnostic ultrasounds, and respiratory therapy.

In 2000, 15.7 million American males and 24.3 million American females underwent hospital procedures. (See Table 3.7.) After miscellaneous diagnostic and therapeutic procedures, men were admitted most frequently for cardiovascular procedures (3.4 million) and women for various obstetrical procedures. A large number of women also underwent cardiovascular procedures (2.5 million). More women (3 million) had digestive system operations than men (2.2 million).

The rate of procedures by age per 10,000 population ranged from 322.5 for patients under 15 years of age to

TABLE 3.3

Number, rate, and average length of stay for discharges from short-stay hospitals by age, region, and sex, 2000

[Discharges of inpatients from non-federal hospitals. Excludes newborn infants]

Selected characteristic	Both sexes		Male		Female	
	Number	Standard error	Number	Standard error	Number	Standard error
	Number in thousands					
Total	31,706	1,218	12,514	541	19,192	703
Age						
Under 15 years	2,383	328	1,333	187	1,050	142
15–44 years	9,969	405	2,680	161	7,289	281
45–64 years	6,958	290	3,424	153	3,534	145
65 years and over	12,396	555	5,077	234	7,319	329
Region						
Northeast	7,103	705	2,979	324	4,123	386
Midwest	7,207	623	2,857	280	4,351	352
South	12,016	689	4,621	286	7,395	421
West	5,380	363	2,057	168	3,323	218
	Rate per 10,000 population					
Total	1,140.1	43.8	920.2	39.7	1,350.5	49.5
Age						
Under 15 years	393.9	54.2	430.8	60.6	355.2	48.2
15–44 years	815.9	33.2	438.7	26.3	1,192.9	45.9
45–64 years	1,141.7	47.6	1,158.0	51.7	1,126.3	46.3
65 years and over	3,595.5	161.1	3,528.3	162.8	3,643.7	163.8
Region						
Northeast	1,354.9	134.4	1,173.5	127.7	1,525.3	142.7
Midwest	1,128.3	97.6	915.3	89.7	1,331.8	107.6
South	1,216.4	69.8	964.2	59.6	1,454.0	82.7
West	853.7	57.6	653.8	53.4	1,053.1	69.1
	Average length of stay in days					
Total	4.9	0.1	5.3	0.1	4.6	0.1
Age						
Under 15 years	4.5	0.2	4.7	0.3	4.3	0.2
15–44 years	3.7	0.1	4.9	0.2	3.2	0.1
45–64 years	5.0	0.1	5.1	0.1	4.8	0.1
65 years and over	6.0	0.1	5.9	0.1	6.0	0.1
Region						
Northeast	5.7	0.2	6.0	0.3	5.4	0.2
Midwest	4.5	0.1	4.8	0.1	4.3	0.1
South	4.9	0.1	5.3	0.1	4.6	0.1
West	4.5	0.2	5.2	0.2	4.1	0.1

SOURCE: Margaret J. Hall and Maria F. Owings, "Table 1. Number, rate, and average length of stay for discharges from short–stay hospitals by age, region, and sex, United States, 2000," in *2000 National Hospital Discharge Survey,* Advance Data From Vital and Health Statistics, No. 329, Centers for Disease Control and Prevention, National Center for Health Statistics, Hyattsville, MD, June 19, 2002

4,274.7 for patients 65 years of age and over. (See Table 3.8.) For patients under age 15, some of the most commonly performed procedures included operations on the nervous system and digestive system, and respiratory therapy. For patients between the ages of 15 and 44 years (not including obstetrical procedures), the most common procedures were on the digestive and cardiovascular systems. Other common procedures included musculoskeletal procedures and diagnostic testing.

For patients age 45 to 64 years, cardiovascular procedures and diagnostic testing were most frequent. (See Table 3.8.) For patients age 65 years and over, cardiovascular, respiratory, and digestive system procedures, as well as diagnostic testing and respiratory therapy were most common.

Organ Transplants

Organ transplants are a viable means of saving lives, and in 2001, 24,076 transplants were performed in 255 hospital transplant centers across the country. The United Network for Organ Sharing (UNOS) compiles data on organ transplants, distributes organ donor cards, and maintains a registry of patients awaiting organ transplants. UNOS reported that as of August 2002, 80,294 Americans were waiting for transplants. According to UNOS about 5,000 people die each year while waiting for an organ transplant because demand for organs continues to outpace supply.

Governors of many states began a variety of programs aimed at increasing public awareness of the lack of donor organs and honoring those who have chosen to become donors. For example, Alabama Governor Don Siegelman created an Alabama Donor Registry, Georgia Governor Roy Barnes designated March 2001 as Eye Donor Month, and Utah Governor Michael O. Leavitt and the state legislature adopted a resolution to improve public awareness

TABLE 3.4

Number of discharges from short-stay hospitals by first-listed diagnosis and age, 2000

[Discharges of inpatients from non-federal hospitals. Excludes newborn infants. Diagnostic groupings and code numbers are based on the *International Classification of Diseases, 9th Revision, Clinical Modification* (ICD–9–CM)]

Category of first-listed diagnosis and ICD–9–CM code		All ages		Under 15 years		15–44 years		45–64 years		65 years and over	
		Number	SE[1]	Number	SE[1]	Number	SE[1]	Number	SE[1]	Number	SE[1]
		Number in thousands									
All conditions		31,706	1,218	2,383	328	9,969	405	6,958	290	12,396	555
Infectious and parasitic diseases	001–139	787	42	160	26	173	12	150	10	305	18
Septicemia	038	326	20	16	3	32	5	62	6	216	14
Neoplasms	140–239	1,587	70	37	11	289	14	566	26	695	38
Malignant neoplasms	140–208, 230–234	1,156	54	27	8	120	8	393	19	617	33
Malignant neoplasm of large intestine and rectum	153–154, 197.5	159	10	*	*	*7	*2	49	4	103	8
Malignant neoplasm of trachea, bronchus, and lung	162, 176.4, 197.0, 197.3	139	9	*	*	8	2	43	4	87	7
Malignant neoplasm of breast	174–175, 198.81	108	8	*	*	12	2	40	4	56	6
Benign neoplasms	210–229	390	20	*	*	163	10	161	11	58	5
Endocrine, nutritional and metabolic diseases, and immunity disorders	240–279	1,455	62	152	21	289	17	381	19	634	30
Diabetes mellitus	250	557	26	22	5	136	10	207	12	192	11
Volume depletion	276.5	485	29	111	16	54	7	59	6	261	17
Diseases of the blood and blood-forming organs	280–289	392	27	70	13	91	8	83	8	149	15
Mental disorders	290–319	2,147	341	103	25	1,255	233	495	74	293	28
Psychoses	290–299	1,445	243	*	*	803	160	343	55	244	25
Alcohol dependence syndrome	303	146	34	*	*	92	23	49	12	6	1
Diseases of the nervous system and sense organs	320–389	471	31	84	16	112	10	109	9	167	13
Diseases of the circulatory system	390–459	6,294	286	30	6	389	19	1,813	89	4,062	191
Heart disease	391–392.0, 393–398, 402, 404, 410–416, 420–429	4,385	211	16	4	244	13	1,271	68	2,854	140
Acute myocardial infarction	410	781	44	*	*	38	4	242	15	499	30
Coronary atherosclerosis	414.0	1,102	77	*	*	50	5	442	33	609	43
Other ischemic heart disease	411–413, 414.1–414.9	283	27	*	*	21	3	105	9	157	19
Cardiac dysrhythmias	427	716	36	8	2	43	4	157	10	508	27
Congestive heart failure	428.0	999	47	*	*	35	4	195	15	767	37
Cerebrovascular disease	430–438	981	46	*	*	37	4	229	14	711	36
Diseases of the respiratory system	460–519	3,444	159	699	95	394	19	648	32	1,703	86
Acute bronchitis and bronchiolitis	466	285	34	201	33	13	2	19	3	52	5
Pneumonia	480–486	1,282	60	173	20	128	9	218	12	763	44
Chronic bronchitis	491	495	32	*	*	18	4	147	13	328	21
Asthma	493	465	38	203	33	111	9	84	6	68	7
Diseases of the digestive system	520–579	3,143	124	217	30	758	32	852	41	1,317	59
Appendicitis	540–543	273	18	68	9	145	11	43	5	16	3
Noninfectious enteritis and colitis	555–558	277	14	49	7	81	6	56	5	91	7
Diverticula of intestine	562	264	15	*	*	30	4	70	6	164	10
Cholelithiasis	574	344	18	*	*	108	7	107	9	127	10
Diseases of the genitourinary system	580–629	1,743	80	83	14	574	29	436	23	650	36
Calculus of kidney and ureter	592	177	15	*	*	80	7	62	7	31	4
Complications of pregnancy, childbirth, and the puerperium[2]	630–677	504	29	*	*	503	29	*	*	—	—
Diseases of the skin and subcutaneous tissue	680–709	514	40	*	*	132	12	133	9	179	11
Cellulitis and abscess	681–682	353	18	28	5	96	8	106	8	124	8
Diseases of the musculoskeletal system and connective tissue	710–739	1,530	92	37	7	322	24	497	29	674	47
Osteoarthrosis and allied disorders	715	441	35	*	*	13	2	125	11	303	27
Intervertebral disc disorders	722	329	22	*	*	140	12	132	12	56	5
Congenital anomalies	740–759	165	29	113	25	33	6	11	2	9	2
Certain conditions originating in the perinatal period	760–779	156	28	155	28	*	*	*	*	*	*
Symptoms, signs, and ill-defined conditions	780–799	267	17	56	8	93	8	74	7	44	6
Injury and poisoning	800–999	2,466	112	228	33	712	39	514	27	1,012	53
Fractures, all sites[3]	800–829	982	56	74	12	223	17	164	12	521	33
Fracture of neck of femur[3]	820	321	23	*	*	*6	*1	24	3	290	21
Poisonings	960–989	192	12	21	4	108	7	39	4	25	3
Supplementary classifications	V01–V82	4,640	191	89	16	3,851	166	196	16	505	58
Females with deliveries	V27	3,738	166	12	2	3,722	165	*3	*1	—	—

* Figure does not meet standard of reliability or precision.
—Category not applicable.
[1]SE is standard error.
[2]First-listed diagnosis for females with deliveries is coded V27, shown under "Supplementary classifications."
[3]Excludes fractures coded as 733.1, pathologic fracture.

SOURCE: Margaret J. Hall and Maria F. Owings, "Table 2. Number of discharges from short–stay hospitals by first-listed diagnosis and age, United States, 2000," in *2000 National Hospital Discharge Survey*, Advance Data From Vital and Health Statistics, No. 329, Centers for Disease Control and Prevention, National Center for Health Statistics, Hyattsville, MD, June 19, 2002

TABLE 3.5

Average length of stay for discharges from short-stay hospitals by age and first-listed diagnosis, 2000

[Discharges of inpatients from non-federal hospitals. Excludes newborn infants. Diagnostic groupings and code numbers are based on the *International Classification of Diseases, 9th Revision, Clinical Modification* (ICD–9–CM)]

Category of first-listed diagnosis and ICD–9–CM code		All ages		Under 15 years		15–44 years		45–64 years		65 years and over	
		ALOS[1]	SE[2]	ALOS[1]	SE[2]	ALOS[1]	SE[2]	ALOS[1]	SE[2]	ALOS[1]	SE[2]
All conditions		4.9	0.1	4.5	0.2	3.7	0.1	5.0	0.1	6.0	0.1
Infectious and parasitic diseases	001–139	6.3	0.2	3.3	0.2	6.6	0.5	6.5	0.3	7.5	0.3
Septicemia	038	8.0	0.3	5.5	0.9	9.6	1.4	8.3	0.6	7.8	0.3
Neoplasms	140–239	5.8	0.1	6.5	0.6	4.2	0.2	5.3	0.2	7.0	0.2
Malignant neoplasms	140–208, 230–234	6.7	0.1	7.6	0.7	6.4	0.4	6.2	0.2	7.2	0.2
Malignant neoplasm of large intestine and rectum	153–154, 197.5	8.6	0.3	*	*	*7.2	*0.9	7.4	0.4	9.2	0.4
Malignant neoplasm of trachea, bronchus, and lung	162, 176.4, 197.0, 197.3	6.7	0.2	*	*	7.3	1.3	6.2	0.3	6.9	0.3
Malignant neoplasm of breast	174–175,198.81	2.9	0.5	*	*	2.3	0.2	2.1	0.1	3.7	0.9
Benign neoplasms	210–229	3.2	0.1	3.0	0.5	2.5	0.1	3.1	0.1	5.2	0.3
Endocrine, nutritional and metabolic diseases, and immunity disorders	240–279	4.5	0.1	2.8	0.2	3.6	0.1	4.8	0.2	5.1	0.2
Diabetes mellitus	250	5.2	0.2	3.1	0.2	3.8	0.2	5.6	0.3	5.9	0.3
Volume depletion	276.5	4.0	0.2	2.2	0.1	3.1	0.2	3.8	0.3	5.0	0.2
Diseases of the blood and blood-forming organs	280–289	4.4	0.2	4.0	0.2	4.7	0.2	4.5	0.3	4.5	0.3
Mental disorders	290–319	7.3	0.4	12.4	2.8	6.5	0.3	7.5	0.4	8.8	0.4
Psychoses	290–299	8.1	0.4	11.5	3.3	7.3	0.4	8.3	0.4	9.6	0.4
Alcohol dependence syndrome	303	5.7	0.5	*	*	5.8	0.6	5.7	0.6	4.6	0.8
Diseases of the nervous system and sense organs	320–389	4.8	0.2	3.9	0.2	4.5	0.3	4.3	0.3	5.7	0.3
Diseases of the circulatory system	390–459	4.8	0.1	5.6	0.9	3.9	0.1	4.2	0.1	5.2	0.1
Heart disease	391–392.0, 393–398, 402, 404, 410–416, 420–429	4.7	0.1	5.4	1.0	3.6	0.1	3.9	0.1	5.1	0.1
Acute myocardial infarction	410	5.7	0.1	*	*	3.8	0.2	4.8	0.2	6.2	0.2
Coronary atherosclerosis	414.0	3.9	0.1	*	*	2.9	0.2	3.3	0.1	4.4	0.2
Other ischemic heart disease	411–413, 414.1–414.9	2.7	0.1	*	*	2.1	0.3	2.3	0.1	3.1	0.1
Cardiac dysrhythmias	427	3.7	0.1	3.5	0.6	2.4	0.2	2.9	0.1	4.1	0.1
Congestive heart failure	428.0	5.5	0.1	*	*	4.4	0.4	4.9	0.3	5.6	0.2
Cerebrovascular disease	430–438	5.4	0.2	*	*	6.4	0.9	5.3	0.3	5.3	0.2
Diseases of the respiratory system	460–519	5.4	0.1	3.3	0.3	4.5	0.2	5.6	0.1	6.4	0.1
Acute bronchitis and bronchiolitis	466	3.4	0.1	3.1	0.2	3.8	0.4	3.0	0.2	4.8	0.3
Pneumonia	480–486	5.9	0.1	3.4	0.2	5.3	0.4	5.9	0.2	6.5	0.2
Chronic bronchitis	491	5.2	0.2	*	*	4.6	0.7	5.1	0.3	5.2	0.2
Asthma	493	3.0	0.1	2.2	0.1	2.9	0.1	3.9	0.2	4.9	0.3
Diseases of the digestive system	520–579	4.7	0.1	3.3	0.2	3.8	0.1	4.7	0.1	5.5	0.1
Appendicitis	540–543	3.3	0.2	3.0	0.2	3.1	0.3	3.6	0.3	5.1	0.5
Noninfectious enteritis and colitis	555–558	4.6	0.2	2.3	0.2	4.5	0.4	4.7	0.4	5.8	0.4
Diverticula of intestine	562	5.5	0.2	*	*	4.4	0.4	4.8	0.2	6.0	0.3
Cholelithiasis	574	3.8	0.1	*	*	2.9	0.2	3.4	0.2	5.0	0.2
Diseases of the genitourinary system	580–629	3.8	0.1	3.3	0.2	2.9	0.2	3.4	0.1	4.8	0.1
Calculus of kidney and ureter	592	2.4	0.2	*	*	2.0	0.1	2.7	0.5	2.8	0.2
Complications of pregnancy, childbirth, and the puerperium[3]	630–677	2.5	0.1	*	*	2.5	0.1	*	*	—	—
Diseases of the skin and subcutaneous tissue	680–709	5.5	0.2	3.1	0.1	4.4	0.3	6.0	0.4	7.0	0.3
Cellulitis and abscess	681–682	5.3	0.2	3.2	0.3	4.1	0.2	5.4	0.3	6.5	0.3
Diseases of the musculoskeletal system and connective tissue	710–739	4.1	0.1	4.4	0.3	3.0	0.1	3.8	0.1	4.9	0.1
Osteoarthrosis and allied disorders	715	4.5	0.1	*	*	3.7	0.2	4.1	0.1	4.7	0.2
Intervertebral disc disorders	722	3.0	0.1	*	*	2.3	0.1	2.8	0.2	4.9	0.6
Congenital anomalies	740–759	5.7	0.6	6.4	0.7	3.9	0.5	4.7	1.0	5.0	0.9
Certain conditions originating in the perinatal period	760–779	10.1	0.8	10.2	0.8	*	*	*	*	*	*
Symptoms, signs, and ill-defined conditions	780–799	2.4	0.1	2.1	0.1	1.9	0.1	2.1	0.2	4.2	0.5
Injury and poisoning	800–999	5.4	0.2	4.1	0.5	4.4	0.2	5.5	0.2	6.4	0.3
Fractures, all sites [4]	800–829	5.8	0.2	3.1	0.3	4.8	0.4	5.6	0.4	6.6	0.4
Fracture of neck of femur[4]	820	7.0	0.3	*	*	*5.1	*0.8	6.3	0.5	7.1	0.3
Poisonings	960–989	2.9	0.3	1.8	0.2	2.5	0.2	3.0	0.3	*	*
Supplementary classifications	V01–V82	3.9	0.2	5.5	0.9	2.6	0.0	8.5	0.5	11.6	0.4
Females with deliveries	V27	2.5	0.0	2.4	0.2	2.5	0.0	*2.9	*0.3	—	—

* Figure does not meet standard of reliability or precision.
—Category not applicable.
[1]ALOS is average length of stay.
[2]SE is standard error of average length of stay.
[3]First-listed diagnosis for females with deliveries is coded V27, shown under "Supplementary classifications."
[4]Excludes fractures coded as 733.1, pathologic fracture.

SOURCE: Margaret J. Hall and Maria F. Owings, "Table 4. Average length of stay for discharges from short–stay hospitals by age and first-listed diagnosis, United States, 2000," in *2000 National Hospital Discharge Survey*, Advance Data From Vital and Health Statistics, No. 329, Centers for Disease Control and Prevention, National Center for Health Statistics, Hyattsville, MD, June 19, 2002

TABLE 3.6

Number of all-listed procedures for discharges from short-stay hospitals by procedure category and age, 2000

[Discharges of inpatients from non-federal hospitals. Excludes newborn infants. Procedure groupings and code numbers are based on the *International Classification of Diseases, 9th Revision, Clinical Modification* (ICD–9–CM)]

Procedure category and ICD–9–CM code		All ages		Under 15 years		15–44 years		45–64 years		65 years and over	
		Number	SE[1]	Number	SE[1]	Number	SE[1]	Number	SE[1]	Number	SE[1]
						Number in thousands					
All procedures		39,981	1,855	1,951	323	13,518	612	9,775	500	14,737	807
Operations on the nervous system	01–05	1,000	77	210	41	309	38	238	18	242	19
Spinal tap	03.31	296	25	131	22	70	7	47	5	48	4
Operations on the endocrine system	06–07	90	6	*	*	27	3	37	5	23	3
Operations on the eye	08–16	80	11	9	2	20	4	20	4	32	6
Operations on the ear	18–20	37	5	22	5	8	2	*4	*1	*4	*1
Operations on the nose, mouth, and pharynx	21–29	261	18	56	10	89	8	57	6	59	7
Operations on the respiratory system	30–34	969	49	57	14	164	14	271	17	477	30
Bronchoscopy with or without biopsy	33.21–33.24, 33.27	248	18	*	*	42	5	73	7	116	10
Operations on the cardiovascular system	35–39	5,939	339	154	31	549	30	2,113	131	3,123	189
Removal of coronary artery obstruction and insertion of stent(s)	36.0	1,025	83	*	*	62	8	437	32	524	51
Coronary artery bypass graft[2]	36.1	519	41	*	*	17	3	216	19	286	23
Cardiac catheterization	37.21–37.23	1,221	101	8	2	96	10	520	43	597	51
Insertion, replacement, removal, and revision of pacemaker leads or device	37.7–37.8	327	22	*	*	*5	*1	45	7	274	19
Hemodialysis	39.95	456	31	*	*	65	6	164	14	226	18
Operations on the hemic and lymphatic system	40–41	315	18	*	*	49	4	108	8	135	11
Operations on the digestive system	42–54	5,145	207	208	39	1,136	51	1,404	65	2,397	109
Endoscopy of small intestine with or without biopsy	45.11–45.14, 45.16	915	40	11	3	120	8	231	13	553	28
Endoscopy of large intestine with or without biopsy	45.21–45.25	541	27	*	*	65	6	125	10	346	19
Partial excision of large intestine	45.7	236	14	*	*	27	4	73	6	134	9
Appendectomy, excluding incidental	47.0	303	19	71	9	167	11	50	5	16	2
Cholecystectomy	51.2	419	21	*	*	138	9	129	9	149	10
Lysis of peritoneal adhesions	54.5	307	17	4	1	123	9	94	7	85	8
Operations on the urinary system	55–59	962	55	35	9	235	20	291	19	401	28
Cystoscopy with or without biopsy	57.31–57.33	181	12	*	*	33	4	47	4	97	8
Operations on the male genital organs	60–64	258	18	19	5	14	3	68	6	157	12
Prostatectomy	60.2–60.6	184	16	*	*	*	*	48	5	134	12
Operations on the female genital organs	65–71	2,061	94	6	1	1,192	58	638	34	225	17
Oophorectomy and salpingo-oophorectomy	65.3–65.6	494	27	*	*	205	14	230	14	57	6
Bilateral destruction or occlusion of fallopian tubes	66.2–66.3	315	19	*	*	315	19	*	*	*	*
Hysterectomy	68.3–68.7, 68.9	633	33	*	*	317	20	254	14	62	5
Obstetrical procedures	72–75	6,209	296	19	3	6,185	295	*5	*1	—	—
Episiotomy with or without forceps or vacuum extraction	72.1, 72.21, 72.31, 72.71, 73.6	944	57	*	*	940	57	*	*	—	—
Artificial rupture of membranes	73.0	833	61	*	*	830	61	*	*	—	—
Cesarean section	74.0–74.2, 74.4,74.99	855	43	*	*	853	43	*	*	—	—
Repair of current obstetric laceration	75.5–75.6	1,136	59	*4	*1	1,130	59	*	*	—	—
Operations on the musculoskeletal system	76–84	3,171	182	172	31	836	49	918	63	1,245	84
Partial excision of bone	76.2–76.3, 77.6–77.8	209	17	11	3	70	6	77	9	51	6
Reduction of fracture	76.7,79.0–79.3	628	41	51	8	187	15	125	10	265	20
Open reduction of fracture with internal fixation	79.3	423	28	15	3	117	10	87	7	203	15
Excision or destruction of intervertebral disc	80.5	296	23	*	*	126	11	128	11	41	5
Total hip replacement	81.51	152	12	*	*	13	2	51	6	88	8
Total knee replacement	81.54	299	28	*	*	*6	*1	82	9	211	22
Operations on the integumentary system	85–86	1,264	87	*	*	355	25	378	21	407	25
Debridement of wound, infection, or burn	86.22,86.28	325	20	17	4	84	8	105	10	120	9
Miscellaneous diagnostic and therapeutic procedures	87–99	12,223	932	837	147	2,349	248	3,226	239	5,812	449
Computerized axial tomography	87.03 ,87.41, 87.71, 88.01, 88.38	754	94	39	10	150	22	182	23	383	54
Arteriography and angiocardiography using contrast material	88.4–88.5	2,005	146	11	3	175	14	821	64	998	76
Diagnostic ultrasound	88.7	886	96	37	10	143	18	232	25	474	59
Respiratory therapy	93.9,96.7	991	89	206	61	129	14	215	18	440	34
Insertion of endotracheal tube	96.04	429	23	40	9	61	5	103	7	226	15
Injection or infusion of cancer chemotherapeutic substance	99.25	199	20	48	13	37	5	68	7	46	6

* Figure does not meet standard of reliability or precision.
—Category not applicable.
[1]SE is standard error.
[2]The number of discharges with a coronary artery bypass graft was 314,000.

SOURCE: Margaret J. Hall and Maria F. Owings, "Table 8. Number of all-listed procedures for discharges from short-stay hospitals by procedure category and age, United States, 2000," in *2000 National Hospital Discharge Survey,* Advance Data From Vital and Health Statistics, No. 329, Centers for Disease Control and Prevention, National Center for Health Statistics, Hyattsville, MD, June 19, 2002

TABLE 3.7

Number of all-listed procedures for discharges from short-stay hospitals by procedure category and sex, 2000

[Discharges of inpatients from non-federal hospitals. Excludes newborn infants. Procedure groupings and code numbers are based on the *International Classification of Diseases, 9th Revision, Clinical Modification* (ICD–9–CM)]

Procedure category and ICD–9–CM code		Both sexes		Male		Female	
		Number	SE[1]	Number	SE[1]	Number	SE[1]
		Number in thousands					
All procedures		39,981	1,855	15,654	852	24,328	1,047
Operations on the nervous system	01–05	1,000	77	458	37	542	49
Spinal tap	03.31	296	25	156	16	141	12
Operations on the endocrine system	06–07	90	6	23	2	67	6
Operations on the eye	08–16	80	11	43	7	37	5
Operations on the ear	18–20	37	5	24	4	13	2
Operations on the nose, mouth, and pharynx	21–29	261	18	158	12	103	8
Operations on the respiratory system	30–34	969	49	526	32	443	24
Bronchoscopy with or without biopsy	33.21–33.24, 33.27	248	18	145	13	103	8
Operations on the cardiovascular system	35–39	5,939	339	3,420	209	2,519	135
Removal of coronary artery obstruction and insertion of stent(s)	36.0	1,025	83	655	54	370	31
Coronary artery bypass graft[2]	36.1	519	41	371	31	148	11
Cardiac catheterization	37.21–37.23	1,221	101	732	61	490	41
Insertion, replacement, removal, and revision of pacemaker leads or device	37.7–37.8	327	22	162	12	165	16
Hemodialysis	39.95	456	31	224	20	232	16
Operations on the hemic and lymphatic system	40–41	315	18	160	11	155	9
Operations on the digestive system	42–54	5,145	207	2,180	98	2,965	121
Endoscopy of small intestine with or without biopsy	45.11–45.14, 45.16	915	40	408	21	508	25
Endoscopy of large intestine with or without biopsy	45.21–45.25	541	27	210	12	331	19
Partial excision of large intestine	45.7	236	14	107	8	129	10
Appendectomy, excluding incidental	47.0	303	19	163	12	140	9
Cholecystectomy	51.2	419	21	134	9	284	15
Lysis of peritoneal adhesions	54.5	307	17	61	5	246	14
Operations on the urinary system	55–59	962	55	450	28	511	34
Cystoscopy with or without biopsy	57.31–57.33	181	12	96	8	85	7
Operations on the male genital organs	60–64	258	18	258	18	—	—
Prostatectomy	60.2–60.6	184	16	184	16	—	—
Operations on the female genital organs	65–71	2,061	94	—	—	2,061	94
Oophorectomy and salpingo-oophorectomy	65.3–65.6	494	27	—	—	494	27
Bilateral destruction or occlusion of fallopian tubes	66.2–66.3	315	19	—	—	315	19
Hysterectomy	68.3–68.7, 68.9	633	33	—	—	633	33
Obstetrical procedures	72–75	6,209	296	—	—	6,209	296
Episiotomy with or without forceps or vacuum extraction	72.1, 72.21, 72.31, 72.71, 73.6	944	57	—	—	944	57
Artificial rupture of membranes	73.0	833	61	—	—	833	61
Cesarean section	74.0–74.2, 74.4, 74.99	855	43	—	—	855	43
Repair of current obstetric laceration	75.5–75.6	1,136	59	—	—	1,136	59
Operations on the musculoskeletal system	76–84	3,171	182	1,546	87	1,624	101
Partial excision of bone	76.2–76.3, 77.6–77.8	209	17	111	9	98	10
Reduction of fracture	76.7, 79.0–79.3	628	41	285	21	344	23
Open reduction of fracture with internal fixation	79.3	423	28	177	14	246	17
Excision or destruction of intervertebral disc	80.5	296	23	162	13	134	12
Total hip replacement	81.51	152	12	69	6	83	7
Total knee replacement	81.54	299	28	115	12	185	17
Operations on the integumentary system	85–86	1,264	87	567	47	697	45
Debridement of wound, infection, or burn	86.22, 86.28	325	20	189	14	136	9
Miscellaneous diagnostic and therapeutic procedures	87–99	12,223	932	5,841	442	6,382	497
Computerized axial tomography	87.03, 87.41, 87.71, 88.01, 88.38	754	94	345	45	409	52
Arteriography and angiocardiography using contrast material	88.4–88.5	2,005	146	1,157	87	848	63
Diagnostic ultrasound	88.7	886	96	385	42	501	56
Respiratory therapy	93.9, 96.7	991	89	507	48	484	43
Insertion of endotracheal tube	96.04	429	23	221	13	209	12
Injection or infusion of cancer chemotherapeutic substance	99.25	199	20	115	15	85	9

* Figure does not meet standard of reliability or precision.
—Category not applicable.
[1]SE is standard error.
[2]The number of discharges with a coronary artery bypass graft was 314,000.

SOURCE: Margaret J. Hall and Maria F. Owings, "Table 10. Number of all-listed procedures for discharges from short–stay hospitals by procedure category and sex, United States, 2000," in *2000 National Hospital Discharge Survey,* Advance Data From Vital and Health Statistics, No. 329, Centers for Disease Control and Prevention, National Center for Health Statistics, Hyattsville, MD, June 19, 2001

TABLE 3.8

Rate of all-listed procedures for discharges from short-stay hospitals by procedure category and age, 2000

[Discharges of inpatients from non-federal hospitals. Excludes newborn infants. Procedure groupings and code numbers are based on the *International Classification of Diseases, 9th Revision, Clinical Modification* (ICD–9–CM)]

Procedure category and ICD–9–CM code		All ages		Under 15 years		15–44 years		45–64 years		65 years and over	
		Number	SE[1]	Number	SE[1]	Number	SE[1]	Number	SE[1]	Number	SE[1]
		Rate per 10,000 population									
All procedures		1,437.7	66.7	322.5	53.4	1,106.3	50.1	1,603.9	82.0	4,274.7	234.2
Operations on the nervous system	01–05	35.9	2.8	34.8	6.7	25.3	3.1	39.1	2.9	70.3	5.6
Spinal tap	03.31	10.6	0.9	21.6	3.7	5.8	0.5	7.8	0.8	13.8	1.3
Operations on the endocrine system	06–07	3.2	0.2	*	*	2.2	0.3	6.1	0.7	6.5	0.8
Operations on the eye	08–16	2.9	0.4	1.5	0.3	1.6	0.3	3.2	0.6	9.3	1.7
Operations on the ear	18–20	1.3	0.2	3.6	0.8	0.6	0.1	*0.6	*0.1	*1.1	*0.3
Operations on the nose, mouth, and pharynx	21–29	9.4	0.7	9.2	1.6	7.3	0.6	9.4	0.9	17.0	2.0
Operations on the respiratory system	30–34	34.8	1.8	9.4	2.3	13.4	1.1	44.4	2.7	138.3	8.7
Bronchoscopy with or without biopsy	33.21–33.24, 33.27	8.9	0.7	*	*	3.5	0.4	12.1	1.2	33.7	2.9
Operations on the cardiovascular system	35–39	213.5	12.2	25.4	5.2	44.9	2.5	346.8	21.4	905.9	54.9
Removal of coronary artery obstruction and insertion of stent(s)	36.0	36.9	3.0	*	*	5.1	0.6	71.7	5.2	152.0	14.7
Coronary artery bypass graft[2]	36.1	18.7	1.5	*	*	1.4	0.2	35.4	3.2	82.9	6.8
Cardiac catheterization	37.21–37.23	43.9	3.6	1.4	0.3	7.8	0.8	85.4	7.0	173.0	14.8
Insertion, replacement, removal, and revision of pacemaker leads or device	37.7–37.8	11.8	0.8	*	*	*0.4	*0.1	7.4	1.2	79.4	5.5
Hemodialysis	39.95	16.4	1.1	*	*	5.3	0.5	26.9	2.3	65.5	5.3
Operations on the hemic and lymphatic system	40–41	11.3	0.7	*	*	4.0	0.4	17.7	1.3	39.1	3.3
Operations on the digestive system	42–54	185.0	7.4	34.4	6.5	93.0	4.2	230.3	10.7	695.2	31.7
Endoscopy of small intestine with or without biopsy	45.11–45.14, 45.16	32.9	1.5	1.8	0.5	9.8	0.7	37.9	2.1	160.5	8.0
Endoscopy of large intestine with or without biopsy	45.21–45.25	9.4	1.0	*	*	5.3	0.5	20.5	1.6	100.5	5.6
Partial excision of large intestine	45.7	8.5	0.5	*	*	2.2	0.3	11.9	1.0	38.8	2.6
Appendectomy, excluding incidental	47.0	10.9	0.7	11.7	1.4	13.6	0.9	8.2	0.9	4.7	0.7
Cholecystectomy	51.2	15.1	0.7	*	*	11.3	0.7	21.2	1.5	43.3	3.0
Lysis of peritoneal adhesions	54.5	11.0	0.6	0.7	0.2	10.1	0.7	15.5	1.1	24.8	2.2
Operations on the urinary system	55–59	34.6	2.0	5.8	1.5	19.3	1.6	47.7	3.1	116.3	8.2
Cystoscopy with or without biopsy	57.31–57.33	6.5	0.4	*	*	2.7	0.3	7.8	0.7	28.0	2.3
Operations on the male genital organs	60–64	9.3	0.6	3.2	0.8	1.2	0.2	11.1	1.1	45.5	3.6
Prostatectomy	60.2–60.6	6.6	0.6	*	*	*	*	7.9	0.9	38.9	3.3
Operations on the female genital organs	65–71	74.1	3.4	0.9	0.2	97.5	4.8	104.7	5.6	65.3	4.8
Oophorectomy and salpingo-oophorectomy	65.3–65.6	17.8	1.0	*	*	16.8	1.1	37.8	2.3	16.6	1.6
Bilateral destruction or occlusion of fallopian tubes	66.2–66.3	11.3	0.7	*	*	25.8	1.5	*	*	*	*
Hysterectomy	68.3–68.7, 68.9	22.8	1.2	*	*	26.0	1.6	41.7	2.4	17.9	1.4
Obstetrical procedures	72–75	223.3	10.6	3.1	0.5	506.2	24.1	*0.8	*0.2	—	—
Episiotomy with or without forceps or vacuum extraction	72.1,72.21,72.31,72.71,73.6	33.9	2.0	*	*	76.9	4.6	*	*	—	—
Artificial rupture of membranes	73.0	30.0	2.2	*	*	67.9	5.0	*	*	—	—
Cesarean section	74.0–74.2, 74.4, 74.99	30.8	1.6	*	*	69.8	3.5	*	*	—	—
Repair of current obstetric laceration	75.5–75.6	40.9	2.1	*0.7	*0.2	92.5	4.8	*	*	—	—
Operations on the musculoskeletal system	76–84	114.0	6.6	28.4	5.1	68.4	4.0	150.6	10.3	361.1	24.2
Partial excision of bone	76.2–76.3, 77.6–77.8	7.5	0.6	1.9	0.5	5.7	0.5	12.7	1.4	14.7	1.6
Reduction of fracture	76.7, 79.0–79.3	22.6	1.5	8.5	1.4	15.3	1.2	20.5	1.7	76.8	5.7
Open reduction of fracture with internal fixation	79.3	15.2	1.0	2.5	0.5	9.5	0.8	14.3	1.2	58.9	4.5
Excision or destruction of intervertebral disc	80.5	10.6	0.8	*	*	10.3	0.9	21.0	1.9	12.0	1.4
Total hip replacement	81.51	5.5	0.4	*	*	1.0	0.2	8.3	1.0	25.7	2.3
Total knee replacement	81.51	10.8	1.0	*	*	*0.5	*0.1	13.5	1.5	61.2	6.3
Operations on the integumentary system	85–86	45.4	3.1	*	*	29.1	2.0	62.0	3.4	118.0	7.1
Debridement of wound, infection, or burn	86.22, 86.28	11.7	0.7	2.9	0.6	6.8	0.6	17.2	1.7	34.7	2.6
Miscellaneous diagnostic and therapeutic procedures	87–99	439.5	33.5	138.3	24.3	192.3	20.3	529.3	39.2	1,685.7	130.3
Computerized axial tomography	87.03, 87.41, 87.71, 88.01, 88.38	27.1	3.4	6.5	1.7	12.3	1.8	29.8	3.8	111.0	15.5
Arteriography and angiocardiography using contrast material	88.4–88.5	72.1	5.3	1.8	0.4	14.3	1.1	134.6	10.5	289.5	21.9
Diagnostic ultrasound	88.7	31.9	3.5	6.1	1.6	11.7	1.5	38.1	4.1	137.6	17.0
Respiratory therapy	93.9,96.7	35.6	3.2	34.1	10.0	10.6	1.1	35.2	3.0	127.7	9.8
Insertion of endotracheal tube	96.04	15.4	0.8	6.5	1.4	5.0	0.4	16.9	1.1	65.5	4.5
Injection or infusion of cancer chemotherapeutic substance	99.25	7.2	0.7	8.0	2.1	3.0	0.4	11.2	1.1	13.3	1.8

* Figure does not meet standard of reliability or precision.
—Category not applicable.
[1]SE is standard error of rate.
[2]The rate per 10,000 population of discharges with a coronary artery bypass graft was 11.3.

SOURCE: Margaret J. Hall and Maria F. Owings, "Table 9. Rate of all-listed procedures for discharges from short–stay hospitals by procedure category and age, United States, 2000," in *2000 National Hospital Discharge Survey*, Advance Data From Vital and Health Statistics, No. 329, Centers for Disease Control and Prevention, National Center for Health Statistics, Hyattsville, MD, June 19, 2002

about organ and tissue donation. Governors of at least nine states forged partnerships with local advocacy, medical, religious, and business groups to strengthen support for transplant programs.

State programs were also reinforced by a national organ donation initiative announced by Health and Human Services (HHS) Secretary Tommy G. Thompson in April 2001. Secretary Thompson vowed to create a national medal to honor families of organ donors and called upon powerful alliances between employers and labor unions to promote donation. Called the "Workplace Partnership for Life," this coalition included some of the largest U.S. employers and organizations such as Aetna, American Airlines, Bank of America, Daimler–Chrysler Corporation, United Auto Workers, Ford Motor Company, General Motors, 3M, MetLife, Verizon, and the United States Postal Service.

In March 1998 UNOS was ordered to change its organ allocation policy to more equitably distribute organs to various regions of the country. Under the previous system, when an organ became available in a local area, that organ was offered to the sickest patient in that area. If no local patient needed the organ, then it was offered regionally, then nationally. The government wanted organs distributed to the sickest patients first, regardless of where they lived. Secretary of Health and Human Services (HHS) at that time, Donna Shalala, claimed, "People are dying unnecessarily, not because they don't have health insurance, not because they don't have access to care, but simply because of where they happen to live in the country. We need a level playing field for all patients."

The new regulations changed the allocation of organs from a regional system to a national system in which medical necessity, rather than geography, was the primary factor determining who received organs. The new rules met with great resistance in Congress. Some members felt that the government should have no role in deciding life and death issues, and others insisted that a national program would result in the closure of smaller transplant centers, forcing some transplant recipients to travel great distances for life-saving care. UNOS opposed the regulations, arguing that the new system would obstruct their ability to supply donated organs.

The new system, based on need rather than location, took effect in March 2000, although the issue of precisely who would decide the allocation of organs remained unresolved until April 2000, when the U.S. House of Representatives passed a proposal to restore decision-making to UNOS, where it has remained. In September 2000, UNOS signed a new three-year contract with the government that compelled the network to put the new rules into effect. By 2002 UNOS policies reflected the shift to a more equitable national organ distribution system.

SURGICAL CENTERS AND URGENT CARE CENTERS

Ambulatory surgery centers, often called surgicenters, are equipped to perform routine surgical procedures that do not require an overnight hospital stay. A surgical center requires less sophisticated and expensive equipment than a hospital operating room. Minor surgery, such as biopsies, abortions, hernia repair, and many cosmetic surgery procedures are performed at outpatient surgical centers. Most procedures are done under local anesthesia, and the patient goes home the same day.

Most ambulatory surgery centers are freestanding, but some are located on hospital campuses or are adjacent to physicians' offices or clinics. Facilities are licensed by the states, and they must be equipped with at least one operating room, an area for preparing patients for procedures, a patient recovery area, and x-ray and clinical laboratory services. Surgical centers must have a registered nurse on the premises when patients are in the facility.

Urgent care centers (also called urgicenters) are usually operated by private for-profit organizations and provide up to 24-hour care on a walk-in basis. These centers fill several special needs in a community. They provide convenient, timely, and easily accessible care in an emergency when the nearest hospital is miles away. The centers are normally open during the hours when most physicians' offices are closed, and they are economical to operate because they do not provide hospital beds. They usually treat problems such as cuts that require sutures, sprains and bruises from accidents, and various infections. Many provide inexpensive immunization, and some offer routine health care for persons who do not have a regular source of medical care. Urgent care tends to be more expensive than a visit to the family physician, but an urgent care center visit is usually less expensive than treatment from a traditional hospital emergency department.

LONG-TERM CARE FACILITIES

Families are still the major caretakers of older, dependent, and disabled members of our society. The number of people age 65 and older living in long-term care facilities such as nursing homes, however, is rising because the population in this age group is increasing rapidly. Even though many older people now live longer, healthier lives, the increase in overall length of life has increased the need for long-term care facilities.

Growth of the home health care industry in the early 1990s only slightly slowed the increase in the numbers of Americans entering nursing homes. Assisted living and continuing-care retirement communities offer other alternatives to nursing home care. When it is possible, many older adults prefer to remain in the community and receive health care in their homes.

TABLE 3.9

Nursing home facility characteristics and measures of utilization, selected years 1973–99

Survey year	Homes	Beds	Beds per nursing home	Current residents	Occupancy rate[1]	Discharges	Discharges per 100 beds[2]
1999	18,000	1,879,600	104.5	1,628,300	86.6	2,522,300	134.2
1997	17,000	1,820,800	106.9	1,608,700	88.4	2,369,000	130.1
1995	16,700	1,770,900	106.1	1,548,600	96.4	—	—
1985	19,100	1,624,200	85.0	1,491,400	80.5	1,223,500	75.3
1977	18,900	1,402,400	74.2	1,303,100	98.4	1,117,500	80.4
1973–74	15,700	1,177,300	75.0	1,075,800	95.3	—	—

—Data not available.
[1]Occupancy rate is calculated by dividing residents by available beds.
[2]Discharge rate is calculated by dividing discharges by available beds.

SOURCE: Adrienne Jones, "Table A. Number and percent of facility characteristics and measures of utilization for nursing homes by survey year: United States, 1973–1974, 1977, 1985, 1997, 1999," in *The National Nursing Home Survey: 1999 Summary,* Data from the National Health Care Survey, Centers for Disease Control and Prevention, Vital and Health Statistics, Series 13, No. 152, Hyattsville, MD, June 2002

Types of Nursing Homes

Nursing homes fall into three broad categories: residential care facilities, intermediate care facilities, and skilled nursing facilities. Each provides a different range and intensity of services:

• A residential care facility (RCF) normally provides meals and housekeeping for its residents, plus some basic medical monitoring, such as administering medications. This type of home is for persons who are fairly independent and do not need constant medical attention but need help with tasks such as laundry and cleaning. Many RCFs also provide social activities and recreational programs for their residents.

• An intermediate care facility (ICF) offers room and board and nursing care as necessary for persons who can no longer live independently. As in the RCF, exercise and social programs are provided, and some ICFs offer physical therapy and rehabilitation programs as well.

• A skilled nursing facility (SNF) provides around-the-clock nursing care, plus on-call physician coverage. The SNF is for patients who need intensive nursing care, as well as such services as occupational therapy, physical therapy, respiratory therapy, and rehabilitation.

Number of Nursing Home Residents Rising

The nation's 18,000 nursing homes had occupancy rates of almost 87 percent in 1999. Nursing homes averaged about 105 beds per facility. (See Table 3.9.) In 1999 about 1.5 million adults age 65 and older were nursing home residents. Of those, most were white (87.1 percent) and female (74.3 percent). (See Table 3.10.) If the 158,700 residents under 65 are added to the total, there were 1.6 million nursing home residents in 1999, with women (nearly 1.2 million) outnumbering men (457,900) by almost three to one. There were more than six times as

many white nursing home residents as blacks and other racial minorities. (See Table 3.11.)

Most residents of nursing homes are the "oldest old." Out of the total 1.6 million nursing home residents in 1999, 90 percent were 65 years old and older. People age 85 and older (the so-called oldest old) are a fast-growing segment of the population, and accounted for almost half (46 percent) of all nursing home residents. (See Table 3.11.)

In 1999, 92 percent of all nursing homes were privately owned. Most (67 percent) nursing homes were company-owned and operated on a for-profit basis. Another 27 percent were operated by nonprofit, volunteer organizations, and only 12 percent were operated by governmental agencies. More than 80 percent were certified (approved for payment) by both Medicare and Medicaid.

About half of all current nursing home residents were admitted directly from a hospital, and about 30 percent came from the community.

Diversification of Nursing Homes

To remain competitive with home health care and the increasing array of alternative living arrangements for the elderly, many nursing homes began to offer alternative services and programs. New services include adult day care and visiting nurse services for persons who still live at home. Other programs include respite plans that allow caregivers who need to travel for business or vacation to leave an elderly relative in the nursing home temporarily.

One of the most popular nontraditional services is subacute care, which is comprehensive inpatient treatment for people recovering from acute illnesses such as pneumonia, injuries such as a broken hip, and chronic diseases such as arthritis that do not require intensive, hospital-level treatment. This level of care also enables nursing homes to expand their markets by offering services for younger patients.

TABLE 3.10

Nursing home residents 65 years of age and over by age, sex, and race, selected years 1973–99

[Data are based on a sample of nursing home residents]

Age, sex, and race	Residents				Residents per 1,000 population			
	1973–74	1985	1995	1999	1973–74	1985	1995	1999
Age								
65 years and over, age adjusted[1]	—	—	—	—	58.5	54.0	45.9	43.3
65 years and over, crude	961,500	1,318,300	1,422,600	1,469,500	44.7	46.2	42.4	42.9
65–74 years	163,100	212,100	190,200	194,800	12.3	12.5	10.1	10.8
75–84 years	384,900	509,000	511,900	517,600	57.7	57.7	45.9	43.0
85 years and over	413,600	597,300	720,400	757,100	257.3	220.3	198.6	182.5
Male								
65 years and over, age adjusted[1]	—	—	—	—	42.5	38.8	32.8	30.6
65 years and over, crude	265,700	334,400	356,800	377,800	30.0	29.0	26.1	26.5
65–74 years	65,100	80,600	79,300	84,100	11.3	10.8	9.5	10.3
75–84 years	102,300	141,300	144,300	149,500	39.9	43.0	33.3	30.8
85 years and over	98,300	112,600	133,100	144,200	182.7	145.7	130.8	116.5
Female								
65 years and over, age adjusted[1]	—	—	—	—	67.5	61.5	52.3	49.8
65 years and over, crude	695,800	983,900	1,065,800	1,091,700	54.9	57.9	53.7	54.6
65–74 years	98,000	131,500	110,900	110,700	13.1	13.8	10.6	11.2
75–84 years	282,600	367,700	367,600	368,100	68.9	66.4	53.9	51.2
85 years and over	315,300	484,700	587,300	612,900	294.9	250.1	224.9	210.5
White only[2]								
65 years and over, age adjusted[1]	—	—	—	—	61.2	55.5	45.4	41.9
65 years and over, crude	920,600	1,227,400	1,271,200	1,279,600	46.9	47.7	42.3	42.1
65–74 years	150,100	187,800	154,400	157,200	12.5	12.3	9.3	10.0
75–84 years	369,700	473,600	453,800	440,600	60.3	59.1	44.9	40.5
85 years and over	400,800	566,000	663,000	681,700	270.8	228.7	200.7	181.8
Black or African American only[2]								
65 years and over, age adjusted[1]	—	—	—	—	28.2	41.5	50.4	55.6
65 years and over, crude	37,700	82,000	122,900	145,900	22.0	35.0	45.2	51.1
65–74 years	12,200	22,500	29,700	30,300	11.1	15.4	18.4	18.2
75–84 years	13,400	30,600	47,300	58,700	26.7	45.3	57.2	66.5
85 years and over	12,100	29,000	45,800	56,900	105.7	141.5	167.1	183.1

—Category not applicable.

[1]Age adjusted by the direct method to the year 2000 population standard using the following three age groups: 65–74 years, 75–84 years, and 85 years and over.

[2]Beginning in 1999 the instruction for the race item on the Current Resident Questionnaire was changed so that more than one race could be recorded. In previous years only one racial category could be checked. Estimates for racial groups presented in this table are for residents for whom only one race was recorded. Estimates for residents where multiple races were checked are unreliable due to small sample sizes and are not shown.

Note: Excludes residents in personal care or domiciliary care homes. Age refers to age at time of interview. Rates are based on the resident population as of July 1. Starting in 1997, population figures are adjusted for net underenumeration using the 1990 National Population Adjustment Matrix from the U.S. Bureau of the Census.

SOURCE: "Table 97. Nursing home residents 65 years of age and over, according to age, sex, and race: United States, 1973–74, 1985, 1995, and 1999," in *Health United States, 2002*, Centers for Disease Control and Prevention, National Center for Health Statistics, Hyattsville, MD, 2002

Innovation Improves Quality of Nursing Home Care

Although industry observers and the media frequently decry the care provided in nursing homes, and publicize instances of elder abuse and other quality of care issues, several organizations have actively sought to develop models of health service delivery that improve the clinical care and quality of life for nursing home residents. In August 2002, the Commonwealth Fund published a report examining one such model in eastern Wisconsin, *Evaluation of the Wellspring Model for Improving Nursing Home Quality*. Researchers from the Institute for the Future of Aging Services and American Association of Homes and Services for the Aging evaluated the Wellspring model of nursing home quality improvement.

Wellspring is a group of 11 not-for-profit nursing homes governed by a group called the Wellspring Alliance. Founded in 1994, the alliance aimed to improve simultaneously clinical care delivered to its nursing home residents and the work environment for its employees. Education and collaboration are hallmarks of the Wellspring philosophy, and this program began by equipping nursing home personnel with the skills needed to perform their jobs and organizing employees in teams working toward shared goals. The Wellspring model of service delivery uses a multidisciplinary clinical team approach—nurse practitioners, social service, food service personnel, nursing assistants, facility and housekeeping personnel—to solve problems and develop approaches to better meet residents' needs. The teams represent an important innovation because they allow health professionals and other workers to interact as peers and share resources, information, and decision-making in a cooperative, supportive environment.

Shared resources, training, ideas, and goals have had a powerful impact on care at the Wellspring facilities. The

TABLE 3.11

Number of nursing home residents by facility characteristics and age, sex, and race of resident, 1999

Facility characteristic	All residents	Under 65 years	Age at interview 65 years and over Total	65–74 years	75–84 years	85 years and over	Sex Male	Female	Race White only	Black and other[1]	Black only	Unknown
All facilities	1,628,300	158,700	1,469,500	194,800	517,600	757,100	457,900	1,170,400	1,394,900	215,900	178,700	17,400
Ownership												
Proprietary	1,049,300	113,000	936,300	133,700	345,500	457,100	305,800	743,500	875,600	162,900	135,100	*10,800
Voluntary nonprofit	445,600	26,300	419,300	40,800	130,000	248,500	103,700	341,900	398,900	40,200	32,300	*6,600
Government and other	133,300	19,400	114,000	20,300	42,200	51,400	48,300	85,000	120,500	*12,900	*11,400	—
Certification												
Certified												
By Medicare and Medicaid	1,415,400	134,600	1,280,800	172,100	454,400	654,300	389,800	1,025,600	1,209,600	189,000	157,400	16,700
By Medicare only	37,100	*	35,700	*	12,900	19,800	13,800	23,300	35,100	*	*	*
By Medicaid only	143,100	20,600	122,500	17,100	40,900	64,500	42,900	100,100	119,200	23,500	19,200	*
Not certified	32,700	*	30,600	*	9,500	18,500	*11,300	21,500	31,100	*	*	—
Beds												
Fewer than 50 beds	58,600	*3,900	53,800	*6,600	17,000	30,100	16,600	42,100	53,000	*5,300	*	*
50–99 beds	414,200	40,200	374,000	44,700	129,300	200,000	122,500	291,600	369,100	41,300	30,800	*
100–199 beds	827,800	75,500	752,300	102,000	267,200	383,000	221,800	606,000	705,100	114,100	98,100	*8,600
200 beds or more	327,700	38,200	289,500	41,400	104,100	144,000	97,000	230,700	267,800	55,200	48,400	*
Geographic region												
Northeast	383,400	34,200	349,200	46,400	118,500	184,300	109,200	274,200	339,000	40,000	33,800	*
Midwest	498,200	45,000	453,200	58,900	153,200	241,100	135,800	362,400	453,400	42,600	37,800	*
South	531,500	51,300	480,100	63,400	179,100	237,700	143,700	387,700	423,600	100,600	95,500	*7,300
West	215,200	28,200	187,000	26,100	66,800	94,000	69,100	146,100	178,900	32,700	11,600	*
Location of agency												
Metropolitan statistical area	1,128,400	118,000	1,010,300	135,200	362,700	512,500	314,600	813,800	946,800	168,800	138,500	12,800
Nonmetropolitan statistical area	499,900	40,700	459,200	59,600	155,000	244,600	143,300	356,600	448,100	47,200	40,200	*
Affiliation[2]												
Chain	978,800	98,100	880,700	120,900	319,100	440,800	277,800	701,000	833,500	136,300	115,700	*9,100
Independent	646,100	60,300	585,900	73,500	197,400	314,900	179,300	466,800	559,100	78,800	62,100	*8,300

– Quantity zero.

* Figure does not meet standard of reliability or precision because the sample size is less than 30. If shown with a number, it should not be assumed reliable because the sample size is between 30 and 59 or is greater than 59, but the estimate has a standard error over 30 percent.

[1] A small number of patients with more than one race indicated have been classified as "other," and are reported in the "Black and other" race category.

[2] Excludes unknown.

Note: Numbers may not add to totals because of rounding.

SOURCE: Adrienne Jones, "Table 7. Number of nursing home residents by selected facility characteristics and age, sex, and race of resident: United States, 1999," in *The National Nursing Home Survey: 1999 Summary*, Data from the National Health Care Survey, Centers for Disease Control and Prevention, Vital and Health Statistics, Series 13, No. 152, Hyattsville, MD, June 2002

researchers observed more cooperation, responsibility, and accountability within the teams and the institutions than observed at other comparable facilities. In addition to finding a strong organizational culture, committed to quality patient care, the researchers also documented measurable improvements in specific areas including:

- Wellspring facilities had lower rates of staff turnover than comparable Wisconsin facilities during the same time period, probably because Wellspring workers felt valued by management and experienced greater job satisfaction than other nursing home personnel.

- The Wellspring model did not require additional resources to institute, and Wellspring facilities operated at lower costs than comparable facilities.

- Wellspring facilities' performance, as measured by a federal survey, improved.

- Generally, Wellspring personnel appeared more attentive to residents' needs and problems and sought to anticipate and promptly resolve problems.

The researchers concluded that the organizational commitment to training and shared decision-making along with improved quality of interactions and relationships among staff and between staff and residents significantly contributed to enhanced quality of life for residents.

MENTAL HEALTH FACILITIES

In earlier centuries, mental illness was often considered a sign of possession by the devil or, at best, moral weakness. A change in these attitudes began in the late eighteenth century, when mental illness began to be perceived as a treatable condition. It was then that the concept of "asylums" was developed, not simply to lock the mentally ill away, but also to provide them with "relief" from the conditions they found troubling.

Who Are the Mentally Ill?

Providers of mental health care distinguish between people who are severely mentally ill (defined by diagnosis), those who are mentally disabled (defined by level of disability), and those who are chronic mental patients (defined by duration of hospitalization). These three dimensions—diagnosis, disability, and duration—are the models used to describe the mentally ill population in the United States.

Mental Health: A Report of the Surgeon General, 1999 defines mental disorders as "health conditions that are characterized by alterations in thinking, mood, or behavior (or some combination thereof) associated with distress and/or impaired functioning." The report distinguishes mental disorders from mental problems, describing the signs and symptoms of mental health problems as less intense and of shorter duration than those of mental health disorders, however it acknowledges that both mental health disorders and problems may be distressing and disabling.

The U.S. Public Health Service uses this definition:

The chronically mentally ill population includes persons who suffer from emotional disorders that interfere with their functional capacities in relation to such primary aspects of daily life as self-care, interpersonal relationships, and work or schooling, and that may often necessitate prolonged mental health care.

The U.S. Surgeon General's Report asserts that at the close of the twentieth century, the nation's ability to prevent, identify, and treat mental disorders had outpaced the system for delivering mental health care to all those in need of it. The report estimated that 1 in 5 Americans suffers from a mental disorder in any given year and 15 percent of adults make use of mental health services during the year—8 percent seek care for a mental disorder and 7 percent have mental health problems.

Where Are the Mentally Ill?

The chronically mentally ill reside either in mental hospitals or in community settings, such as with families, in boarding homes and shelters, in single-room-occupancy hotels (usually cheap hotels or boardinghouses), in jail, or even on the streets as part of the homeless population. The institutionalized mentally ill are those persons with psychiatric diagnoses who have lived in mental hospitals for more than one year or those with diagnosed mental conditions who are living in nursing homes.

Between 1986 and 1998, the number of patients housed in county mental health institutions declined, although the number of mental health organizations rose by almost 1,000 during this time. The total number of beds dropped from 267,613 to 261,903, and from 111.7 beds to 97.4 beds per 100,000 persons. State and county mental hospital beds were reduced most dramatically, by more than one-half, from 50 to 24 beds per 100,000 persons. (See Table 3.12.) This is not necessarily a result of better treatment for the mentally ill, but rather a consequence of reduced funding for those institutions and individuals. Unfortunately, many of the patients who were once housed in mental institutions (including some who had been lifelong residents in these facilities) now fend for themselves on the streets or in prisons.

Declining mental health expenditures have resulted in fewer available services for specific populations of the mentally ill, particularly those who could benefit from inpatient or residential care. Even for persons without conditions requiring institutional care there are barriers to access. The Surgeon General's Report describes the U.S. mental health service system as largely uncoordinated and fragmented, in part because it involves so many different sectors—health and social welfare agencies, public and private hospitals, housing, criminal justice, education—and it is funded through many different sources. Finally, inequalities in insurance coverage for mental health, coupled with the stigma associated with mental illness and treatment also have limited access to services

HOME HEALTH CARE

The concept of home health care began as post-acute care after hospitalization, an alternative to longer, costlier hospital lengths-of-stay. Home health care services have grown tremendously since the 1980s when prospective payment (payments made before, rather than after care is received) for Medicare patients sharply reduced hospital lengths-of-stay. During the mid-1980s Medicare began to reimburse hospitals using a rate scale based on diagnosis related groups (DRGs)—hospitals received a fixed amount for providing services to Medicare patients based on their diagnoses. This form of payment gave hospitals powerful financial incentives to utilize fewer resources since they could keep the difference between the prepayment and the amount they actually spent to provide care. Hospitals suffered losses when patients had longer lengths of stay and used more services than were covered by the standardized DRG prospective payment.

Home health care grew faster in the early 1990s than any other segment of health services. Its growth may be attributable to the observation that in many cases, caring for patients at home is preferable to and more cost-effective than care provided in a hospital, nursing home, or some

TABLE 3.12

Mental health organizations and beds for 24-hour hospital and residential treatment according to type of organization, selected years 1986–98

[Data are based on inventories of mental health organizations]

Type of organization	1986	1990	1992	1994[1]	1998[1]
	Number of mental health organizations				
All organizations	4,747	5,284	5,498	5,392	5,722
State and county mental hospitals	285	273	273	256	229
Private psychiatric hospitals	314	462	475	430	348
Non-Federal general hospital psychiatric services	1,351	1,674	1,616	1,612	1,707
Department of Veterans Affairs medical centers[2]	139	141	162	161	145
Residential treatment centers for emotionally disturbed children	437	501	497	459	461
All other organizations[3]	2,221	2,233	2,475	2,474	2,832
	Number of beds				
All organizations	267,613	272,253	270,867	290,604	261,903
State and county mental hospitals	119,033	98,789	93,058	81,911	63,525
Private psychiatric hospitals	30,201	44,871	43,684	42,399	33,635
Non-Federal general hospital psychiatric services	45,808	53,479	52,059	52,984	54,266
Department of Veterans Affairs medical centers[2]	26,874	21,712	22,466	21,146	13,301
Residential treatment centers for emotionally disturbed children	24,547	29,756	30,089	32,110	33,483
All other organizations[3]	21,150	23,646	29,511	60,054	63,693
	Beds per 100,000 civilian population				
All organizations	111.7	111.6	107.5	112.1	97.4
State and county mental hospitals	49.7	40.5	36.9	31.6	23.6
Private psychiatric hospitals	12.6	18.4	17.3	16.4	12.5
Non-Federal general hospital psychiatric services	19.1	21.9	20.7	20.4	20.2
Department of Veterans Affairs medical centers[2]	11.2	8.9	8.9	8.2	4.9
Residential treatment centers for emotionally disturbed children	10.3	12.2	11.9	12.4	12.4
All other organizations[3]	8.8	9.7	11.7	23.2	23.7

[1]Beginning in 1994 data for supportive residential clients (moderately staffed housing arrangements such as supervised apartments, group homes, and halfway houses) are included in the totals and all other organizations. This change affects the comparability of trend data prior to 1994 with data for 1994 and later years.
[2]Includes Department of Veterans Affairs (VA) neuropsychiatric hospitals, VA general hospital psychiatric services, and VA psychiatric outpatient clinics.
[3]Includes freestanding psychiatric outpatient clinics, partial care organizations, and multiservice mental health organizations.
Note: Some numbers in this table have been revised and differ from previous editions of *Health, United States*. These data exclude mental health care provided in non-psychiatric units of hospitals such as general medical units.

SOURCE: "Table 109. Mental health organizations and beds for 24-hour hospital and residential treatment according to type of organization: United States, selected years 1986–98," in *Health, United States, 2001*, Centers for Disease Control and Prevention, National Center for Health Statistics, National Vital Statistics System, Hyattsville, MD, 2002

other residential facility. Oftentimes, older adults are more comfortable and much happier living in their own homes or with family members. Disabled persons may also be able to function better at home with limited assistance than in a residential setting with full-time monitoring. ("Home Health Care," *Family Economics and Nutrition Review,* vol. 9, no. 2, 1996.)

Home health care agencies provide a wide variety of services. Services range from helping with activities of daily living, such as bathing, light housekeeping, and meals, to skilled nursing care, such as the nursing care needed by AIDS or cancer patients. About 20 percent of the personnel employed by home health agencies are registered nurses, another 7 percent are licensed practical nurses, and 13 percent are nursing or home health aides. Other personnel involved in home health care include physical therapists, social workers, and speech-language pathologists.

In 1972 Medicare extended home care coverage to persons under 65 years of age only if they were disabled or suffered from end stage renal disease (ESRD). Prior to the year 2000, Medicare coverage for home health care was limited to patients immediately following discharge from the hospital. By the year 2000 Medicare covered beneficiaries' home health care services with no requirement for prior hospitalization. There were also no limits to the number of professional visits or to the length of coverage. As long as the patient's condition warranted it, the following services were provided:

• Part-time or intermittent skilled nursing and home health aide services

• Speech-language pathology services

• Physical and occupational therapy

• Medical social services

FIGURE 3.1

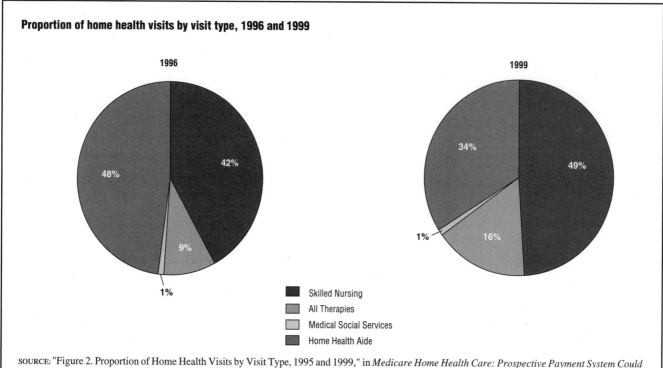

Proportion of home health visits by visit type, 1996 and 1999

1996

1999

Skilled Nursing
All Therapies
Medical Social Services
Home Health Aide

SOURCE: "Figure 2. Proportion of Home Health Visits by Visit Type, 1995 and 1999," in *Medicare Home Health Care: Prospective Payment System Could Reverse Recent Declines in Spending,* U.S. General Accounting Office, Washington, DC, September 2000

• Medical supplies

• Durable medical equipment (with a 20 percent co-payment)

Over time, the population receiving home care services has changed. Today much of home health care is associated with rehabilitation from critical illnesses, and fewer users are long-term patients with chronic conditions. Compared with acute care users, the long-term patients are older, more functionally disabled, more likely to be incontinent, and more expensive to serve.

In 1996, 48 percent of home health users received home health aide services, 42 percent received skilled nursing care, 1 percent received medical social services, and 9 percent received all of these therapies. (See Figure 3.1.) By 1999, home health aide visits dropped to 34 percent, skilled nursing rose to 49 percent, medical social services stayed at 1 percent, and 16 percent received all therapies. In 1999 the proportion of visits in which all therapies were included nearly doubled from nine percent in 1996 to 16 percent. This changing pattern of utilization reflects a shift from longer-term care for chronic conditions to short-term, post-acute care.

From 1989 to 1997 annual Medicare spending for home health care rose 30 percent. Relaxed eligibility criteria for home health care, including elimination of the requirement of an acute hospitalization before receiving home care, enabled an increased number of beneficiaries to use services.

Home health care utilization among those over 65 peaked in 1996 and began to decline during 1997. (See Figure 3.2.)

Medicare Limits Home Care Services

The Balanced Budget Act of 1997 (PL 105-33) aimed to cut approximately $16.2 billion from the federal government's home care expenditures over a period of five years. The act sought to return home health care to its original concept of short-term care plus skilled nursing and therapy services. According to Medicare's administrator, Nancy-Ann DeParle, some of the 4.8 million Medicare beneficiaries who receive home health care would lose certain personal care services, such as assistance with bathing, dressing, and eating.

The Balanced Budget Act sharply curtailed the growth in home-care spending, greatly affecting health care providers. Annual Medicare home health care spending fell 32 percent between 1998 and 1999 in response to tightened eligibility requirements for skilled nursing services, limited per visit payments, and increasingly stringent claims review. (See Table 3.13.) The changes forced many agencies to close and transfer their patients to other home-health companies. Nationwide, it was estimated that 1,200 agencies went out of business during 1998.

HOSPICE CARE

In medieval times, hospices were refuges for the sick, the needy, and travelers. The modern hospice movement

FIGURE 3.2

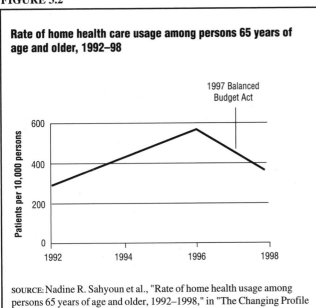

Rate of home health care usage among persons 65 years of age and older, 1992–98

SOURCE: Nadine R. Sahyoun et al., "Rate of home health usage among persons 65 years of age and older, 1992–1998," in "The Changing Profile of Nursing Home Residents, 1985–1997," in *Trends in Health and Aging*, Centers for Disease Control and Prevention, National Center for Health Statistics, Hyattsville, MD, no. 4, March 2001

TABLE 3.13

History of Medicare home health care spending growth, 1985–99

Period	Annual spending rate	Significant change shaping service use
1985-88	1%	Tightened interpretation of coverage criteria; increased emphasis on medical review of home health claims.
1989-97	30%	Loosening of coverage criteria allowed more beneficiaries to receive more services.
1998-99	-32%	IPS limited per visit payments and limited aggregate agency payments; heightened scrutiny of claims; changed qualifying criteria for "skilled" services.

SOURCE: "Table 5. History of Medicare Home Health Care Spending Growth, 1985–99," in *Medicare Home Health Care: Prospective Payment System Could Reverse Recent Declines in Spending*, U.S. General Accounting Office, Washington, DC, September 2000

developed in response to the need to provide humane care to terminally ill patients, while at the same time offering support to their families. An English physician, Dame Cicely Saunders, introduced the hospice concept in the United States. The care provided by hospice workers is called palliative care, and it aims to relieve patients' pain and the accompanying symptoms of terminal illness without seeking to cure the illness.

Hospice is a philosophy, an approach to care for the dying, and it is not necessarily a physical facility. Hospice may refer to a place—a freestanding facility or designated floor in a hospital or nursing home—or to a program such as hospice-home care, where a team of health professionals helps the dying patient and family at home. Hospice teams may involve physicians, nurses, social workers, pastoral counselors, and trained volunteers. The goal of hospice care is to provide support and care for people at the end of life enabling them to remain as comfortable as possible.

Hospice workers consider the patient and family as the "unit of care" and focus their efforts on attending to emotional, psychological, and spiritual needs as well as physical comfort and well-being. The programs provide respite care, which offers relief at any time for families who may be overwhelmed and exhausted by the demands of caregiving and may be neglecting their own needs for rest and relaxation. Finally, hospice programs work to prepare relatives and friends for the loss of their loved ones. Hospice offers bereavement support groups and counseling to help deal with grief and may even help with funeral arrangements.

The hospice concept is different from most other health care services because it focuses on care rather than cure. Hospice workers try to minimize the two greatest fears associated with dying: fear of isolation and fear of pain. Potent, effective medications are offered to patients in pain, with the goal of controlling pain without impairing alertness so that patients may be as comfortable as possible.

Hospice care also emphasizes living life to its fullest. Patients are encouraged to stay active for as long as possible, to do things they enjoy, and to learn something new each day. Quality of life, rather than length of life, is the focus. In addition, whenever it is possible, family and friends are urged to be the primary caregivers in the home. Care at home helps both patients and family members enrich their lives and face death together.

Dr. Ira Byock, former president of the American Academy of Hospice and Palliative Medicine, explains the concept of hospice care in *Dying Well: The Prospect for Growth at the End of Life* (G. P. Putnam's Sons, New York, 1997):

> . . . [H]ospice care differs noticeably from the modern medical approach to dying. Typically, as a hospice patient nears death, the medical details become almost automatic and attention focuses on the personal nature of this final transition—what the patient and family are going through emotionally and spiritually. In the more established system, even as people die, medical procedures remain the first priority. With hospice, they move to the background as the personal comes to the fore.

Studies show that about 80 percent of terminally ill patients die in a hospital or a nursing home, many of them the object of over-treatment. The Institute of Medicine's Committee on Care at the End of Life described this over-treatment as involving both care that is inappropriate and care that is not wanted by the patient, even if some clinical benefit could be expected.

Hospice Isn't the Answer for Everyone

Hospice, however, is not the ideal program for everyone. To some choosing hospice care might mean giving up hope and succumbing to death. Others might wish to endure their pain and suffering out of religious or philosophical convictions. Still others might opt for quantity rather than quality of life, as reported by Joel Tsevat et al. in "Health Values of Hospitalized Patients 80 Years or Older" (*Journal of the American Medical Association,* vol. 279, no. 5, February 4, 1998). In this study, 414 hospitalized patients age 80–98 were interviewed. Nearly 41 percent of patients were unwilling to exchange any time in their current state of health for a shorter life in excellent health.

MANAGED CARE ORGANIZATIONS

Managed health care is the sector of the health insurance industry in which health care providers are not independent businesses run by, for example, private medical practitioners, but by administrative firms that manage the allocation of health care benefits. In contrast to conventional indemnity insurers that do not govern the provision of medical care services and simply pay for them, managed care firms have a significant voice in how services are administered to enable them to exert better control over health care costs. (Indemnity insurance is traditional fee-for service coverage in which providers are paid according to the service performed.)

Managed care, which has a primary purpose of controlling service utilization and costs, represents a rapidly growing segment of the health care industry. The beneficiaries of employer-funded health plans (persons who receive health benefits from their employers), as well as Medicare and Medicaid recipients, often find themselves in this type of health care program. The term "managed care organization" covers several types of health care delivery systems, such as health maintenance organizations (HMOs), preferred provider organizations (PPOs), and "utilization review" (UR) groups that oversee diagnoses, recommend treatments, and manage costs for their beneficiaries.

Health Maintenance Organizations

Health maintenance organizations (HMOs) began to grow in the 1970s as alternatives to traditional health insurance, which was becoming more and more expensive. The HMO Act of 1973 was a federal law requiring employers with more than 24 employees to offer an alternative to conventional indemnity insurance in the form of a federally qualified HMO. The intent of the act was to stimulate HMO development, and the federal government has been promoting HMOs since the President Richard Nixon Administration, maintaining that groups of physicians following certain rules of practice could slow rising medical costs and improve health care quality.

HMOs are health insurance programs organized to provide complete coverage for subscribers' (also known as enrollees or members) health needs for negotiated, prepaid prices. The subscribers (and/or their employers) pay a fixed amount each month; in turn, the HMO group provides, at no extra charge or at a very minimal charge, preventive care, such as routine checkups and immunizations, and care for any illness or accident. Inpatient hospitalization and referral services are also covered by the monthly fee. HMO members benefit from reduced out-of-pocket costs (they do not pay deductibles), they do not have to file claims or fill out insurance forms, and they generally pay only a small copayment for each office visit. Members are usually "locked into" the plan for a specified period—usually one year. If the necessary service is available within the HMO, patients normally must use an HMO doctor. There are several types of HMOs:

- Staff model HMO—the "purest" form of managed care. All primary care physicians are employees of the HMO and practice in a centralized location such as an outpatient clinic that also may house laboratory, pharmacy, and facilities for other diagnostic testing. The staff model offers the HMO the greatest opportunities to manage both cost and quality of health care services.

- Group model—in which the HMO contracts with a group of primary care and multi-specialty health providers. The group is paid a fixed amount per patient to provide specific services. This model is the one used by Kaiser Permanente and Group Health Cooperative of Puget Sound (Group Health Cooperative of Puget Sound affiliated with Kaiser Permanente in 2000), early pioneers in the HMO movement. The administration of the medical group determines how the HMO payments will be distributed among the physicians and other health care providers. Group model HMOs are usually located in hospitals or clinic settings and have on-site pharmacies. Participating physicians usually do not have any fee-for-service patients.

- Network model—in which the HMO contracts with two or more groups of health providers that agree to provide health care at negotiated prices to all members enrolled in the HMO.

- Independent practice association model (IPA)—in which the HMO contracts with individual physicians or medical groups that then provide medical care to HMO members at their own offices. The individual physicians agree to follow the practices and procedures of the HMO when caring for the HMO members, however, they generally also maintain their own private practices and see fee-for-service patients as well as HMO members. IPA physicians are paid by capitation (literally, "per head") for the HMO patients and by conventional methods for their fee-for-service

TABLE 3.14

Health maintenance organizations (HMO's) and enrollment, according to model type, geographic region, and federal program, selected years, 1976–2001

[Data are based on a census of health maintenance organizations]

Plans and enrollment	1976	1980	1990	1995	1996	1997	1998	1999	2000	2001
Plans					Number					
All plans	174	235	572	562	630	652	651	643	568	541
Model type:[1]										
Individual practice association[2]	41	97	360	332	367	284	317	309	278	257
Group[3]	122	138	212	108	122	98	116	123	101	104
Mixed	—	—	—	122	141	258	212	208	188	180
Geographic region:										
Northeast	29	55	115	100	111	110	107	110	98	96
Midwest	52	72	160	157	182	184	185	179	161	190
South	23	45	176	196	218	236	237	239	203	158
West	70	63	121	109	119	121	122	115	106	97
Enrollment[1]					Number of persons in millions					
Total	6.0	9.1	33.0	50.9	59.1	66.8	76.6	81.3	80.9	79.5
Model type:[1]										
Individual practice association[2]	0.4	1.7	13.7	20.1	26.0	26.7	32.6	32.8	33.4	33.1
Group[3]	5.6	7.4	19.3	13.3	14.1	11.0	13.8	15.9	15.2	15.6
Mixed	—	—	—	17.6	19.0	29.0	30.1	32.6	32.3	30.9
Federal program:[4]										
Medicaid[5]	—	0.3	1.2	3.5	4.7	5.6	7.8	10.4	10.8	11.4
Medicare	—	0.4	1.8	2.9	3.7	4.8	5.7	6.5	6.6	6.1
					Percent of HMO enrollees					
Model type:[1]										
Individual practice association[2]	6.6	18.7	41.6	39.4	44.1	39.9	42.6	40.3	41.3	41.6
Group[3]	93.4	81.3	58.4	26.0	23.7	16.5	18.0	19.6	18.9	19.5
Mixed	—	—	—	34.5	32.2	43.4	39.2	40.1	39.9	38.8
Federal program:[4]										
Medicaid[5]	—	2.9	3.5	6.9	8.0	8.2	10.2	12.7	13.3	14.3
Medicare	—	4.3	5.4	5.7	6.3	7.2	7.4	8.0	8.1	10.2
					Percent of population enrolled in HMO's					
Total	2.8	4.0	13.4	19.4	22.3	25.2	28.6	30.1	30.0	28.3
Geographic region:										
Northeast	2.0	3.1	14.6	24.4	25.9	32.4	37.8	36.7	36.5	35.1
Midwest	1.5	2.8	12.6	16.4	18.8	19.5	22.7	23.3	23.2	21.7
South	0.4	0.8	7.1	12.4	15.2	17.9	21.0	23.9	22.6	21.0
West	9.7	12.2	23.2	28.6	33.2	36.4	39.1	41.4	41.7	40.7

—Data not available.

[1]Enrollment or number of plans may not equal total because some plans did not report these characteristics.

[2]An HMO operating under an individual practice association model contracts with an association of physicians from various settings (a mixture of solo and group practices) to provide health services.

[3]Group includes staff, group, and network model types.

[4]Federal program enrollment in HMO's refers to enrollment by Medicaid or Medicare beneficiaries, where the Medicaid or Medicare program contracts directly with the HMO to pay the appropriate annual premium.

[5]Data for 1990 and later include enrollment in managed care health insuring organizations.

Note: Data as of June 30 in 1976–80, and January 1 from 1990 onwards. Open-ended enrollment in HMO plans, amounting to 9 million on Jan. 1, 2001, is included from 1994 onwards. HMO's in Guam are included starting in 1994; HMO's in Puerto Rico, starting in 1998. In 2001 HMO enrollment in Guam was 97,000 and in Puerto Rico, 1,265,000.

SOURCE: "Table 132. Health maintenance organizations (HMO's) and enrollment, according to model type, geographic region, and Federal program: United States, selected years, 1976–2001," in *Health, United States, 2002*, Centers for Disease Control and Prevention, National Center for Health Statistics, Hyattsville, MD, 2002

patients. Physician members of the IPA guarantee that the care for each HMO member for which they are responsible will be delivered within a fixed budget. They guarantee this by allowing the HMO to withhold an amount of their payments (usually about 20 percent per year). If at year's end, the physician's cost for providing care falls within the preset amount, then the physician receives all the monies withheld. If the physician's costs of care exceed the agreed upon amount, the HMO may retain any portion of the monies it has withheld. This arrangement places physicians and other providers such as hospitals, labo-

ratories, and imaging centers "at risk" for keeping down treatment costs, and this "at risk" formula is key to HMO cost-containment efforts.

An HMO may offer an open-ended or point-of-service (POS) option that allows members to choose their own physicians and hospitals, either within or outside the HMO. A member who chooses an outside provider, however, will generally have to pay a larger portion of the expenses. Physicians not contracting with the HMO but who see HMO patients are paid according to the services performed. POS members are incentivized to seek care from contracted network physicians and other health care providers through comprehensive coverage offerings.

The number of people enrolled in HMOs more than tripled between 1980 and 1990. In 1980 HMOs covered only 9.1 million people. By 1990, 33 million Americans were enrolled in HMOs. Enrollment continued to explode through the 1990s, and by 1999, there were 643 HMOs covering 81.3 million persons—more than one quarter of the American population. (See Table 3.14.) Both the number of HMOs and the number of people covered dropped in both 2000 and 2001. By 2001, the number of HMOs had declined by over 100, to 541, and enrollment had declined by almost 2 million, to 79.5 million.

HMOs Have Fans and Critics

HMOs have been the subject of considerable debate among physicians, payers, policymakers, and health care consumers. Many physicians feel HMOs interfere in the physician-patient relationship and effectively prevent them from practicing medicine the way they have traditionally practiced. These physicians claim they know their patients' conditions and are, therefore, in the best position to recommend treatment. The physicians resent being advised and overruled by insurance administrators. (Physicians can recommend the treatment they believe is best, but if the insurance company will not cover the costs, patients may be unwilling to undergo the recommended treatment.)

The HMO industry counters that its evidence-based determinations (judgments about the appropriateness of care that reflect scientific research) are based on the experiences of many thousands of physicians and, therefore, it knows which treatment is most likely to be successful. The industry generally claims that, in the past, physicians' chosen treatments have not been scrutinized or even assessed for effectiveness, and as a result most physicians do not really know whether the treatment they have prescribed is optimal for the specific medical condition.

Further, the HMO industry cited the slower increase in health care expenses as another indicator of its management success. Industry spokespersons noted that any major change in how the industry is run would lead to increasing costs. They claimed that HMOs and other managed care programs were bringing a more rational approach to the health care industry while maintaining health care quality and controlling costs.

Still, many physicians resent that, with a few exceptions, HMOs are not financially liable for their decisions. When a physician chooses to forgo a certain procedure and is wrong, the physician may well be held legally accountable. When an HMO informs a physician that it will not cover a recommended procedure and the HMO's decision is found to be wrong, it cannot be held directly

liable. Many physicians assert that because HMOs make such choices, they are practicing medicine, and should, therefore, be held accountable. The HMOs counter that these are administrative decisions, and they deny that they are practicing medicine.

The legal climate, however, began to change for HMOs during the mid 1990s. Both the Third Circuit Federal Court of Appeals in *Dukes v. U.S. Healthcare* (64 LW 2007, 1995) and the Tenth Circuit Federal Court of Appeals in *PacifiCare of Oklahoma, Inc., v. Burrage* (59 F.3rd 151, 1995) agreed that HMOs were liable for malpractice and negligence claims against the HMO and HMO physicians. In *Frappier Estate v. Wishnov* (Florida District Court of Appeals, Fourth District, No. 95-0669, May 8, 1996), the Florida court agreed with the earlier findings. It seemed these decisions would be backed by new laws when both houses of Congress passed legislation (the "Patients' Bill of Rights") giving patients more recourse to contest the decisions of HMOs, although the House of Representatives and the Senate disagreed about the specific rights and the actions patients could take to enforce their rights.

The Senate-passed bill ensured that patients could hold their HMOs accountable when their actions resulted in injury or death. The bill allows patients to sue their HMOs in state court over denied benefits or to contest quality of care issues. It also allows federal court lawsuits for issues unrelated to quality of care. The bill does not limit damages in state court but damages are capped at $5 million in federal court.

The House version of the bill limits patients' access to courts and their ability to sue their HMOs by permitting lawsuits in state courts under restrictive rules, and caps non-economic damages at $1.5 million. Critics of the House-passed bill contended that it placed special interests above the interests of insured Americans.

By August 2002 the prospects for a patients' rights law passing during 2002 dimmed as senators and members of the House failed to resolve their differences about the legislation. The central issue that stalled the negotiations about the bill was the question of how much recourse patients should have in court when they believe their HMOs have not provided adequate care. Although the legislation was not officially "dead," and a conference committee was appointed to attempt to resolve the issues, many industry observers decided the talks, and White House actions to encourage consensus, had failed.

Preferred Provider Organizations

During the 1990s, in response to HMOs and other efforts by insurance groups to cut costs, physicians began forming or joining preferred provider organizations (PPOs). PPOs are managed care organizations that offer integrated delivery systems—networks of providers—available through a wide array of health plans and are readily accountable to purchasers for access, cost, quality, and services of their networks. They use provider selection standards, utilization management, and quality assessment programs to complement negotiated fee reductions (discounted rates from participating physicians, hospitals, and other health care providers) as effective strategies for long-term cost control. Under a PPO benefit plan, covered persons retain the freedom of choice of providers but are offered financial incentives such as lower out-of-pocket costs to use the preferred provider network. PPO members may use other physicians and hospitals, but they usually have to pay a higher proportion of the costs. PPOs are marketed directly to employers and to third party administrators (TPAs) who then market PPOs to their employer clients.

Exclusive provider organizations (EPOs) are a more restrictive variation of PPOs in which members must seek care from providers on the EPO panel. If a member visits an outside provider who is not on the EPO panel, then the EPO will offer either very limited or no coverage for the office or hospital visit.

CHAPTER 4

RESEARCHING, MEASURING, AND MONITORING
THE QUALITY OF HEALTH CARE

More than 2,500 agencies, institutions, and organizations are dedicated to researching, quantifying (measuring), monitoring, and improving health in the United States. Some are federally funded public entities such as the many institutes and agencies governed by the U.S. Department of Health and Human Services (HHS). Others are professional societies and organizations that develop standards of care, represent the views and interests of health care providers, and ensure the quality of health care facilities such as the American Medical Association (AMA) and the Joint Commission on Accreditation of Healthcare Organizations (JCAHO). Still other voluntary health organizations such as the American Heart Association, American Cancer Society, and the March of Dimes promote research and education about prevention and treatment of specific diseases.

THE U.S. DEPARTMENT OF HEALTH AND HUMAN SERVICES

The U.S. Department of Health and Human Services (HHS) is the nation's lead agency for ensuring the health of Americans by planning, operating, and funding delivery of essential human services, especially for society's most vulnerable populations. HHS consists of more than 300 programs, operated by 11 divisions, including 8 agencies in the U.S. Public Health Service. It is the largest grant-making agency in the federal government, funding about 60,000 grants each year and the HHS Medicare program, the nation's largest health insurer, which processes more than 900 million claims per year. For fiscal year 2002, HHS had a budget of $460 billion dollars and 65,100 employees.

HHS Milestones

HHS has a long, illustrious history beginning with the 1798 opening of the first Marine Hospital in Boston to care for sick and injured merchant seamen. Under President Abraham Lincoln, the agency that would become the Food and Drug Administration was established in 1862.

The 1935 enactment of the Social Security Act spurred the development of the Federal Security Agency in 1939 to direct programs in health, human services, insurance, and education. In 1946 the Communicable Disease Center, which would become the Centers for Disease Control and Prevention (CDC) was established and almost 20 years later, in 1965, Medicare and Medicaid were enacted to improve access to health care for older, disabled, and low-income Americans. The same year, the "Head Start" program was developed to provide education, health, and social services to preschool-age children.

In 1970 the National Health Service Corps was established to help meet the health care needs of underserved areas and populations; the following year the National Cancer Act became law. In 1984 the human immunodeficiency virus (HIV), the virus that causes acquired immunodeficiency syndrome (AIDS), was identified by the U.S. Public Health Service and French research scientists. The National Organ Transplant Act became law in 1984, and in 1990, the Human Genome Project was initiated.

During 1994, NIH-funded research isolated the genes responsible for inherited breast cancer, colon cancer, and the most frequently occurring kidney cancer. In 1998 efforts were launched to eliminate racial and ethnic disparities (differences) in health, and in 2000 the human genome sequencing was published. In 2001 the Health Care Financing Administration (HCFA) was replaced by the Centers for Medicaid & Medicare Services and HHS responded to the first reported cases of bioterrorism—the anthrax attacks—and developed new strategies to prevent and detect threats of bioterrorism.

HHS Agencies and Institutes Provide Comprehensive Health and Social Services

In addition to the CDC and NIH, the following HHS agencies research, plan, direct, oversee, administer, and provide health care services:

FIGURE 4.1

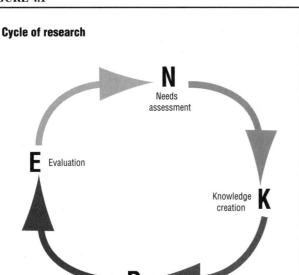

SOURCE: "Cycle of Research," in *Quality Research for Quality Health Care,* U.S. Department of Health and Human Services, Agency for Healthcare Research and Quality, Rockville, MD, 2002 [Online] http://www.ahcpr.gov.about/qualres.pdf [accessed August 10, 2002]

FIGURE 4.2

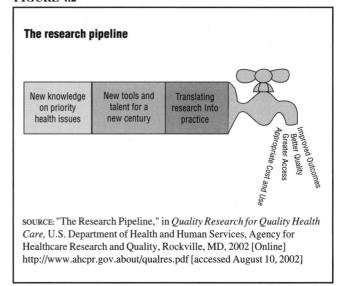

SOURCE: "The Research Pipeline," in *Quality Research for Quality Health Care,* U.S. Department of Health and Human Services, Agency for Healthcare Research and Quality, Rockville, MD, 2002 [Online] http://www.ahcpr.gov.about/qualres.pdf [accessed August 10, 2002]

• Administration on Aging (AoA) provides services aimed at helping older Americans retain their independence. The AoA develops policies that support older adults and directs programs that provide transportation, in-home services, and other health and social services. In fiscal year 2002 the AoA had a budget of $1.3 billion and 124 employees.

• Administration for Children and Families (ACF) provides services for families and children in need, administers "Head Start," and works with state foster care and adoption programs. ACF ran about 60 programs with a budget of $44 billion and 1,537 employees in 2002.

• Agency for Healthcare Research and Quality (AHRQ) researches access to health care, quality of care, and efforts to control health care costs. It also looks at the safety of health care services and ways to prevent medical errors. Figure 4.1 shows how AHRQ researches health system problems by performing a continuous process of needs assessment, gaining knowledge, interpreting and communicating information, and evaluating the effects of this process on the health problem. Figure 4.2 shows the process that transforms new information about health care issues into actions to improve access, costs, outcomes (what happens to patients as a result of the care they have received), and quality. AHRQ had a budget of $91 billion in fiscal year 2002 and 294 employees. AHRQ's six major categories of patient safety initiatives for 2001 were: identifying methods for reporting medical errors data; using computers and information technology to prevent medical errors; understanding the impact of working conditions on patient safety; developing innovative approaches to improving patient safety; disseminating research results; and additional patient safety research initiatives.

• Agency for Toxic Substances and Disease Registry (ATSDR) seeks to prevent exposure to hazardous waste.

• Centers for Medicare & Medicaid Services (CMMS) administer entitlement programs that provide health insurance for about 75 million Americans who are either age 65 or older or in financial need. It also operates the State Children's Health Insurance Program (SCHIP) that covers about 10 million uninsured children and regulates all laboratory testing, except testing performed for research purposes, in the United States. CMMS had a $374.7 billion budget in fiscal year 2002 and 4,569 employees.

• Food and Drug Administration (FDA) acts to ensure the safety and efficacy of pharmaceutical drugs and medical devices, and monitors food safety and purity. The FDA had a budget of $1.3 billion in fiscal year 2002 and nearly 10,000 employees.

• Health Resource and Service Administration (HRSA) provides services for medically underserved populations such as migrant workers, the homeless, and residents in public housing. HRSA oversees the nation's organ transplant program, directs efforts to improve maternal and child health, and delivers services to persons with AIDS through the Ryan White CARE Act. More than 2,000 people work for HRSA; its fiscal year 2002 budget was $6.5 billion.

• Indian Health Service (IHS) serves more than 550 tribes through a network of 37 hospitals, 60 health centers, 3 school health programs, 46 health stations, and

34 urban Indian health centers. IHS employed 14,794 workers in 2002 and had a budget of $2.9 billion.

• Office of the Secretary of Health and Human Services (OSHHS) provides the department's leadership and oversees the 11 operating divisions of HHS and advises the president about health, welfare, human service, and income security issues.

• Program Support Center (PSC) administers operations, financial management, and human resources for HHS as well as other departments and federal agencies. The PSC staff of about 1,200 processes approximately $195 billion in grant payments, provides personnel and payroll services for more than 65,000 HHS employees, and performs accounting, management, information technology, and telecommunication services.

• Substance Abuse and Mental Health Service Administration (SAMHSA) seeks to improve access to, and availability of, substance abuse prevention and treatment programs as well as other mental health services. SAMHSA was budgeted $2.9 billion in fiscal year 2002 and has 607 employees.

HHS agencies work with state, local, and tribal governments as well as public and private organizations to coordinate and deliver a wide range of services including:

• Preventive health services such as surveillance to detect outbreaks of disease and immunization programs through efforts directed by the (CDC) and the National Institutes of Health (NIH)

• Ensuring food, drug, and cosmetic safety through efforts of the Food and Drug Administration (FDA)

• Improving maternal and child health and preschool education in programs such as "Head Start," which served more than 877,000 children in 2002

• Preventing child abuse, domestic violence, and substance abuse, as well as funding substance abuse treatment through programs directed by the Administration for Children and Families (ACF)

• Assuring delivery of health care services to nearly 1.5 million Native Americans and Alaska Natives through the Indian Health Service (IHS), a network of hospitals, health centers, and other programs and facilities

• Medicare (federal health insurance program for older adults and persons with disabilities) and Medicaid (state and federal health insurance for low-income people) are administered by the Centers for Medicare & Medicaid Services (CMMS)

• Financial assistance and support services for low-income and older Americans, such as home-delivered meals ("Meals on Wheels") coordinated by the Administration on Aging (AoA).

FIGURE 4.3

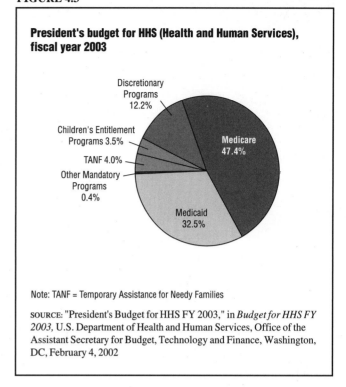

President's budget for HHS (Health and Human Services), fiscal year 2003

Discretionary Programs 12.2%

Children's Entitlement Programs 3.5%

TANF 4.0%

Other Mandatory Programs 0.4%

Medicare 47.4%

Medicaid 32.5%

Note: TANF = Temporary Assistance for Needy Families

SOURCE: "President's Budget for HHS FY 2003," in *Budget for HHS FY 2003,* U.S. Department of Health and Human Services, Office of the Assistant Secretary for Budget, Technology and Finance, Washington, DC, February 4, 2002

SUBSTANTIAL BUDGET HELPS HHS TO ACHIEVE ITS OBJECTIVES. Figure 4.3 displays how the FY 2003 HHS budget will be allocated, and Table 4.1 shows budgets for the HHS agencies during 2001, 2002, and 2003. Almost 80 percent of the FY 2003 HHS budget is designated for the Medicare and Medicaid programs. The FY 2003 budget aims to provide additional funds to assist state and local public health agencies to protect the nation against bioterrorism. The budget also is intended to strengthen Medicare, advance welfare reform efforts by supporting the Temporary Assistance to Needy Families (TANF) program, and improve public health by intensifying prevention programs to reduce the occurrence of diabetes, asthma, and obesity. HHS agencies also plan to improve budget and management performance of the agencies and to add 586 employees to their ranks in 2003.

THE U.S. PUBLIC HEALTH SERVICE COMMISSIONED CORPS. The uniformed service component of the early Marine Hospital Service adopted a military model for a group of career health professionals who traveled from one marine hospital to another as their services were needed. A law enacted in 1889 established this group as the Commissioned Corps, and throughout the twentieth century, the corps grew to include a wide range of health professionals. In addition to physicians, the corps contained nurses, dentists, research scientists, planners, pharmacists, sanitarians, engineers, and other public health professionals. The corps assisted the Marine Hospital Service to prevent infectious diseases from entering the country by examining newly arrived immigrants and directing state quarantine (the

TABLE 4.1

President's budget, fiscal year 2003

Line	Titles	FY 2001 APPROP Comp. to 03	FY 2002 APPROP Comp. to 03	FY 2003 Pres. Budg.
55000	DEPARTMENT OF HEALTH AND HUMAN SERVICES			
55003				
55005	FOOD AND DRUG ADMINISTRATION			
55010	Budget Authority/Appropriation	1,139,535	1,413,258	1,432,136
55012	*Program Level*	*1,317,215*	*1,604,645*	*1,727,300*
55015	Outlays	1,116,000	1,326,000	1,440,000
55020				
55105	HEALTH RESOURCES AND SERVICES ADMINISTRATION			
55115	Budget Authority/Appropriation	6,304,499	6,271,499	5,531,741
55130	*Program Level*	*6,368,758*	*6,568,199*	*6,175,045*
55140	Outlays	5,119,000	5,672,000	5,711,000
55145				
55205	INDIAN HEALTH SERVICE			
55206	Budget Authority/Appropriation	2,789,008	2,924,116	2,984,143
55208	*Program Level*	*3,273,059*	*3,438,093*	*3,498,901*
55210	Outlays	2,617,000	2,867,000	3,044,000
55212				
55255	CENTERS FOR DISEASE CONTROL AND PREVENTION			
55260	Budget Authority/Appropriation	3,812,557	4,184,730	4,015,341
55280	*Program Level*	*4,242,462*	*6,765,661*	*5,765,289*
55340	Outlays	3,172,000	3,731,000	4,215,000
55357				
55400	NATIONAL INSTITUTES OF HEALTH			
55420	Budget Authority/Appropriation	20,534,582	23,720,084	27,432,075
55430	*Program Level*	*20,544,082*	*23,729,584*	*27,432,075*
55460	Outlays	17,310,000	20,943,000	23,573,000
55475				
55560	SUBSTANCE ABUSE & MENTAL HEALTH SVCS. ADMIN.			
55570	Budget Authority/Appropriation	2,966,078	3,140,551	3,197,704
55580	*Program Level*	*2,994,078*	*3,150,551*	*3,207,704*
55630	Outlays	2,740,000	2,916,000	3,084,000
55640				
55710	AGENCY FOR HEALTHCARE RESEARCH AND QUALITY			
55711	Budget Authority/Appropriation	106,072	2,688	—
55712	*Program Level*	*271,334*	*300,359*	*251,700*
55718	Outlays	36,000	91,000	96,000
55722				
55740	PHS/Trust Funds - BA/Approp	70,000	70,000	70,000
55745	*PHS/Trust Funds - Prog. Lvl*	*70,000*	*70,000*	*70,000*
55780	Outlays	53,000	78,000	72,000
55790				
55800	Retirement Pay & Med. Benefits for Comm. Ofcrs. - BA/Approp	249,956	262,075	250,741
55805	Retirement Pay & Med. Benefits for Comm. Ofcrs. - Prog.Lvl.	*249,956*	*262,075*	*250,741*
55820	Outlays	240,000	256,000	252,000
55840				
55990	CENTERS FOR MEDICARE & MEDICAID SERVICES			
56348	Appropriation	210,842,142	232,255,018	245,810,185
56350	Budget Authority	352,800,940	378,002,818	396,334,485
56355	*Program Level*	*353,545,946*	*378,768,016*	*397,268,073*
56360	Outlays	350,396,997	374,843,871	397,497,234
59620				
59995	ADMINISTRATION FOR CHILDREN AND FAMILIES			
60000	Appropriation	43,244,885	44,586,412	46,966,455
60010	Budget Authority	43,244,885	44,586,412	46,966,455
60320	*Program Level*	*42,853,822*	*44,136,812*	*46,515,855*
60330	Outlays	43,114,000	44,637,000	46,912,000
60340				
60515	ADMINISTRATION ON AGING			
60518	Budget Authority/Appropriation	1,253,898	1,350,433	1,342,357
60520	*Program Level*	*1,256,698*	*1,352,433*	*1,345,357*
60522	Outlays	1,103,000	1,287,000	1,295,000
60543				
60700	DEPARTMENTAL MANAGEMENT			
60710	Budget Authority/Appropriation	899,541	3,342,029	2,875,414
60720	*Program Level*	*1,167,469*	*3,826,886*	*3,794,425*
60730	Outlays	737,000	1,687,800	2,343,500
61035				

TABLE 4.1

President's budget, fiscal year 2003 [CONTINUED]

Line	Titles	FY 2001 APPROP Comp. to 03	FY 2002 APPROP Comp. to 03	FY 2003 Pres. Budg.
61140	OFFICE OF INSPECTOR GENERAL			
61148	Budget Authority/Appropriation	171,627	189,603	209,972
61149	*Program Level*	*171,627*	*189,603*	*209,972*
61150	Outlays	34,000	42,000	50,000
61164				
61190	OFFICE FOR CIVIL RIGHTS			
61197	Budget Authority/Appropriation	29,605	33,753	35,574
61198	*Program Level*	*29,605*	*33,753*	*35,574*
61199	Outlays	22,000	28,000	29,800
61201				
61240	OTHER PROGRAMS AND SERVICES:			
61249	Adjustments for Proprietary Receipts	(888,000)	(797,000)	(828,007)
61250	Outlays	(888,000)	(797,000)	(828,007)
61255				
61260	*Program Support Center (non-add)*	*414,047*	*414,551*	*452,083*
61265	*Outlays (non-add)*	*293,000*	*334,000*	*453,000*
61270				
61287	Financing Offset 1% Evaluation (program level)	(258,504)	(360,509)	(338,234)
61336				
61406	Total, Health and Human Services-Appropriation	293,525,985	322,949,249	341,325,831
61410	Total, Health and Human Services-BA/Income	435,484,783	468,697,049	491,850,131
61415	*Total, Health and Human Services - Program Level*	*438,097,607*	*473,836,161*	*497,209,777*
61430	Total, Health and Human Services-Outlays	426,921,997	459,608,671	488,786,527
61450	SUMMARY:			
61455				
61460	BUDGET AUTHORITY:			
61465	Discretionary Programs	53,642,900	61,615,708	64,019,137
61470	Mandatory Programs	381,841,883	407,081,341	427,830,994
61475				
61480	*PROGRAM LEVEL:*			
61485	*Discretionary Programs*	*55,108,835*	*65,713,145*	*68,266,776*
61490	*Mandatory Programs*	*382,988,772*	*408,123,016*	*428,943,001*
61495				
61500	OUTLAYS:			
61505	Discretionary Programs	44,318,000	52,077,800	57,179,300
61510	Mandatory Programs	382,603,997	407,530,871	431,607,227
61515				

SOURCE: "FY 2003 President's Budget," in *Summary of Comparable President's Budget–FY 2003,* U.S. Department of Health and Human Services, Office of the Assistant Secretary for Budget, Technology and Finance, Washington, DC, February 4, 2002

period of time and place where persons suspected of having contagious diseases are detained and isolated) functions.

By 1912 the Marine Hospital Service was renamed the Public Health Service (PHS) to reflect its broader scope of activities. Today PHS is part of the Department of Health and Human Services. PHS commissioned officers played important roles in disease prevention and detection, acted to ensure food and drug safety, conducted research, provided medical care to underserved groups such as Native Americans and Alaska Natives, and assisted in disaster relief programs. One of the uniformed services in the United States (others are the Navy, Army, Marines, Air Force, and Coast Guard), the PHS Commissioned Corps continues to perform all of these functions and also identifies environmental threats to health and safety, promotes healthy lifestyles for Americans, and is involved with international agencies to help address global health problems.

In 2002 the PHS Commissioned Corps numbered 6,000 health professionals. These people report to the U.S. surgeon general, who holds the rank of vice admiral in the U.S. PHS Commissioned Corps. Corps officers work in PHS agencies and at other agencies including the Bureau of Prisons, U.S. Coast Guard, Environmental Protection Agency, and the Commission on Mental Health of the District of Columbia. The surgeon general is the physician appointed by the president of the United States to serve in a medical leadership position in the nation for a 4-year term of office. The surgeon general reports to the assistant secretary for health, and the Office of the Surgeon General is part of the Office of Public Health and Science. Eve E. Slater, MD, FACC, has served as the assistant secretary of HHS since January 2002. Sixteen surgeon generals have served. In 2002 Dr. Richard Carmona was sworn into this key office.

CENTERS FOR DISEASE CONTROL AND PREVENTION

The Centers for Disease Control and Prevention (CDC) is the primary HHS agency responsible for ensuring the health and safety of the nation's citizens in the United States

FIGURE 4.4

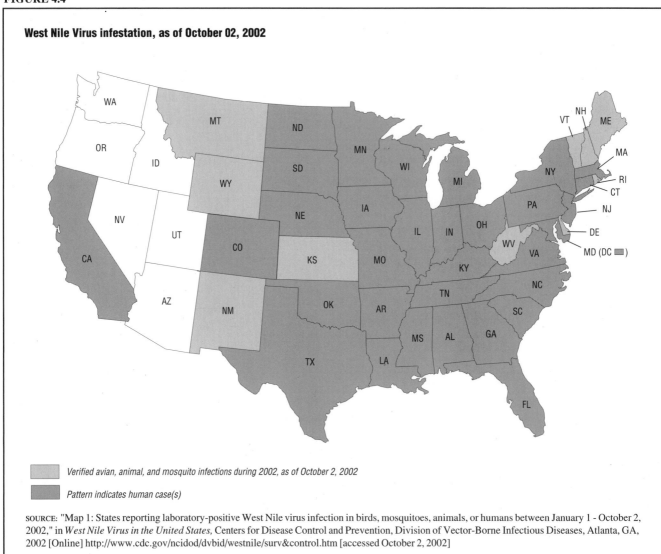

West Nile Virus infestation, as of October 02, 2002

Verified avian, animal, and mosquito infections during 2002, as of October 2, 2002

Pattern indicates human case(s)

SOURCE: "Map 1: States reporting laboratory-positive West Nile virus infection in birds, mosquitoes, animals, or humans between January 1 - October 2, 2002," in *West Nile Virus in the United States,* Centers for Disease Control and Prevention, Division of Vector-Borne Infectious Diseases, Atlanta, GA, 2002 [Online] http://www.cdc.gov/ncidod/dvbid/westnile/surv&control.htm [accessed October 2, 2002]

and abroad. CDC responsibilities include researching and monitoring health, detecting and investigating health problems, researching and instituting prevention programs, developing health policies, ensuring environmental health and safety, and offering education and training.

CDC headquarters are located in Atlanta, Georgia. However, 2,000 of the more than 8,500 CDC employees, representing 170 disciplines, serve throughout the country at 47 state health departments and 45 locations outside the United States. In addition to research scientists, physicians, nurses, and other health practitioners, CDC employs epidemiologists—scientists trained to measure the occurrence of disease in human populations. Epidemiologists measure disease occurrences, such as incidence and prevalence of disease, and work with clinical researchers to answer questions about causation—how particular diseases arise and the factors that contribute to their development, whether new treatments are effective, and how to prevent specific diseases.

Twelve centers, institutes, and offices make up the CDC—among the best known are the National Center for Health Statistics, which collects vital statistics, and the National Institute for Occupational Safety and Health (NIOSH), which seeks to prevent workplace injuries and accidents through research and prevention. Julie Louise Gerbering, MD, MPH, was named director of the CDC in 2002.

CDC Actions to Protect the Health of the Nation

The CDC is part of the first response to natural disasters, outbreaks of disease, and other public health emergencies. One recent CDC action is the 1999 identification of the West Nile virus (encephalitis), and methods to control this disease. Figure 4.4 is a map created by the CDC Division of Vector-Borne Diseases that shows the distribution of confirmed cases of West Nile virus infection as of August 9, 2002. Other examples are identification and education about effective strategies for preventing school and domestic violence and the National Breast and Cervical Cancer Early Detection Program, which detected breast cancer and prevented cervical cancer in more than 40,000 women from 1991 to September 1999.

Examples of CDC efforts to educate and communicate vital health information are its publications *Morbidity and Mortality Weekly Report (MMWR)* and the *Emerging Infectious Disease Journal* that alert the medical community to the presence of health risks, outbreaks, and preventive measures. In addition to providing vital statistics (births, deaths, and related health data), the CDC monitors Americans' health using surveys to measure the frequency of behaviors that increase health risk, such as smoking, substance abuse, and physical inactivity, and compiles data about the use of health care resources such as inpatient hospitalization rates and visits to hospital emergency departments.

CDC partners with public and private, national, state, and local agencies and organizations to deliver services. Examples of these collaborative efforts include the global battle against HIV/AIDS via *Leadership and Investment in Fighting an Epidemic (LIFE)* and a ten-agency initiative to address the problem of preventing further increases in antimicrobial infections—infections that resist treatment with antibiotics.

NATIONAL INSTITUTES OF HEALTH (NIH)

The NIH, which began as a one-room laboratory in 1887, is the world's premier medical research center. NIH conducts research in its own facilities and supports research in universities, medical schools, and hospitals throughout and outside the United States. NIH trains research scientists and other investigators and serves to communicate medical and health information to professional and consumer audiences.

Part of the U.S. Public Health Service, NIH is composed of 27 centers and institutes and is housed in more than 75 buildings on a 300-acre campus in Bethesda, Maryland. Among the better-known centers and institutes are the National Cancer Institute, National Human Genome Research Institute, National Institute of Mental Health, and the newer National Center for Complementary and Alternative Medicine. Figure 4.5 is an organizational chart of the NIH and shows all of its centers and institutes.

Patients arrive at the NIH Warren Grant Magnuson Clinical Center in Bethesda, Maryland, to participate in clinical research trials—about 7,000 patients per year are treated as inpatients and an additional 72,000 receive outpatient treatment. The National Library of Medicine, which produces the *Index Medicus,* a monthly listing of articles from the world's top medical journals, and maintains *Medline,* a comprehensive medical bibliographic database, is in the NIH Lister Hill Center.

The NIH budget has increased from about $300 per year in 1887 to almost $23.4 billion in 2002. NIH works to achieve its ambitious research objectives of "acquiring new knowledge to help prevent, detect, diagnose, and treat disease and disability, from the rarest genetic disorder to the common cold" by investing in promising biomedical research. NIH makes grants and contracts to support research and training in every state in the country, at more than 2,000 institutions.

Establishing Research Priorities

By law, all 27 institutes of the NIH must be funded and each institute must allocate its funding to specific areas and aspects of research within its domain. About half of each institute's budget is dedicated to supporting the best research proposals presented, in terms of their potential to contribute to advances that will combat the diseases the institute is charged with researching. Some of the other criteria used to determine research priorities include:

- Public health need—The NIH responds to health problems and diseases based on their incidence (the rate of development of a disease in a group during a given period of time), severity, and the costs associated with them. Examples of other measures used to weigh and assess need are the mortality rate (the number of deaths caused by the disease), the morbidity rate (the degree of disability caused by the disease), the economic and social consequences of the disease, and whether rapid action is required to control the spread of the disease.

- Rigorous peer review—proposals are scrutinized by accomplished researchers to determine their potential to return on the investment of resources.

- Flexibility and expansiveness—NIH experience has demonstrated that important findings for commonly occurring diseases may come from research about rarer ones. NIH attempts to fund the broadest possible array of research opportunities to stimulate creative solutions to pressing problems.

- Commitment to human resources and technology—NIH invests in people, equipment, and even some construction projects in the pursuit of scientific advancements.

Since not even the most gifted scientists can accurately predict the next critical discovery or stride in biomedical research, NIH must analyze each research opportunity in terms of competition for the same resources, public interests, scientific merit, the potential to build upon current knowledge. Figure 4.6 shows all of the stakeholders whose interests and opinions are considered when NIH resource allocation and grant funding decisions are made.

NIH Achievements

As of 2002, NIH supports about 1,000 principal investigators—researchers directing projects and 45,000

FIGURE 4.5

National Institutes of Health organizational chart

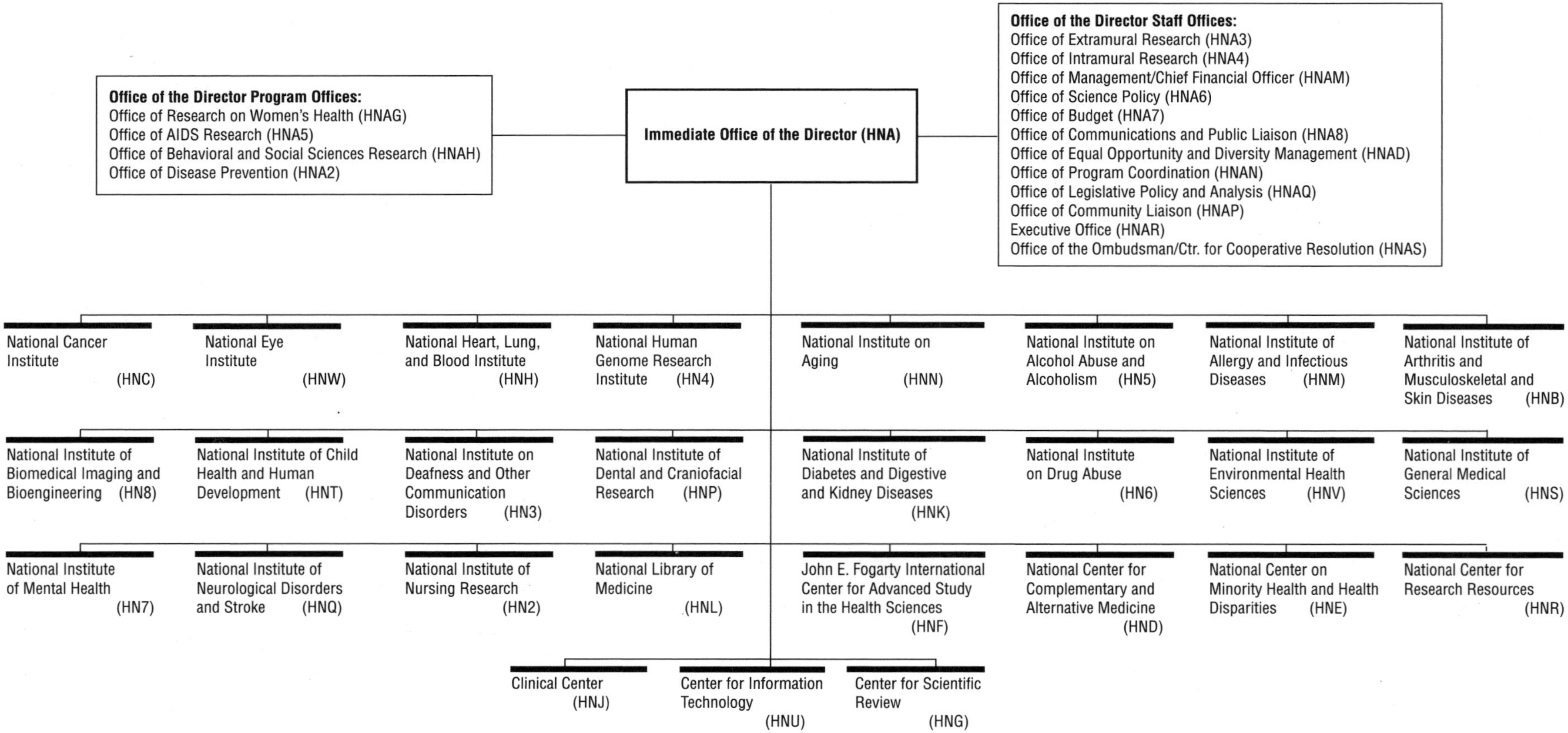

SOURCE: "National Institutes of Health," U.S. Department of Health and Human Services, National Institutes of Health, Bethesda, MD [Online] http://www1.od.nih.gov/oma/manualchapters/management/1123/nih.pdf [accessed August 12, 2002]

FIGURE 4.6

Setting research priorities, every voice counts

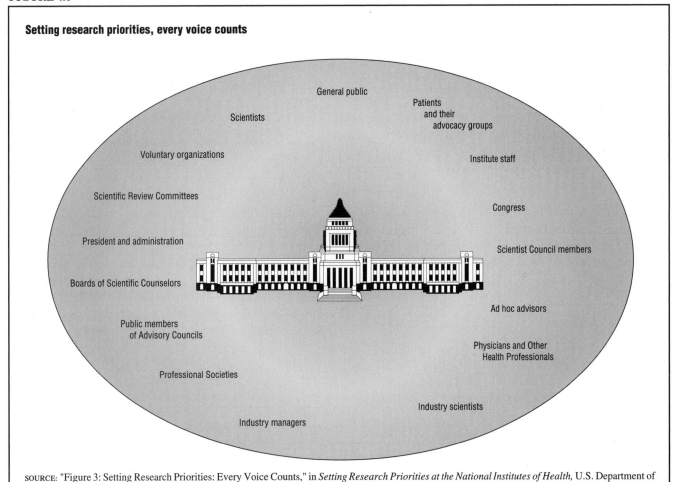

General public

Scientists

Patients
and their
advocacy groups

Voluntary organizations

Institute staff

Scientific Review Committees

Congress

President and administration

Scientist Council members

Boards of Scientific Counselors

Ad hoc advisors

Public members
of Advisory Councils

Physicians and Other
Health Professionals

Professional Societies

Industry scientists

Industry managers

SOURCE: "Figure 3: Setting Research Priorities: Every Voice Counts," in *Setting Research Priorities at the National Institutes of Health,* U.S. Department of Health and Human Services, National Institutes of Health, Bethesda, MD [Online] http://www.nih.gov/about/researchpriorities.htm [accessed October 1, 2002]

trainees at academic institutions and research laboratories across the United States. The NIH recruits and attracts the most capable research scientists in the world. In fact, 104 scientists who conducted NIH research or were supported by NIH grants have received Nobel Prizes. Five Nobel winners made their prize-winning discoveries in NIH laboratories.

Equally important, NIH research has contributed to great improvements in the health of the nation. Examples of past achievements credited to NIH effort include:

• U.S. deaths from cardiovascular disease—heart disease and stroke—were reduced significantly between 1977 and 1999, with heart disease deaths declining by 36 percent and stroke deaths by 50 percent.

• Better detection and treatment increased the 5-year survival rates for persons with cancer to 60 percent.

• Effective medication to enable the estimated 19 millions Americans suffering from depression to regain quality of life.

• Immunization against a host of infectious diseases has markedly reduced deaths and disability among children and adults.

• Gene therapy, performed by NIH researchers for the first time in 1990, promises to produce more effective screening for genetic disorders and gene therapies for cancer and other diseases.

During 2001 alone, NIH scientists reported significant findings resulting from more than 30 research projects. Some of these important findings were:

• A diet that is low in sodium and fats and rich in fruits, vegetables, and low-fat dairy foods lowered blood pressure for all people studied, not just those with high blood pressure.

• HIV, the virus that causes AIDS, must attach to cholesterol-rich parts of a cell's membrane to infect the cell. This finding may lead to an approach to block the virus from entering cells.

- The shape of his sperm appears to determine a man's fertility.

- Persons at risk for developing age-related vision loss from macular degeneration can reduce their risk by taking high doses of zinc, vitamins A and C, and beta carotene.

- The genome of *Streptococcus pneumoniae* was sequenced, which may lead to development of new drugs to combat this bacteria that causes pneumonia and meningitis and has become increasingly resistant to treatment with antibiotics.

- Mouse embryonic stem cells were turned into cells that produce insulin. This achievement may produce an effective new treatment for diabetes, a disorder of glucose metabolism that affects 16 million people in the United States.

- Persons at risk for developing type 2 diabetes can sharply reduce their risk by losing 5 to 7 percent of their body weight and exercising for 30 minutes every day.

- A vaccine that protects children ages two to five from typhoid fever was developed and tested. Typhoid fever strikes about 16 million people per year worldwide and 600,000 die from it.

ACCREDITATION

Accreditation of health care providers—facilities and organizations—provides consumers, payers, and other stakeholders with the assurance that accredited facilities and organizations have been certified as meeting or exceeding predetermined standards. Accreditation refers to both the process during which the quality of care delivered is measured and the resulting official endorsement that quality standards have been met. In addition to promoting accreditation to health care consumers and other purchasers of care such as employer groups, accreditation assists health care facilities and organizations to recruit and retain qualified staff, increase organizational efficiencies in order to reduce costs, identify ways to improve service delivery, and reduce liability insurance premiums.

Joint Commission on Accreditation of Healthcare Organizations

As of 2002, the Joint Commission on Accreditation of Healthcare Organizations (JCAHO) surveys and accredits more than 17,000 health care organizations and programs throughout the United States. JCAHO is a not-for-profit organization, headquartered in Oakbrook Terrace, Illinois, with a satellite office in Washington, D.C. JCAHO has more than 1,000 surveyors—physicians, nurses, pharmacists, hospital and health care organization administrators, and other health professionals—who are qualified and trained to evaluate specific aspects of health care quality.

Working closely with medical and other professional societies, purchasers of health care services, and management experts as well as other accrediting organizations, JCAHO develops the standards that health care organizations are expected to meet. In addition to developing benchmarks and standards of organizational quality, JCAHO is credited with promoting improvement in infection control, safety, and patients' rights.

JCAHO GROWS TO BECOME THE PREEMINENT ACCREDITING BODY. Early efforts to standardize and evaluate care delivered in hospitals began in 1910 by the American College of Surgeons, a group that 40 years later would start the present day Joint Commission on Accreditation of Healthcare Organizations, originally dubbed the Joint Commission on Accreditation of Hospitals (JCAH) in 1953. In 1965 JCAH began to offer long-term care facilities accreditation as well as hospitals, and in 1972 the Social Security Act was amended to require the secretary of HHS to validate JCAH findings and include them in the HHS annual report to the U.S. Congress.

In 1975 JCAH expanded its purview to include accreditation of ambulatory health care facilities, and in 1978 it began to evaluate and offer accreditation to hospital laboratories. In 1983 accreditation of hospice care organizations began and the accreditation schedule was changed from a two-year cycle to three years for hospitals, psychiatric facilities, substance abuse programs, community mental health centers, and long-term care organizations. In 1987 JCAH was renamed the Joint Commission on Accreditation of Healthcare Organizations (JCAHO) to reflect its greatly expanded scope of accreditation services.

In 1990 hospice accreditation was integrated into home health care accreditation processes and accreditation for managed care organizations was initiated within the ambulatory care accreditation program. During the 1990s JCAHO moved to emphasize performance improvement standards, required accredited hospitals to prohibit smoking in the hospital, and began performing random, "surprise" surveys—unannounced site visits to accredited organizations. JCAHO also offered accreditation to health care networks, preferred provider organizations (PPOs), and managed behavioral health care organizations.

On April 1, 1998, in a move intended to stem the rising tide of medical errors, JCAHO revised its sentinel event policy, the requirement that accredited organizations immediately report and investigate the causes of medical errors and institute preventive and corrective measures. In 1999 JCAHO launched a toll-free telephone complaint hotline to encourage patients, families, caregivers, and other concerned citizens to report concerns about quality of care at accredited organizations.

During 2000 JCAHO established standards and survey requirements for agencies that provide foster care services and developed cooperative agreements with professional organizations that certify and accredit blood banks, cancer centers, and hospital rehabilitation programs. JCAHO also added standards for assisted-living facilities, pain assessment and management programs, and office-based surgery programs. In 2001, following the terrorist attacks of September 11, JCAHO set up a command center to provide round-the-clock advice and counsel to accredited hospitals and health care organizations.

On July 1, 2002, JCAHO required hospitals to begin collecting and reporting data about the care they provide for four specific diagnoses—acute myocardial infarction (heart attack), heart failure, community-acquired pneumonia, and pregnancy and related medical conditions. JCAHO has termed these "core measure data" and will use them to compare facilities and assess the quality of service delivered. In 2002 JCAHO also moved to make its recommendations more easily understood by consumers so they could make informed choices about health care providers.

National Committee for Quality Assurance

The National Committee for Quality Assurance (NCQA) is another well-respected accrediting organization that focuses its attention on the managed care industry. NCQA began surveying and accrediting managed care organizations in 1991. By 2000 half of all health maintenance organizations (HMOs) in the United States had been reviewed by NCQA, and 23 states accepted NCQA accreditation in place of state review since accreditation indicated that the managed care plans met specific regulatory requirements.

When a managed care organization undergoes a NCQA survey, it is assessed using more than 60 different standards, each focusing on a specific aspect of health plan operations. The standards address access and service, the qualifications of providers, the organization's commitment to prevention programs and health maintenance, the quality of care delivered to members when they are ill or injured, and the organization's approaches for helping members manage chronic diseases such as diabetes, heart disease, and asthma.

To ensure fair comparisons between managed health care plans and to track their progress and improvement over time, NCQA uses a tool called the Health Plan Employer Data and Information Set (HEDIS). The more than 60 HEDIS measures look at health care delivery issues such as:

- Management of asthma and effective use of medication

- Controlling hypertension (high blood pressure)

- Effective and appropriate use of antidepressant medications

- The frequency and consistency with which smokers are counseled to quit

- Rates of breast cancer screening

- The frequency and consistency with which beta blocker (drug treatment) is used following heart attack

- Rates of immunization among children and teens

NCQA combines HEDIS data with national and regional benchmarks of quality in a national database called Quality Compass. This national database enables employers and health care consumers to compare health plans to one another and make choices about coverage based on quality and value rather than simply price and participating providers (physicians, hospitals, and other providers that offer services to the managed care plan members).

NCQA issues health plan "report cards," rating HMOs and other managed care organizations (MCOs) that health care consumers and other stakeholders can access at the NCQA Web site. After NCQA review, MCOs may be granted NCQA's full accreditation for three years, indicating a level of excellence that exceeds NCQA standards. Those that need some improvement are granted one-year accreditation with recommendations about areas that need improvement, and those MCOs that meet some but not all NCQA standards may be denied accreditation or granted provisional accreditation.

In 2001 NCQA reported that managed care quality had improved dramatically for the second consecutive year. Between 2000 and 2001, participating health plans' performance on every measure was better than the previous year's results.

Accreditation Association for Ambulatory Health Care, Inc.

Another accrediting organization, the Accreditation Association for Ambulatory Health Care, Inc. (AAAHC) was incorporated in 1979 and focuses exclusively on ambulatory (outpatient) facilities and programs. Outpatient clinics, group practices, college health services, occupational medicine clinics, and ambulatory surgery centers are among the organizations that are evaluated by AAAHC. The AAAHC accreditation process involves a self-assessment by the organization seeking accreditation and a survey conducted by AAAHC surveyors who are all practicing professionals. AAAHC grants accreditation for periods ranging from six months to three years.

In April 2002 the AAAHC and JCAHO signed a collaborative accreditation agreement that permits ambulatory health care organizations to use their AAAHC accreditation to satisfy JCAHO requirements. In June 2002 the Centers for Medicare & Medicaid Services (CMMS) granted AAAHC authority to review health plans that provide coverage for Medicare beneficiaries. HMOs, PPOs, and ambulatory surgery centers are now considered Medicare-certified upon their receipt of accreditation from the AAAHC.

PROFESSIONAL SOCIETIES

There are professional and membership organizations and societies for all health professionals such as physicians, nurses, psychologists, hospital administrators as well as for institutional health care providers such as hospitals, managed care plans, and medical groups. These professional organizations represent the interests and concerns of their members, advocate on their behalf, and frequently compile data and publish information about working conditions, licensing, accreditation, compensation, and scientific advancements of interest to members.

The American Medical Association

The American Medical Association (AMA) is a powerful voice for U.S. physicians' interests. The AMA concerns itself with a wide range of health-related issues including medical ethics, medical education, physician and patient advocacy, and development of national health policy. The AMA publishes the highly regarded *Journal of the American Medical Association (JAMA)* and the *AMNews,* as well as journals in ten specialty areas called *Archives Journals.* The organization also maintains a Web site with full-text journal articles for its members.

Founded in 1847, the AMA has worked to upgrade medical education by expanding medical school curricula and establishing standards for licensing and accreditation of practitioners and postgraduate training programs. Recent activities of the AMA are advocating for passage of comprehensive Patients Bill of Rights legislation, co-hosting a world conference on preventing tobacco use, launching a "health literacy" campaign to improve patient-physician relationships, and managing a project aimed at reducing underage drinking.

The American Nurses Association

The American Nurses Association (ANA) is a professional organization that represents 2.6 million registered nurses (RNs) and promotes high standards of nursing practice and education as well as the roles and responsibilities of nurses in the workplace and the community. On behalf of its members, the ANA works to protect patients' rights, lobbies to advocate for nurses' interests, champions workplace safety, and provides career and continuing education opportunities. The ANA publishes the *American Journal of Nursing,* and actively seeks to improve the public image of nurses among health professionals and the community at large.

The American Hospital Association

The American Hospital Association (AHA) represents nearly 5,000 hospitals, health care systems, networks, and other health care providers as well as 37,000 individual members. Originally established as a membership organization for hospital superintendents in 1899, the AHA had expanded its mission by 1917 to address all facets of hospital care and quality. In addition to national advocacy activities and participation in the development of health policy, the AHA oversees research and pilot programs to improve health service delivery. It also gathers and disseminates hospital and other related health care data, publishes information of interest to its members, and sponsors educational opportunities for health care managers and administrators.

VOLUNTARY HEALTH ORGANIZATIONS

The American Heart Association

The mission of the American Heart Association is "to reduce disability and death from cardiovascular diseases and stroke." The association's national headquarters is in Dallas, Texas, and 15 regional affiliate offices serve the balance of the United States. More than 22.5 million volunteers and supporters were involved with association programs and activities during 2001.

The American Heart Association was started by a group of physicians and social workers in New York City in 1915. The early efforts of this group, called the Association for the Prevention and Relief of Heart Disease, were to educate physicians and the general public about heart disease. The first fundraising efforts were launched in 1948 during a radio broadcast, and since then the AHA has raised millions of dollars to fund research, education, and treatment programs.

In addition to research, fundraising, and generating public awareness about reducing the risk of developing heart disease, the American Heart Association has published many best-selling cookbooks featuring heart-healthy recipes and meal planning ideas. The American Heart Association also is considered one of the world's most trusted authorities about heart health among physicians and scientists. The organization publishes five print journals and one online professional journal, including *Circulation, Stroke, Hypertension,* and *Atherosclerosis, Thrombosis, and Vascular Biology.*

The American Cancer Society

The American Cancer Society (ACS) makes its headquarters in Atlanta, Georgia, and has more than 3,400 offices across the country. The ACS mission is "to eliminate cancer as a major health problem by preventing cancer, saving lives, and diminishing suffering from cancer, through research, education, advocacy, and service."

The ACS is the biggest source of private, not-for-profit funding for cancer research—second only to the federal government. By 2000 the ACS had invested more than $2 billion in cancer research at leading centers throughout the United States. It also supports epidemiological research to provide cancer surveillance information about occurrence rates, risk factors, mortality, and availability of treatment services. The ACS publishes an array of patient information brochures and four clinical journals for health professionals—*Cancer, Cancer Cytopathology, CA—A Cancer Journal for Clinicians,* and *Cancer Practice.* The ACS also maintains a 24-hour consumer telephone line staffed by trained cancer information specialists and a Web site with information for professionals, patients and families, and the media.

In addition to education, prevention, and patient services, the ACS advocates for the more than 8 million cancer survivors, their families, and every potential cancer patient. The ACS seeks to obtain support and passage of laws, policies, and regulations that benefit persons affected by cancer. The ACS is especially concerned with developing strategies to better serve the poor and persons with little formal education, who historically have been disproportionately affected by cancer.

The March of Dimes

The March of Dimes was founded in 1938 by President Franklin Roosevelt to help protect America's young people from polio. In addition to supporting the research that produced the polio vaccine, the March of Dimes has advocated birth defects research and the fortification of food supplies with folic acid to prevent neural tube defects. The March of Dimes also has supported increasing access to quality prenatal care and the growth of neonatal intensive care units (NICUs) to help improve the chances of survival for babies born prematurely or those with serious medical conditions.

The March of Dimes continues to partner volunteers, scientific researchers, educators and community outreach workers to help prevent birth defects. March of Dimes funds genetic research, investigates the causes and treatment of premature birth, educates pregnant women, and provides health care services for women and children including immunization, checkups, and treatment for childhood illnesses.

In 2000 the March of Dimes set forth the following four goals for the immediate future:

• To reduce birth defects, the leading cause of infant mortality in the United States, by 10 percent.

• To reduce infant mortality to 7 deaths per 1,000 live births. The United States ranks 25th in terms of infant mortality, trailing 24 countries where babies have greater chances of living until their first birthdays.

• To reduce low-birthweight babies (less than 5.5 pounds) to no more than 5 percent of all live births since these babies are less likely to live until their first birthdays and when they do, may suffer serious health consequences.

• Increase the proportion of women receiving prenatal care during the first trimester (the first three months of pregnancy) to 90 percent because early prenatal care is linked to healthier pregnancies and infants.

CHAPTER 5

THE INCREASING COST OF HEALTH CARE

HOW MUCH DOES HEALTH CARE COST?

American society places a high value on human life, and generally wants—and expects—quality medical care. But quality care comes with an increasingly high cost. In 1970 the United States spent 7 percent of its gross domestic product (GDP; the value of all the goods and services produced by the nation) on health care. By 1999 health care had risen to 13 percent ($1,211 trillion) of the GDP, and in 2000 health care expenditures reached 13.2 percent ($1.3 trillion) of the GDP. Table 5.1 shows the growth in health care expenditures, the growth in the GDP, and the annual percent change from the previous year for the years from 1960 to 2000. As a proportion of GDP, health care spending showed little change from 1994 to 2000, averaging slightly more than 13 percent, but both the GDP and health care cost continued to rise. (See Table 5.2.) Though costs continued to increase each year, the rate of their rise slowed during the late 1990s.

For many years, the consumer price index (CPI; a measure of the average change in prices paid by consumers) increased at a greater rate for medical care than for any other commodity. From 1980 to 1990, the average annual increase in the overall CPI was 4.7 percent, while the average annual increase in the medical care index stood at 8.1 percent. By 1998 the average annual growth in the medical care index had fallen to 3.2 percent, but had risen again to 4.6 percent in 2001. The medical care index has consistently outpaced the CPI in each decade, and continued to do so in 2001, when the CPI annual growth was 2.8. (See Table 5.3.) Of all the components of health care delivery, the sharpest price increases in 2001 were in hospital and related services at 6.6 percent and prescription drugs at 5.4 percent.

The Health Care Financing Administration (HCFA; now called the Center for Medicare & Medicaid Services), an agency of the U.S. Department of Health and Human Services (HHS), has projected that the national health expenditure will grow to $2.8 trillion by 2011, nearly twice as much as the 2001 projection of $1.4 trillion. (See Table 5.4.) (Since the numbers in Table 5.4 are projections, they necessarily differ from the actual numbers presented in some other tables and figures.) Medicare was projected to reach $450.1 billion by 2011, responsible for almost 16 percent of all health care expenditures.

Generally, projections are most accurate for the near future and least accurate for the distant future. For example, predictions for 2030 should be viewed more cautiously than predictions for 2005. Since it is unlikely that the conditions on which the projections were based will remain the same, the HCFA cautioned that its projections should not be viewed as predictions for the future. Rather, they were intended to help policymakers evaluate the costs or savings of proposed legislative or regulatory changes.

Total Health Care Spending

The Center for Medicare & Medicaid Services (CMMS, formerly the Health Care Financing Administration or HCFA), along with the Centers for Disease Control and Prevention (CDC) and the General Accounting Office (GAO), maintain most of the nation's statistics on health care costs. The CMMS reported that the United States spent nearly $1.3 trillion for health care in 2000, up 6.9 percent from the previous year. (See Table 5.2.) This rate was higher than the lowest rates of increase since the late 1960s, which were documented in 1998 and 1999, but was not among the highest annual increases observed, such as the 11 percent rise in 1990.

About 54.8 percent of 2000 health care expenditures, or $712.3 billion, came from private funds, while the remaining 45.2 percent ($587.2 billion) was paid with public money. (See Table 5.2.) This means that nearly 55 cents of every dollar spent on health care came from private funds, and the remainder came from federal (32

TABLE 5.1

Gross domestic product, federal and state and local government expenditures, national health expenditures, and average percent change, selected years 1960–2000

[Data are compiled by the Centers for Medicare & Medicaid Services]

Gross domestic product, government health expenditures, and national health expenditures	1960	1970	1980	1990	1995	1997	1998	1999	2000
					Amount in billions				
Gross domestic product (GDP)	$527	$1,040	$2,796	$5,803	$7,400	$8,318	$8,782	$9,269	$ 9,873
Government expenditures									
Federal	85.8	198.6	576.6	1,228.7	1,575.7	1,678.8	1,705.9	1,753.6	1,828.3
Health	2.8	17.6	71.3	192.7	322.0	358.8	367.7	384.8	411.5
State and local	38.1	107.5	307.8	660.8	902.5	980.3	1,033.7	1,101.7	1,189.8
Health	3.8	10.0	33.5	89.8	134.2	143.6	153.3	164.2	175.7
Source of funds for health expenditures									
National health expenditures	26.7	73.1	245.8	696.0	990.3	1,091.2	1,149.8	1,215.6	1,299.5
Private	20.1	45.4	140.9	413.5	534.1	588.8	628.8	666.5	712.3
Public	6.6	27.6	104.8	282.5	456.2	502.4	520.9	549.0	587.2
Per capita health expenditures					Amount per capita				
National health expenditures	143	348	1,067	2,738	3,698	4,001	4,177	4,377	4,637
Private	108	216	612	1,627	1,994	2,159	2,285	2,400	2,542
Public	35	131	455	1,111	1,704	1,842	1,893	1,977	2,096
Percent									
National health expenditures as percent of GDP	5.1	7.0	8.8	12.0	13.4	13.1	13.1	13.1	13.2
Health expenditures as a percent of total government expenditures									
Federal	3.3	8.9	12.4	15.7	20.4	21.4	21.6	21.9	22.5
State and local	9.9	9.3	10.9	13.6	14.9	14.6	14.8	14.9	14.8
Percent distribution									
National health expenditures	100.0	100.0	100.0	100.0	100.0	100.0	100.0	100.0	100.0
Private	75.2	62.2	57.3	59.4	53.9	54.0	54.7	54.8	54.8
Public	24.8	37.8	42.7	40.6	46.1	46.0	45.3	45.2	45.2
Growth					Average annual percent change from previous year shown				
Gross domestic product	—	7.0	10.4	7.6	5.0	6.0	5.6	5.5	6.5
Government expenditures									
Federal	—	8.8	11.2	7.9	5.1	3.2	1.6	2.8	4.3
Health	—	20.1	15.0	10.5	10.8	5.6	2.5	4.7	6.9
State and local	—	10.9	11.1	7.9	6.4	4.2	5.4	6.6	8.0
Health	—	10.2	12.8	10.4	8.4	3.4	6.8	7.1	7.0
Health expenditures									
National health expenditures	—	10.6	12.9	11.0	7.3	5.0	5.4	5.7	6.9
Private	—	8.5	12.0	11.4	5.2	5.0	6.8	6.0	6.9
Public	—	15.4	14.3	10.4	10.1	4.9	3.7	5.4	7.0
Per capita health expenditures									
National health expenditures	—	9.3	11.9	9.9	6.2	4.0	4.4	4.8	6.0
Private	—	7.2	11.0	10.3	4.2	4.0	5.8	5.0	5.9
Public	—	14.0	13.2	9.3	8.9	4.0	2.7	4.4	6.0

—Category not applicable.

Note: These data include revisions in health expenditures and differ from previous editions of *Health, United States*. They reflect U.S. Bureau of the Census resident population estimates as of July 2001. Federal and state and local government total expenditures reflect October 2001 revisions from the Bureau of Economic Analysis.

SOURCE: "Table 113. Gross domestic product, Federal and State and local expenditures, national health expenditures, and annual percent change: United States, selected years 1960–2000," in *Health, United States, 2002*, Centers for Disease Control and Prevention, National Center for Health Statistics, Hyattsville, MD, 2002

cents) or state and local governments (13.5 cents). The 2000 per capita cost for health care (the average per individual if spending was divided equally among all persons in the country) was $4,637. (See Table 5.2.)

A comparison of the sources of funds spent on health care in 1994 and 2000 reveals few changes. During 2000, private insurance paid just 1 percent more and Medicaid 2 percent more for health care services, and Americans' out-of-pocket expenses dropped by 3 percent from 1994.

Of the almost $1.3 trillion spent on health care in 2000, $1.13 trillion (87 percent) was spent on personal health services (expenses incurred by individuals as opposed to institutions). Some of the services included hospital care, physician and dental services, nursing and home health care, prescription drugs, and durable medical equipment. (See Table 5.5.)

Table 5.5 shows the trends and annual percent changes in personal health care expenditures by category. In 2000

TABLE 5.2

National health expenditures, aggregate and per capita amounts, percent distribution, and average annual percent growth, by source of funds, selected calendar years, 1980–2000

Item	1980	1988	1990	1993	1994	1995	1996	1997	1998	1999	2000
						Amount in Billions					
National Health Expenditures	$245.8	$558.1	$696.0	$888.1	$937.2	$990.3	$1,040.0	$1,091.2	$1,149.8	$1,215.6	$1,299.5
Private	140.9	331.7	413.5	497.7	510.3	534.1	558.2	588.8	628.8	666.5	712.3
Public	104.8	226.4	282.5	390.4	427.0	456.2	481.8	502.4	520.9	549.0	587.2
Federal	71.3	154.1	192.7	274.4	298.5	322.0	343.9	358.8	367.7	384.8	411.5
State and Local	33.5	72.3	89.8	116.0	128.5	134.2	137.8	143.6	153.3	164.2	175.7
						Number in Millions					
U.S. Population[1]	230	249	254	263	265	268	270	273	275	278	280
						Amount in Billions					
Gross Domestic Product[2]	$2,796	$5,108	$5,803	$6,642	$7,054	$7,400	$7,813	$8,318	$8,782	$9,269	$9,873
						Per Capita Amount					
National Health Expenditures	$1,067	$2,243	$2,738	$3,381	$3,534	$3,698	$3,849	$4,001	$4,177	$4,377	$4,637
Private	612	1,333	1,627	1,895	1,924	1,994	2,066	2,159	2,285	2,400	2,542
Public	455	910	1,111	1,486	1,610	1,704	1,783	1,842	1,893	1,977	2,096
Federal	310	619	758	1,045	1,125	1,202	1,273	1,316	1,336	1,385	1,468
State and Local	146	290	353	442	485	501	510	526	557	591	627
						Percent Distribution					
National Health Expenditures	100.0	100.0	100.0	100.0	100.0	100.0	100.0	100.0	100.0	100.0	100.0
Private	57.3	59.4	59.4	56.0	54.4	53.9	53.7	54.0	54.7	54.8	54.8
Public	42.7	40.6	40.6	44.0	45.6	46.1	46.3	46.0	45.3	45.2	45.2
Federal	29.0	27.6	27.7	30.9	31.8	32.5	33.1	32.9	32.0	31.7	31.7
State and Local	13.6	13.0	12.9	13.1	13.7	13.6	13.3	13.2	13.3	13.5	13.5
						Percent of Gross Domestic Product					
National Health Expenditures	8.8	10.9	12.0	13.4	13.3	13.4	13.3	13.1	13.1	13.1	13.2
						Average Annual Percent Growth from Previous Year Shown					
National Health Expenditures	11.7[3]	10.8	11.7	8.5	5.5	5.7	5.0	4.9	5.4	5.7	6.9
Private	10.2[3]	11.3	11.7	6.4	2.5	4.7	4.5	5.5	6.8	6.0	6.9
Public	14.8[3]	10.1	11.7	11.4	9.4	6.9	5.6	4.3	3.7	5.4	7.0
Federal	17.5[3]	10.1	11.8	12.5	8.8	7.9	6.8	4.3	2.5	4.7	6.9
State and Local	11.5[3]	10.1	11.4	8.9	10.8	4.5	2.7	4.2	6.8	7.1	7.0
U.S. Population	1.1[3]	1.0	1.1	1.1	1.0	1.0	0.9	0.9	0.9	0.9	0.9
Gross Domestic Product	8.7[3]	7.8	6.6	4.6	6.2	4.9	5.6	6.5	5.6	5.5	6.5

[1]July 1 Census resident based population estimates for each year 1960-2000.
[2]U.S. Department of Commerce, Bureau of Economic Analysis.
[3]Average annual growth between 1960 and 1980.
Note: Numbers and percents may not add to totals because of rounding.

SOURCE: "Table 1: National Health Expenditures Aggregate and per Capita Amounts, Percent Distribution, and Average Annual Percent Growth, by Source of Funds: Selected Calendar Years 1980–2000," U.S. Department of Health and Human Services, Centers for Medicare & Medicaid Services, Baltimore, MD, [Online] http://www.cms.hhs.gov/statistics/nhe/historical/t1.asp [accessed October 2, 2002]

the nation spent $422.1 billion on professional services, by far the largest chunk of health care spending, followed by $412.1 billion (about 32 percent of all health expenditures) on hospital costs. This expense was followed by $286.4 billion for physician and clinical services, $121.8 billion for prescription drugs, and $92.2 billion for nursing home care. (See Table 5.5.) Figure 5.1 shows general percentages for how much was paid for medical spending in 2000.

WHO PAYS THE BILL?

In general, the government is the fastest-growing payer of health care expenses. From 1990 to 2000, total public share of the nation's total health care bill rose from 40.6 percent to 45.2 percent. (See Table 5.2.) This represented the largest increase in the government's contribution to health care since Medicare began covering the disabled population in the early 1970s.

In 2000 private health insurance, the major non-government payer of health care costs, paid approximately 34 percent of all health expenditures, a proportion that has not changed significantly since 1990. The share of health care spending from private, out-of-pocket (paid by the patient) funds remained stable from 1995 to 2000, also, at about 15 percent. (See Table 5.6.)

Different sectors paid more for different types of health services. The public sector paid for more than half (59 percent) of all hospital costs, with the federal government providing 46.8 percent of the nation's hospital bill. The public sector also paid 60.6 percent of all nursing home care and 52.2 percent of all home health care. Private health insurance paid for 47.7 percent of all physicians' services and 50.2 percent of dental bills. Patients paid 44.8 percent of their dental bills and 32.1 percent of their drug and prescription bills out-of-pocket. (See Table 5.6.)

TABLE 5.3

Consumer Price Index and average annual percent change for all items, selected items, and medical care components, selected years 1960–2001

[Data are based on reporting by samples of providers and other retail outlets]

Items and medical care components	1960	1970	1980	1990	1995	1998	1999	2000	2001
	Consumer Price Index (CPI)								
All items	29.6	38.8	82.4	130.7	152.4	163.0	166.6	172.2	177.1
All items excluding medical care	30.2	39.2	82.8	128.8	148.6	158.6	162.0	167.3	171.9
All services	24.1	35.0	77.9	139.2	168.7	184.2	188.8	195.3	203.4
Food	30.0	39.2	86.8	132.4	148.4	160.7	164.1	167.8	173.1
Apparel	45.7	59.2	90.9	124.1	132.0	133.0	131.3	129.6	127.3
Housing	—	36.4	81.1	128.5	148.5	160.4	163.9	169.6	176.4
Energy	22.4	25.5	86.0	102.1	105.2	102.9	106.6	124.6	129.3
Medical care	22.3	34.0	74.9	162.8	220.5	242.1	250.6	260.8	272.8
Components of medical care									
Medical care services	19.5	32.3	74.8	162.7	224.2	246.8	255.1	266.0	278.8
Professional services	—	37.0	77.9	156.1	201.0	222.2	229.2	237.7	246.5
Physicians' services	21.9	34.5	76.5	160.8	208.8	229.5	236.0	244.7	253.6
Dental services	27.0	39.2	78.9	155.8	206.8	236.2	247.2	258.5	269.0
Eye glasses and eye care[1]	—	—	—	117.3	137.0	144.1	145.5	149.7	154.5
Services by other medical professionals[1]	—	—	—	120.2	143.9	155.4	158.7	161.9	167.3
Hospital and related services	—	—	69.2	178.0	257.8	287.5	299.5	317.3	338.3
Hospital services[2]	—	—	—	—	—	105.0	109.3	115.9	123.6
Inpatient hospital services[2]	—	—	—	—	—	104.0	107.9	113.8	121.0
Outpatient hospital services[1]	—	—	—	138.7	204.6	233.2	246.0	263.8	281.1
Hospital rooms	9.3	23.6	68.0	175.4	251.2	—	—	—	—
Other inpatient services[1]	—	—	—	142.7	206.8	—	—	—	—
Nursing homes and adult day care	—	—	—	—	—	107.1	111.6	117.0	121.8
Medical care commodities	46.9	46.5	75.4	163.4	204.5	221.8	230.7	238.1	247.6
Prescription drugs and medical supplies	54.0	47.4	72.5	181.7	235.0	258.6	273.4	285.4	300.9
Nonprescription drugs and medical supplies[1]	—	—	—	120.6	140.5	147.7	148.5	149.5	150.6
Internal and respiratory over-the-counter drugs	—	42.3	74.9	145.9	167.0	175.4	175.9	176.9	178.9
Nonprescription medical equipment and supplies	—	—	79.2	138.0	166.3	174.9	176.7	178.1	178.2
	Average annual percent change from previous year shown								
All items	...	4.3	8.9	4.7	3.1	2.3	2.2	3.4	2.8
All items excluding medical care	...	4.1	8.8	4.5	2.9	2.2	2.1	3.3	2.7
All services	...	5.6	10.2	6.0	3.9	3.0	2.5	3.4	4.1
Food	...	4.0	7.7	4.3	2.3	2.7	2.1	2.3	3.2
Apparel	...	4.4	4.6	3.2	1.2	0.3	−1.3	−1.3	−1.8
Housing	...	—	9.9	4.7	2.9	2.6	2.2	3.5	4.0
Energy	...	2.2	15.4	1.7	0.6	−0.7	3.6	16.9	3.8
Medical care	...	6.2	9.5	·8.1	6.3	3.2	3.5	4.1	4.6
Components of medical care									
Medical care services	...	7.3	9.9	8.1	6.6	3.3	3.4	4.3	4.8
Professional services	...	—	8.9	7.2	5.2	3.4	3.2	3.7	3.7
Physicians' services	...	6.6	9.7	7.7	5.4	3.2	2.8	3.7	3.6
Dental services	...	5.3	8.2	7.0	5.8	4.5	4.7	4.6	4.1
Eye glasses and eye care[1]	...	—	—	—	3.2	1.7	1.0	2.9	3.2
Services by other medical professionals[1]	...	—	—	—	3.7	2.6	2.1	2.0	3.3
Hospital and related services	...	—	—	9.9	7.7	3.7	4.2	5.9	6.6
Hospital services[2]	...	—	—	—	—	—	4.1	6.0	6.6
Inpatient hospital services[2]	...	—	—	—	—	—	3.8	5.5	6.3
Outpatient hospital services[1]	...	—	—	—	8.1	4.5	5.5	7.2	6.6
Hospital rooms	...	13.9	12.2	9.9	7.4	—	—	—	—
Other inpatient services[1]	...	—	—	—	7.7	—	—	—	—
Nursing homes and adult day care	...	—	—	—	—	—	4.2	4.8	4.1
Medical care commodities	...	0.7	7.2	8.0	4.6	2.7	4.0	3.2	4.0
Prescription drugs and medical supplies	...	-0.2	7.2	9.6	5.3	3.2	5.7	4.4	5.4
Nonprescription drugs and medical supplies[1]	...	—	—	—	3.1	1.7	0.5	0.7	0.7
Internal and respiratory over-the-counter drugs	...	1.6	7.7	6.9	2.7	1.6	0.3	0.6	1.1
Nonprescription medical equipment and supplies	...	—	—	5.7	3.8	1.7	1.0	0.8	0.1

—Data not available.
... Category not applicable.
[1]Dec. 1986 = 100.
[2]Dec. 1996 = 100.
Note: 1982–84 = 100, except where noted.

SOURCE: "Table 114. Consumer Price Index and average annual percent change for all items, selected items, and medical care components: United States, selected years 1960–2001," in *Health, United States, 2001,* Centers for Disease Control and Prevention, National Center for Health Statistics, Hyattsville, MD, 2001

TABLE 5.4

National health expenditure amounts, percent distribution, and average annual percent change, by source of funds, selected years 1980–2011

Year	Total	Out-of-Pocket Payments	Third-Party Payments						Medicare[2]	Medicaid[3]
			Total	Private Health Insurance	Other Private Funds	Public				
						Total	Federal[1]	State and Local[1]		
Historical Estimates						*Amount in Billions*				
1980	$245.8	$58.2	$187.5	$68.2	$14.5	$104.8	$71.3	$33.5	$37.4	$26.0
1990	696.0	137.3	558.7	233.5	42.8	282.5	192.7	89.8	110.2	73.6
1995	990.3	146.5	843.7	330.1	57.4	456.2	322.0	134.2	182.7	144.0
1998	1,149.8	174.5	975.3	383.2	71.1	520.9	367.7	153.3	209.5	171.4
1999	1,215.6	184.4	1,031.2	409.4	72.7	549.0	384.8	164.2	212.6	186.7
2000	1,299.5	194.5	1,104.9	443.9	73.8	587.2	411.5	175.7	224.4	202.7
Projected										
2001	1,423.8	210.4	1,213.3	486.7	78.6	648.1	452.9	195.2	245.6	226.1
2002	1,545.9	226.9	1,319.0	537.3	84.5	697.1	484.1	213.0	259.3	246.8
2003	1,653.4	242.7	1,410.7	580.1	90.0	740.6	510.8	229.8	269.6	266.2
2004	1,773.4	259.2	1,514.2	624.4	96.0	793.8	545.7	248.1	286.2	289.3
2005	1,902.2	276.2	1,626.0	671.6	101.9	852.5	584.6	267.9	305.0	314.8
2006	2,036.6	293.6	1,743.0	719.5	108.0	915.5	625.8	289.7	324.3	342.4
2007	2,174.9	311.0	1,863.8	766.9	113.9	983.0	669.8	313.2	344.3	372.9
2008	2,320.0	329.9	1,990.1	813.3	120.1	1,056.7	718.7	338.0	367.7	405.6
2009	2,476.1	350.9	2,125.2	862.0	126.7	1,136.4	771.4	365.0	392.8	441.2
2010	2,639.2	372.4	2,266.9	912.2	132.6	1,222.0	828.1	393.9	419.8	479.8
2011	2,815.8	395.6	2,420.2	966.1	138.4	1,315.7	890.5	425.2	450.1	521.8
Historical Estimates						*Per Capita Amount*				
1980	$1,067	$253	$814	$296	$63	$455	$310	$146	(4)	(4)
1990	2,738	540	2,198	919	168	1,111	758	353	(4)	(4)
1995	3,698	547	3,151	1,233	214	1,704	1,202	501	(4)	(4)
1998	4,177	634	3,543	1,392	258	1,893	1,336	557	(4)	(4)
1999	4,377	664	3,713	1,474	262	1,977	1,385	591	(4)	(4)
2000	4,637	694	3,943	1,584	264	2,096	1,468	627	(4)	(4)
Projected										
2001	5,039	745	4,295	1,722	278	2,294	1,603	691	(4)	(4)
2002	5,427	797	4,630	1,886	297	2,447	1,700	748	(4)	(4)
2003	5,757	845	4,912	2,020	314	2,579	1,779	800	(4)	(4)
2004	6,126	895	5,230	2,157	331	2,742	1,885	857	(4)	(4)
2005	6,519	947	5,572	2,302	349	2,921	2,003	918	(4)	(4)
2006	6,926	998	5,927	2,447	367	3,113	2,128	985	(4)	(4)
2007	7,338	1,049	6,289	2,588	384	3,317	2,260	1,057	(4)	(4)
2008	7,768	1,105	6,664	2,723	402	3,538	2,407	1,132	(4)	(4)
2009	8,228	1,166	7,062	2,864	421	3,776	2,563	1,213	(4)	(4)
2010	8,704	1,228	7,476	3,008	437	4,030	2,731	1,299	(4)	(4)
2011	9,216	1,295	7,921	3,162	453	4,306	2,915	1,392	(4)	(4)
Historical Estimates						*Percent Distribution*				
1980	100.0	23.7	76.3	27.8	5.9	42.7	29.0	13.6	15.2	10.6
1990	100.0	19.7	80.3	33.5	6.1	40.6	27.7	12.9	15.8	10.6
1996	100.0	14.8	85.2	33.3	5.8	46.1	32.5	13.6	18.4	14.5
1998	100.0	15.2	84.8	33.3	6.2	45.3	32.0	13.3	18.2	14.9
1999	100.0	15.2	84.8	33.7	6.0	45.2	31.7	13.5	17.5	15.4
2000	100.0	15.0	85.0	34.2	5.7	45.2	31.7	13.5	17.3	15.6
Projected										
2001	100.0	14.8	85.2	34.2	5.5	45.5	31.8	13.7	17.3	15.9
2002	100.0	14.7	85.3	34.8	5.5	45.1	31.3	13.8	16.8	16.0
2003	100.0	14.7	85.3	35.1	5.4	44.8	30.9	13.9	16.3	16.1
2004	100.0	14.6	85.4	35.2	5.4	44.8	30.8	14.0	16.1	16.3
2005	100.0	14.5	85.5	35.3	5.4	44.8	30.7	14.1	16.0	16.5
2006	100.0	14.4	85.6	35.3	5.3	45.0	30.7	14.2	15.9	16.8
2007	100.0	14.3	85.7	35.3	5.2	45.2	30.8	14.4	15.8	17.1
2008	100.0	14.2	85.8	35.1	5.2	45.5	31.0	14.6	15.8	17.5
2009	100.0	14.2	85.8	34.8	5.1	45.9	31.2	14.7	15.9	17.8
2010	100.0	14.1	85.9	34.6	5.0	46.3	31.4	14.9	15.9	18.2
2011	100.0	14.1	85.9	34.3	4.9	46.7	31.6	15.1	16.0	18.5

TABLE 5.4

National health expenditure amounts, percent distribution, and average annual percent change, by souce of funds, selected years 1980–2011 [CONTINUED]

Year	Total	Out-of-Pocket Payments	Third-Party Payments						Medicare[2]	Medicaid[3]
			Total	Private Health Insurance	Other Private Funds	Public				
						Total	Federal[1]	State and Local[1]		
Historical Estimates										
			Average Annual Percent Change from Previous Year Shown							
1980	—	—	—	—	—	—	—	—	—	—
1990	11.0	9.0	11.5	13.1	11.4	10.4	10.5	10.4	11.4	11.0
1995	7.3	1.3	8.6	7.2	6.1	10.1	10.8	8.4	10.6	14.4
1998	5.1	6.0	4.9	5.1	7.4	4.5	4.5	4.5	4.7	6.0
1999	5.7	5.7	5.7	6.8	2.3	5.4	4.7	7.1	1.5	8.9
2000	6.9	5.5	7.2	8.4	1.5	7.0	6.9	7.0	5.6	8.6
Projected										
2001	9.6	8.2	9.8	9.6	6.4	10.4	10.1	11.1	9.5	11.5
2002	8.6	7.8	8.7	10.4	7.6	7.6	6.9	9.1	5.6	9.2
2003	7.0	6.9	7.0	8.0	6.5	6.2	5.5	7.9	4.0	7.8
2004	7.3	6.8	7.3	7.6	6.6	7.2	6.8	8.0	6.2	8.7
2005	7.3	6.5	7.4	7.6	6.2	7.4	7.1	8.0	6.6	8.8
2006	7.1	6.3	7.2	7.1	6.0	7.4	7.1	8.2	6.3	8.8
2007	6.8	5.9	6.9	6.6	5.5	7.4	7.0	8.1	6.2	8.9
2008	6.7	6.1	6.8	6.1	5.4	7.5	7.3	7.9	6.8	8.8
2009	6.7	6.4	6.8	6.0	5.5	7.5	7.3	8.0	6.8	8.8
2010	6.6	6.1	6.7	5.8	4.7	7.5	7.3	7.9	6.9	8.8
2011	6.7	6.2	6.8	5.9	4.4	7.7	7.5	7.9	7.2	8.7

[1]Includes Medicaid SCHIP (State Children's Health Insurance Program) Expansion and SCHIP.
[2]Subset of federal funds.
[3]Subset of federal and state and local funds. Includes Medicaid SCHIP Expansion.
[4]Calculation of per capita estimates is inappropriate.
Note: Per capita amounts based on July 1 Census resident based population estimates. Numbers and percents may not add to totals because of rounding. The health spending projections were based on the 2000 version of the National Health Expenditures (NHE) released in January 2002.

SOURCE: "Table 3. National Health Expenditures Aggregate and per Capita Amounts, Percent Distribution and Average Annual Percent Change by Source of Funds: Selected Calendar Years 1980–2011," Centers for Medicare & Medicaid Services, Baltimore, MD, 2002 [Online] http://cms.hhs.gov/statistics/nhe/projections-2001/t3.asp [accessed October 28, 2002]

The Personal Health Care Bill

Much of the increase in government spending has occurred in the area of personal health care. In 1980 government sources paid 40.4 percent of personal health care expenditures; by 2000 they covered 43.3 percent ($489 billion) of the nearly $1.13 trillion spent on personal health care services. (See Table 5.7.) Of the total expenditures, 32.8 percent came from the federal government and 10.5 percent from state and local governments. A large proportion of the federal increase was attributed to Medicare spending, which grew from 11.4 percent of all personal health care expenditures in 1970 to 19.2 percent in 2000.

WHY DID HEALTH CARE COSTS AND SPENDING INCREASE?

The increase in the cost of medical care is challenging to analyze because the methods and quality of health care change constantly and as a result are often not comparable. A hospital stay in 1960 did not include the same services offered in 2000. Further, the care received in a physician's office today is in no way comparable to that received a generation ago. One contributing factor to the

rising cost of health care is the increase in biomedical technology, much of which is now available for use outside of a hospital.

Many other factors also contribute to the increase in health care costs. These include population growth, high salaries for physicians and some other health care workers, and the expense of malpractice insurance. Escalating malpractice insurance costs and professional liability premiums have prompted some physicians and other health care practitioners to refrain from performing high-risk procedures that increase their vulnerability or have caused them to relocate to states where malpractice premiums are lower. Further, to protect themselves from malpractice suits, many health care practitioners routinely order diagnostic tests and prescribe treatments that are not medically necessary and do not serve to improve their patients' health. This practice is known as "defensive medicine," and while its precise contribution to rising health care costs is difficult to gauge, industry observers agree that it is a significant factor.

Although physicians have historically been the most vocal protesters of rising malpractice insurance premi-

TABLE 5.5

National health expenditures aggregate amounts and average annual percent change, by type of expenditure, selected calendar years 1980–2000

Type of expenditure	1980	1988	1990	1993	1994	1995	1996	1997	1998	1999	2000
						Amount in Billions					
National Health Expenditures	$245.8	$558.1	$696.0	$888.1	$937.2	$990.3	$1,040.0	$1,091.2	$1,149.8	$1,215.6	$1,299.5
Health Services and Supplies	233.5	535.4	669.6	856.3	904.8	957.7	1,005.7	1,053.9	1,111.5	1,175.0	1,255.5
Personal Health Care	214.6	493.3	609.4	775.8	816.5	865.7	911.9	959.2	1,009.9	1,062.6	1,130.4
Hospital Care	101.5	209.4	253.9	320.0	332.4	343.6	355.9	367.5	379.2	392.2	412.1
Professional Services	67.3	176.3	216.9	280.7	297.5	316.5	332.9	352.3	375.7	397.0	422.1
Physician and Clinical Services	47.1	127.4	157.5	201.2	210.5	220.5	229.4	241.0	256.8	270.2	286.4
Other Professional Services	3.6	14.3	18.2	24.5	25.7	28.5	30.9	33.4	35.5	36.7	39.0
Dental Services	13.3	27.3	31.5	38.9	41.4	44.5	46.8	50.2	53.2	56.4	60.0
Other Personal Health Care	3.3	7.3	9.6	16.1	19.9	22.9	25.8	27.8	30.2	33.7	36.7
Nursing Home and Home Health	20.1	48.9	65.3	87.6	94.4	105.1	113.5	119.6	122.7	121.6	124.7
Home Health Care	2.4	8.4	12.6	21.9	26.1	30.5	33.6	34.5	33.6	32.3	32.4
Nursing Home Care	17.7	40.5	52.7	65.7	68.3	74.6	79.9	85.1	89.1	89.3	92.2
Retail Outlet Sales of Medical Products	25.7	58.7	73.3	87.5	92.2	100.5	109.5	119.8	132.3	151.8	171.5
Prescription Drugs	12.0	30.6	40.3	51.3	54.6	60.8	67.2	75.7	87.2	103.9	121.8
Other Medical Products	13.7	28.1	33.1	36.2	37.6	39.7	42.4	44.0	45.1	48.0	49.7
Durable Medical Equipment	3.9	8.7	10.6	12.8	13.3	14.2	15.3	16.2	16.5	17.6	18.5
Other Non-Durable Medical Products	9.8	19.4	22.5	23.4	24.3	25.6	27.1	27.9	28.6	30.4	31.2
Government Administration and Net Cost of Private Health Insurance	12.1	26.6	40.0	53.3	58.3	60.6	60.9	59.2	63.7	71.5	80.9
Government Public Health Activities	6.7	15.5	20.2	27.2	30.0	31.4	33.0	35.5	37.9	40.9	44.2
Investment	12.3	22.7	26.4	31.8	32.5	32.6	34.2	37.2	38.3	40.5	43.9
Research[1]	5.5	10.8	12.7	15.6	16.3	17.1	17.8	18.7	20.6	23.1	25.3
Construction	6.8	11.9	13.7	16.2	16.2	15.5	16.4	18.5	17.7	17.5	18.6
					Average Annual Percent Change From Previous Year Shown						
National Health Expenditures	11.7[2]	10.8	11.7	8.5	5.5	5.7	5.0	4.9	5.4	5.7	6.9
Health Services and Supplies	11.8[2]	10.9	11.8	8.5	5.7	5.9	5.0	4.8	5.5	5.7	6.9
Personal Health Care	11.7[2]	11.0	11.1	8.4	5.2	6.0	5.3	5.2	5.3	5.2	6.4
Hospital Care	12.8[2]	9.5	10.1	8.0	3.9	3.4	3.6	3.3	3.2	3.4	5.1
Professional Services	11.0[2]	12.8	10.9	9.0	6.0	6.4	5.2	5.8	6.7	5.7	6.3
Physician and Clinical Services	11.5[2]	13.2	11.2	8.5	4.6	4.8	4.0	5.0	6.6	5.2	6.0
Other Professional Services	11.7[2]	18.8	12.7	10.4	4.8	11.3	8.2	8.1	6.4	3.3	6.3
Dental Services	10.0[2]	9.4	7.4	7.3	6.6	7.4	5.2	7.2	6.0	6.1	6.3
Other Personal Health Care	8.6[2]	10.5	15.0	18.7	23.3	15.3	12.6	7.6	8.8	11.7	8.9
Nursing Home and Home Health	16.8[2]	11.8	15.5	10.3	7.8	11.3	8.0	5.4	2.6	-0.9	2.5
Home Health Care	20.6[2]	17.1	22.1	20.3	19.1	17.1	10.1	2.8	-2.8	-3.7	0.3
Nursing Home Care	16.4[2]	10.9	14.1	7.6	4.0	9.1	7.2	6.4	4.7	0.2	3.3
Retail Outlet Sales of Medical Products	8.6[2]	10.9	11.8	6.0	5.4	9.0	9.0	9.4	10.4	14.8	13.0
Prescription Drugs	7.8[2]	12.4	14.7	8.4	6.6	11.2	10.5	12.8	15.1	19.2	17.3
Other Medical Products	9.4[2]	9.4	8.5	3.1	3.7	5.8	6.6	3.9	2.5	6.3	3.7
Durable Medical Equipment	9.3[2]	10.7	10.4	6.5	4.1	6.5	7.8	5.8	2.3	6.3	5.4
Other Non-Durable Medical Products	9.4[2]	8.9	7.7	1.4	3.6	5.4	6.0	2.9	2.6	6.3	2.7
Government Administration and Net Cost of Private Health Insurance	12.2[2]	10.3	22.7	10.0	9.3	3.9	0.5	-2.7	7.5	12.3	13.1
Government Public Health Activities	15.3[2]	11.0	14.2	10.4	10.3	4.7	5.0	7.5	6.8	7.8	8.3
Investment	10.4[2]	8.0	7.8	6.4	2.1	0.3	5.1	8.8	2.9	5.8	8.4
Research[1]	10.9[2]	8.9	8.2	7.2	4.3	5.2	4.3	5.0	10.1	11.9	10.0
Construction	10.0[2]	7.2	7.4	5.7	0.1	-4.5	5.9	13.0	-4.4	-1.3	6.4

[1]Research and development expenditures of drug companies and other manufacturers and providers of medical equipment and supplies are excluded from research expenditures. These research expenditures are implicitly included in the expenditure class in which the product falls, in that they are covered by the payment received for that product.
[2]Average annual growth between 1960 and 1980.
Note: Numbers may not add to totals because of rounding.

SOURCE: "Table 2: National Health Expenditures Aggregate Amounts, and Average Annual Percent Change, by Type of Expenditure: Selected Calendar Years 1980–2000," U.S. Department of Health and Human Services, Centers for Medicare & Medicaid Services, Baltimore, MD [Online] http://www.cms.hhs.gov/statistics/nhe/historical/t2.asp [accessed August 13, 2002]

ums, hospitals and other health care providers also must purchase malpractice insurance to protect them from financial ruin in the event of lawsuits. An August 24, 2002 article in the *New York Times* reported that some hospitals had closed obstetric wards (units devoted to care of expectant mothers), clinics, and trauma services in response to soaring malpractice costs. The article cited an American Hospital Association (AHA) survey finding that more than 1,300 health care institutions had been affected by the costs of malpractice insurance and the AHA claimed that in some states, such as New Jersey, insurance costs nearly doubled during 2001.

Other factors include advanced biomedical procedures requiring high-technology expertise and equipment; redundant (excessive and unnecessary) technology in

FIGURE 5.1

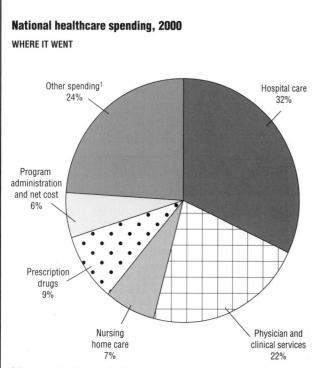

National healthcare spending, 2000
WHERE IT WENT

Other spending[1] 24%

Hospital care 32%

Program administration and net cost 6%

Prescription drugs 9%

Nursing home care 7%

Physician and clinical services 22%

[1]"Other spending" includes dentist services, other professional services, home health, durable medical products, over-the-counter medicines and sundries, public health, research and construction.

SOURCE: "Where It Went," U.S. Department of Health and Human Services, Centers for Medicare & Medicaid Services, Office of the Actuary, National Health Statistics Group, Baltimore, MD [Online] http://www.cms.hhs.gov/statistics/nhe/historical/chart.asp [accessed August 13, 2002]

FIGURE 5.2

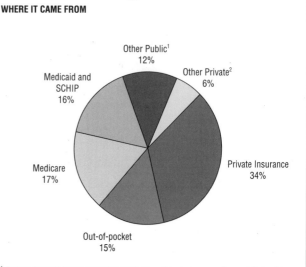

National healthcare funding, 2000
WHERE IT CAME FROM

Other Public[1] 12%

Other Private[2] 6%

Medicaid and SCHIP 16%

Medicare 17%

Private Insurance 34%

Out-of-pocket 15%

[1]"Other public" includes programs such as workers' compensation, public health activity, Department of Defense, Department of Veterans' Affairs, Indian Health Service, and state and local government hospital subsidy and school health.
[2]"Other private" includes industrial in-plant, privately funded construction, and non-patient venues, including philanthropy.

SOURCE: "Where It Came From," U.S. Department of Health and Human Services, Centers for Medicare & Medicaid Services, Office of the Actuary, National Health Statistics Group, Baltimore, MD [Online] http://www.cms.hhs.gov/statistics/nhe/historical/chart.asp [accessed August 13, 2002]

hospitals; cumbersome medical insurance programs and consumer demand for less restrictive insurance plans (that offer more choices, benefits, and coverage, but usually mean higher premiums); and consumer demand for the latest and comprehensive testing and treatment. Legislation that increased Medicare spending and the growing number of older adults who utilize a disproportionate amount of health care services also acted to accelerate health care spending.

In an article in the August 10, 2002 issue of the *New York Times*, Drew Altman, president of the Kaiser Family Foundation, a health care research organization, expressed a concern shared by many health care industry observers. "No one has a big new answer about what to do about health care costs. And it's all made worse because health costs are rising in bad economic times," Altman said. Some industry observers believe that combating health care inflation requires a major shift in how American health care providers and consumers approach health care delivery. They feel Americans must learn to use health care services wisely, choosing only treatments that have proven effective and accepting that bigger facilities and more treatment do not necessarily produce better health.

CONTROLLING HEALTH CARE SPENDING

In 1996 national health expenditures topped $1 trillion for the first time, and by 2000 national health expenditures approached $1.3 trillion. Despite the continuing growth in health care spending from year to year from 1997 to 2000—from 4.9 percent in 1997 to 6.9 percent in 2000—these figures represent a decline from the skyrocketing costs that marked the beginning of the 1990s. In 1990, for instance, health costs grew at a staggering 11.7 percent from the previous year. (See Table 5.2.)

In order to achieve these results, the nation's health care system underwent some dramatic changes. Beginning in the late 1980s, employers began looking for new ways to contain health benefit costs for their workers. Many enrolled their employees in managed care programs as alternatives to traditional, fee-for-service insurance. Managed care programs offered lower premiums by keeping a tighter control on costs and utilization, and by emphasizing the importance of preventive care. This allowed insurers to negotiate discounts with providers (physicians, hospitals, clinical laboratories, and others) in exchange for guaranteed access to employer-insured groups. Private insurance pays for about 34 percent of the nation's health costs, with public sources picking up about 45 percent of the nation's costs, and 15 percent of the costs coming directly from citizen's pockets. (See Figure 5.2.)

TABLE 5.6

National health expenditures, by source of funds and type of expenditure, 1995–2000

		Private					Public		
			Consumer						
Year and Type of Expenditure	Total	All Private Funds	Total	Out-of-Pocket Payments	Private Health Insurance	Other	Total	Federal	State and Local
1995					Amount in Billions				
National Health Expenditures	$990.3	$534.1	$476.7	$146.5	$330.1	$57.4	$456.2	$322.0	$134.2
Health Services and Supplies	957.7	521.6	476.7	146.5	330.1	44.9	436.1	307.7	128.4
Personal Health Care	865.7	479.9	435.7	146.5	289.1	44.3	385.8	295.0	90.8
Hospital Care	343.6	137.1	122.4	10.5	111.9	14.7	206.5	166.2	40.3
Professional Services	316.5	217.9	194.4	53.4	140.9	23.5	98.6	72.8	25.7
Physician and Clinical Services	220.5	151.0	133.4	26.3	107.2	17.6	69.5	56.2	13.3
Other Professional Services	28.5	21.2	18.6	7.8	10.8	2.6	7.3	4.6	2.8
Dental Services	44.5	42.4	42.4	19.4	23.0	0.1	2.0	1.2	0.9
Other Personal Health Care	22.9	3.3	—	—	—	3.3	19.7	10.9	8.7
Nursing Home and Home Health	105.1	41.7	35.7	24.5	11.2	6.0	63.4	44.4	19.1
Home Health Care	30.5	11.2	10.0	4.4	5.6	1.2	19.4	15.8	3.5
Nursing Home Care	74.6	30.5	25.7	20.1	5.6	4.8	44.1	28.5	15.5
Retail Outlet Sales of Medical Products	100.5	83.2	83.2	58.1	25.1	—	17.3	11.5	5.7
Prescription Drugs	60.8	48.5	48.5	26.0	22.6	—	12.2	6.6	5.6
Other Medical Products	39.7	34.7	34.7	32.1	2.6	—	5.0	4.9	0.1
Durable Medical Equipment	14.2	10.2	10.2	7.7	2.6	—	4.0	3.8	0.1
Other Non-Durable Medical Products	25.6	24.5	24.5	24.5	—	—	1.1	1.1	—
Government Administration and Net Cost of Private Health Insurance	60.6	41.7	41.0	—	41.0	0.7	18.9	9.1	9.8
Government Public Health Activities	31.4	—	—	—	—	—	31.4	3.6	27.8
Investment	32.6	12.5	—	—	—	12.5	20.1	14.3	5.8
Research	17.1	1.4	—	—	—	1.4	15.7	13.2	2.5
Construction	15.5	11.1	—	—	—	11.1	4.4	1.1	3.3
1996									
National Health Expenditures	$1,040.0	$558.2	$496.8	$152.1	$344.8	$61.4	$481.8	$343.9	$137.8
Health Services and Supplies	1,005.7	545.0	496.8	152.1	344.8	48.2	460.8	329.2	131.6
Personal Health Care	911.9	502.8	455.4	152.1	303.3	47.5	409.0	315.6	93.5
Hospital Care	355.9	139.7	123.7	10.6	113.1	16.0	216.2	175.5	40.8
Professional Services	332.9	227.9	202.7	55.4	147.4	25.2	105.0	78.3	26.7
Physician and Clinical Services	229.4	156.7	137.9	26.9	110.9	18.8	72.7	59.2	13.5
Other Professional Services	30.9	23.1	20.3	8.3	12.0	2.8	7.8	4.9	2.9
Dental Services	46.8	44.7	44.6	20.2	24.4	0.1	2.1	1.2	0.9
Other Personal Health Care	25.8	3.4	—	—	—	3.4	22.4	13.0	9.4
Nursing Home and Home Health	113.5	45.0	38.7	25.5	13.2	6.3	68.6	48.7	19.8
Home Health Care	33.6	12.9	11.6	5.1	6.5	1.3	20.7	17.0	3.7
Nursing Home Care	79.9	32.1	27.1	20.4	6.7	5.0	47.8	31.7	16.1
Retail Outlet Sales of Medical Products	109.5	90.3	90.3	60.6	29.7	—	19.2	13.1	6.2
Prescription Drugs	67.2	53.3	53.3	26.5	26.9	—	13.8	7.8	6.0
Other Medical Products	42.4	37.0	37.0	34.1	2.8	—	5.4	5.3	0.1
Durable Medical Equipment	15.3	11.0	11.0	8.1	2.8	—	4.3	4.2	0.1
Other Non-Durable Medical Products	27.1	26.0	26.0	26.0	—	—	1.1	1.1	—
Government Administration and Net Cost of Private Health Insurance	60.9	42.2	41.4	—	41.4	0.7	18.7	9.9	8.9
Government Public Health Activities	33.0	—	—	—	—	—	33.0	3.8	29.3
Investment	34.2	13.2	—	—	—	13.2	21.0	14.8	6.3
Research	17.8	1.6	—	—	—	1.6	16.2	13.6	2.7
Construction	16.4	11.6	—	—	—	11.6	4.8	1.2	3.6
1997									
National Health Expenditures	$1,091.2	$588.8	$521.8	$162.3	$359.4	$67.0	$502.4	$358.8	$143.6
Health Services and Supplies	1,053.9	573.9	521.8	162.3	359.4	52.1	480.1	343.2	136.9
Personal Health Care	959.2	533.9	482.5	162.3	320.2	51.4	425.3	328.5	96.9
Hospital Care	367.5	144.9	126.9	11.2	115.7	18.0	222.6	181.0	41.6
Professional Services	352.3	242.1	215.3	60.4	154.9	26.8	110.2	82.7	27.5
Physician and Clinical Services	241.0	165.1	145.0	28.7	116.2	20.1	75.9	62.4	13.5
Other Professional Services	33.4	25.5	22.5	9.5	13.0	3.0	7.9	5.0	2.9
Dental Services	50.2	47.9	47.8	22.2	25.6	0.1	2.3	1.3	0.9
Other Personal Health Care	27.8	3.6	—	—	—	3.6	24.1	14.0	10.2
Nursing Home and Home Health	119.6	48.8	42.2	27.7	14.5	6.6	70.8	49.9	20.9
Home Health Care	34.5	14.8	13.4	5.9	7.5	1.4	19.8	15.9	3.9
Nursing Home Care	85.1	34.0	28.8	21.7	7.1	5.2	51.1	34.1	17.0
Retail Outlet Sales of Medical Products	119.8	98.1	98.1	63.1	35.0	—	21.7	14.8	6.9

TABLE 5.6

National health expenditures, by source of funds and type of expenditure, 1995–2000 [CONTINUED]

Year and Type of Expenditure	Total	All Private Funds	Private				Public		
			Consumer						
			Total	Out-of-Pocket Payments	Private Health Insurance	Other	Total	Federal	State and Local
1997 [CONTINUED]					Amount in Billions				
Prescription Drugs	75.7	60.0	60.0	27.9	32.2	—	15.7	9.0	6.8
Other Medical Products	44.0	38.1	38.1	35.2	2.9	—	6.0	5.9	0.1
Durable Medical Equipment	16.2	11.3	11.3	8.5	2.9	—	4.8	4.7	0.1
Other Non-Durable Medical Products	27.9	26.7	26.7	26.7	—	—	1.2	1.2	—
Government Administration and Net Cost of Private Health Insurance	59.2	40.0	39.3	—	39.3	0.8	19.2	10.8	8.4
Government Public Health Activities	35.5	—	—	—	—	—	35.5	3.9	31.6
Investment	37.2	14.9	—	—	—	14.9	22.3	15.6	6.7
Research	18.7	1.6	—	—	—	1.6	17.1	14.3	2.8
Construction	18.5	13.3	—	—	—	13.3	5.2	1.3	3.9
1998									
National Health Expenditures	$1,149.8	$628.8	$557.7	$174.5	$383.2	$71.1	$520.9	$367.7	$153.3
Health Services and Supplies	1,111.5	613.3	557.7	174.5	383.2	55.6	498.2	351.0	147.2
Personal Health Care	1,009.9	571.9	517.2	174.5	342.7	54.7	438.0	334.2	103.8
Hospital Care	379.2	154.0	134.5	11.9	122.6	19.5	225.1	179.9	45.2
Professional Services	375.7	257.2	228.0	64.9	163.1	29.2	118.5	89.4	29.2
Physician and Clinical Services	256.8	175.2	153.1	30.7	122.4	22.1	81.6	67.6	14.0
Other Professional Services	35.5	27.3	24.2	10.6	13.6	3.1	8.2	5.2	3.0
Dental Services	53.2	50.8	50.7	23.7	27.0	0.1	2.3	1.4	1.0
Other Personal Health Care	30.2	3.8	—	—	—	3.8	26.4	15.2	11.2
Nursing Home and Home Health	122.7	52.9	46.8	31.2	15.6	6.0	69.8	48.5	21.3
Home Health Care	33.6	16.1	14.7	6.5	8.2	1.4	17.5	13.4	4.1
Nursing Home Care	89.1	36.8	32.1	24.7	7.4	4.7	52.3	35.1	17.2
Retail Outlet Sales of Medical Products	132.3	107.8	107.8	66.4	41.4	—	24.5	16.4	8.1
Prescription Drugs	87.2	68.7	68.7	30.4	38.3	—	18.5	10.5	7.9
Other Medical Products	45.1	39.1	39.1	36.0	3.1	—	6.0	5.9	0.1
Durable Medical Equipment	16.5	11.7	11.7	8.6	3.1	—	4.8	4.7	0.1
Other Non-Durable Medical Products	28.6	27.4	27.4	27.4	—	—	1.2	1.2	—
Government Administration and Net Cost of Private Health Insurance	63.7	41.4	40.6	—	40.6	0.9	22.3	12.8	9.5
Government Public Health Activities	37.9	—	—	—	—	—	37.9	4.0	33.9
Investment	38.3	15.5	—	—	—	15.5	22.8	16.6	6.1
Research	20.6	2.0	—	—	—	2.0	18.6	15.6	3.0
Construction	17.7	13.6	—	—	—	13.6	4.1	1.0	3.1
1999									
National Health Expenditures	$1,215.6	$666.5	$593.8	$184.4	$409.4	$72.7	$549.0	$384.8	$164.2
Health Services and Supplies	1,175.0	651.1	593.8	184.4	409.4	57.3	524.0	366.1	157.9
Personal Health Care	1,062.6	604.6	548.3	184.4	363.9	56.3	458.0	346.8	111.3
Hospital Care	392.2	160.7	140.0	12.6	127.4	20.6	231.5	183.9	47.7
Professional Services	397.0	267.7	238.2	67.5	170.7	29.5	129.4	97.4	31.9
Physician and Clinical Services	270.2	181.8	159.4	31.5	127.8	22.4	88.5	73.4	15.0
Other Professional Services	36.7	28.1	25.1	11.1	14.0	3.0	8.6	5.4	3.3
Dental Services	56.4	53.9	53.7	24.9	28.8	0.1	2.5	1.5	1.0
Other Personal Health Care	33.7	4.0	—	—	—	4.0	29.8	17.2	12.6
Nursing Home and Home Health	121.6	52.9	46.7	31.3	15.4	6.1	68.7	46.6	22.1
Home Health Care	32.3	15.8	14.2	6.4	7.8	1.6	16.5	12.3	4.2
Nursing Home Care	89.3	37.1	32.5	24.9	7.5	4.6	52.2	34.3	17.9
Retail Outlet Sales of Medical Products	151.8	123.4	123.4	73.0	50.5	—	28.4	18.9	9.6
Prescription Drugs	103.9	81.7	81.7	34.7	47.1	—	22.2	12.7	9.4
Other Medical Products	48.0	41.7	41.7	38.3	3.4	—	6.3	6.1	0.2
Durable Medical Equipment	17.6	12.5	12.5	9.1	3.4	—	5.1	4.9	0.2
Other Non-Durable Medical Products	30.4	29.2	29.2	29.2	—	—	1.2	1.2	—
Government Administration and Net Cost of Private Health Insurance	71.5	46.5	45.5	—	45.5	1.0	25.1	14.9	10.2
Government Public Health Activities	40.9	—	—	—	—	—	40.9	4.4	36.4
Investment	40.5	15.5	—	—	—	15.5	25.0	18.7	6.4
Research	23.1	2.2	—	—	—	2.2	20.9	17.8	3.1
Construction	17.5	13.3	—	—	—	13.3	4.2	0.9	3.3

There is heightened interest in developing treatments and technologies designed to reduce the health system's dependence on expensive, inpatient hospital care. After professional services ($422.1 billion), hospital care expenditures were the single-largest spending component of total health care expenses ($412.1), accounting for 32 percent of all national health care expenditures. (See Table 5.5 and Figure 5.1.) The annual hospital cost growth rate dropped from 12.8 percent per year in 1980 to around 3.3 percent between 1995 and

TABLE 5.6

National health expenditures, by source of funds and type of expenditure, 1995–2000 [CONTINUED]

Year and Type of Expenditure	Total	All Private Funds	Private				Public		
			Consumer						
			Total	Out-of-Pocket Payments	Private Health Insurance	Other	Total	Federal	State and Local
2000				Amount in Billions					
National Health Expenditures	$1,299.5	$712.3	$638.4	$194.5	$443.9	$73.8	$587.2	$411.5	$175.7
Health Services and Supplies	1,255.5	695.6	638.4	194.5	443.9	57.2	559.9	391.2	168.7
Personal Health Care	1,130.4	641.4	585.3	194.5	390.7	56.1	489.0	370.4	118.6
Hospital Care	412.1	168.9	146.9	13.0	133.9	22.0	243.2	192.9	50.3
Professional Services	422.1	282.3	253.7	71.8	181.8	28.6	139.8	105.6	34.3
Physician and Clinical Services	286.4	191.3	169.9	33.2	136.7	21.3	95.2	79.2	16.0
Other Professional Services	39.0	29.6	26.7	11.7	15.0	2.9	9.4	5.9	3.4
Dental Services	60.0	57.2	57.0	26.9	30.1	0.2	2.8	1.6	1.1
Other Personal Health Care	36.7	4.2	—	—	—	4.2	32.5	18.9	13.7
Nursing Home and Home Health	124.7	51.8	46.3	31.2	15.1	5.5	72.8	50.4	22.5
Home Health Care	32.4	15.5	14.0	6.4	7.6	1.5	16.9	12.6	4.3
Nursing Home Care	92.2	36.3	32.3	24.9	7.4	4.0	55.9	37.8	18.2
Retail Outlet Sales of Medical Products	171.5	138.4	138.4	78.5	59.9	—	33.1	21.6	11.5
Prescription Drugs	121.8	95.3	95.3	39.0	56.3	—	26.5	15.2	11.3
Other Medical Products	49.7	43.1	43.1	39.5	3.6	—	6.6	6.4	0.2
Durable Medical Equipment	18.5	13.3	13.3	9.6	3.6	—	5.3	5.1	0.2
Other Non-Durable Medical Products	31.2	29.8	29.8	29.8	—	—	1.3	1.3	—
Government Administration and Net Cost of Private Health Insurance	80.9	54.2	53.1	—	53.1	1.0	26.7	15.9	10.8
Government Public Health Activities	44.2	—	—	—	—	—	44.2	4.9	39.3
Investment	43.9	16.7	—	—	—	16.7	27.3	20.3	7.0
Research	25.3	2.3	—	—	—	2.3	23.0	19.6	3.4
Construction	18.6	14.3	—	—	—	14.3	4.3	0.7	3.6

Note: Research and development expenditures of drug companies and other manufacturers and providers of medical equipment and supplies are excluded from research expenditures. These research expenditures are implicitly included in the expenditure class in which the product falls, in that they are covered by the payment received for that product. Numbers may not add to totals because of rounding.

SOURCE: "Table 3: National Health Expenditures, by Source of Funds and Type of Expenditure: Calendar Years 1995–2000," U.S. Department of Health and Human Services, Centers for Medicare & Medicaid Services, Baltimore, MD [Online] http://www.cms.hhs.gov/statistics/nhe/historical/t3.asp [accessed August 13, 2002]

1998. However, in 2000 it spiked to 5.1 percent. (See Table 5.5.)

Further, higher hospital prices in 2001 resulted in the greatest increase in health care spending in a decade. Total health care costs increased 8.7 percent in 2001, compared with a 7.3 percent increase in 2000, and hospital care was responsible for nearly half of the increase. Economic analysis of the increase attributable to hospitals revealed that less than 40 percent was caused by rising hospital prices and slightly more than 60 percent by increased utilization of hospital services.

Physician and clinical services accounted for 22 percent ($286.4 billion) of 2000 national health spending. (See Table 5.5 and Figure 5.1.) The average annual physician spending, however, dropped steadily from 13.2 percent in 1988 to 4 percent in 1996. From 1997 to 2000, it fluctuated between 5 and 6.6 percent. (See Table 5.5.) Managed care has played a large role in the slowed growth observed in this sector of health care delivery.

In 2000 spending for nursing home care totaled $92.2 billion, and spending for home health care reached $32.4 billion. (See Table 5.5.) Although in 2000 nursing home expenses increased just 3.3 percent, this increase followed four consecutive years of decelerating growth from a high of 9.1 percent annual growth in 1995. The increase was caused by legislation that increased Medicare payments to nursing homes for selected complex medical conditions and for facilities specializing in the care of patients with AIDS.

Home health care expenses also slowed, from 20.3 percent annual growth in 1993 to 2.8 percent in 1997. In 1998 and 1999 the annual growth was actually negative, but rose 0.3 percent in 2000. (See Table 5.5.) Like nursing home expenditures, home health spending increased in 2000 after several years of decelerating growth. Medicare home health expenditures rose 0.8 percent in 2000, the first increase in four years.

However, the fastest-growing component of health care was the market for prescription drugs. In 2000 Americans spent $121.8 billion on prescription medication—a 17.3 percent increase from 1999. (See Table 5.5.) A large part of the increase was financed by private insurers, which paid 46.2 percent of drug costs in 2000, up from 37.2 percent in 1995. (See Table 5.6.) Growth in this

TABLE 5.7

Personal health care expenditures aggregate and per capita amounts and percent distributions, by source of funds, selected calendar years 1980–2000

Year	Total	Out-of-Pocket Payments	Total	Private Health Insurance	Other Private Funds	Total	Federal[1]	State and Local[1]	Medicare[2]	Medicaid[3]
						Third-Party Payments — Public				
						Amount in Billions				
1980	$214.6	$58.2	$156.4	$60.6	$9.2	$86.6	$62.8	$23.8	$36.3	$24.7
1988	493.3	118.9	374.4	157.0	27.6	189.8	138.4	51.4	$86.4	$52.2
1990	609.4	137.3	472.1	203.6	30.6	237.9	174.2	63.7	107.3	69.7
1993	775.8	146.9	628.8	259.9	38.4	330.5	250.6	79.9	144.4	115.7
1994	816.5	143.9	672.5	271.8	40.1	360.6	273.0	87.6	161.6	126.2
1995	865.7	146.5	719.2	289.1	44.3	385.8	295.0	90.8	178.2	135.3
1996	911.9	152.1	759.8	303.3	47.5	409.0	315.6	93.5	192.2	144.5
1997	959.2	162.3	796.9	320.2	51.4	425.3	328.5	96.9	202.2	151.7
1998	1,009.9	174.5	835.4	342.7	54.7	438.0	334.2	103.8	203.4	160.0
1999	1,062.6	184.4	878.2	363.9	56.3	458.0	346.8	111.3	205.3	173.5
2000	1,130.4	194.5	935.9	390.7	56.1	489.0	370.4	118.6	217.0	187.6
						Per Capita Amount				
1980	931	253	679	263	40	376	272	103	(4)	(4)
1988	1,982	478	1,504	631	111	763	556	207	(4)	(4)
1990	2,398	540	1,858	801	120	936	685	251	(4)	(4)
1993	2,954	559	2,394	989	146	1,258	954	304	(4)	(4)
1994	3,079	543	2,536	1,025	151	1,360	1,030	330	(4)	(4)
1995	3,233	547	2,686	1,080	165	1,441	1,101	339	(4)	(4)
1996	3,375	563	2,812	1,123	176	1,514	1,168	346	(4)	(4)
1997	3,517	595	2,922	1,174	188	1,560	1,204	355	(4)	(4)
1998	3,669	634	3,035	1,245	199	1,591	1,214	377	(4)	(4)
1999	3,826	664	3,162	1,310	203	1,649	1,249	401	(4)	(4)
2000	4,034	694	3,340	1,394	200	1,745	1,322	423	(4)	(4)
						Percent Distribution				
1980	100.0	27.1	72.9	28.3	4.3	40.3	29.3	11.1	16.9	11.5
1988	100.0	24.1	75.9	31.8	5.6	38.5	28.0	10.4	17.5	10.6
1990	100.0	22.5	77.5	33.4	5.0	39.0	28.6	10.5	17.6	11.4
1993	100.0	18.9	81.1	33.5	5.0	42.6	32.3	10.3	18.6	14.9
1994	100.0	17.6	82.4	33.3	4.9	44.2	33.4	10.7	19.8	15.5
1995	100.0	16.9	83.1	33.4	5.1	44.6	34.1	10.5	20.6	15.6
1996	100.0	16.7	83.3	33.3	5.2	44.9	34.6	10.2	21.1	15.9
1997	100.0	16.9	83.1	33.4	5.4	44.3	34.2	10.1	21.1	15.8
1998	100.0	17.3	82.7	33.9	5.4	43.4	33.1	10.3	20.1	15.8
1999	100.0	17.4	82.6	34.2	5.3	43.1	32.6	10.5	19.3	16.3
2000	100.0	17.2	82.8	34.6	5.0	43.3	32.8	10.5	19.2	16.6

[1]Includes Medicaid SCHIP Expansion & SCHIP.
[2]Subset of federal funds.
[3]Subset of federal and state and local funds.
[4]Calculation of per capita estimates is inappropriate.
Note: Per capita amounts based on July 1 Census resident based population estimates for each year 1980-2000. Numbers and percents may not add to totals because of rounding.

SOURCE: "Table 4: Personal Health Care Expenditures, Aggregate and per Capita Amounts and Percent Distribution, by Source of Funds: Selected Calendar Years 1980–2000," U.S. Department of Health and Human Services, Centers for Medicare & Medicaid Services, Baltimore, MD [Online] http://www.cms.hhs.gov/statistics/nhe/historical/t4.asp [accessed August 13, 2002]

sector of health services has been fueled by the fact that today, prescription drugs are more often substituted for other types of health care. For example, antidepressant drugs have demonstrated effectiveness in place of more expensive psychotherapy.

HEALTH CARE FOR OLDER ADULTS, PERSONS WITH DISABILITIES, AND THE POOR

The United States is one of the few industrialized nations that does not have national health care programs. In most other developed countries, government programs cover almost all health-related costs, from maternity care to long-term care.

In the United States, the major government health care entitlement programs are Medicare and Medicaid. They provide financial assistance for persons age 65 and older, the poor, and persons with disabilities. Before the existence of these programs, a large number of older Americans could not afford adequate medical care. For older adults who are beneficiaries, the Medicare program provides reimbursement for hospital and physician care, while Medicaid pays for the cost of nursing home care.

TABLE 5.8

Medicare enrollees and expenditures and percent distribution, according to type of service, U.S. and other areas, selected years, 1970–2000

[Data are compiled by the Centers for Medicare & Medicaid Services]

Type of Service	1970	1980	1990	1995	1996	1997	1998	1999	2000[1]
Enrollees					Number in millions				
Total[2]	20.4	28.4	34.3	37.6	38.1	38.5	38.9	39.2	39.6
Hospital insurance	20.1	28.0	33.7	37.2	37.7	38.1	38.5	38.8	39.2
Supplementary medical insurance	19.5	27.3	32.6	35.6	36.1	36.4	36.8	37.0	37.3
Expenditures					Amount in billions				
Total	$7.5	$36.8	$111.0	$184.2	$200.3	$213.6	$213.4	$213.0	$221.8
Total hospital insurance (HI)	5.3	25.6	67.0	117.6	129.9	139.5	135.8	130.6	131.1
HI payments to managed care organizations[3]	- - -	0.0	2.7	6.7	11.8	16.3	19.0	20.9	21.4
HI payments for fee-for-service utilization	5.3	25.6	64.3	110.9	118.2	123.1	116.8	109.8	109.7
Inpatient hospital	4.8	24.1	56.9	82.3	86.1	89.2	87.4	86.8	87.6
Skilled nursing facility	0.2	0.4	2.5	9.1	10.9	12.8	12.9	10.5	11.0
Home health agency	0.1	0.5	3.7	16.2	17.7	17.5	11.8	7.3	3.7
Home health agency transfer[4]	...	...	...	...	...	...	0.5	0.6	1.7
Hospice	...	...	0.3	1.9	2.0	2.1	2.2	2.6	3.0
Administrative expenses[5]	0.2	0.5	0.9	1.4	1.5	1.9	2.0	2.0	2.8
Total supplementary medical insurance (SMI)	2.2	11.2	44.0	66.6	70.4	74.1	77.6	82.3	90.7
SMI payments to managed care organizations[3]	0.0	0.2	2.8	6.6	9.6	11.0	15.3	17.7	18.4
SMI payments for fee-for-service utilization[6]	2.2	11.0	41.2	60.0	60.8	63.2	62.3	64.6	72.3
Physician/supplies[7]	1.8	8.2	29.6	- - -	- - -	- - -	- - -	- - -	- - -
Outpatient hospital[8]	0.1	1.9	8.5	- - -	- - -	- - -	- - -	- - -	- - -
Independent laboratory[9]	0.0	0.1	1.5	- - -	- - -	- - -	- - -	- - -	- - -
Physician fee schedule	- - -	- - -	- - -	31.7	31.6	31.9	32.4	33.3	36.9
Durable medical equipment	- - -	- - -	- - -	3.7	3.8	4.2	4.0	4.3	4.7
Laboratory[10]	- - -	- - -	- - -	4.3	3.9	3.9	3.6	3.8	4.0
Other[11]	- - -	- - -	- - -	9.9	10.8	12.2	12.3	12.2	13.7
Hospital[12]	- - -	- - -	- - -	8.7	8.6	9.4	8.7	8.8	8.4
Home health agency	0.0	0.2	0.1	0.2	0.2	0.2	0.2	1.2	4.4
Home health agency transfer[4]	- - -	- - -	- - -	- - -	- - -	- - -	−0.5	−0.6	−1.7
Administrative expenses[5]	0.2	0.6	1.5	1.6	1.8	1.4	1.5	1.6	1.8
					Percent distribution of expenditures				
Total hospital insurance (HI)	100.0	100.0	100.0	100.0	100.0	100.0	100.0	100.0	100.0
HI payments to managed care organizations[3]	- - -	0.0	4.0	5.7	9.1	11.7	14.0	16.0	16.3
HI payments for fee-for-service utilization	100.0	100.0	96.0	94.3	90.9	88.3	86.0	84.0	83.7
Inpatient hospital	90.6	94.1	84.9	70.0	66.5	63.9	64.3	66.4	66.8
Skilled nursing facility	3.8	1.6	3.7	7.8	8.4	9.0	9.5	8.0	8.4
Home health agency	1.9	2.0	5.5	13.8	13.5	12.5	8.7	5.6	2.8
Home health agency transfer[4]	...	...	...	...	...	...	0.4	0.5	1.3
Hospice	...	...	0.4	1.6	1.6	1.5	1.6	2.0	2.3
Administrative expenses[5]	3.8	2.0	1.3	1.2	1.1	1.3	1.5	1.6	2.1

Medicare

The Medicare program, enacted under Title XVIII (Health Insurance for the Aged) of the Social Security Act (PL 89-97), went into effect on July 1, 1966. The program is composed of two parts:

- Part A provides hospital insurance. Coverage includes physicians' fees, nursing services, meals, semiprivate rooms, special-care units, operating room costs, laboratory tests, and some drugs and supplies. Part A also covers rehabilitation services, limited post-hospital care in a skilled nursing facility, home health care, and hospice care for the terminally ill.

- Part B (Supplemental Medical Insurance, or SMI) is elective medical insurance; that is, enrollees must pay premiums to obtain coverage. SMI covers outpatient physicians' services, diagnostic tests, outpatient hospital services, outpatient physical therapy, speech pathology services, home health services, and medical equipment and supplies.

In 2000 close to $222 million was spent to provide coverage for the almost 40 million persons enrolled in Medicare. (See Table 5.8.) Most Medicare recipients were 65 and older; more than half of these older adults were between the ages of 65 and 74; a third were between the ages of 75 and 84; and 12.1 percent were 85 and older. The CMMS estimated that by 2050, 69 million people age 65 and older would be eligible for Medicare; of those, 15 million would be 85 or older.

In general, Medicare reimburses physicians on a fee-for-service basis, as opposed to per capita (per head) or per

TABLE 5.8

Medicare enrollees and expenditures and percent distribution, according to type of service, U.S. and other areas, selected years, 1970–2000 [CONTINUED]

[Data are compiled by the Centers for Medicare & Medicaid Services]

Type of Service	1970	1980	1990	1995	1996	1997	1998	1999	2000[1]
				Percent distribution of expenditures					
Total supplementary medical insurance (SMI)	100.0	100.0	100.0	100.0	100.0	100.0	100.0	100.0	100.0
SMI payments to managed care organizations[3]	0.0	1.8	6.4	9.9	13.6	14.8	19.8	21.5	20.2
SMI payments for fee-for-service utilization[6]	100.0	98.2	93.6	90.1	86.4	85.2	80.2	78.5	79.8
Physician/supplies[7]	81.8	73.2	67.3	---	---	---	---	---	---
Outpatient hospital[8]	4.5	17.0	19.3	---	---	---	---	---	---
Independent laboratory[9]	0.0	0.9	3.4	---	---	---	---	---	---
Physician fee schedule	---	---	---	47.6	44.9	43.0	41.8	40.5	40.7
Durable medical equipment	---	---	---	5.5	5.4	5.7	5.2	5.2	5.2
Laboratory[10]	---	---	---	6.4	5.5	5.2	4.7	4.6	4.4
Other[11]	---	---	---	14.8	15.4	16.4	15.9	14.8	15.1
Hospital[12]	---	---	---	13.0	12.2	12.6	11.2	10.6	9.3
Home health agency	0.0	1.8	0.2	0.3	0.3	0.3	0.2	1.5	4.8
Home health agency transfer[4]	---	---	---	---	---	---	-0.7	-0.7	-1.9
Administrative expenses[5]	9.1	5.4	3.4	2.4	2.6	1.9	2.0	2.0	2.0

- - - Data not available.
. . . Category not applicable.
0.0 Quantity greater than 0 but less than 0.05.
[1]Preliminary figures; home health agency expenditures for 2000 reflect annual home health HI to SMI transfer amounts.
[2]Average number enrolled in the hospital insurance and/or supplementary medical insurance programs for the period.
[3]Medicare-approved managed care organizations.
[4]Reflects annual home health HI to SMI transfer amounts for 1998 and later.
[5]Includes research, costs of experiments and demonstration programs, and peer review activity.
[6]Type of service reporting categories for fee-for-service reimbursement differ before and after 1991.
[7]Includes payment for physicians, practitioners, durable medical equipment, and all suppliers other than Independent laboratory, which is shown separately through 1990. Beginning in 1991, those physician services subject to the Physician fee schedule are so broken out. Payments for laboratory services paid under the Laboratory fee schedule and performed in a physician office are included under "Laboratory" beginning in 1991. Payments for durable medical equipment are broken out and so labeled beginning in 1991. The remaining services from the "Physician" category are included in "Other."
[8]Includes payments for hospital outpatient department services, for skilled nursing facility outpatient services, for Part B services received as an inpatient in a hospital or skilled nursing facility setting, and for other types of outpatient facilities. Beginning 1991, payments for hospital outpatient department services, except for laboratory services, are listed under "Hospital." Hospital outpatient laboratory services are included in the "Laboratory" line.
[9]Beginning in 1991 those independent laboratory services that were paid under the Laboratory fee schedule (most of independent lab) are included in the "Laboratory" line; the remaining services are included in "Physician fee schedule" and "Other" lines.
[10]Payments for laboratory services paid under the Laboratory fee schedule performed in a physician office, independent lab, or in a hospital outpatient department.
[11]Includes payments for physician-administered drugs, free-standing ambulatory surgical center facility services; ambulance services; supplies; free-standing end-stage renal disease (ESRD) dialysis facility services; rural health clinics; outpatient rehabilitation facilities; psychiatric hospitals; and federally qualified health centers.
[12]Includes the hospital facility costs for Medicare Part B services that are predominantly in the outpatient department, with the exception of hospital outpatient laboratory services, which are included on the "Laboratory" line. The physician reimbursement is included on the "Physician fee schedule" line.
Note: Table includes service disbursements as of January 2002 for Medicare enrollees residing in Puerto Rico, Virgin Islands, Guam, other outlying areas, foreign countries, and unknown residence. Totals do not necessarily equal the sums of rounded components. Some numbers in this table have been revised and differ from revious editions of *Health, United States*.

SOURCE: "Table 134. Medicare enrollees and expenditures and percent distribution, according to type of service: United States and other areas, selected years 1970–2000," in *Health, United States, 2002*, Centers for Disease Control, National Center for Health Statistics, Hyattsville, MD, 2002

member per month (PMPM). In response to the increasing administrative burden of paperwork, reduced compensation, and delays in reimbursements, some physicians opt out of Medicare participation—they do not provide services under the Medicare program and choose not to accept Medicare patients into their practices. Others still provide services to Medicare beneficiaries, however they do not "accept assignment," meaning that patients must pay out-of-pocket for services and then seek reimbursement from Medicare.

Because of these problems, the Tax Equity and Fiscal Responsibility Act of 1982 (PL 97-248) authorized a "risk managed care" option for Medicare, based on agreed-upon prepayments. Beginning in 1985, the HCFA could contract to pay health care providers, such as HMOs or health care prepayment plans, to serve Medicare and Medicaid patients. These groups are paid a predetermined cost per patient for their services.

Medicare-Risk HMOs Control Costs, But Some Senior Health Plans Do Not Survive

During the 1980s and 1990s the federal government, employers that provided health coverage for retiring employees, and many states sought to control costs by encouraging Medicare and Medicaid beneficiaries to enroll in HMOs. From the early 1980s through the late 1990s, "Medicare-risk HMOs" did contain costs because essentially, the federal government paid the health plans that operated them with fixed fee per member per month (PMPM). For this fixed fee, Medicare recipients were to receive a fairly comprehensive, preset array of benefits. PMPM payment financially incentivized Medicare-risk

HMO physicians to control costs, unlike physicians who were reimbursed on a fee-for-service basis (paid for each visit, procedure, or treatment delivered).

Although Medicare recipients were generally pleased with these HMOs (even when enrolling meant they had to change physicians and thereby end longstanding relationships with their family doctors), many of the health plans did not fare as well. The health plans suffered for a variety of reasons: some plans had underestimated the service utilization rates of older adults, and some were unable to provide the stipulated range of services as cost effectively as they had believed possible. Other plans found that the PMPM payment was simply not sufficient to enable them to cover all the clinical services and their administrative overhead.

Still, the health plans providing these "senior HMOs" competed fiercely to market to and enroll older adults. Some health plans feared that closing their Medicare-risk programs would be viewed negatively by employer groups, which, when faced with the choice of plans that offered coverage for both younger workers and retirees or one that only covered the younger workers, would choose the plans that covered both. Despite losing money, most health plans maintained their Medicare-risk programs to avoid alienating the employers they depended on to enroll workers who were younger, healthier, and less expensive to serve than the older adults.

About ten years into operations some of the Medicare-risk plans faced a challenge that proved unbeatable. Their enrollees had aged and required even more health care services than they had previously. For example, a senior HMO member who had joined as a healthy 65-year old could now be a frail 75-year-old with multiple chronic health conditions, requiring many costly health services. While the PMPM had increased over the years, for some plans it was simply insufficient to cover their costs. Many Medicare-risk plans, especially those operated by smaller health plans, were forced to end their programs abruptly, leaving thousands of older adults scrambling to join other health plans. Others have endured to year 2002, offering older adults comprehensive care and generating substantial cost savings for employers and the federal government.

The Balanced Budget Act of 1997 produced another plan for Medicare recipients called "Medicare+Choice." These plans offer Medicare beneficiaries a wider range of managed care plan options than just HMOs—older adults may join preferred provider organizations (PPOs) and provider-sponsored organizations (PSOs) that generally offer greater freedom of choice of providers (physicians and hospitals) than available through HMO membership.

Medicaid

Medicaid was enacted by Congress in 1965 under "Grants to States for Medical Assistance Programs," Title XIX of the Social Security Act. It is a joint federal/state program that provides medical assistance to selected categories of low-income Americans: the aged, persons who are blind, persons who are disabled, or families with dependent children. Medicaid covers hospitalization, physicians' fees, laboratory fees, X rays, and long-term care in nursing homes.

In 1998, 40.6 million people received Medicaid services—an 88 percent increase over 1980. Of Medicaid dollars spent in 1998, 22.4 percent went to nursing facilities, while 15.1 percent was spent in inpatient general hospitals. (See Table 5.9.)

The Personal Responsibility and Work Opportunity Reconciliation Act (PL 104-193)—federal welfare reform—was signed into law in August 1996, replacing the American Families with Dependent Children program (AFDC) with Temporary Assistance for Needy Families (TANF). Under TANF, Medicaid coverage was no longer guaranteed, as it had been for recipients of AFDC. The new law, however, required states to continue benefits to those who would have been eligible under the AFDC requirements that each state had in place on July 16, 1996.

Medicaid is the largest third-party payer of long-term care in the United States, financing about one half of all nursing home care in 1999. Under current law, an elderly person must have less than $2,500 in savings or assets (with some exceptions) to qualify for nursing home care paid for by Medicaid. Although home health services currently account for a small share of Medicaid expenditures for older adults, they are the fastest-growing expense.

LONG-TERM HEALTH CARE

One of the most urgent health care problems facing Americans today is the growing need for long-term care. Long-term care refers to health and social services for persons with chronic illnesses or mental or physical conditions so disabling that they cannot live independently without assistance—they require care on a daily basis. Longer life spans and improved life-sustaining technologies are increasing the likelihood that more people than ever before may eventually require costly, long-term care.

Limited and Expensive Options

Caring for chronically ill or elderly patients presents difficult and expensive choices for Americans: they must either provide long-term care at home or rely on nursing homes. Home health care was the fastest-growing segment of the health care industry during the first half of the 1990s. Although the rate of growth slowed during the late 1990s, the home health care sector was expected to more than double, from $29.3 billion to $68 billion by 2005.

The situation for disabled older adults who remain at home can be grim. Nine out of 10 must rely on their

TABLE 5.9

Medicaid recipients and medical vendor payments, according to type of service, selected fiscal years, 1972–98

[Data are compiled by the Centers for Medicare & Medicaid Services]

Type of Service	1972	1975	1980	1985	1990	1995	1996	1997	1998[1]
Recipients					Number in millions				
All recipients	17.6	22.0	21.6	21.8	25.3	36.3	36.1	34.9	40.6
					Percent of recipients				
Inpatient general hospitals	16.1	15.6	17.0	15.7	18.2	15.3	14.8	13.6	10.5
Inpatient mental hospitals	0.2	0.3	0.3	0.3	0.4	0.2	0.3	0.3	0.3
Mentally retarded intermediate care facilities	- - -	0.3	0.6	0.7	0.6	0.4	0.4	0.4	0.3
Nursing facilities	- - -	- - -	- - -	- - -	- - -	4.6	4.4	4.6	4.0
Skilled	3.1	2.9	2.8	2.5	2.4	- - -	- - -	- - -	- - -
Intermediate care	- - -	3.1	3.7	3.8	3.4	- - -	- - -	- - -	- - -
Physician	69.8	69.1	63.7	66.0	67.6	65.6	63.3	60.7	45.6
Dental	13.6	17.9	21.5	21.4	18.0	17.6	17.2	17.0	12.2
Other practitioner	9.1	12.1	15.0	15.4	15.3	15.2	14.8	14.7	10.7
Outpatient hospital	29.6	33.8	44.9	46.2	49.0	46.1	44.0	39.1	29.9
Clinic	2.8	4.9	7.1	9.7	11.1	14.7	14.0	13.5	13.0
Laboratory and radiological	20.0	21.5	14.9	29.1	35.5	36.0	34.9	31.8	23.1
Home health	0.6	1.6	1.8	2.5	2.8	4.5	4.8	5.3	3.0
Prescribed drugs	63.3	64.3	63.4	63.8	68.5	65.4	62.5	60.1	47.6
Family planning	. . .	5.5	5.2	7.5	6.9	6.9	6.6	6.0	4.9
Early and periodic screening	. . .	. . .	. . .	8.7	11.7	18.2	18.2	18.5	15.2
Rural health clinic	. . .	. . .	. . .	0.4	0.9	3.4	3.9	4.1	- - -
Prepaid health care	- - -	- - -	- - -	- - -	- - -	- - -	- - -	- - -	49.7
Other care	14.4	13.2	11.9	15.5	20.3	31.5	36.3	35.5	36.0
Vendor payments [2]					Amount in billions				
All payments	$6.3	$12.2	$23.3	$37.5	$64.9	$120.1	$121.7	$124.4	$142.3
Percent distribution									
Total	100.0	100.0	100.0	100.0	100.0	100.0	100.0	100.0	100.0
Inpatient general hospitals	40.6	27.6	27.5	25.2	25.7	21.9	20.7	18.6	15.1
Inpatient mental hospitals	1.8	3.3	3.3	3.2	2.6	2.1	1.7	1.6	2.0
Mentally retarded intermediate care facilities	- - -	3.1	8.5	12.6	11.3	8.6	7.9	7.9	6.7
Nursing facilities	- - -	- - -	- - -	- - -	- - -	24.2	24.3	24.5	22.4
Skilled	23.3	19.9	15.8	13.5	12.4	- - -	- - -	- - -	- - -
Intermediate care	- - -	15.4	18.0	17.4	14.9	- - -	- - -	- - -	- - -
Physician	12.6	10.0	8.0	6.3	6.2	6.1	5.9	5.7	4.3
Dental	2.7	2.8	2.0	1.2	0.9	0.8	0.8	0.8	0.6
Other practitioner	0.9	1.0	0.8	0.7	0.6	0.8	0.9	0.8	0.4
Outpatient hospital	5.8	3.0	4.7	4.8	5.1	5.5	5.3	5.0	4.0
Clinic	0.7	3.2	1.4	1.9	2.6	3.6	3.5	3.4	2.8
Laboratory and radiological	1.3	1.0	0.5	0.9	1.1	1.0	1.0	0.8	0.7
Home health.	0.4	0.6	1.4	3.0	5.2	7.8	8.9	9.8	1.9
Prescribed drugs	8.1	6.7	5.7	6.2	6.8	8.1	8.8	9.6	9.5
Family planning	. . .	0.5	0.3	0.5	0.4	0.4	0.4	0.3	0.3
Early and periodic screening	. . .	. . .	. . .	0.2	0.3	1.0	1.1	1.3	0.9
Rural health clinic	. . .	. . .	. . .	0.0	0.1	0.2	0.2	0.2	- - -
Prepaid health care	- - -	- - -	- - -	- - -	- - -	- - -	- - -	- - -	13.6
Other care	1.8	1.9	1.9	2.5	3.7	7.7	8.4	8.9	13.6
Vendor payments per recipient [2]					Amount				
Total payment per recipient	$358	$556	$1,079	$1,719	$2,568	$3,311	$3,369	$3,568	$3,501
Inpatient general hospitals	903	983	1,742	2,753	3,630	4,735	4,696	4,877	5,031
Inpatient mental hospitals	2,825	6,045	11,742	19,867	18,548	29,847	21,873	22,990	20,701
Mentally retarded intermediate care facilities	- - -	5,507	16,438	32,102	50,048	68,613	68,232	72,033	74,960
Nursing facilities	- - -	- - -	- - -	- - -	- - -	17,424	18,589	19,029	19,379
Skilled	2,665	3,864	6,081	9,274	13,356	- - -	- - -	- - -	- - -
Intermediate care	- - -	2,764	5,326	7,882	11,236	- - -	- - -	- - -	- - -
Physician	65	81	136	163	235	309	317	333	327
Dental	71	86	99	98	130	160	166	175	182
Other practitioner	37	48	61	75	96	178	205	190	135
Outpatient hospital	70	50	113	178	269	397	409	453	474
Clinic	82	358	209	337	602	804	833	902	742
Laboratory and radiological	23	27	38	53	80	90	96	93	100
Home health	229	204	847	2,094	4,733	5,740	6,293	6,575	2,206

TABLE 5.9

Medicaid recipients and medical vendor payments, according to type of service, selected fiscal years, 1972–98 [CONTINUED]

[Data are compiled by the Centers for Medicare & Medicaid Services]

Type of Service	1972	1975	1980	1985	1990	1995	1996	1997	1998[1]
Vendor payments per recipient [2]					Amount				
Prescribed drugs	46	58	96	166	256	413	474	571	699
Family planning	...	55	72	119	151	206	200	200	223
Early and periodic screening	...	...	...	45	67	177	212	251	216
Rural health clinic	...	...	...	81	154	174	215	213	- - -
Prepaid health care	- - -	- - -	- - -	- - -	- - -	- - -	- - -	- - -	955
Other care	44	80	172	274	465	807	782	891	1,331

- - - Data not available.
. . . Category not applicable.
[1]Prior to 1998 recipient counts exclude those individuals who only received coverage under prepaid health care and for whom no direct vendor payments were made during the year. Prior to 1998 vendor payments exclude payments to health maintenance organizations and other prepaid health plans ($19.3 billion in 1998 and $18 billion in 1997). The total number of persons who were Medicaid eligible and enrolled was 41.4 million in 1998, 41.6 million in 1997, and 41.2 million in 1996 (HCFA Medicaid Statistics, Program and Financial Statistics FY1996, FY1997, and FY1998, unpublished).
[2]Payments exclude disproportionate share hospital payments ($16 billion in 1997 and $15 billion in 1998).
Note: 1972 and 1975 data are for fiscal year ending June 30. All other years are for fiscal year ending September 30. Some numbers in this table have been revised and differ from the previous edition of *Health, United States*.

SOURCE: "Table 138. Medicaid recipients and medical vendor payments, according to type of service: United States, selected fiscal years 1972–98," in *Health, United States, 2002*, Centers for Disease Control, National Center for Health Statistics, Hyattsville, MD, 2002

families for some portion of their care, and 80 percent rely totally on their families, often creating tremendous financial and emotional drains. Women are usually the caregivers, whether the older adults are their own parents or their in-laws, and sometimes they must sacrifice their jobs and incomes to care for elderly dependents. Hiring an unskilled worker to care for the sick or elderly in the home can cost more than $25,000 a year; skilled in-home care is more expensive.

High Costs of Nursing Home Care

With the elderly population growing rapidly, the problems of long-term care and its costs have become urgent public policy and social issues. Nursing home care costs about $40,000 per year, and in some homes the costs can exceed $80,000 a year. Medicare does not cover routine nursing home care, and Medicaid is intended to cover expenses only for the poor. In 1999, the average daily charge was $116 and the average length of stay was 272 days. Table 5.10 shows average nursing home charges and sources of payment for nursing home services.

To be eligible for Medicaid, a person must have no more than $2,500 in assets. (In the case of a married couple where only one spouse is in a nursing home, the remaining spouse can retain a house, a car, up to $75,000 in assets, and $2,000 in monthly income.) Many elderly persons must "spend down" to deplete their entire life savings in order to qualify for Medicaid assistance.

Although the Medigap policies available through private insurers pay for some costs not covered by Medicare, most of these policies do not cover the average nursing home stay. Many older adults are eager to buy private insurance policies for long-term care. The average policy,

covering two years of care after a one-hundred-day waiting period, costs about $300 a month for a couple in which the husband is in his early seventies and the wife in her late sixties. For many older adults with fixed incomes, the cost of long-term care insurance prevents them from obtaining it.

Coverage provided by these private policies varies widely. Some insurers refuse to pay for the first 20 days in a nursing home, and others require a waiting period of 100 days before they will pay. Some offer coverage for only one year; others allow longer stays. Because of the variations and limitations on coverage, some policyholders have had their claims denied or their policies cancelled. The purchasers of such policies must be very careful to understand the specific provisions and terms of their benefits.

A combination of federal, state, and private monies finance nursing home care. According to the Administration on Aging (AoA), in 2000 almost half of the funds came from Medicaid, 25 percent were from Medicare, and the balance came from private payment and private insurance.

HIV/AIDS—Treatment Is Costly

HIV/AIDS treatment, like treatment of cancer and other chronic diseases, is expensive. Even though newer drug treatments—highly active antiretroviral therapy (HAART)—had higher per unit costs, their introduction in 1996 reduced total health care spending by reducing the rate of hospitalization and use of outpatient care. According to a study conducted by the Rand Corporation and published in the March 15, 2001 issue of the *New England Journal of Medicine*, the average HIV patient incurred costs of about $1,410 per month in 1998. In 1998 a year's worth of treatment for HIV could cost as much as

TABLE 5.10

Average daily charge and number of nursing home residents by primary expected source of payment in month before interview and selected facility characteristics, 1999

Facility characteristic	All sources		Private sources[1]		Medicare		Medicaid		All other sources[2]	
	Average daily charge	Number of residents	Average daily charge	Number of residents	Average daily charge	Number of residents	Average daily charge	Number of residents	Average daily charge	Number of residents
All residents	$115.91	1,628,300	$115.00	386,400	$166.37	238,700	$106.39	955,700	$110.98	47,400
Ownership										
Proprietary	107.17	1,049,300	115.68	211,700	128.22	149,000	100.37	659,900	114.12	28,700
Voluntary nonprofit	134.74	445,600	117.46	150,200	257.78	73,500	115.97	212,300	*124.35	*9,600
Government and other	121.14	133,300	95.45	24,600	143.01	16,100	127.82	83,500	*94.52	*9,100
Certification										
Certified										
By Medicare and Medicaid	120.79	1,415,400	121.40	304,600	172.06	219,800	109.77	854,400	126.55	36,500
By Medicare only	121.70	37,100	121.84	26,500	*128.25	*7,800	*	*	*	*
By Medicaid only	78.73	143,100	78.74	31,300	*82.74	*8,000	78.20	99,500	*	*
Not certified	70.42	32,700	77.64	24,100	*	*	*	*	*	*
Beds										
Fewer than 50 beds	104.76	58,600	100.71	23,600	113.05	9,300	107.39	24,900	*	*
50–99 beds	100.78	414,200	108.28	117,100	117.22	51,200	94.28	235,700	*98.14	*10,200
100–199 beds	119.78	827,800	119.19	179,900	200.06	124,600	104.78	504,800	112.85	18,500
200 beds or more	126.58	327,700	120.67	65,800	143.90	53,600	125.00	190,300	115.05	18,000
Geographic region										
Northeast	139.82	383,400	149.30	68,900	160.74	63,000	132.35	239,000	*149.76	*12,500
Midwest	117.90	498,200	103.53	163,900	247.14	66,400	99.64	254,800	116.85	13,100
South	95.35	531,500	101.73	102,100	113.30	79,400	90.81	337,400	78.45	*12,500
West	120.35	215,200	133.33	51,500	130.87	29,900	113.34	124,400	*112.74	*9,300
Location of agency										
Metropolitan statistical area	118.67	1,128,400	122.79	270,400	137.76	180,700	112.70	637,000	116.03	40,300
Nonmetropolitan statistical area	110.04	499,900	97.86	116,000	252.07	58,100	94.31	318,700	*74.11	*7,200
Affiliation[3]										
Chain	115.35	978,800	115.68	211,500	187.23	148,600	101.43	594,800	99.96	24,000
Independent	116.78	646,100	114.23	174,800	133.08	90,000	114.46	358,100	123.26	23,300

*Figure does not meet standard of reliability or precision because the sample size is less than 30. If shown with a number, it should not be assumed reliable because the sample size is between 30 and 59 or is greater than 59, but the estimate has a standard error over 30 percent.

[1]Includes private insurance, own income, family support, Social Security benefits, and retirement funds.

[2]Includes Supplemental Security Income (SSI), religious organizations, foundations, agencies, Veterans Administration (VA) contracts, pensions, or other VA compensation, payment source not yet determined, and other and unknown sources.

[3]Excludes unknown.

Note: Numbers may not add to totals because of rounding.

SOURCE: Adrienne Jones, "Table 12. Average daily charge and number of nursing home residents, by primary expected source of payment in month before interview by selected facility characteristics: United States, 1999," in *The National Nursing Home Survey: 1999 Summary*, National Health Care Survey, Centers for Disease Control and Prevention, Vital and Health Statistics, Series 13, No. 152, Hyattsville, MD, June 2002

$18,000 per patient. Persons with AIDS could spend up to $77,000 per year on medication alone.

Some HIV/AIDS patients rely on health insurance to help pay these costs, but many patients are not insured. Many policies exclude or deny coverage to persons with pre-existing conditions and as a result, many HIV-positive people are denied private health insurance.

Medicaid pays the costs of approximately half of all adults and nearly 90 percent of children living with HIV/AIDS, according to the Office of National AIDS Policy, a White House agency. Medicaid eligibility requirements vary from state to state; it generally covers people with incomes of less than $625 per month who cannot engage in substantial gainful employment due to physical or mental impairment that is expected to last at least one year or result in death. Medicaid programs vary widely by jurisdiction; many states supplement federal funding with state funds and each state determines not only the eligibility criteria for its program but also the benefits—the number and type of treatments—provided through the program.

Some expenses, however, have actually been reduced by relocating services from the hospital to a variety of outpatient settings. Examples of cost-saving services include outpatient transfusions and outpatient treatment for opportunistic infections such as *Pneumocystis carinii* pneumonia (PCP) and cryptococcal meningitis. Increased volunteer-based social service programs that enable patients to be cared for at home also serve to prevent prolonged, expensive hospital stays.

Federal government spending on HIV-related care and activities has increased steadily since 1985. In 2000 the Budget Office of the Public Health Service estimated that federal spending for HIV-related expenses was nearly $11 billion, $6.3 billion of which was spent on medical care. Other government costs included research ($2.1 billion), education and prevention ($1 billion), and cash assistance ($1.4 billion), which is provided through the Social Security Administration and the Department of Housing and Urban Development.

The High Costs of Research

Medical and pharmaceutical research to develop and conduct clinical trials of antiretroviral drugs is expensive. In 2002 the National Institutes of Health (NIH) spent an estimated $2.5 billion for HIV/AIDS research, while spending about $630 million to investigate breast cancer, and $263 million for research about stroke.

Decisions about how much is spent to research a particular disease are not based solely on how many people develop the disease or die from it. Rightly or wrongly, economists base the societal value of an individual on his or her earning potential and productivity—the ability to contribute to society as a worker. The bulk of the people who die from heart disease, stroke, and cancer are older adults. Many have retired from the workforce, and their potential economic productivity is usually low or even nil. (This is not an observation about how society values older adults; instead it is simply an economic measure of present and future financial productivity.)

In contrast, AIDS patients are usually much younger, dying in their twenties, thirties, and forties. Until they developed AIDS, their potential productivity, measured in economic terms, was high. The number of work years lost when they die is considerable. Using this economic equation to determine how disease research should be funded, it may be considered economically wise to invest more money to research AIDS since the losses, measured in potential work years rather than lives, is so much greater.

The primary goals of HIV/AIDS therapy are to prolong life and improve its quality. Few researchers expect any drug to cure HIV infection; their objective is to make the virus less deadly by foiling its efforts to reproduce within the body. A major obstacle to the discovery of such treatments is the cost of drug research and development. Pharmaceutical manufacturers spend millions of dollars researching and developing new medicines. According to the Pharmaceutical Research and Manufacturers of America, U.S. pharmaceutical companies spend more money each year on research and development activities than the annual budget of the NIH.

Once a new drug receives Federal Food and Drug Administration (FDA) approval, its manufacturer is ordinarily allowed to hold the patent on the drug in order to recoup its investment. During that time, the drug is priced much higher than if other manufacturers were allowed to compete by producing generic versions of the same drug. After the patent expires, competition between pharmaceutical manufacturers generally lowers the price. HIV/AIDS drugs are granted seven years of exclusivity under legislation aimed at encouraging research and promoting development of new treatments.

The pharmaceutical manufacturer must cover the cost not only of research and development for the approximately 3 out of 10 drugs that succeed, but also for many—7 out of 10—that have failed. In contrast, the producer of generic drugs has the formula and must simply manufacture the drugs properly. The generic manufacturer does not have to pay for successful and unsuccessful research and development of new drugs nor does it have to pursue the complicated, time-consuming process of seeking and obtaining FDA approval.

Cancer

Cancer, in all its forms, is extremely expensive to treat. Americans often resort to many different methods of treatment in search of a cure. In addition, it can be costly to treat the adverse side effects of radiation, chemotherapy, and other therapies. Pain management is also expensive for cancer patients. The National Institutes of Health (NIH) estimated the overall annual cost of cancer in 2000 as more than $180 billion, of which $60 billion goes for direct medical costs. The balance is indirect cost associated with lost productivity due to illness or death.

Generally, the younger a patient, the higher the cost, since younger patients can often fight the disease longer than older patients can. Most expenses for cancer treatment occur at the end of life: hospitalization for the initial phase of treatment costs only 38 percent as much as terminal care.

THE HARDSHIP OF HIGH HEALTH CARE COSTS ON FAMILIES

Families USA is a national, nonprofit, non-partisan consumer organization based in Washington, D.C., dedicated to achieving affordable, quality health care and long-term care for all American families. The organization describes itself as "the voice for American consumers," and contends that American families pay about two-thirds of the nation's health care bill, while American businesses pay the other third. This ratio is based on the premise that families and businesses pay for health care in several ways:

• Directly, through out-of-pocket payments and insurance expenses, such as premiums, deductibles (annual amounts that must be paid by the employee before the insurance plan begins paying), and copayments.

- Indirectly, through Medicare payroll, income, and other federal, state, and local taxes that support public health programs. These include veterans' health benefits, military health benefits, the Medicaid program, and a variety of smaller public health programs.

As a result, Families USA estimates of per capita health spending differ from other reports, such as those from the CMMS (formerly HCFA) and the U.S. Census Bureau, which take into account only direct payments.

Families also purchase insurance themselves when they work for employers that do not offer group health insurance, or when insurers refuse to insure certain groups they consider to be at high risk (such as persons with chronic diseases). Workers who retire before reaching age 65 and are not yet eligible for Medicare coverage also must purchase insurance on their own. Further, many Medicare beneficiaries pay insurance premiums for supplemental (Medigap) insurance to cover the difference in charges that Medicare does not pay, as well as uncovered costs, such as prescription drugs.

The High Cost of Prescription Drugs

Spending for prescription drugs is the fastest-growing component of health care spending. Families USA decried the escalating costs of prescription drugs in a study that found that between January 2001 and January 2002 the prices of the 50 most commonly prescribed drugs for older adults rose nearly three times the rate of inflation. Since many older adults live on fixed incomes, these dramatic price increases may prevent them from obtaining life-saving medications. The Families USA report *Bitter Pill: The Rising Prices of Prescription Drugs for Older Americans* (June 2002), observed that drug prices have outpaced inflation for at least a decade and that that generic drug prices rose more slowly than brand-name pharmaceuticals.

Families USA also refuted the pharmaceutical companies' claims that high drug prices simply reflect the companies' efforts to recoup their investments in drug research and development. Families USA asserted that prices for drugs that have been on the market for more than ten years continued to rise more sharply than the rate of inflation, long after the pharmaceutical companies should have regained their initial investments and realized substantial profits. Their 2001 analysis of the nine U.S. pharmaceutical companies that manufacture or market the 50 top-selling drugs for older adults revealed that profits consistently exceeded spending on research and development. Table 5.11 shows 2001 revenues for these pharmaceutical companies, and the percent of revenues devoted to marketing, advertising, administration, research and development, and profits.

To control prescription drug expenditures, many hospitals, health plans, employers, and other group pur-chasers have attempted to obtain discounts and rebates for bulk purchases from pharmaceutical companies. Some have developed programs to encourage health care practitioners and consumers to use less costly generic drugs and others have limited, reduced, or even eliminated prescription drug coverage.

MANY OLDER ADULTS CANNOT AFFORD PRESCRIPTION DRUGS. A survey of nearly 11,000 older adults in eight states conducted in 2001 by the Kaiser Family Foundation, the Commonwealth Fund, and Tufts-New England Medical Center found that cost prevented almost one quarter of all survey respondents from filling their prescriptions or caused them to skip doses of prescribed medications. The study also found that the percentage of all older adults surveyed who did not have prescription drug coverage varied among the eight states from highs of 31 percent in Illinois and Texas to lows of California (18 percent) and New York (19 percent).

Figure 5.3 shows the percentage of older adults in eight states at or 200 percent below the federal poverty level without prescription drug coverage in 2001. Michigan and Texas, with 38 percent each, had the highest rates of older adults without prescription drug coverage, and Illinois had the second highest percentage of persons without coverage, with 34 percent.

Figure 5.4 shows that in the same states, among those at or well below the federal poverty level, the percent of older adults who did not fill a prescription or skipped drug doses was considerably higher, with Ohio and Texas reporting 40 and 44 percent respectively. Medicaid beneficiaries with drug coverage fared better—the percent of older adults who skipped doses or did not fill prescriptions ranged from a low of 13 percent in Colorado to a high of 35 percent in Texas. (See Figure 5.5.)

RATIONING HEALTH CARE

When health care rationing—allocating medical resources—is defined as "all care that is expected to be beneficial is not always available to all patients," most health care practitioners, policymakers, and consumers accept that rationing has been, and will continue to be a feature of the American health care system. Most American opinion leaders and industry observers accept that even a country as wealthy as the United States cannot afford all the care that is likely to benefit its citizens. Today, the practical considerations of allocating health care resources involve establishing priorities and determining how these resources should be rationed.

Opponents of Rationing

There is widespread agreement among Americans that rationing according to patients' ability to pay for health care services or insurance is unfair. Ideally, health

TABLE 5.11

Revenue figures for corporations marketing the top 50 drugs for seniors, 2001

Company	Revenue (net sales in millions of dollars)	Percent of revenue allocated to:		
		Marketing/ advertising/ administration	R&D	Profit (net income)
Merck & Co., Inc.	$47,716	13%	5%	15%
Pfizer, Inc.	$32,259	35%	15%	24%
Bristol-Myers Squibb Company	$19,423	27%	12%	27%
Abbott Laboratories	$16,285	23%	10%	10%
Wyeth	$14,129	37%	13%	16%
Pharmacia Corporation	$13,837	44%	16%	11%
Eli Lilly & Co.	$11,543	30%	19%	24%
Schering-Plough Corporation	$9,802	36%	13%	20%
Allergan, Inc.	$1,685	42%	15%	13%
Total*	**$166,678**	**27%**	**11%**	**18%**
(Dollars in millions)		$45,413	$19,076	$30,599

*Totals may not add due to rounding.

SOURCE: "Table 1. 2001 Financials for U.S. Corporations Marketing the Top 50 Drugs for Seniors," in *Profiting from Pain: Where Prescription Drug Dollars Go,* Families USA Foundation, Washington DC, 2002

FIGURE 5.4

Percent of seniors in eight states with incomes at or below 200% of the poverty level who either didn't fill a prescription one or more times or skipped doses of a medicine to make it last longer, 2001

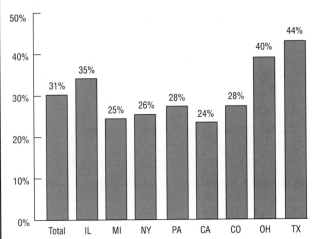

Note: Analysis of seniors in sample with classifiable drug coverage. States included in survey were California, Colorado, Illinois, Michigan, New York, Ohio, Pennsylvania, and Texas.

SOURCE: "Figure 17: Percent of Seniors in Eight States with Incomes at or Below 200% of Poverty Who Either Didn't Fill a Prescription One or More Times or Skipped Doses of a Medicine to Make it Last Longer," in *Seniors and Prescription Drugs: Findings from a 2001 Survey of Seniors in Eight States,* The Henry J. Kaiser Family Foundation, The Commonwealth Fund, and Tufts–New England Medical Center, 2002

FIGURE 5.3

Percent of seniors in eight states with incomes at or below 200% of the poverty level who lack drug coverage, 2001

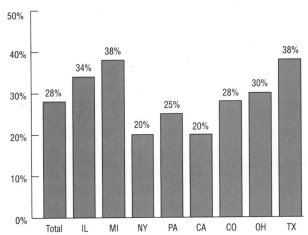

Note: Analysis of seniors in sample with classifiable drug coverage. States included in survey were California, Colorado, Illinois, Michigan, New York, Ohio, Pennsylvania, and Texas.

SOURCE: "Figure 6: Percent of Seniors in Eight States with Incomes at or Below 200% of Poverty Who Lack Drug Coverage," in *Seniors and Prescription Drugs: Findings from a 2001 Survey of Seniors in Eight States,* The Henry J. Kaiser Family Foundation, The Commonwealth Fund, and Tufts–New England Medical Center, 2002

FIGURE 5.5

Percent of seniors in eight states with Medicaid drug coverage who skipped doses of a medication or didn't fill a prescription one or more times, 2001

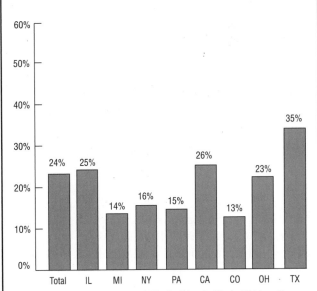

Note: States included in survey were California, Colorado, Illinois, Michigan, New York, Ohio, Pennsylvania, and Texas.

SOURCE: "Figure 21: Percent of Seniors in Eight States with Medicaid Drug Coverage Who Skipped Doses of a Medication or Didn't Fill a Prescription One or More Times," in *Seniors and Prescription Drugs: Findings from a 2001 Survey of Seniors in Eight States,* The Henry J. Kaiser Family Foundation, The Commonwealth Fund, and Tufts–New England Medical Center, 2002

care should be equitably allocated on the basis of need and the potential benefit derived from the care. Those who argue against rationing fear that society's most vulnerable populations—older adults, the poor, and persons with chronic illnesses—suffer most from the present rationing of health care.

Many observers believe that improving the efficiency of the U.S. health care system would save enough money to supply basic health care services to all Americans. They suggest that since expenditures for the same medical procedures vary greatly in different areas of the country, standardizing fees and costs could realize great savings. They also believe that money could be saved if greater emphasis was placed on preventive care and on effective strategies to prevent or reduce behaviors that increase health risk such as smoking, alcohol and drug abuse, and unsafe sexual practices. Further, they insist that the high cost of administering the American health system could be streamlined by using a single payer for health care—as in the Canadian system.

Supporters of Rationing

Those who endorse rationing argue that the spiraling cost of health care stems from more than simple inefficiency. They attribute escalating costs to the aging population, rapid technological innovation, and the increasing price tags for labor and supplies. Rationing supporters believe that the nation's health care system charges too much for the services it delivers, and that it fails altogether to deliver to millions of uninsured. In fact, they point out that the United States already rations health care by not covering the uninsured.

Some health care rationing advocates argue that the problem is one of basic cultural assumptions, not the economics of the health care industry. Americans value human life, believe in the promise of health and quality health care for all, and insist that diseases can be cured. They contend that the issue is not whether health care should be rationed but rather how care is rationed. They believe that the United States spends too much on health compared to other societal needs; too much on the old rather than the young; more on curing and not enough on caring; too much on extending the length of life and not enough on enhancing the quality of life. Supporters of rationing argue instead for a system that guarantees a minimally acceptable level of health care for all, while reining in the expensive excesses of the current system, which often acts to prolong life at any cost.

THE OREGON PLAN. In 1987 the state of Oregon designed a new, universal health care plan that would simultaneously expand coverage and contain costs by limiting services. Unlike other states, which trimmed budgets by eliminating people from Medicaid eligibility, Oregon chose to eliminate low-priority services. The Oregon Health Plan, approved in August 1993, aimed to provide

Medicaid to 120,000 additional residents living below the federal poverty level. The plan also established a high risk insurance pool for persons refused health insurance coverage because of pre-existing medical conditions, offered more insurance options for small businesses, and improved employees' abilities to retain their health insurance benefits when they changed jobs. A 10-cent increase in the state cigarette tax (providing approximately $45 million annually) helped fund the additional estimated $400 million needed over the next several years.

Oregon developed a table of health care services and performed a cost-benefit analysis to rank them. (See Figure 5.6.) It was decided that Oregon Medicaid would cover the top 565 services on a list of 696 medical procedures. Services that fell below the cutoff point and thus would not be covered included liver transplants for patients with liver cancer; nutritional counseling for obese people; fertility services; and treatment for the common cold, chronic back pain, and viral hepatitis.

When setting the priorities, disease prevention and quality of life were the factors that most influenced the ranking of the treatments. Quality of life (quality of well being, or QWB, in the Oregon plan) drew fire from those who felt such judgments could not be decided subjectively. Active medical or surgical treatment of terminally ill patients also ranked low on the QWB scale, while comfort and hospice care ranked high. The Oregon Health Services Commission emphasized that their QWB judgments were not based on an individual's quality of life at a given time; such judgments were considered ethically questionable. Instead they focused on the potential for change in an individual's life, posing questions such as, "After treatment, how much better or worse off would the patient be?"

Critics countered that the plan obtained its funding by reducing services that were currently offered to Medicaid recipients (often poor women and children) rather than by emphasizing cost control. Others objected to the ranking and the ethical questions raised by choosing to support some treatments over others.

By 1998 the Oregon Health Plan had encountered major problems. The state was no longer promising universal care; physicians were seeking and finding ways to get around the rationing restrictions; and friction with federal Medicaid regulators was blocking Oregon's efforts to deny more treatments. A plan to require that employers insure all their workers or contribute to a fund to cover them failed. Spending for the health plan climbed to $2.1 billion in the 1997–99 state budget period, up from $1.7 billion in the 1995–97 period. Higher cigarette taxes did not offset the increase, requiring more money from the state's general fund.

The Oregon Health Plan did serve to reduce the percentage of uninsured Oregonians, from 17 percent in 1992 to 11 percent in 1996, placing Oregon among the states with the lowest rates of uninsured residents. Still by 1998, five years after the Oregon plan was initiated with the goal of having no uninsured people in the state, coverage was far from universal. Despite the Oregon plan's best efforts, there were still approximately 350,000 people in Oregon who had no insurance. The plan's supporters observed that the downward trend in the rates of uninsured was a measure of the plan's success and hailed the state's pioneering efforts.

In 2001 the Oregon Health Plan was given a three-year grant of nearly $1.5 million from the Robert Wood Johnson Foundation, the nation's largest philanthropy devoted solely to health and health care, to help expand coverage to new populations within the state. The grant money acknowledges the success of the Oregon plan and supports statewide research and evaluation as the state moves to cover more people. During 2001 the Robert Wood Johnson Foundation also recognized the innovative and successful efforts of Arkansas, New Mexico, and Rhode Island to improve health care coverage for their residents.

The Oregon Health Services Commission (HSC) continued to modify the plan's covered benefits. The Commission's most recent effort to refine the list of covered services began in January 2002. The HSC sought to reduce the overall costs of the plan by eliminating less effective treatments and determining if any covered medical conditions could be more effectively treated using standardized clinical practice guidelines (step-by-step instructions for diagnosis and treatment of specific illnesses or disorders) while preserving basic coverage. The benefit review process will be ongoing with the HSC submitting a new prioritized list of benefits on July 1 of each even-numbered year for review by legislative assembly.

Rationing by HMOs

Until 2000, steadily increasing numbers of Americans received their health care from health maintenance organizations (HMOs) or other managed care systems. By 1999 national enrollment in HMOs topped 81 million, nearly four times as many as were enrolled just a decade earlier (21 million). However, the number of enrollees declined during 2000 (78.9 million enrollees) and in July 2001 HMO enrollment was down to 78 million. The number of HMOs operating in the United States also dropped from 560 in July 2000 to 531 in 2002.

Managed care programs have sought to control costs by limiting coverage for expensive experimental, duplicative, and unnecessary treatments. Before physicians can perform experimental procedures or prescribe new treatment plans, they must obtain prior authorization—approval from the patient's managed care plan to ensure that the expenses will be covered.

Increasingly, patients and physicians are battling HMOs for approval to use and receive reimbursement for

FIGURE 5.6

Health care service categories and rankings

Rank	Category ID No.
"Essential" Services	
1. Acute fatal, prevents death, full recovery	15
Examples: Repair of deep, open wound of neck. Appendectomy for appendicitis. Medical therapy for myocarditis.	
2. Maternity care (including care for newborn in first 28 days of life)	12
Examples: Obstetrical care for pregnancy. Medical therapy for drug reactions and intoxications specific to newborn. Medical therapy for low birthweight babies.	
3. Acute fatal, prevents death, w/o full recovery	16
Examples: Surgical treatment for head injury with prolonged loss of consciousness. Medical therapy for acute bacterial meningitis. Reduction of an open fracture of a joint.	
4. Preventive care for children	01
Examples: Immunizations. Medical therapy for streptococcal sore throat and scarlet fever (reduces disability, prevents spread). Screening for specific problems such as vision or hearing problems, or anemia.	
5. Chronic fatal, improves life span and QWB (Quality of Well-Being)	20
Examples: Medical therapy for Type I Diabetes Mellitus. Medical and surgical treatment for treatable cancer of the uterus. Medical therapy for asthma.	
6. Reproductive services (excluding maternity and infertility)	13
Examples: Contraceptive management, vasectomy, tubal ligation.	
7. Comfort care	26
Example: Palliative therapy for conditions in which death is imminent.	
8. Preventive dental (children and adults)	03/07
Example: Cleaning and flouride.	
9. Preventive care for adults (A-B-C)	04
Examples: Mammograms, blood pressure screening, medical therapy and chemoprophylaxis for primary tuberculosis.	
"Very Important" Services	
10. Acute nonfatal, return to previous health	17
Examples: Medical therapy for acute thyroiditis. Medical therapy for vaginitis. Restorative dental service for dental caries.	
11. Chronic nonfatal, one time treatment improves QWB	23
Examples: Hip replacement. Laser surgery for diabetic retinopathy. Medical therapy for rheumatic fever.	
12. Acute nonfatal, w/o return to previous health	18
Examples: Relocation of dislocation of elbow. Arthroscopic repair of internal derangement of knee. Repair of corneal laceration.	
13. Chronic nonfatal, repetitive treatment improves QWB	24
Examples: Medical therapy for chronic sinusitis. Medical therapy for migraine. Medical therapy for psoriasis.	
Services "Valuable to Certain Individuals"	
14. Acute nonfatal, expedites recovery	19
Examples: Medical therapy for diaper rash. Medical therapy for acute conjunctivitis. Medical therapy for acute pharyngitis.	
15. Infertility services	14
Examples: Medical therapy for anovulation. Microsurgery for tubal disease. In-vitro fertilization.	
16. Preventive care for adults (D-E)	05
Examples: Dipstick urinalysis for hematuria in adults less than 60 years of age. Sigmoidoscopy for persons less than 40 years of age. Screening of nonpregnant adults for Type I Diabetes Mellitus.	
17. Fatal or nonfatal, minimal or no improvement in QWB (non-self-limited)	25
Examples: Repair fingertip avulsion that does not include fingernail. Medical therapy for gallstones without cholecystitis. Medical therapy for viral warts.	

SOURCE: "Health care service categories and rankings," in Oregon Basic Health Services Program, February 22, 1991

new technology and experimental treatments. Judges and juries, moved by the desperate situations of patients, have generally decided cases against HMOs, regardless of whether the new treatment had been shown to be effective.

"SILENT RATIONING." Physicians and health care consumers are concerned that limiting coverage for new, high-cost technology will discourage research and development for new treatments before they have even been developed. This has been called "silent rationing," because patients will never know what they have missed.

While new technology is thought to contribute heavily to the growth of the nation's health care bill, its precise toll is unknown. Some estimates have put the share at 30–50 percent. Yet, new technologies often save money by increasing the efficiency and effectiveness of medical care. These savings may, however, be offset when the new technology increases the volume of services delivered, resulting in an increase in total spending.

In an effort to control costs, some HMOs have discouraged physicians from informing patients about certain treatment options—those that are very expensive or not covered by the HMO. This has proved to be a highly controversial issue, both politically and ethically. In December 1996 HHS ruled that HMOs and other health plans cannot prevent physicians from telling Medicare patients about all available treatment options.

IS LESS HEALTH CARE BETTER THAN MORE?. Although health care providers and consumers fear that rationing that sharply limits access to medical care will ultimately result in poorer health among affected Americans, researchers are also concerned about the effects of too much care on the health of the nation. Several recent studies suggest that an oversupply of medical care may be as harmful as an under-supply. They assert that supply appears to drive demand—in areas with more physicians and hospitals, people visit physicians more often and spend more days in hospitals with no apparent improvement in their health status.

Dr. John Wennberg, a physician and epidemiologist, and his colleagues at Dartmouth Medical School found tremendous regional variation in both utilization and the cost of health care that the researchers believe is explained, at least in part, by the distribution of health care providers. In an article published in the March 2002 issue of *Health Affairs,* Dr. Wennberg also suggests that variations in physicians' practice styles—whether they favor outpatient treatment over hospitalization for specific procedures such as biopsies (surgical procedures to examine tissue to detect cancer cells)—greatly affects demand for hospital care.

Variation in demand for health care services in turn produces variation in health care expenditures. Dr. Wennberg and his colleagues reported wide geographic variation in Medicare spending. Medicare paid more than twice as much to care for a 65-year old in Miami where the supply of health care providers is overabundant as it spent on care for a 65-year old in Minneapolis, a city with an average supply of health care providers. To be certain that the difference was not simply higher fees and charges in Miami, the investigators also compared rates of utilization and found that older adults in Miami visited physicians and hospitals much more often than their counterparts in Minneapolis.

The researchers also wanted to be sure that the differences were not caused by the severity of illness, so they compared care during the last six months of life to control for any underlying regional differences in the health of the population. Remarkably, the widest variations were observed in care during the last six months of life when older adults in Miami saw physician specialists six times as often as those in Minneapolis. Dr. Wennberg, who has studied variations in health service utilization for more than two decades, asserted that higher expenditures, particularly at the end of life, do not purchase better care. Instead they finance generally unpleasant and futile interventions intended to prolong life rather than improve the quality of patients' lives.

The researchers concluded that areas with more medical care, higher utilization, and higher costs fared no better in terms of life expectancy, morbidity, or mortality, and the care they received was no different in quality from care received by persons in areas with average supplies of health care providers. The Dartmouth research and similar studies pose two important and as yet unanswered questions: "How much health care is needed to deliver the best health to a population?" and "Are Americans getting the best value for the dollars spent on health care?"

CHAPTER 6

INSURANCE—THOSE WITH AND THOSE WITHOUT

In 1798 Congress established the U.S. Marine Hospital Services for seamen. It was the first time an employer offered health insurance in the United States. Payments for hospital services were deducted from the sailors' salaries.

Today, many factors affect the availability of health insurance, including employment, income, personal health status, and age. As a result, an individual's or family's health insurance status often changes as circumstances change. In 2001, 7 of every 10 Americans (70.9 percent) were covered during all or some part of the year by private insurance, mostly through their employers (62.6 percent). Medicare, the government's health insurance program for older adults and persons with disabilities, covered 13.5 percent of Americans, and Medicaid, the government health insurance program for the poor, covered 11.2 percent. (See Figure 6.1.) (Note that percentages come close to 100 percent because some persons are covered by more than one type of insurance program, yet in 2001 14.6 percent of people were not covered by any type of insurance.)

In 2001, the 14.6 percent of the American population without health coverage showed a slight increase from the 14.2 percent uninsured in 2000, but a decrease from the 16.3 percent uninsured in 1998. (See Table 6.1.) The year 1998 was the first year since 1987 that the share of the population without health insurance declined. In the 11-year period from 1987 (the first year comparable health statistics were available) to 1998, the uninsured rate either increased or remained unchanged from one year to the next. The number of uninsured children dropped in 2000, from 12.6 percent in 1999 to 11.6 percent (Robert J. Mills, "Health Insurance Coverage 2000," in *Current Population Reports*, U.S. Census Bureau, September 2001).

WHO WAS UNINSURED IN 2000?

Not surprisingly, the poor were the income group most likely to be without insurance coverage. In 2001,

FIGURE 6.1

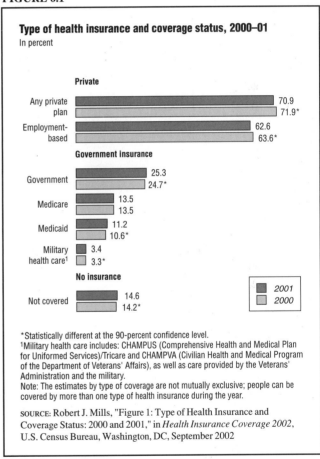

Type of health insurance and coverage status, 2000–01
In percent

*Statistically different at the 90-percent confidence level.
[1]Military health care includes: CHAMPUS (Comprehensive Health and Medical Plan for Uniformed Services)/Tricare and CHAMPVA (Civilian Health and Medical Program of the Department of Veterans' Affairs), as well as care provided by the Veterans' Administration and the military.
Note: The estimates by type of coverage are not mutually exclusive; people can be covered by more than one type of health insurance during the year.

SOURCE: Robert J. Mills, "Figure 1: Type of Health Insurance and Coverage Status: 2000 and 2001," in *Health Insurance Coverage 2002*, U.S. Census Bureau, Washington, DC, September 2002

30.7 percent of the nation's poor went without insurance. (See Figure 6.2 and Table 6.2.) Across every demographic category—age, race, citizenship status, education, and work experience—higher proportions of the nation's poor were uninsured in 2001.

Gender, Age, and Race/Ethnicity

More males than females lacked insurance in 2001— 15.8 percent of males lacked insurance, compared to 13.5

TABLE 6.1

People without health insurance for the entire year by selected characteristics, 2000–01

Numbers in thousands

| Characteristic | 2001 | | | | 2000 | | | | Difference, 2001 less 2000[1] | | |
| | | Uninsured | | | | Uninsured | | | | Uninsured | |
	Total	Number	Percent[1]	Percent 90-pct C.I. (±)	Total	Number	Percent[1]	Percent 90-pct C.I. (±)	Number	Percent	Percent 90-pct C.I. (±)
People											
Total	282,082	41,207	14.6	0.2	279,517	39,804	14.2	0.2	*1,403	*0.4	0.1
Sex											
Male	137,871	21,722	15.8	0.2	136,559	20,791	15.2	0.2	*931	*0.5	0.2
Female	144,211	19,485	13.5	0.2	142,958	19,013	13.3	0.2	*472	*0.2	0.2
Race and Ethnicity											
White	230,071	31,193	13.6	0.2	228,208	30,075	13.2	0.2	*1,118	*0.4	0.1
Non-Hispanic	194,822	19,409	10.0	0.2	193,931	18,683	9.6	0.2	*726	*0.3	0.1
Black	36,023	6,833	19.0	0.3	35,597	6,683	18.8	0.3	150	0.2	0.5
Asian and Pacific Islander	12,500	2,278	18.2	0.7	12,693	2,287	18.0	0.7	−9	0.2	0.8
Hispanic[2]	37,438	12,417	33.2	0.3	36,093	11,883	32.9	0.3	*534	0.2	0.4
Age											
Under 18 years	72,628	8,509	11.7	0.2	72,314	8,617	11.9	0.2	−108	−0.2	0.2
18 to 24 years	27,312	7,673	28.1	0.5	26,815	7,406	27.6	0.5	*267	0.5	0.6
25 to 34 years	38,670	9,051	23.4	0.3	38,865	8,507	21.9	0.3	*544	*1.5	0.4
35 to 44 years	44,284	7,131	16.1	0.3	44,566	6,898	15.5	0.3	*233	*0.6	0.4
45 to 64 years	65,419	8,571	13.1	0.2	63,391	8,124	12.8	0.2	*447	*0.3	0.3
65 years and over	33,769	272	0.8	0.2	33,566	251	0.7	0.2	21	0.1	0.1
Nativity											
Native	249,629	30,364	12.2	0.2	247,706	29,529	11.9	0.2	*835	*0.2	0.1
Foreign born	32,453	10,843	33.4	0.5	31,811	10,275	32.3	0.5	*568	*1.1	0.6
Naturalized citizen	11,962	2,060	17.2	0.7	11,785	1,930	16.4	0.7	*131	*0.9	0.8
Not a citizen	20,491	8,782	42.9	0.7	20,026	8,345	41.7	0.7	*437	*1.2	0.8
Region											
Northeast	53,300	6,399	12.0	0.2	53,046	6,372	12.0	0.2	27	—	0.3
Midwest	63,779	6,840	10.7	0.2	63,631	6,703	10.5	0.2	136	0.2	0.2
South	100,652	16,712	16.6	0.2	99,420	16,000	16.1	0.2	*712	*0.5	0.3
West	64,351	11,257	17.5	0.3	63,420	10,728	16.9	0.3	*528	*0.6	0.3
Household Income											
Less than $25,000	62,209	14,474	23.3	0.3	61,792	14,094	22.8	0.3	*380	*0.5	0.4
$25,000 to $49,999	76,226	13,516	17.7	0.2	77,084	13,385	17.4	0.2	131	*0.4	0.3
$50,000 to $74,999	58,114	6,595	11.3	0.2	59,089	6,513	11.0	0.2	81	*0.3	0.3
$75,000 or more	85,532	6,623	7.7	0.2	81,553	5,812	7.1	0.2	*811	*0.6	0.2
Education											
(18 years and older)											
Total	209,454	32,698	15.6	0.2	207,203	31,186	15.1	0.2	*1,512	*0.6	0.2
No high school diploma	35,423	9,776	27.6	0.5	34,994	9,406	26.9	0.5	*370	*0.7	0.5
High school graduate only	66,682	11,618	17.4	0.3	66,327	11,137	16.8	0.3	*481	*0.6	0.3
Some college, no degree	40,282	5,815	14.4	0.3	40,298	5,400	13.4	0.3	*415	*1.0	0.4
Associate degree	16,183	1,754	10.8	0.5	16,075	1,721	10.7	0.5	34	0.1	0.5
Bachelor's degree or higher	50,884	3,734	7.3	0.2	49,510	3,522	7.1	0.2	*212	0.2	0.2
Work Experience											
(18 to 64 years old)											
Total	175,685	32,426	18.5	0.2	173,638	30,935	17.8	0.2	*1,491	*0.6	0.2
Worked during year	142,474	24,230	17.0	0.2	142,447	23,525	16.5	0.2	*704	*0.5	0.2
Worked full-time	118,776	19,014	16.0	0.2	119,067	18,707	15.7	0.2	307	*0.3	0.3
Worked part-time	23,698	5,216	22.0	0.5	23,381	4,818	20.6	0.5	*398	*1.4	0.7
Did not work	33,211	8,197	24.7	0.5	31,190	7,410	23.8	0.5	*787	*0.9	0.6

—Represents zero or rounds to zero.
*Statistically significant at the 90-percent confidence level.
[1]All numbers are derived from unrounded numbers. Some numbers and percentages may therefore appear to be slightly higher or lower than those computed with rounded figures from other columns.
[2]Hispanics may be of any race.
Note: C.I. is confidence interval.

SOURCE: Robert J. Mills, "Table 1. People Without Health Insurance for the Entire Year by Selected Characteristics: 2000 and 2001," in *Health Insurance Coverage 2001*, U.S. Census Bureau, Washington, DC, September 2002

FIGURE 6.2

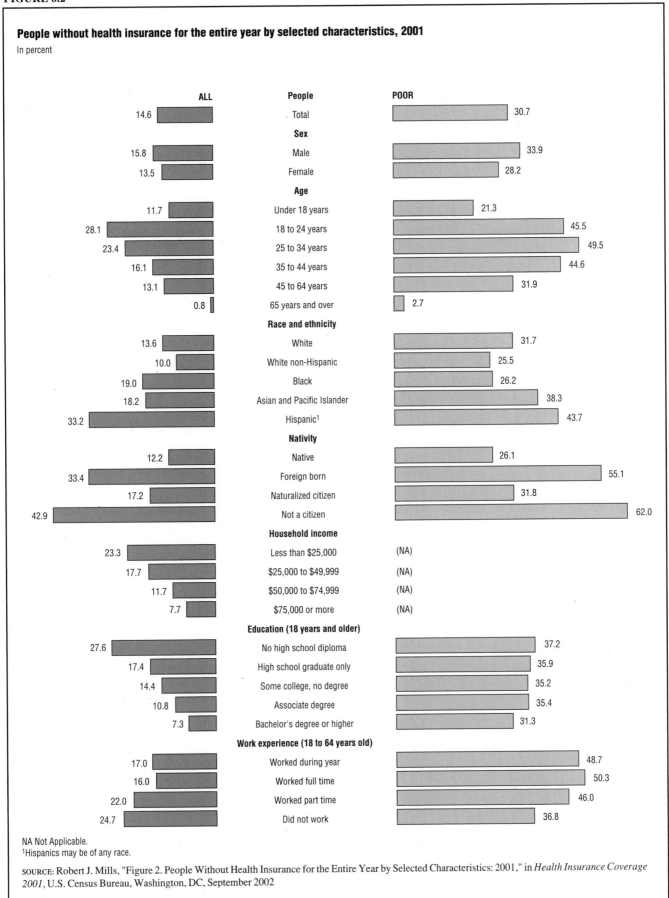

People without health insurance for the entire year by selected characteristics, 2001

In percent

	ALL	People	POOR	
14.6		Total	30.7	
		Sex		
15.8		Male	33.9	
13.5		Female	28.2	
		Age		
11.7		Under 18 years	21.3	
28.1		18 to 24 years	45.5	
23.4		25 to 34 years	49.5	
16.1		35 to 44 years	44.6	
13.1		45 to 64 years	31.9	
0.8		65 years and over	2.7	
		Race and ethnicity		
13.6		White	31.7	
10.0		White non-Hispanic	25.5	
19.0		Black	26.2	
18.2		Asian and Pacific Islander	38.3	
33.2		Hispanic[1]	43.7	
		Nativity		
12.2		Native	26.1	
33.4		Foreign born	55.1	
17.2		Naturalized citizen	31.8	
42.9		Not a citizen	62.0	
		Household income		
23.3		Less than $25,000	(NA)	
17.7		$25,000 to $49,999	(NA)	
11.7		$50,000 to $74,999	(NA)	
7.7		$75,000 or more	(NA)	
		Education (18 years and older)		
27.6		No high school diploma	37.2	
17.4		High school graduate only	35.9	
14.4		Some college, no degree	35.2	
10.8		Associate degree	35.4	
7.3		Bachelor's degree or higher	31.3	
		Work experience (18 to 64 years old)		
17.0		Worked during year	48.7	
16.0		Worked full time	50.3	
22.0		Worked part time	46.0	
24.7		Did not work	36.8	

NA Not Applicable.
[1]Hispanics may be of any race.

SOURCE: Robert J. Mills, "Figure 2. People Without Health Insurance for the Entire Year by Selected Characteristics: 2001," in *Health Insurance Coverage 2001*, U.S. Census Bureau, Washington, DC, September 2002

TABLE 6.2

Poor people without health insurance for the entire year by selected characteristics, 2000 and 2001

(Numbers in thousands.)

Characteristic	Total	2001 Uninsured			Total	2000 Uninsured			Difference, 2001 less 2000[1] Uninsured		
		Number	Percent[1]	Percent 90-pct C.I. (±)		Number	Percent[1]	Percent 90-pct C.I. (±)	Number	Percent	Percent 90-pct C.I. (±)
People											
Total	32,907	10,093	30.7	1.0	31,581	9,548	30.2	1.0	*545	0.4	1.0
Sex											
Male	14,327	4,854	33.9	1.5	13,536	4,461	33.0	2.1	*393	0.9	2.0
Female	18,580	5,239	28.2	1.3	18,045	5,086	28.2	1.3	152	—	1.3
Race and Ethnicity											
White	22,739	7,206	31.7	1.2	21,645	6,804	31.4	1.2	*402	0.3	1.3
Non-Hispanic	15,271	3,893	25.5	1.3	14,366	3,576	24.9	1.3	*316	0.6	1.4
Black	8,136	2,131	26.2	1.8	7,982	2,038	25.5	1.8	93	0.7	1.9
Asian and Pacific Islander	1,275	489	38.3	5.1	1,258	464	36.8	5.1	25	1.5	5.4
Hispanic[2]	7,997	3,496	43.7	2.1	7,747	3,356	43.3	2.1	140	0.4	1.8
Age											
Under 18 years	11,733	2,497	21.3	1.3	11,587	2,602	22.5	1.3	−106	−1.2	1.3
18 to 24 years	4,449	2,025	45.5	1.8	4,036	1,793	44.4	1.8	*232	1.1	1.9
25 to 34 years	4,255	2,108	49.5	1.8	4,087	1,968	48.1	1.8	*140	1.4	1.9
35 to 44 years	3,822	1,703	44.6	1.8	3,660	1,568	42.8	2.0	*135	1.7	2.0
45 to 64 years	5,234	1,669	31.9	1.5	4,887	1,527	31.2	1.5	*142	0.6	1.6
65 years and over	3,414	91	2.7	0.7	3,323	88	2.7	0.7	2	—	0.7
Nativity											
Native	27,698	7,223	26.1	1.0	26,680	6,904	25.9	1.0	318	0.2	1.1
Foreign born	5,209	2,870	55.1	3.0	4,901	2,643	53.9	3.1	227	1.2	3.2
Naturalized citizen	1,186	377	31.8	5.8	1,060	349	32.9	6.3	28	−1.1	6.3
Not a citizen	4,023	2,493	62.0	3.3	3,841	2,294	59.7	3.5	199	2.2	3.5
Region											
Northeast	5,687	1,504	26.4	2.1	5,474	1,255	22.9	2.0	*249	*3.5	2.2
Midwest	5,966	1,546	25.9	2.0	5,916	1,573	26.6	2.1	−26	−0.7	2.2
South	13,515	4,366	32.3	1.6	12,705	4,183	32.9	1.6	183	−0.6	1.7
West	7,739	2,677	34.6	2.3	7,485	2,537	33.9	2.3	140	0.7	2.4
Education											
(18 years and older)											
Total	21,174	7,596	35.9	1.3	19,994	6,945	34.7	1.3	*651	1.1	1.3
No high school diploma	8,033	2,992	37.2	2.0	7,865	2,841	36.1	2.0	150	1.1	2.1
High school graduate only	7,029	2,523	35.9	2.1	6,536	2,282	34.9	2.3	*241	1.0	2.3
Some college, no degree	3,392	1,194	35.2	3.1	3,040	1,022	33.6	3.3	*172	1.6	3.3
Associate degree	886	314	35.4	6.1	870	266	30.6	5.9	48	4.8	6.3
Bachelor's degree or higher	1,832	574	31.3	4.1	1,684	534	31.7	4.3	40	−0.4	4.4
Work Experience											
(18 to 64 years old)											
Total	17,760	7,506	42.3	1.5	16,671	6,857	41.1	1.5	*649	1.1	1.5
Worked during year	8,172	3,978	48.7	2.1	8,100	3,692	45.6	2.1	*286	*3.1	2.2
Worked full-time	5,121	2,575	50.3	2.6	5,088	2,485	48.8	2.6	90	1.5	2.8
Worked part-time	3,051	1,403	46.0	3.5	3,012	1,208	40.1	3.5	*195	*5.9	3.6
Did not work	9,588	3,528	36.8	1.8	8,571	3,165	36.9	2.0	*363	−0.1	2.0

—Represents zero or rounds to zero.
*Statistically significant at the 90-percent confidence level.
[1]All numbers are derived from unrounded numbers. Some numbers and percentages may therefore appear to be slightly higher or lower than those computed with rounded figures from other columns.
[2]Hispanics may be of any race.
Note: C.I. is confidence interval.

SOURCE: Robert J. Mills, "Table 2. Poor People Without Health Insurance for the Entire Year by Selected Characteristics: 2000 and 2001," in *Health Insurance Coverage 2001*, U.S. Census Bureau, Washington, DC, September 2002

percent of females. (See Table 6.1.) As would be expected, those age 65 and over were most likely to be covered by insurance, since almost all of them qualified for Medicare. (Some older adults also qualified for Medicaid.) Less than 1 percent of those over 65 went without health insurance in 2001. Persons 18 to 24 years of age were the least likely to have insurance coverage—28.1 percent of Americans in that age group lacked health insurance in 2001. Hispanics were more likely than those of other ethnicities to be uninsured (33.2 percent), followed by blacks (19 percent), and Asians and Pacific Islanders (18.2 percent). Only 10 percent of non-Hispanic whites had no coverage. (See Figure 6.2.)

While only 12.2 percent of native-born Americans went without coverage in 2001, 33.4 percent of foreign-born persons went uninsured. Those who were not citizens had an even higher chance of going uninsured—42.9 percent lacked health insurance in 2001. (See Table 6.1.)

Effects of Education Level, Income, and Employment

Education levels and health coverage are closely related. Generally, the better educated a person, the more likely he or she is to have a job that offers health insurance and other benefits. In 2001 those who had not completed high school were nearly four times as likely to be uninsured as those who held a bachelor's or higher degree (27.6 percent versus 7.3 percent). (See Table 6.1.)

As household income increases, the chances of being uninsured drop dramatically. Figure 6.2 shows the 2001 percentages of uninsured persons according to income level and other selected characteristics. While only 7.7 percent of individuals with an income of $75,000 or more lacked insurance, 23.3 percent of those with incomes under $25,000 were uninsured. The same was true in 1999—only 7 percent of high-income individuals were uninsured, while 23.2 percent of Americans in the lowest income bracket went without insurance.

Not surprisingly, persons who worked full-time were most likely to have health insurance. In 2001 about 16 percent of full-time workers were uninsured, compared to 22 percent of part-time workers and 24.7 percent of those who did not work. (See Table 6.1.) Among the poor population however, the percentage of uninsured workers, even those who worked full-time, was considerably higher—50.3 percent of poor full-time workers were uninsured in 2001. (See Figure 6.2.)

About 56.3 percent of workers age 18–64 had insurance coverage through their employer. Large companies were more likely to provide health insurance coverage than were smaller firms. Employees of firms with 1,000 or more workers were more than twice as likely to receive health insurance benefits as those in firms with 25 or fewer employees (69.6 and 31.3 percent, respectively). (See Figure 6.3.) Many small firms claim they cannot afford health insurance for their employees. Insurers charge higher premiums for small firms because of the higher administrative costs of small groups.

SOURCES OF HEALTH INSURANCE

Persons under Age 65

For persons under age 65, there are two principal sources of health insurance coverage: private insurance (from employers or private policies) and Medicaid (the government program for low-income or disabled persons). From 1984 to 1994, the proportion of those covered by private insurance declined from 77.1 to 70.3 percent. (See Table 6.3.) During this time, the percentage covered by Medicaid increased (from 6.7 percent in 1984 to 11 percent in 1994) and the proportion of uninsured increased (from 14.3 percent in 1984 to 16.8 percent in 1994). (See Table 6.4

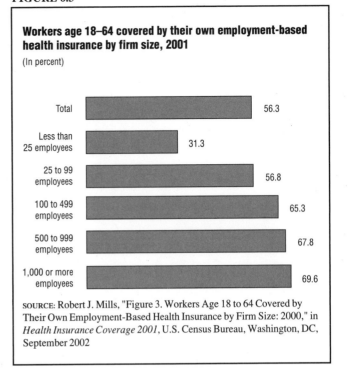

FIGURE 6.3

Workers age 18–64 covered by their own employment-based health insurance by firm size, 2001

(In percent)

Total	56.3
Less than 25 employees	31.3
25 to 99 employees	56.8
100 to 499 employees	65.3
500 to 999 employees	67.8
1,000 or more employees	69.6

SOURCE: Robert J. Mills, "Figure 3. Workers Age 18 to 64 Covered by Their Own Employment-Based Health Insurance by Firm Size: 2000," in *Health Insurance Coverage 2001*, U.S. Census Bureau, Washington, DC, September 2002

and Table 6.5.) The percentage of those privately insured remained between 70.9 and 72.9 percent in the years from 1995 to 2000, while those on Medicaid decreased (from 11.3 percent in 1995 to 9.4 in 2000). Persons under 65 without health insurance accounted for 16.8 percent of the population in 2000, up from 14.3 percent in 1984, but down from a high of 17.4 in 1997. (See Table 6.5.)

In 2000 the National Center for Health Statistics estimated that about 71.7 percent of the under-65 population had private health policies, with 67 percent covered through the workplace, a decrease from the 68.1 percent covered by employers in 1999. (See Table 6.3.) Although the percentage of persons who received health insurance coverage through the workplace rose slowly from 1994 to 1999, it did not rise to levels observed during the 1980s when close to 70 percent of workers obtained private insurance through their employers. Considerable variation by geographic region persists, with workers in the Northeast (72.2 percent) more likely to receive private insurance at the workplace than those in the West (61.1 percent) in 2000.

Three major factors contributed to the long-term decline in private health insurance. The first is the rising cost of health care, which frequently leads to greater cost sharing between employers and employees. Some workers simply can not afford the higher premiums and copayments (the share of medical bills the employee pays for each health service). A second factor is the shift in American commerce from the goods-producing sector, where health benefits have traditionally been provided, to the service sector, where many employers do not offer health insurance.

TABLE 6.3

Private health insurance coverage among persons under age 65, by selected characteristics, selected years, 1984–2000

[Data are based on household interviews of a sample of the civilian noninstitutionalized population]

Characteristic	1984	1989	1994[1]	1995	1996	1997[1]	1998	1999	2000
					Number in millions				
Total[2]	157.5	162.7	159.8	164.2	165.6	165.8	170.8	174.3	173.0
					Percent of population				
Total, age adjusted[2,3]	77.1	76.2	70.3	71.6	71.5	70.9	72.3	72.9	71.7
Total, crude[2]	76.8	75.9	69.9	71.3	71.2	70.7	72.1	72.8	71.7
Age									
Under 18 years	72.6	71.8	63.2	65.2	66.2	66.1	68.4	68.8	67.0
Under 6 years	68.1	67.9	57.6	59.5	60.8	61.3	64.7	64.7	63.1
6–17 years	74.9	74.0	66.3	68.3	68.9	68.5	70.2	70.9	68.9
18–44 years	76.5	75.5	69.4	70.9	70.5	69.4	71.1	72.0	70.9
18–24 years	67.4	64.5	57.9	60.8	60.3	59.3	61.5	63.2	60.9
25–34 years	77.4	75.9	69.0	70.1	69.4	68.1	70.6	71.2	70.6
35–44 years	83.9	82.7	76.9	77.7	77.4	76.4	76.9	77.9	77.1
45–64 years	83.3	82.5	80.2	80.1	79.4	79.0	79.0	79.3	78.7
45–54 years	83.3	83.4	81.2	80.9	80.4	80.4	80.0	80.4	80.0
55–64 years	83.3	81.6	78.7	79.0	78.0	76.9	77.3	77.7	76.6
Sex[3]									
Male	77.7	76.5	70.9	72.1	71.9	71.2	72.5	73.0	72.1
Female	76.5	75.9	69.8	71.1	71.1	70.6	72.1	72.8	71.4
Race[3,4]									
White only	80.1	79.3	73.8	74.7	74.5	74.3	75.9	76.8	75.8
Black or African American only	59.2	58.7	52.2	54.9	55.9	56.1	55.9	58.1	56.9
American Indian and Alaska Native only	#	#	#	#	#	#	#	41.3	44.2
Asian only	70.9	71.6	67.5	68.4	68.3	68.2	72.2	73.2	71.9
Native Hawaiian and Other Pacific Islander only	- - -	- - -	- - -	- - -	- - -	- - -	- - -	*	*
2 or more races	- - -	- - -	- - -	- - -	- - -	- - -	- - -	63.5	63.1
Hispanic origin and race[3,4]									
Hispanic or Latino	57.1	53.2	49.0	48.0	48.2	47.9	49.9	50.3	49.0
Mexican	54.9	48.5	46.1	44.3	44.3	43.9	45.6	48.0	46.6
Puerto Rican	51.0	46.8	48.8	48.9	52.4	48.2	52.7	51.4	52.6
Cuban	72.1	70.0	63.5	63.4	65.6	70.7	71.7	71.4	63.6
Other Hispanic or Latino	62.0	62.4	52.8	52.9	53.2	51.2	52.8	53.4	51.6
Not Hispanic or Latino	#	#	#	#	#	#	#	76.3	75.1
White only	82.4	82.5	77.4	78.6	78.6	78.0	79.6	80.3	79.3
Black or African American only	59.4	58.8	52.6	55.3	56.3	56.3	56.1	58.2	57.0
Age and percent of poverty level[5]									
All ages:[3]									
Below 100 percent	33.0	27.5	22.6	23.0	21.8	23.4	24.1	26.1	25.8
100–149 percent	61.8	54.2	46.0	47.9	46.6	42.0	43.3	40.1	39.5
150–199 percent	77.2	70.6	64.1	65.2	65.8	63.6	61.4	59.4	58.4
200 percent or more	91.6	91.0	88.0	88.4	88.4	87.6	88.3	88.7	87.2
Under 18 years:									
Below 100 percent	28.7	22.3	15.2	16.9	17.0	17.3	18.9	19.5	18.9
100–149 percent	66.2	59.6	47.3	48.5	48.5	42.5	45.8	40.4	37.9
150–199 percent	80.9	75.9	68.0	67.4	72.1	66.8	66.5	61.6	59.8
200 percent or more	92.3	92.7	89.0	89.5	89.8	88.9	89.9	90.4	88.0
Geographic region[3]									
Northeast	80.7	82.1	75.0	75.5	75.4	74.3	76.4	77.1	76.5
Midwest	80.9	81.7	77.2	77.5	78.7	77.3	79.1	80.2	78.9
South	74.5	71.7	65.7	67.1	66.5	67.5	67.8	68.0	67.0
West	72.3	71.8	65.7	68.1	67.7	65.8	67.8	68.9	67.1
Location of residence[3]									
Within MSA[6]	77.8	76.8	70.9	72.5	72.9	71.5	73.2	74.3	72.7
Outside MSA[6]	75.5	74.0	68.4	68.1	66.3	68.5	68.9	67.8	67.7

A third factor is the changing nature of the relationship between employers and employees. In the past, many companies took a paternalistic (fatherly) approach to employee welfare to promote a healthy workforce and foster employee loyalty. Since the mid-1990s, many companies have assumed less responsibility for their workers' health and have found that measures to cut health care costs effectively reduce business expenditures ("Sources of Health Insurance and Characteristics of the Uninsured," *EBRI Issue Brief,* no. 170, February 1996).

RACE AND ETHNICITY. In the under-65 age group, more than three-fourths of non-Hispanic whites (79.3 percent) had private health insurance in 2000, down from 82.4 percent in 1984. More than half (57 percent) of non-Hispanic blacks had private health insurance policies in

TABLE 6.3

Private health insurance coverage among persons under age 65, by selected characteristics, selected years, 1984–2000 [CONTINUED]

[Data are based on household interviews of a sample of the civilian noninstitutionalized population]

Characteristic	Private insurance obtained through workplace[7]								
	1984	1989	1994[1]	1995	1996	1997[1]	1998	1999	2000
	Number in millions								
Total[2]	141.8	146.3	145.8	150.7	151.1	155.6	159.3	162.6	161.6
	Percent of population								
Total, age adjusted[2,3]	69.2	68.4	64.1	65.6	65.2	66.5	67.4	68.1	67.0
Total, crude[2]	69.1	68.3	63.8	65.4	65.0	66.3	67.3	68.0	67.0
Age									
Under 18 years	66.5	65.8	58.5	60.4	60.8	62.7	64.1	64.6	63.1
Under 6 years	62.1	62.3	53.3	55.1	56.2	58.2	60.9	60.8	59.2
6–17 years	68.7	67.7	61.3	63.3	63.2	64.9	65.7	66.5	65.0
18–44 years	69.6	68.4	63.5	65.3	64.6	65.5	66.5	67.7	66.5
18–24 years	58.7	55.3	50.4	53.5	52.2	54.7	55.7	57.8	55.5
25–34 years	71.2	69.5	63.7	65.0	64.3	64.5	66.7	67.2	66.6
35–44 years	77.4	76.2	71.4	72.7	71.9	72.6	72.5	73.8	72.8
45–64 years	71.8	71.6	71.7	72.2	71.4	72.6	72.7	72.7	72.5
45–54 years	74.6	74.4	74.4	74.7	73.9	75.4	75.1	75.1	75.3
55–64 years	69.0	68.3	67.8	68.4	67.5	68.3	69.1	69.2	68.1
Sex[3]									
Male	70.1	68.9	64.7	66.3	65.7	66.9	67.6	68.1	67.4
Female	68.4	67.9	63.6	65.0	64.7	66.1	67.2	68.0	66.6
Race[3,4]									
White only	72.0	71.2	67.2	68.5	67.8	69.6	70.8	71.6	70.8
Black or African American only	53.3	53.6	49.5	51.1	52.7	53.9	53.2	55.4	54.1
American Indian and Alaska Native only	#	#	#	#	#	#	#	38.4	42.0
Asian only	64.4	60.2	57.5	59.8	59.4	61.7	63.8	65.3	64.9
Native Hawaiian and Other Pacific Islander only	---	---	---	---	---	---	---	*	*
2 or more races	---	---	---	---	---	---	---	59.9	61.2
Hispanic origin and race[3]									
Hispanic or Latino[4]	52.9	48.6	44.8	44.6	44.4	45.1	46.8	47.3	46.1
Mexican	51.7	45.6	44.1	42.3	41.3	42.1	43.4	45.4	44.3
Puerto Rican	48.3	43.4	45.6	45.6	49.8	46.1	50.2	48.3	50.6
Cuban	57.6	56.3	45.6	53.8	54.7	58.1	60.3	63.7	53.5
Other Hispanic or Latino	57.7	55.7	46.8	47.7	48.2	48.2	49.4	50.0	48.0
Not Hispanic or Latino	#	#	#	#	#	#	#	71.1	70.1
White only	74.0	74.0	70.5	72.1	71.5	73.1	74.2	74.8	73.9
Black or African American only	53.4	53.7	49.8	51.5	53.1	54.1	53.4	55.5	54.2
Age and percent of poverty level[5]									
All ages:[3]									
Below 100 percent	23.8	19.7	16.9	17.6	16.7	19.9	19.8	22.2	21.2
100–149 percent	51.1	45.0	39.7	41.7	40.4	37.3	38.5	35.9	35.0
150–199 percent	68.6	61.9	57.3	58.6	58.9	59.0	55.7	53.9	53.6
200 percent or more	85.0	83.9	81.7	82.4	81.8	83.6	83.7	84.5	83.1
Under 18 years:									
Below 100 percent	23.2	17.5	12.3	13.6	13.9	15.5	16.5	16.7	15.9
100–149 percent	58.3	52.5	42.7	43.6	43.0	38.9	41.8	37.4	34.8
150–199 percent	75.8	70.1	62.5	61.8	66.8	63.8	62.1	57.2	56.4
200 percent or more	86.9	86.7	83.5	84.4	83.6	85.5	85.3	86.5	84.3

2000, while 59.4 percent were insured in 1984. In 2000 more than two-thirds (71.9 percent) of Asians had private policies, an increase from the 70.9 covered in 1984.

The most dramatic drop in private coverage was among Hispanics. In 2000 less than half (49 percent) of Hispanic Americans had private health insurance coverage, down from 57.1 percent in 1984. (See Table 6.3.)

INCOME AND LOCATION. Persons under 65 with higher incomes in 2000 were more likely to have private health insurance. All income levels, however, were less likely to have private insurance than in 1984. In 1984, more than half (61.8 percent) of individuals living at 100–149 percent of the poverty level had private insurance; by 2000 the proportion sank to 35.5 percent. For people earning 200 percent or more above the poverty line, 91.6 percent were covered by private insurance in 1984, compared to 87.2 percent in 2000. (See Table 6.3.)

From 1984 to 2000, all geographic regions showed overall decreases in the percentage of persons under 65 covered by private health insurance and increases in the percentages of uninsured and Medicaid recipients. In 2000 persons in the South and West were least likely to have private insurance and the most likely to be uninsured. In 1984 and in 2000, more people living within

TABLE 6.3

Private health insurance coverage among persons under age 65, by selected characteristics, selected years, 1984–2000 [CONTINUED]

[Data are based on household interviews of a sample of the civilian noninstitutionalized population]

Characteristic	Private insurance obtained through workplace[7]								
	1984	1989	1994[1]	1995	1996	1997[1]	1998	1999	2000
Geographic region[3]	Percent of population								
Northeast	74.1	75.1	69.7	69.9	69.1	71.0	73.0	73.5	72.2
Midwest	72.1	73.4	70.9	71.4	72.5	72.6	73.7	75.4	74.7
South	66.2	63.8	59.7	62.0	60.8	63.0	63.3	63.7	62.4
West	64.9	64.2	58.6	60.8	60.1	60.9	61.6	61.9	61.1
Location of residence[3]									
Within MSA[6]	71.0	69.8	56.1	66.9	66.9	67.4	68.5	69.6	68.1
Outside MSA[6]	65.3	63.5	60.6	60.8	58.9	62.8	63.0	62.0	62.3

\# Estimates calculated upon request.
* Estimates are considered unreliable. Data not shown have a relative standard error of greater than 30 percent.
- - - Data not available.
[1]The questionnaire changed compared with previous years.
[2]Includes all other races not shown separately and unknown poverty level.
[3]Estimates are age adjusted to the year 2000 standard using three age groups: under 18 years, 18–44 years, and 45–64 years.
[4]Starting with data year 1999, estimates by race and Hispanic origin are tabulated using the 1997 Standards for Federal data on race and ethnicity; prior to data year 1999 the 1977 Standards are used. Estimates for specific race groups are shown when they meet requirements for statistical reliability and confidentiality. Starting with data year 1999, the categories "White only," "Black or African American only," "American Indian and Alaska Native (AI/AN) only," "Asian only," and "Native Hawaiian and Other Pacific Islander only" include persons who reported only one racial group; and the category "2 or more races" includes persons who reported more than one of the five racial groups in the 1997 Standards or one of the five racial groups and "Some other race." Prior to data year 1999, estimates for the race categories shown include persons who reported one race or who reported more than one race and identified one race as best representing their race; and the category "Asian only" includes Native Hawaiian and Other Pacific Islander. Because of the differences between the two Standards, race-specific estimates starting with data year 1999 are not strictly comparable with estimates for earlier years. To estimate change between 1998 and 1999, race-specific estimates for 1999 based on the 1977 Standards can be used. In comparison with the 1999 estimates based on the 1997 Standards, estimates of the age-adjusted percent with private health insurance based on the 1977 Standards are: 0.1 percentage points lower for the white group; 0.1 percentage points higher for the black group; 0.9 percentage points lower for the Asian and Pacific Islander group; and 0.2 percentage points higher for the AI/AN group.
[5]Prior to 1997 percent of poverty level is based on family income and family size using Bureau of the Census poverty thresholds. Beginning in 1997 percent of poverty level is based on family income, family size, number of children in the family, and, for families with two or fewer adults, the age of adults in the family. Missing family income data were imputed for 17 percent of the sample under age 65 years in 1994, 15 percent in 1995, and 16 percent in 1996. Percent of poverty level was unknown for 19 percent of sample persons under 65 in 1997, 24 percent in 1998, 27 percent in 1999, and 26 percent in 2000.
[6]MSA is metropolitan statistical area.
[7]Private insurance originally obtained through a present or former employer or union. Starting in 1997 also includes private insurance obtained through workplace, self-employed, or professional association.

SOURCE: "Table 127. Private health insurance coverage among persons under 65 years of age, according to selected characteristics: United States, selected years 1984–2000," in *Health, United States, 2002,* Centers for Disease Control and Prevention, National Center for Health Statistics, Hyattsville, MD, 2002

metropolitan statistical areas (large cities and their surrounding suburbs) had private insurance than did those living in rural areas. (See Table 6.3.)

Accompanying the declines in private health insurance for those under 65 from 1984 to 2000 was the significant increase in the proportion of individuals receiving Medicaid health benefits at all income levels. Most surprising was the sharp increase in Medicaid participation by people living above the poverty level—persons who qualify for the federal program as a result of their disabilities. (See Table 6.4.)

Persons Age 65 and Over

There are three sources of health insurance for persons age 65 and over: private insurance, Medicare, and Medicaid. Medicare is the federal government's primary health program for those 65 years old and older, and all persons in this age group are eligible for certain basic benefits under Medicare. Medicaid is the government's program for the poor and persons with disabilities. In 2000 a scant 0.8 percent of adults age 65 or older went without some type of health insurance. (See Table 6.1.)

Older adults may be covered by a combination of private health insurance and Medicare, or Medicare and Medicaid, depending on their incomes and levels of disability.

Almost all of those over 65 are covered by Medicare. Thus, in 2000, the 63.1 percent of all adults age 65 or older who had private insurance were covered by a combination of their private insurance and Medicare. Another 7.6 percent had a combination of Medicare and Medicaid and 26.7 percent had Medicare only. (See Table 6.6.)

Whites were far more likely to have both Medicare and private insurance (66.9 percent) than any other ethnic or racial group. Only 23.4 percent of Hispanics, and 35.6 percent of blacks had both Medicare and private coverage. (See Table 6.6.)

CHILDREN

In 2001, 8.5 million children, or 11.7 percent of children under the age of 18, were uninsured. Among poor children under the age of 18, 21.3 percent had no health insurance. Hispanic children were the most likely to be uninsured—24.1 percent in 2001, followed by 13.9 percent of black children and 11.7 percent of API children. (See Figure 6.4.) Just 7.4 percent of non-Hispanic white children had no health care coverage, making them the least likely children to be uninsured in 2001. Older children, age 12 through 17, were more likely to be uninsured (13.1 percent)

TABLE 6.4

Medicaid coverage among persons under 65 years of age, according to selected characteristics, selected years, 1984–2000

[Data are based on household interviews of a sample of the civilian noninstitutionalized population]

Characteristic	1984	1989	1994[1]	1995	1996	1997[1]	1998	1999	2000
					Number in millions				
Total[2]	14.0	15.4	25.7	26.6	25.8	22.9	21.1	21.9	22.9
					Percent of population				
Total, age adjusted[2,3]	6.7	7.1	11.0	11.3	10.9	9.6	8.8	9.0	9.4
Total, crude[2]	6.8	7.2	11.2	11.5	11.1	9.7	8.9	9.1	9.5
Age									
Under 18 years	11.9	12.6	21.2	21.5	20.7	18.4	17.1	18.1	19.4
Under 6 years	15.5	15.7	28.4	29.3	28.2	24.7	22.4	23.5	24.3
6–17 years	10.1	10.9	17.2	17.4	16.9	15.2	14.5	15.5	17.0
18–44 years	5.1	5.2	7.8	7.8	7.6	6.6	5.8	5.7	5.6
18–24 years	6.4	6.8	10.2	10.4	9.7	8.8	8.0	8.1	8.1
25–34 years	5.3	5.2	8.3	8.2	7.8	6.8	5.7	5.7	5.5
35–44 years	3.5	4.0	5.9	5.9	6.2	5.2	4.6	4.3	4.3
45–64 years	3.4	4.3	4.7	5.6	5.3	4.6	4.5	4.4	4.5
45–54 years	3.2	3.8	4.0	5.1	4.9	4.0	4.1	3.9	4.2
55–64 years	3.6	4.9	5.7	6.4	5.9	5.6	5.0	5.3	4.9
Sex[3]									
Male	5.2	5.6	8.8	9.2	8.9	8.1	7.5	7.7	8.0
Female	8.0	8.6	13.0	13.3	12.8	11.0	10.1	10.4	10.8
Race[3,4]									
White only	4.6	5.1	8.3	8.8	8.7	7.5	6.7	6.9	7.2
Black or African American only	18.9	17.8	26.1	26.0	23.0	20.5	19.6	18.7	19.4
American Indian and Alaska Native only	#	#	#	#	#	#	#	41.3	44.2
Asian only	9.1	11.3	9.9	10.7	*11.5	9.4	6.7	8.4	7.8
Native Hawaiian and Other Pacific Islander only	---	---	---	---	---	---	---	*	*
2 or more races	---	---	---	---	---	---	---	15.8	15.6
Hispanic origin and race[3,4]									
Hispanic or Latino	12.2	12.7	18.6	19.8	18.5	16.0	14.1	14.1	14.2
Mexican	11.1	11.5	17.4	18.8	17.6	15.3	12.6	12.4	12.5
Puerto Rican	28.6	26.9	35.3	31.1	31.3	28.9	24.5	27.0	27.6
Cuban	4.8	7.8	*8.6	13.8	*13.1	8.2	*9.1	8.3	9.7
Other Hispanic or Latino	7.4	10.4	15.2	16.9	15.0	13.9	13.9	13.8	14.1
Not Hispanic or Latino	#	#	#	#	#	#	#	8.2	8.6
White only	3.7	4.2	6.7	7.1	7.0	6.2	5.7	6.0	6.3
Black or African American only	19.1	17.8	26.1	25.6	22.7	20.3	19.4	18.7	19.3
Age and percent of poverty level[5]									
All ages:[3]									
Below 100 percent	30.5	35.3	42.7	44.7	42.9	38.8	37.9	36.8	37.2
100–149 percent	7.5	11.0	15.9	18.0	17.4	17.5	16.0	18.6	20.3
150–199 percent	3.1	5.0	6.4	7.9	8.0	7.4	7.2	9.8	10.8
200 percent or more	0.6	1.1	1.6	1.8	1.7	1.7	1.8	2.0	2.3
Under 18 years:									
Below 100 percent	43.1	47.8	64.3	66.0	65.2	59.7	58.7	59.9	60.9
100–149 percent	9.0	12.3	24.3	27.2	26.6	30.2	25.9	33.5	37.1
150–199 percent	4.4	6.1	10.0	13.1	12.2	12.2	12.8	18.0	21.5
200 percent or more	0.8	1.6	2.9	3.3	2.8	2.9	3.2	3.7	4.7

than children under 12 (10.7 percent of children under 6 and 11.2 percent of those 6–11 were uninsured).

In 2001, 68.4 percent of American children were insured under private health insurance plans, either privately purchased or obtained through the parents' workplace, and nearly one-quarter (22.7 percent) were covered by Medicaid. (See Figure 6.5.) Medicaid covered a higher percentage of black children (38.3 percent) and Hispanic children (34.9 percent) than API (18 percent) or non-Hispanic white children (15.3 percent). (See Figure 6.5.)

Some health care industry observers believed that the 1996 welfare reform law, the Personal Responsibility and Work Opportunity Reconciliation Act (PL 104-193), would reduce enrollment in Medicaid. Under the 1996 law, federal money once dispensed through the American Families with Dependent Children (AFDC) program was now given as a block grant (a lump sum of money) to states. In addition, the law no longer required that children who received cash assistance automatically enroll in the Medicaid program. The law gave states greater leeway in defining their requirements for AFDC eligibility, and in some states, some families were no longer eligible for Medicaid.

Although it did not prove to reduce Medicaid enrollment dramatically, after three previous years of fairly steady enrollment, the percentage of children under 18

TABLE 6.4

Medicaid coverage among persons under 65 years of age, according to selected characteristics, selected years, 1984–2000 [CONTINUED]

[Data are based on household interviews of a sample of the civilian noninstitutionalized population]

Characteristic	1984	1989	1994[1]	1995	1996	1997[1]	1998	1999	2000
Geographic region [3]					Percent of population				
Northeast	8.5	6.8	11.4	11.7	11.5	11.2	9.8	10.1	10.5
Midwest	7.2	7.5	10.2	10.3	8.7	8.2	7.5	7.3	7.9
South	5.0	6.4	10.6	11.1	11.1	8.6	8.6	8.9	9.4
West	6.9	8.2	11.9	12.4	12.4	11.4	9.7	10.3	10.2
Location of residence [3]									
Within MSA [6]	7.1	7.0	11.1	11.1	10.4	9.5	8.5	8.4	8.8
Outside MSA [6]	5.9	7.8	10.4	12.0	12.7	9.9	9.8	11.5	11.9

Estimates calculated upon request.
* Estimates are considered unreliable. Data preceded by an asterisk have a relative standard error of 20–30 percent. Data not shown have a relative standard error of greater than 30 percent.
- - - Data not available.
[1] The questionnaire changed compared with previous years.
[2] Includes all other races not shown separately and unknown poverty level.
[3] Estimates are age adjusted to the year 2000 standard using three age groups: under 18 years, 18–44 years, and 45–64 years.
[4] Starting with data year 1999, estimates by race and Hispanic origin are tabulated using the 1997 Standards for federal data on race and ethnicity; prior to data year 1999 the 1977 Standards are used. Estimates for specific race groups are shown when they meet requirements for statistical reliability and confidentiality. Starting with data year 1999, the categories "White only," "Black or African American only," "American Indian and Alaska Native (AI/AN) only," "Asian only," and "Native Hawaiian and Other Pacific Islander only" include persons who reported only one racial group; and the category "2 or more races" includes persons who reported more than one of the five racial groups in the 1997 Standards or one of the five racial groups and "Some other race." Prior to data year 1999, estimates for the race categories shown include persons who reported one race or who reported more than one race and identified one race as best representing their race; and the category "Asian only" includes Native Hawaiian and Other Pacific Islander. Because of the differences between the two Standards, race-specific estimates starting with data year 1999 are not strictly comparable with estimates for earlier years. To estimate change between 1998 and 1999, race-specific estimates for 1999 based on the 1977 Standards can be used. In comparison with the 1999 estimates based on the 1997 Standards, estimates of the age-adjusted percent with Medicaid based on the 1977 Standards are: 0.1 percentage points higher for the white group; 0.1 percentage points lower for the black group; 0.8 percentage points higher for the Asian and Pacific Islander group; and 0.8 percentage points higher for the AI/AN group.
[5] Prior to 1997 percent of poverty level is based on family income and family size using Bureau of the Census poverty thresholds. Beginning in 1997 percent of poverty level is based on family income, family size, number of children in the family, and, for families with two or fewer adults, the age of adults in the family. Missing family income data were imputed for 17 percent of the sample under 65 years of age in 1994, 15 percent in 1995, and 16 percent in 1996. Percent of poverty level was unknown for 19 percent of sample persons under 65 in 1997, 24 percent in 1998, 27 percent in 1999, and 26 percent in 2000.
[6] MSA is metropolitan statistical area.
Note: Medicaid includes other public assistance through 1996. Starting in 1997 includes state-sponsored health plans. Starting in 1999 includes Child Health Insurance Program (CHIP). In 2000, 8.1 percent were covered by Medicaid, 0.7 percent by state-sponsored health plans, and 0.6 percent by CHIP.

SOURCE: "Table 128. Medicaid coverage among persons under 65 years of age, according to selected characteristics: United States, selected years 1984–2000," in *Health, United States, 2002,* Centers for Disease Control and Prevention, National Center for Health Statistics, Hyattsville, MD, 2002

enrolled in Medicaid dropped from 20.1 percent in 1996, when the welfare reform legislation was enacted, to 18.1 percent in 1999. For the same years, Medicaid enrollment dropped from 11.8 percent to 10.2 percent among the general population, but in 2000 Medicaid enrollment grew to 10.6 percent. By 2001, 11.2 percent of the general population was covered by this entitlement program.

Some industry analysts attributed the declining proportion of uninsured children and children covered by Medicaid in the late 1990s to expansion of the State Children's Health Insurance Program (SCHIP) that targeted low income children and was instituted during the late 1990s. Others feel that the economic boom of the late 1990s may have played a role in preventing enrollment growth in Medicaid, and accurately predicted that the economic downturn and uncertainty of the early years of the twenty-first century would reverse the downward trend in both the share of the population without health insurance and Medicaid enrollment.

HEALTH INSURANCE PORTABILITY AND ACCOUNTABILITY ACT OF 1996

On August 21, 1996, President William Clinton signed the Health Insurance Portability and Accountability Act (PL 104-

191). Also known as the Kennedy-Kassebaum Act (for its sponsors senators Edward Kennedy and Nancy Kassebaum) or HIPPA, this legislation aimed to provide better portability (transfer) of employer-sponsored insurance from one job to another. By preventing "job lock"—the need to remain in the same position or with the same employer or risk losing health care coverage, it hoped to afford American workers greater career mobility and the freedom to pursue job opportunities. Industry observers and policymakers viewed HIPPA as an important first step in the federal initiative to reduce significantly the number of uninsured people in the United States.

HIPPA stipulated that American workers who had previous insurance coverage were immediately eligible for new coverage. The law prohibited group health plans from denying new coverage based on past or present poor health and guaranteed that employees could retain their health care coverage even after they left their jobs. New employers could still require a routine waiting period (usually no more than three months) before paying for health benefits, but the new employee who applied for insurance coverage could be continuously covered during the waiting period.

The following sections describe some of the major provisions of HIPPA. In addition to these provisions dis-

TABLE 6.5

No health care coverage among persons under age 65, by selected characteristics, selected years, 1984–2000

[Data are based on household interviews of a sample of the civilian noninstitutionalized population]

Characteristic	1984	1989	1994[1]	1995	1996	1997[1]	1998	1999	2000
					Number in millions				
Total[2]	29.8	33.4	40.0	37.1	38.6	41.0	39.2	38.5	40.5
					Percent of population				
Total, age adjusted[2,3]	14.3	15.3	17.2	15.9	16.5	17.4	16.5	16.1	16.8
Total, crude[2]	14.5	15.6	17.5	16.1	16.6	17.5	16.6	16.1	16.8
Age									
Under 18 years	13.9	14.7	15.0	13.4	13.2	14.0	12.7	11.9	12.4
Under 6 years	14.9	15.1	13.4	11.8	11.7	12.5	11.5	11.0	11.7
6–17 years	13.4	14.5	15.8	14.3	13.9	14.7	13.3	12.3	12.8
18–44 years	17.1	18.4	21.7	20.4	21.1	22.4	21.4	21.0	22.0
18–24 years	25.0	27.1	30.8	28.0	29.3	30.1	29.0	27.4	29.7
25–34 years	16.2	18.3	21.9	21.1	22.4	23.8	22.2	22.1	22.7
35–44 years	11.2	12.3	15.9	15.1	15.2	16.7	16.4	16.3	16.8
45–64 years	9.6	10.5	12.0	10.9	12.1	12.4	12.2	12.2	12.7
45–54 years	10.5	11.0	12.5	11.6	12.4	12.8	12.6	12.8	12.8
55–64 years	8.7	10.0	11.2	9.9	11.6	11.8	11.4	11.4	12.5
Sex[3]									
Male	15.0	16.4	18.5	17.2	17.8	18.5	17.5	17.2	17.8
Female	13.6	14.3	16.1	14.6	15.2	16.2	15.5	15.0	15.8
Race[3,4]									
White only	13.4	14.2	16.6	15.3	15.8	16.3	15.2	14.6	15.2
Black or African American only	20.0	21.4	19.7	18.2	19.6	20.2	20.7	19.5	20.0
American Indian and Alaska Native only	#	#	#	#	#	#	#	38.3	38.2
Asian only	18.0	18.5	20.1	18.2	19.0	19.3	18.1	16.4	17.3
Native Hawaiian and Other Pacific Islander only	- - -	- - -	- - -	- - -	- - -	- - -	- - -	*	*
2 or more races	- - -	- - -	- - -	- - -	- - -	- - -	- - -	16.8	18.4
Hispanic origin and race[3,4]									
Hispanic or Latino	29.1	32.4	31.8	31.5	32.4	34.3	34.0	33.9	35.4
Mexican	33.2	38.8	36.2	36.2	37.5	39.2	40.0	38.0	39.9
Puerto Rican	18.1	23.3	15.7	18.3	15.1	19.4	19.4	19.8	16.4
Cuban	21.6	20.9	27.4	22.1	18.8	20.5	18.4	19.7	25.2
Other Hispanic or Latino	27.5	25.2	30.7	29.7	30.5	32.9	31.1	30.8	32.7
Not Hispanic or Latino	#	#	#	#	#	#	#	13.5	14.1
White only	11.8	11.9	14.4	12.9	13.3	13.7	12.5	12.1	12.5
Black or African American only	19.7	21.3	19.3	18.1	19.5	20.1	20.7	19.4	20.0
Age and percent of poverty level[5]									
All ages:[3]									
Below 100 percent	34.7	35.8	33.1	31.7	34.5	34.4	34.6	34.4	34.2
100–149 percent	27.0	31.3	35.0	31.7	33.3	36.1	36.5	35.8	36.5
150–199 percent	17.4	21.8	26.1	24.0	24.3	25.9	26.7	27.7	27.3
200 percent or more	5.8	6.8	9.2	8.6	8.6	8.8	8.0	7.7	8.7
Under 18 years:									
Below 100 percent	28.9	31.6	22.1	20.0	21.0	22.4	21.5	21.6	20.4
100–149 percent.	22.8	26.1	27.7	24.8	25.0	26.1	28.0	24.9	25.6
150–199 percent	12.7	15.8	19.1	18.0	16.0	19.7	17.3	18.8	16.8
200 percent or more	4.2	4.4	7.1	6.4	6.1	6.1	5.0	4.4	5.5

cussed, the act clarified current law and stiffened penalties for fraud and abuse. The law applies to both group and individual health insurance policies.

Preexisting Medical Conditions

In the past, insurers could refuse to cover treatment for a preexisting disease or medical condition—an illness or condition that had been diagnosed or treated before a person enrolled in the health insurance program. Under the new law, if the preexisting condition had been diagnosed or treated within six months of the patient's enrollment in the insurance program, the insurance company could withhold coverage for that condition for no longer than 12 months. If the preexisting condition had not been diagnosed or treated within six months of changing insurance, there was no

waiting period beyond the short time an employer may require before providing benefits to a new employee.

This provision, along with the portability provision, means that insured employees are no longer trapped by the fear of losing their health insurance coverage if they lose or leave their jobs. In the past, many workers stayed in unsatisfactory jobs because they were ill or had dependents with existing medical conditions. They were afraid to change jobs for fear of losing coverage or having to wait a long time before obtaining new coverage.

Pregnancies are exempt from the 12-month waiting period and are covered within 30 days. Newborns and adopted children are also covered within 30 days. This provision aimed to better accommodate the needs of

TABLE 6.5

No health care coverage among persons under age 65, by selected characteristics, selected years, 1984–2000 [CONTINUED]

[Data are based on household interviews of a sample of the civilian noninstitutionalized population]

Characteristic	1984	1989	1994[1]	1995	1996	1997[1]	1998	1999	2000
Geographic region[3]					Percent of population				
Northeast	10.1	10.7	13.6	13.1	13.5	13.4	12.3	12.2	12.1
Midwest	11.1	10.5	12.2	12.1	12.2	13.1	11.9	11.5	12.3
South	17.4	19.4	21.0	19.2	20.0	20.7	20.0	19.8	20.4
West.	17.8	18.4	20.4	17.7	18.6	20.4	19.9	18.6	20.2
Location of residence[3]									
Within MSA[6]	13.3	14.9	16.7	15.2	15.6	16.7	15.8	15.3	16.3
Outside MSA[6]	16.4	16.9	19.0	18.7	19.7	19.9	19.2	18.9	18.8

\# Estimates calculated upon request.
* Estimates are considered unreliable. Data not shown have a relative standard error of greater than 30 percent.
- - - Data not available.
[1]The questionnaire changed compared with previous years.
[2]Includes all other races not shown separately and unknown poverty level.
[3]Estimates are age adjusted to the year 2000 standard using three age groups: under 18 years, 18–44 years, and 45–64 years.
[4]Starting with data year 1999, estimates by race and Hispanic origin are tabulated using the 1997 Standards for federal data on race and ethnicity; prior to data year 1999 the 1977 Standards are used. Estimates for specific race groups are shown when they meet requirements for statistical reliability and confidentiality. Starting with data year 1999, the categories "White only," "Black or African American only," "American Indian and Alaska Native (AI/AN) only," "Asian only," and "Native Hawaiian and Other Pacific Islander only" include persons who reported only one racial group; and the category "2 or more races" includes persons who reported more than one of the five racial groups in the 1997 Standards or one of the five racial groups and "Some other race." Prior to data year 1999, estimates for the race categories shown include persons who reported one race or who reported more than one race and identified one race as best representing their race; and the category "Asian only" includes Native Hawaiian and Other Pacific Islander. Because of the differences between the two Standards, race-specific estimates starting with data year 1999 are not strictly comparable with estimates for earlier years. To estimate change between 1998 and 1999, race-specific estimates for 1999 based on the 1977 Standards can be used. In comparison with the 1999 estimates based on the 1997 Standards, estimates of the age-adjusted percent with no health care coverage based on the 1977 Standards are: 0.1 percentage points higher for the white group; identical for the black group; 0.1 percentage points lower for the Asian and Pacific Islander group; and 1.5 percentage points higher for the AI/AN group.
[5]Prior to 1997 percent of poverty level is based on family income and family size using Bureau of the Census poverty thresholds. Beginning in 1997 percent of poverty level is based on family income, family size, number of children in the family, and, for families with two or fewer adults, the age of adults in the family. Missing family income data were imputed for 17 percent of the sample under 65 years of age in 1994, 15 percent in 1995, and 16 percent in 1996. Percent of poverty level was unknown for 19 percent of sample persons under 65 in 1997, 24 percent in 1998, 27 percent in 1999, and 26 percent in 2000.
[6]MSA is metropolitan statistical area.
Note: Persons not covered by private insurance, Medicaid, Child Health Insurance Program (CHIP), public assistance (through 1996), state-sponsored or other government-sponsored health plans (starting in 1997), Medicare, or military plans are included.

SOURCE: "Table 129. No health care coverage among persons under 65 years of age, according to selected characteristics: United States, selected years 1984–2000," in *Health, United States, 2002,* Centers for Disease Control and Prevention, National Center for Health Statistics, Hyattsville, MD, 2002

working mothers and ensure access to, and availability of, uninterrupted prenatal care for expectant mothers.

Medical Savings Accounts

The 1996 law also authorized a pilot program—a five-year demonstration project designed to test the concept of medical savings accounts (MSAs). Beginning January 1, 1997, about 750,000 people with high-deductible health plans (high-deductible plans must carry a deductible of $1,600 to $2,400 for an individual or $3,200 to $4,800 for families) could make tax-deductible contributions into interest-bearing savings accounts. The funds deposited into these accounts may be used to purchase health insurance policies, and pay copayments and deductibles. Persons using MSAs also may deduct any employer contributions into the accounts as tax-deductible income. Any unspent money remaining in the MSA at the end of the year is carried over to the next year, allowing the account to grow.

MSAs are similar to individual retirement accounts (IRAs). To be eligible to create a MSA, individuals must be less than 65 years old, self-employed and uninsured, or must work in a firm with 50 or fewer employees that does not offer health care coverage. Withdrawals to cover out-of-pocket medical expenses are tax-free and the money

invested grows on a tax-deferred basis. Using MSA funds for any purpose unrelated to medical care or disability results in a 15 percent penalty. However, when MSA users reach age 65, the money may be withdrawn for any purpose and is taxed at the same rate as ordinary income.

Supporters of MSAs believed that consumers would be less likely to seek unnecessary or duplicative medical care if they knew they could keep the money left in their accounts for themselves at the end of the year. Experience has demonstrated that MSAs can simultaneously help to contain health care costs, allow consumers greater control and freedom of choice of health care providers, enable consumers to save for future medical and long-term care expenses, and improve access to medical care.

Critics felt that the HIPPA legislation created unnecessarily complicated MSAs. They blamed Congress for simply renaming MSAs (they are now known as "Archer MSAs" to honor Bill Archer, the Texas legislator who advocated their enactment) and failing to simplify MSAs when in December 2000, it renewed the MSA through December 31, 2002.

In February 2001 President George W. Bush advocated more liberal rules governing MSAs and proposed making them available to all eligible Americans permanently.

TABLE 6.6

Health care coverage for persons aged 65 and older, by type of coverage and selected characteristics, selected years, 1989–2000

[Data are based on household interviews of a sample of the civilian noninstitutionalized population]

Characteristic	Private insurance[1]						Private insurance obtained through workplace[1,2]					
	1989	1995[3]	1997[3]	1998	1999	2000	1989	1995[3]	1997[3]	1998	1999	2000
	Number in millions											
Total[4]	22.4	23.5	22.3	21.5	20.8	20.6	11.2	12.4	12.0	11.8	11.3	11.7
	Percent of population											
Total, age adjusted[4,5]	76.1	74.5	69.5	66.7	64.0	63.1	37.3	38.9	37.0	36.5	34.6	35.6
Total, crude[4]	76.5	74.6	69.5	66.7	64.1	63.1	38.4	39.5	37.5	36.7	34.9	35.8
Age												
65–74 years	78.2	75.1	69.9	66.6	64.5	62.7	43.7	43.3	42.0	39.7	38.6	39.4
75 years and over	73.9	73.9	69.1	66.8	63.5	63.6	30.2	34.1	31.6	33.0	30.3	31.4
75–84 years	75.9	75.7	70.2	68.1	64.6	64.6	32.0	36.0	33.2	35.1	32.3	33.1
85 years and over	65.5	67.3	64.7	61.8	59.6	59.5	22.8	27.3	25.6	25.3	23.2	24.7
Sex[5]												
Male	77.4	76.6	72.1	68.5	64.5	64.3	42.1	43.3	42.0	40.7	38.6	39.7
Female	75.4	73.2	67.7	65.5	63.8	62.2	34.0	35.8	33.5	33.6	31.8	32.5
Race[5,6]												
White only	79.8	78.3	72.7	70.3	67.6	66.9	38.7	40.4	37.9	37.9	35.8	37.2
Black or African American only	42.3	40.3	42.5	40.3	39.9	35.6	23.7	24.6	30.8	27.3	27.5	25.0
American Indian and Alaska Native only	*	*	*	*	*	*	*	*	*	*	*	*
Asian only	#	#	#	#	33.1	43.3	#	#	#	#	21.4	23.2
Native Hawaiian and Other Pacific Islander only	---	---	---	---	*	*	---	---	---	---	*	*
2 or more races	---	---	---	---	56.0	63.1	---	---	---	---	26.9	48.4
Hispanic origin and race[5,6]												
Hispanic or Latino	42.3	39.8	30.6	29.1	26.9	23.4	22.2	18.4	17.7	17.8	17.4	15.1
Mexican	33.5	31.8	31.8	26.5	27.4	20.3	20.2	15.9	17.7	17.2	16.9	12.8
Not Hispanic or Latino	#	#	#	#	66.2	65.5	#	#	#	#	35.7	36.8
White only	81.0	80.3	74.9	72.3	69.7	69.1	39.3	41.7	39.0	38.8	36.8	38.3
Black or African American only	42.4	40.1	42.6	40.5	40.1	35.6	23.7	24.4	30.7	27.6	27.6	25.0
Percent of poverty level[5,7]												
Below 100 percent	46.1	40.0	31.9	32.8	28.3	29.9	11.6	13.8	7.2	10.0	8.8	10.8
100–149 percent	67.7	67.6	54.5	48.7	44.6	44.2	22.2	26.7	17.4	19.1	14.7	16.1
150–199 percent	81.1	76.0	69.8	65.6	62.0	63.1	39.0	38.7	33.3	30.9	27.2	29.8
200 percent or more	85.5	85.3	81.8	78.6	75.5	74.4	49.4	49.3	48.5	49.1	45.4	47.3
Geographic region[5]												
Northeast	76.1	76.2	72.7	72.0	66.0	66.7	42.2	44.6	42.3	43.0	39.7	38.7
Midwest	81.9	82.3	78.5	78.3	77.0	75.9	40.0	44.7	40.7	40.7	38.5	41.2
South	73.0	70.7	66.0	62.0	60.2	58.4	32.0	33.7	32.9	33.1	31.0	31.9
West.	74.7	68.8	59.9	54.9	51.5	51.5	37.1	33.6	33.6	30.3	30.6	31.7
Location of residence[5]												
Within MSA[8]	76.6	74.7	68.4	65.5	62.8	61.4	39.9	40.9	38.6	38.2	36.0	36.9
Outside MSA[8]	74.8	73.9	73.2	70.6	68.2	68.5	30.2	32.2	31.8	31.1	30.0	31.5
	Number in millions											
Total[4]	2.0	3.0	2.5	2.6	2.4	2.5	4.5	4.6	6.7	7.5	8.5	8.7
	Percent of population											
Total, age adjusted[4,5]	7.2	9.6	7.9	8.1	7.4	7.6	15.7	14.8	20.8	23.3	26.3	26.7
Total, crude[4]	7.0	9.4	7.9	8.1	7.3	7.6	15.4	14.7	20.8	23.2	26.3	26.7
Age												
65–74 years	6.3	8.4	7.5	7.8	6.6	7.7	13.8	14.4	20.3	22.7	25.9	26.3
75 years and over	8.2	10.9	8.4	8.4	8.1	7.5	17.8	15.2	21.5	24.0	26.8	27.2
75–84 years	7.9	9.9	7.9	7.8	7.2	7.2	16.2	14.1	20.5	22.9	26.3	26.3
85 years and over	9.7	14.3	10.2	10.5	11.4	8.6	24.9	19.2	25.2	27.9	28.5	30.9
Sex[5]												
Male	5.2	5.8	5.1	6.2	5.3	5.5	14.9	14.3	19.6	21.9	26.2	26.1
Female	8.6	12.2	9.9	9.5	8.8	9.2	16.2	15.0	21.7	24.3	26.3	27.3

Congress reviewed the president's proposed reforms and during its 2001–2 session lowered the minimum annual deductible to increase the number of eligible Americans, allowed annual MSA contributions up to 65 percent of the maximum deductible for individuals and 75 percent for families, and extended the availability of the Archer MSA through December 31, 2003.

Tax Benefits of HIPPA

HIPPA also changed several tax provisions involving health expenses:

• Health premium tax deductions for the self-employed increased. Formerly, self-employed persons could deduct only 30 percent of their premiums from their taxes. The

TABLE 6.6

Health care coverage for persons aged 65 and older, by type of coverage and selected characteristics, selected years, 1989–2000 [CONTINUED]

[Data are based on household interviews of a sample of the civilian noninstitutionalized population]

Characteristic	Private insurance[1]						Private insurance obtained through workplace[1,2]					
	1989	1995[3]	1997[3]	1998	1999	2000	1989	1995[3]	1997[3]	1998	1999	2000
Race[5,6]					Percent of population							
White only	5.6	7.4	6.5	6.4	5.6	5.6	13.9	13.5	19.3	21.8	25.0	25.4
Black or African American only	21.2	28.4	19.7	18.0	18.2	19.6	34.9	29.0	34.8	38.1	37.2	40.0
American Indian and Alaska Native only	*	*	*	*	*	*	*	*	*	*	*	*
Asian only	#	#	#	#	28.2	21.3	#	#	#	#	32.2	28.4
Native Hawaiian and Other Pacific Islander only	- - -	- - -	- - -	- - -	*	*	- - -	- - -	- - -	- - -	*	*
2 or more races	- - -	- - -	- - -	- - -	*	*	- - -	- - -	- - -	- - -	*28.0	*25.1
Hispanic origin and race[5,6]												
Hispanic or Latino	26.4	32.7	29.0	27.2	24.0	29.6	22.7	23.6	35.1	38.4	42.5	40.0
Not Hispanic or Latino	#	#	#	#	6.4	6.3	#	#	#	#	25.3	25.9
White only	4.9	6.1	5.4	5.4	4.7	4.6	13.6	12.9	18.4	20.9	24.0	24.5
Black or African American only	21.1	28.5	19.5	18.0	18.1	19.5	34.9	29.1	34.8	37.9	37.3	40.1
Percent of poverty level[5,7]												
Below 100 percent	28.2	36.4	40.0	36.7	35.7	35.0	26.4	23.4	27.0	28.4	32.7	31.3
100–149 percent	9.0	12.8	13.9	14.1	15.3	16.2	20.7	18.6	28.3	33.2	35.9	34.4
150–199 percent	4.7	5.9	5.1	6.1	4.2	4.7	13.6	16.8	22.7	26.1	31.5	28.5
200 percent or more	2.4	2.4	2.7	3.5	2.9	2.8	11.0	10.8	14.6	16.7	19.7	21.0
Geographic region[5]					Percent of population							
Northeast	5.4	8.9	6.5	7.5	7.3	7.4	17.4	15.3	19.8	19.3	25.5	24.5
Midwest	3.7	5.8	5.0	4.9	5.7	4.5	13.8	11.0	15.4	16.3	15.7	17.9
South	9.7	11.8	10.0	9.6	8.2	9.4	16.6	15.9	21.6	26.0	29.0	29.4
West	9.4	11.5	9.9	10.2	8.2	8.6	14.4	17.2	28.3	31.4	36.4	35.8
Location of residence[5]												
Within MSA[8]	6.5	8.9	7.5	8.0	6.9	7.2	15.9	14.9	22.3	24.4	28.0	28.8
Outside MSA[8]	8.8	11.7	9.4	8.4	8.8	9.0	15.5	14.2	15.9	19.7	20.6	20.5

* Estimates are considered unreliable. Data preceded by an asterisk have a relative standard error of 20–30 percent. Data not shown have a relative standard error of greater than 30 percent.

Estimates calculated upon request.

- - - Data not available

[1]Almost all persons 65 years of age and over are covered by Medicare also. In 2000, 91 percent of older persons with private insurance also had Medicare.

[2]Private insurance originally obtained through a present or former employer or union. Starting in 1997 also includes private insurance obtained through workplace, self-employed, or professional association.

[3]The questionnaire changed in 1993 and 1997 compared with previous years.

[4]Includes all other races not shown separately and unknown poverty level.

[5]Estimates are age adjusted to the year 2000 standard using two age groups: 65–74 years and 75 years and over.

[6]Starting with data year 1999, estimates by race and Hispanic origin are tabulated using the 1997 Standards for Federal data on race and ethnicity; prior to data year 1999 the 1977 Standards are used. Estimates for specific race groups are shown when they meet requirements for statistical reliability and confidentiality. Starting with data year 1999, the categories "White only," "Black or African American only," "American Indian and Alaska Native (AI/AN) only," "Asian only," and "Native Hawaiian and Other Pacific Islander only" include persons who reported only one racial group; and the category "2 or more races" includes persons who reported more than one of the five racial groups in the 1997 Standards or one of the five racial groups and "Some other race." Prior to data year 1999, estimates for the race categories shown include persons who reported one race or who reported more than one race and identified one race as best representing their race; and the category "Asian only" includes Native Hawaiian and Other Pacific Islander. Because of the differences between the two Standards, race-specific estimates starting with data year 1999 are not strictly comparable with estimates for earlier years. To estimate change between 1998 and 1999, race-specific estimates for 1999 based on the 1977 Standards can be used. In comparison with the 1999 estimates based on the 1997 Standards, estimates of the age-adjusted percent with private health insurance based on the 1977 Standards are: 0.1 percentage points lower for the white group; 0.3 percentage points higher for the black group; and 1 percentage point higher for the Asian and Pacific Islander group.

[7]Prior to 1997 percent of poverty level is based on family income and family size using Bureau of the Census poverty thresholds. Beginning in 1997 percent of poverty level is based on family income, family size, number of children in the family, and, for families with two or fewer adults, the age of adults in the family. Missing family income data were imputed for 25 percent of the sample 65 years of age and over in 1994, 22 percent in 1995, and 24 percent in 1996. Percent of poverty level was unknown for 29 percent of sample persons 65 or older in 1997, 34 percent in 1998, 38 percent in 1999, and 39 percent in 2000.

[8]MSA is metropolitan statistical area.

[9]Includes public assistance through 1996. Starting in 1997 includes state-sponsored health plans. In 2000 the age-adjusted percent of the population 65 years of age and over covered by Medicaid was 7.3 percent, and 0.4 percent were covered by state-sponsored health plans.

[10]Persons covered by Medicare but not covered by private health insurance, Medicaid, public assistance (through 1996), state-sponsored or other government-sponsored health plans (starting in 1997), or military plans.

Note: Percents do not add to 100 because persons with both private health insurance and Medicaid appear in more than one column, and because the percent of persons without health insurance (1.4 percent in 2000) is not shown. Data for additional years are available

SOURCE: "Table 130. Health care coverage among persons 65 years of age and over, according to type of coverage and selected characteristics: United States, selected years 1984–2000," in *Health, United States, 2002,* Centers for Disease Control and Prevention, National Center for Health Statistics, Hyattsville, MD, 2002

new law set up a graduated increasing scale of deductions—45 percent in 1998, 60 percent in 1999–2001, 70 percent in 2002, and 100 percent thereafter.

• Long-term care plan contributions. When an employer contributes to a long-term health care plan for a worker, a spouse, and dependents, those contributions will not be counted as taxable employee income. Long-term care includes rehabilitative care and personal care, such as feeding, bathing, and dressing, for a chronically ill person, defined as a person who has been unable for 12 months to per-

FIGURE 6.4

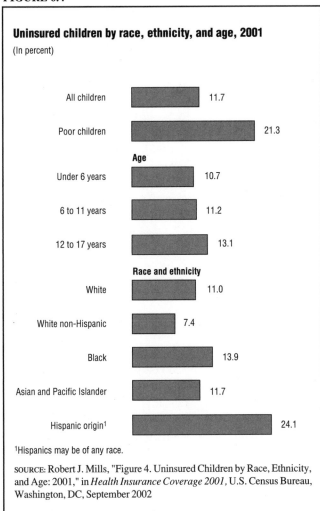

Uninsured children by race, ethnicity, and age, 2001

(In percent)

All children	11.7
Poor children	21.3
Age	
Under 6 years	10.7
6 to 11 years	11.2
12 to 17 years	13.1
Race and ethnicity	
White	11.0
White non-Hispanic	7.4
Black	13.9
Asian and Pacific Islander	11.7
Hispanic origin[1]	24.1

[1]Hispanics may be of any race.

SOURCE: Robert J. Mills, "Figure 4. Uninsured Children by Race, Ethnicity, and Age: 2001," in *Health Insurance Coverage 2001*, U.S. Census Bureau, Washington, DC, September 2002

FIGURE 6.5

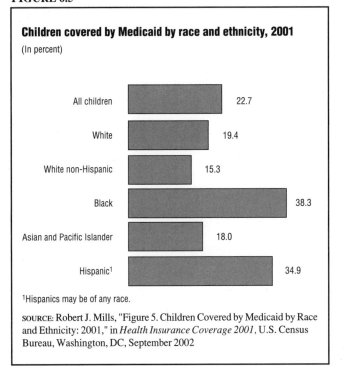

Children covered by Medicaid by race and ethnicity, 2001

(In percent)

All children	22.7
White	19.4
White non-Hispanic	15.3
Black	38.3
Asian and Pacific Islander	18.0
Hispanic[1]	34.9

[1]Hispanics may be of any race.

SOURCE: Robert J. Mills, "Figure 5. Children Covered by Medicaid by Race and Ethnicity: 2001," in *Health Insurance Coverage 2001*, U.S. Census Bureau, Washington, DC, September 2002

form the activities of daily living, such as eating and bathing.

• Individual retirement account (IRA) withdrawals. Ordinarily, withdrawals from an IRA before age 59 carry a 10 percent penalty. If medical expenses, however, exceed 7.5 percent of a person's annual income, he or she may withdraw funds from an IRA without penalty. This provision also allows persons who have collected federal or state unemployment benefits for at least 12 weeks to withdraw money from their IRAs without penalty.

MEDICARE C

Medicare C, also known as "Medicare+Choice," became available to Medicare recipients on January 1, 1999. Medicare C came about as a result of the Balanced Budget Act of 1997 and was designed to supplement Medicare Parts A and B. Medicare C offers beneficiaries a wider variety of health plan options than previously available. These options include traditional (fee-for-service) Medicare, Medicare health maintenance organizations

(HMOs), preferred provider organizations (PPOs), provider-sponsored organizations (PSOs), and medical savings accounts (MSAs).

Medicare provider-sponsored organizations are organized and operate the same way that HMOs do. However, they are administered by providers—physicians and hospitals. Medicare preferred provider organizations are similar to HMOs but permit patients to see providers outside the network and do not require their members to choose a network primary care physician to coordinate their care. Patients in PPOs may seek care from any physician associated with the plan. Medicare private fee-for-service plans are more like traditional Medicare, except patients may pay more out-of-pocket expenses. Medical savings accounts (MSAs) have two parts—an insurance policy and a savings account. Medicare will pay the insurance premium and deposit a fixed amount in an MSA each year to pay for an individual's health care.

Changing Medicare Reimbursement

Medicare reimbursement varies in different parts of the country, despite the fact that everyone pays the same amount to Medicare through taxes. As a result, older adults in some geographic regions have access to a more comprehensive range of services such as prescription drug coverage and coverage for eyeglasses while those in other areas do not receive these benefits.

Describing this practice as "unfair and outdated," legislators called for more equitable reimbursement formulas in August 2002. U.S. Representative Leonard Boswell, a

Democrat from Idaho, and Republican Congressman Tom Osborne from Nebraska introduced bipartisan legislation to ensure that no state receives Medicare reimbursement greater than 5 percentage points above or below the national average. In 2002, 35 states, including Iowa, received less than average reimbursement while states with higher health care costs received above average reimbursement.

HEALTH INSURANCE COSTS CONTINUE TO SKYROCKET

An employer health benefit survey released in September 2002 found that employees' health insurance costs rose 27 percent during 2002 for individuals and 16 percent for families. Employers' costs rose 13 percent, the sharpest increase since 1990. In addition to growing insurance premiums, workers also experienced increases in their deductibles and copayments. Deductibles for PPO members increased 37 percent from 2001, from an average of $201 to $286 dollars per year.

In 2002 the average insurance premium was $3,060 per year for an individual, with the employee paying about $459 (15 percent) of the premium. The annual premium for family coverage was $7,954, with the employee's contribution about 26 percent, or $2,084. The authors projected that the average cost of employer-sponsored health insurance will jump from nearly $8,000 per year for a family in 2002 to about $11,000 per year by 2005.

According to a survey conducted by the Kaiser Family Foundation and the Health Research and Educational Trust, 2002 was the second consecutive year of double-digit increases in insurance costs. The increase was attributed to larger insurance claims resulting from higher prices for hospital care and prescription drugs coupled with increasing consumer demand for, and utilization of, health care services. The researchers reported that more than three-quarters of 3,262 employers surveyed said they would likely have to increase the amounts their employees must pay for heath care coverage in 2003. Further, employers are extremely concerned about continuing increased in health care costs, with more than half of those surveyed identifying health insurance the "greatest concern for the company."

The researchers and other industry analysts observe that if there is no relief from premium increases in the near future, some employers may stop offering health benefits to their employees and some workers may be forced to drop their coverage because they are unable to contribute their share of the cost. During 2002, 9 percent of firms with more than 200 employees eliminated retirement benefits for newly hired or existing employees and for the first time in four years, more employees had their benefits reduced rather than increased. Industry observers and policymakers fear that rising insurance premiums will swell the ranks of Americans without insurance coverage.

CHAPTER 7
INTERNATIONAL COMPARISONS OF HEALTH CARE

International comparisons are often difficult to interpret, because definitions of terms and reliability of data as well as cultures and values differ. What is important in one society may be unimportant or even nonexistent in another. A political or human right that is important in one nation may be meaningless in a neighboring state. Evaluating the quality of health care systems is an example of the difficulties involved in comparing one culture to another.

Even within the United States, there are cultural and regional variations in health care delivery. A visit to a busy urban urgent care center might begin with the patient completing a brief medical history, five or ten minutes with a nurse who measures and records the patient's vital signs (pulse, respiration, temperature) and conclude with a fifteen-minute visit during which the physician diagnoses the problem and prescribes treatment. In contrast, on the Islands of Hawaii, a visit with a healer may last several hours and culminate with a prayer, song, or an embrace. Hawaiian healers, called "kahunas," are unhurried and offer an array of herbal remedies, bodywork (massage, touch, and manipulative therapies), and talk therapies (counseling and guidance) because they believe that the healing quality of the encounter, independent of any treatment offered, improves health and well-being.

While comparing the performance of health care systems and health outcomes (how people fare as a result of receiving health care services) is of benefit to health care planners, administrators, and policymakers, the subjective nature of such assessments should be duly considered.

A COMPARISON OF HEALTH CARE SPENDING, RESOURCES, AND UTILIZATION

The Organisation for Economic Cooperation and Development (OECD) provides information about, and to, 30 member countries that are governed democratically and participate in the global market economy. It collects and publishes data about a wide range of economic and social issues including health and health care policy. The OECD member nations are generally considered the wealthier, more developed nations in the world. The OECD includes the Western European nations, Canada, the United States, Japan, Australia, New Zealand, Mexico, the Czech Republic, Korea, Poland, Hungary, and the Slovak Republic (the Slovak Republic joined the OECD in 2000).

Percentage of Gross Domestic Product Spent on Health Care

Although health has always been a concern for Americans, the growth in the health care industry since the mid-1970s has made it a major factor in the American economy. For many years, the United States has spent a larger proportion of its gross domestic product (GDP) on health care than have other nations with similar economic development. From 1970 through 1990, total health care expenditures as a percentage of the U.S. GDP rose from 6.9 to 11.9 percent. (See Table 7.1.) From 1990 to 2000, expenditures rose to 13 percent, the highest rate in the OECD. Other nations that spent large percentages of GDP on health care in 2000 included Germany (10.6 percent), Switzerland (10.7 percent), France (9.5 percent), and Canada (9.1 percent). Of the member nations that reported health care expenditure data in 2000, Korea (5.9 percent), Mexico (5.4 percent), and the Slovak Republic (5.9 percent) spent the least in the OECD.

The exponential growth in health care spending in the United States during the 1990s was not an international trend, however. Several other countries also experienced significant increases in the percentage of GDP spent on health care from 1990 to 2000. These included the Czech Republic (from 5.0 to 7.2 percent), Germany (from 8.7 to 10.6 percent), Japan (from 5.9 to 7.8 percent), Korea (from 4.8 to 5.9 percent), Portugal (from 6.2 to 8.2 percent), and Switzerland (from 8.5 to 10.7). (See Table 7.1.) These countries, however, were spending a relatively small

TABLE 7.1

Total expenditures on health in OECD countries as a percent of gross domestic product (GDP), 1960–2000

	1960	1970	1980	1990	1995	1996	1997	1998	1999	2000
Australia	4.3	4.9[1]	7.0	7.8	8.2	8.3	8.4	8.5	8.4	8.3
Austria	4.3	5.3	7.6	7.1	8.6	8.7	8.0	8.0	8.1	8.0
Belgium		4.0	6.4	7.4	8.7	8.8	8.5	8.5	8.7	8.7
Canada	5.4	7.0	7.1	9.0	9.1	8.9	8.9	9.1	9.2	9.1
Czech Republic				5.0	7.3	7.1	7.1	7.1	7.2	7.2
Denmark		8.0[2]	9.1	8.5	8.2	8.3	8.2	8.4	8.5	8.3
Finland	3.9	5.6	6.4	7.9	7.5	7.7	7.3	6.9	6.9	6.6
France				8.6	9.6	9.6	9.4	9.3	9.4	9.5
Germany	4.8	6.3	8.8	8.7	10.6	10.9	10.7	10.6	10.7	10.6
Greece		6.1	6.6	7.5	8.9	8.9	8.7	8.7	8.7	8.3
Hungary				7.1[3]	7.5	7.2	7.0	6.9	6.8	6.8
Iceland	3.3	4.9	6.1	7.9	8.2	8.2	8.0	8.3	8.7	8.9
Ireland	3.6	5.1	8.4	6.6	7.2	7.0	6.9	6.8	6.8	6.7
Italy				8.0	7.4	7.5	7.7	7.7	7.8	8.1
Japan	3.0	4.5	6.4	5.9	7.0	7.0	7.2	7.1	7.4	7.8
Korea				4.8	4.7	4.9	5.0	5.1	5.6	5.9
Luxembourg		3.6	5.9	6.1	6.4	6.4	5.9	5.8	6.0	
Mexico				4.4	5.6	5.3	5.3	5.3	5.4	5.4
Netherlands		6.9[4]	7.5	8.0	8.4	8.3	8.2	8.1	8.2	8.1
New Zealand		5.1	5.9	6.9	7.2	7.2	7.5	7.9	7.9	8.0
Norway	2.9	4.4	7.0	7.8	8.0	8.0	8.0	8.5	8.5	7.5
Poland				5.3	6.0	6.4	6.1	6.4	6.2	
Portugal		2.6	5.6	6.2	8.3	8.5	8.6	8.3	8.4	8.2
Slovak Republic							6.1	5.9	5.8	5.9
Spain	1.5	3.6	5.4	6.6	7.7	7.7	7.6	7.6	7.7	7.7
Sweden	4.5	6.9	9.1	8.5	8.1	8.4	8.1	7.9		
Switzerland	4.9	5.6	7.6	8.5	10.0	10.4	10.4	10.6	10.7	10.7
Turkey		2.4	3.3	3.6	3.4	3.9	4.2	4.8		
United Kingdom	3.9	4.5	5.6	6.0	7.0	7.0	6.8	6.8	7.1	7.3
United States	5.1	6.9	8.7	11.9	13.3	13.2	13.0	12.9	13.0	13.0

[1]Data from 1969
[2]Data from 1971
[3]Data from 1991
[4]Data from 1972

SOURCE: "Table 10: Total expenditure on health. % GDP," in *OECD Health Data: A Comprehensive Analysis of 30 Countries: 2002 Edition (CD-ROM Windows/ Single User)*, Organisation for Economic Co-operation and Development, Paris, France, July 2002

percentage of their GDP on health care in 1990. Three countries—Denmark, Finland, and Norway—spent less of their GDP on health care in 2000 than they did in 1990. The majority of other countries experienced small increases.

Per Capita Spending on Health Care

In 2000 the United States also enjoyed the highest per capita spending for health care services, spending an average of $4,631 per citizen. (See Table 7.2.) No other country came close to spending that amount per capita in 2000: Switzerland spent $3,222 per citizen; Germany, $2,748; Iceland, $2,608; Canada, $2,535; and Denmark, $2,420. In 2000 Mexico spent the least per capita of any OECD nation on health care ($490) followed by the Slovak Republic ($690), Hungary ($841), and Korea ($893).

Who Pays for Health Care?

Public expenditures for health care services, as a percent of the GDP, vary widely between the OECD member nations. In 2000 Germany spent the most (8 percent of its GDP) on public expenditures for health and Mexico the least, just 2.5 percent. (See Table 7.3.) The United States

was comparable to other nations in terms of public expenditures for health care. In 2000, 5.8 percent of the U.S. GDP went to public health expenditures, and most of the other OECD nations ranged between 5 and 7 percent.

Of the 12 OECD nations that reported out-of-pocket, per capita payments in 2000, the United States again far exceeded other countries. U.S. citizens spent an average of $707 out-of-pocket for health care, about 50 percent more than the per capita amount of Italy ($466) and nearly ten times the per capita amount spent by citizens of the Slovak Republic ($72). (See Table 7.4.)

Private health insurance fills the gap between public expenditures and out-of-pocket costs. Only ten OECD member nations reported private insurance expenditures for health care in 2000. However, among the countries declaring private insurance as a percentage of total expenditures for health, the United States far exceeded the others. At 34.8 percent, the U.S. private insurance expenditure was more than twice that of France (12.8) and Germany (12.5) and far outstripped the other countries—Austria (7.0), Denmark (1.6), Finland (2.5), Hungary (0.2), Ireland

TABLE 7.2

Total expenditures on health in OECD countries, 1960–2000

Per capita in U.S. dollars

	1960	1970	1980	1990	1995	1996	1997	1998	1999	2000
Australia	87	175[1]	658	1,300	1,765	1,854	1,950	2,058	2,141	2,211
Austria	64	159	662	1,206	1,831	1,940	1,873	1,968	2,061	2,162
Belgium		130	577	1,245	1,896	1,982	2,013	2,008	2,144	2,269
Canada	109	260	710	1,676	2,114	2,091	2,181	2,285	2,428	2,535
Czech Republic				576	902	917	930	944	972	1,031
Denmark		318[2]	819	1,453	1,882	2,004	2,100	2,241	2,358	2,420
Finland	54	161	509	1,295	1,415	1,487	1,550	1,529	1,605	1,664
France				1,517	1,980	1,997	2,046	2,109	2,226	2,349
Germany	90	223	824	1,600	2,264	2,341	2,465	2,520	2,616	2,748
Greece		98	348	712	1,131	1,179	1,224	1,307	1,375	1,399
Hungary				534[3]	677	671	693	751	787	841
Iceland	50	137	576	1,376	1,823	1,911	1,988	2,204	2,409	2,608
Ireland	36	99	454	777	1,300	1,318	1,526	1,576	1,752	1,953
Italy				1,321	1,486	1,566	1,684	1,774	1,882	2,032
Japan	26	130	522	1,083	1,631	1,699	1,831	1,735	1,844	2,012
Korea				355	535	611	657	630	758	893
Luxembourg		148	605	1,492	2,122	2,192	2,204	2,361	2,613	
Mexico				260	388	381	411	431	452	490
Netherlands		284[4]	668	1,333	1,787	1,818	1,958	2,040	2,172	2,246
New Zealand		174	458	937	1,244	1,267	1,364	1,450	1,526	1,623
Norway	46	131	632	1,363	1,864	2,042	2,220	2,421	2,453	2,268
Poland				258	420	469	461	543	557	
Portugal		40	265	611	1,146	1,211	1,360	1,345	1,402	1,441
Slovak Republic							608	641	649	690
Spain	14	83	328	813	1,184	1,238	1,294	1,384	1,469	1,556
Sweden	89	270	850	1,492	1,622	1,716	1,770	1,748		
Switzerland	136	288	881	1,836	2,555	2,615	2,841	2,952	3,080	3,222
Turkey		23	75	171	190	234	272	303		
United Kingdom	74	144	444	972	1,315	1,422	1,481	1,527	1,666	1,763
United States	144	349	1,058	2,739	3,703	3,854	4,005	4,178	4,373	4,631

[1]Data from 1969
[2]Data from 1971
[3]Data from 1991
[4]Data from 1972

SOURCE: "Table 9: Total expenditure on health. Per capita in US$ PPP," in *OECD Health Data: A Comprehensive Analysis of 30 Countries: 2002 Edition (CD-ROM Windows/Single User)*, Organisation for Economic Co-operation and Development, Paris, France, July 2002

(7.1), Italy (0.9), and New Zealand (6.3). Since the United States is the only developed country without a national health care program, U.S. private insurance expenditures cover the costs generally assumed by government programs that finance health care delivery in comparable OECD member nations.

Spending for Hospitalization and Pharmaceutical Drugs

Interestingly, though the United States spends more on health care than other OECD nations, it devoted a smaller percentage of total health expenditures (39.6) to inpatient hospitalization than all the other countries except for Germany (31.1) and the Czech Republic (32) that reported inpatient expenditures in 2000. (See Table 7.5.) This finding is attributable to lower rates of hospitalization, shorter average lengths of stay, and a rise in outpatient hospital and other ambulatory care services in the United States.

In 2000 the United States spent 12 percent of its health care dollars on pharmaceutical drugs and durable medical supplies and equipment. (See Table 7.6.) This number was comparable to the percent of total expenditures that Denmark, Germany, Ireland, the Netherlands, and Switzerland spent on pharmaceuticals. The other six countries reporting pharmaceutical expenditures spent considerably more—the Czech Republic spent 25.2 percent, Italy spent 22.6 percent, and France spent 20.1 percent.

Hospital Utilization Statistics

Of all OECD countries reporting hospital utilization data, Switzerland and Japan had the highest number of inpatient hospital beds in 2000 (17.9 and 16.5 beds per 1,000 population, respectively). (See Table 7.7.) This is probably because neither of these countries distinguishes between acute and long-term (nursing home and rehabilitation) care beds. Norway had the next-highest number of beds, at 14.6 per 1,000 population in 2000. The United States was among the lowest, 3.6 in 2000, trailed only by Turkey and Mexico with 2.6 and 1.1 beds, respectively, per 1,000 population.

Hospital lengths of stay have consistently declined since 1960, in part because increasing numbers of illnesses

TABLE 7.3

Public expenditures on health in OECD countries as a percent of gross domestic product (GDP), 1960–2000

	1960	1970	1980	1990	1995	1996	1997	1998	1999	2000
Australia	2.2	2.8[1]	4.4	5.2	5.5	5.5	5.7	5.9	6.0	6.0
Austria	3.0	3.3	5.2	5.2	6.1	6.1	5.6	5.7	5.6	5.6
Belgium					6.0	6.4	6.0	6.0	6.2	6.2
Canada	2.3	4.9	5.4	6.7	6.5	6.3	6.2	6.5	6.5	6.5
Czech Republic				4.8	6.8	6.5	6.5	6.5	6.5	6.6
Denmark		6.7[2]	8.0	7.0	6.8	6.8	6.8	6.9	7.0	6.8
Finland	2.1	4.1	5.0	6.4	5.7	5.8	5.6	5.3	5.2	5.0
France				6.6	7.3	7.3	7.2	7.1	7.1	7.2
Germany	3.2	4.6	6.9	6.7	8.1	8.4	8.1	7.9	8.0	8.0
Greece		2.6	3.7	4.7	4.8	4.9	4.8	4.7	4.7	4.6
Hungary				6.4[3]	6.3	5.9	5.6	5.5	5.3	5.1
Iceland	2.5	4.0	5.4	6.8	6.9	6.8	6.7	7.0	7.4	7.5
Ireland	2.8	4.2	6.8	4.8	5.3	5.1	5.3	5.2	5.2	5.1
Italy				6.4	5.3	5.4	5.6	5.6	5.7	5.9
Japan	1.8	3.1	4.6	4.6	5.5	5.6	5.7	5.5	5.7	5.9
Korea					1.7	1.7	1.9	2.1	2.4	2.4	2.6
Luxembourg		3.2	5.5	5.7	5.9	5.9	5.4	5.4	5.6	
Mexico				1.8	2.3	2.2	2.3	2.6	2.6	2.5
Netherlands		4.2[4]	5.2	5.4	6.0	5.5	5.5	5.5	5.4	5.5
New Zealand		4.1	5.2	5.7	5.6	5.5	5.8	6.1	6.1	6.2
Norway	2.3	4.0	5.9	6.4	6.7	6.6	6.7	7.1	7.0	6.2
Poland				4.8	4.4	4.7	4.4	4.2	4.6	
Portugal		1.6	3.6	4.1	5.1	5.5	5.5	5.6	5.9	5.8
Slovak Republic							5.6	5.4	5.2	5.3
Spain	0.9	2.3	4.3	5.2	5.5	5.5	5.4	5.4	5.4	5.4
Sweden	3.3	6.0	8.4	7.6	6.9	7.1	6.8	6.6		
Switzerland	2.4	3.3	4.8	5.7	5.4	5.7	5.7	5.8	5.9	6.0
Turkey		0.9	0.9	2.2	2.4	2.7	3.0	3.5		
United Kingdom	3.3	3.9	5.0	5.0	5.8	5.8	5.4	5.5	5.7	5.9
United States	1.2	2.5	3.6	4.7	6.0	6.0	5.9	5.8	5.7	5.8

[1]Data from 1969
[2]Data from 1971
[3]Data from 1991
[4]Data from 1992

SOURCE: "Table 12: Public expenditures. % GDP," in *OECD Health Data: A Comprehensive Analysis of 30 Countries: 2002 Edition (CD-ROM Windows/Single User),* Organisation for Economic Co-operation and Development, Paris, France, July 2002

could be treated as effectively in outpatient settings and because many countries have reduced inpatient hospitalization rates and average length of stay (ALOS) to control health care costs. In 2000, Korea had the longest acute-care, ALOS of the OECD nations reporting (11.0 days), followed by Germany and Switzerland with ALOS of 9.6 and 9.3 days respectively. (See Table 7.8.) The shortest hospital stays in 2000 occurred in Finland, where ALOS averaged 4.4 days. The OECD did not include statistics for the United States for 2000, however it documented a low U.S. ALOS of 5.9 days in 1999.

Medical practice, particularly the types and frequency of procedures performed, also varies from one country to another. The OECD looked at rates of Caesarian section (also known as C-section, delivery of a baby through an incision in the abdomen, as opposed to vaginal delivery) per 1,000 births and found considerable variation in the rates for this surgical procedure. In 1999, the highest rates for Caesarian section were reported in Mexico (356.5), Italy (311.1), the United States (220), and Australia (217). (See Table 7.9.) Although data were not available for all OECD countries in 2000, Mexico and the United States had the highest rates of those reporting, with 363.4 and 229 per 1,000 live births, respectively. Since Caesarian section is performed in the hospital and generally involves at least an overnight stay, the frequency with which it and other surgical procedures are performed contributes to hospitalization rates and expenditures.

Physicians' Numbers Are Increasing

Since 1960, the OECD member nations have all enjoyed growing physician populations. In 2000, of those countries reporting, Italy reported the highest ratio of practicing physicians, 6 per 1,000 population, with most countries ranging between 2 and 4 physicians per 1,000 population. (See Table 7.10.) In 2000 the fewest practicing physicians were found in Turkey and Korea—both countries reported just 1.3 physicians per 1,000 people followed by the United Kingdom (1.8), Mexico (1.8), and Japan (1.9). Though figures were not reported from the United States for 2000, the number from 1999 was 2.8 physicians for 1,000 people.

The ratio of physicians to population is a limited measure of health care quality because many other factors such

TABLE 7.4

Out of pocket payments for health in OECD countries, 1960–2000

U.S. dollars per capita

	1960	1970	1980	1990	1995	1996	1997	1998	1999	2000
Australia	31	51[1]	106	216	281	307	313	378		
Austria					267	296	323	330	375	401
Canada				242	335	337	367	370	392	
Czech Republic				16[2]	66	68	77	77	83	89
Denmark		44	93	232	307	325	343	372	382	396
Finland	23	38	94	201	290	301	308	299	328	343
France				174	219	212	214	220	229	240
Germany		31	85	178	225	235	267	282	284	290
Hungary				58[2]	109	123	130	130	148	178
Iceland	8	22	68	184	283	308	324	354	365	
Ireland			73[3]	140	206	178	198	191	206	214
Italy			76	202	363	379	406	435	452	466
Japan								311	316	
Korea				188	273	300	303	262	324	
Luxembourg			44	82	131	158	164	179	185	
Mexico				154	214	207	219	207	238	
New Zealand			48	135	201	207	213	236	243	249
Norway				198	280	314	336	378	385	
Slovak Republic							51	54	69	72
Spain				182[2]	309	319	333	362	387	
Turkey				61[4]	56	72				
United Kingdom			38	103	143	156				
United States	72	123	256	550	558	573	606	646	676	707

[1]Data from 1969
[2]Data from 1991
[3]Data from 1983
[4]Data from 1992

SOURCE: "Table 16: Out of pocket payments. Per capita US$PPP," in *OECD Health Data: A Comprehensive Analysis of 30 Countries: 2002 Edition (CD-ROM Windows/Single User),* Organisation for Economic Co-operation and Development, Paris, France, July 2002

TABLE 7.5

Total expenditures on in-patient health care in OECD countries as a percent of total expenditures on health, 1960–2000

	1960	1970	1980	1990	1995	1996	1997	1998	1999	2000
Australia	43.0	44.1[1]	51.6	46.5	43.4	43.1	43.4	37.0		
Austria					48.4	47.0	43.7	42.9	41.8	41.5
Belgium		25.7	33.1	32.8	33.5	34.8	35.0			
Canada	43.7	52.6	53.8	49.0	44.7	44.3	43.3	42.9	42.1	42.0
Czech Republic					29.6	33.8	35.6	35.4	30.8	32.0
Denmark			61.6	56.7	55.0	55.3	54.7	54.3	53.9	53.5
Finland	39.9	46.4	46.3	44.7	42.0	41.8	41.4	41.1	40.5	39.9
France				46.0	45.5	45.5	45.4	44.6	43.6	42.8
Germany		30.8	33.2	34.7	30.0	30.2	31.1	31.5	31.1	31.1
Hungary				65.2[2]	54.8	52.4				
Iceland	33.3	47.8	59.1	54.9	55.2	55.1	54.9	55.1	55.7	
Italy				42.7	44.8	41.7	42.5	41.5	41.7	42.3
Japan	34.1	26.4	30.9	33.0	29.3	30.6	29.8	38.1	37.8	
Korea				21.7	23.1	24.3	25.7	26.4	28.1	
Luxembourg			31.3	26.4	31.3	32.4	36.0	30.7	29.8	
Mexico									32.9	
Netherlands		45.8[3]	54.6	49.2	49.1	49.6	49.9	49.9	49.5	49.2
Norway	38.1	68.2	63.9	61.7	37.3	37.4	37.8	38.7	39.5	
Spain		24.1[3]	54.1	44.1	43.6	43.6	43.3	42.8	42.3	
Switzerland	34.7	44.0	47.4	47.9	44.4	45.0	45.0	44.3	43.9	44.2
Turkey				33.4	28.7	28.2	28.8	29.3		
United States	38.6	44.8	49.6	44.9	43.0	42.6	42.2	41.5	40.4	39.6

[1]Data from 1969
[2]Data from 1991
[3]Data from 1972

SOURCE: "Table 13: Total expenditure on in-patient care. % total expenditure on health," in *OECD Health Data: A Comprehensive Analysis of 30 Countries: 2002 Edition (CD-ROM Windows/Single User),* Organisation for Economic Co-operation and Development, Paris, France, July 2002

TABLE 7.6

Total expenditures on pharmaceuticals and other medical durables in OECD countries as a percent of total expenditures on health, 1960–2000

	1960	1970	1980	1990	1995	1996	1997	1998	1999	2000
Australia	22.6	17.8[1]	8.0	9.0	11.3	11.5	11.4	11.6		
Belgium		28.1	17.4	15.5	16.3	15.6	16.3			
Canada	12.9	11.3	8.5	11.4	13.7	13.9	14.6	15.0	15.1	15.2
Czech Republic				21.0	25.6	25.5	25.3	25.5	26.5	25.2
Denmark			6.0	7.5	9.1	8.9	9.0	9.2	9.0	9.2
Finland	17.1	12.6	10.7	9.4	14.0	14.4	14.8	14.6	15.1	15.5
France				16.8	17.5	17.5	17.9	18.5	19.2	20.1
Germany		16.2	13.4	14.3	12.5	12.6	12.7	13.2	13.5	13.6
Greece		25.5	18.8	14.5	17.3	17.9	17.1	14.0	15.8	18.4
Hungary				27.6[2]	25.0	26.0	25.9			
Iceland	16.7	16.1	15.9	15.7	15.6	16.6	16.3	15.5	15.4	
Ireland		22.2	10.9	11.3	9.7	9.6	9.3	9.7	9.9	9.6
Italy				21.2	20.9	21.1	21.3	21.8	22.2	22.6
Japan			21.2	21.4	21.5	21.3	20.0	17.0	16.5	
Korea				25.7	21.9	19.8	17.0	13.8	14.0	
Luxembourg		19.7	14.5	14.9	12.0	11.5	12.6	12.3	11.7	
Mexico									20.0	
Netherlands		10.3[3]	8.0	9.6	11.0	11.0	11.0	11.4	11.6	11.8
New Zealand		11.4[4]	11.9	13.8	14.8	14.5	14.4			
Norway	9.7[5]	7.8	8.7	7.2	9.0	9.0	9.1			
Portugal		13.4	19.9	24.9	23.2	23.6	23.5	23.5		
Spain			21.0	17.8	17.7	18.2	19.0			
Sweden		6.6	6.5	8.0	12.5	12.9	12.8			
Switzerland				10.2	10.0	10.0	10.3	10.2	10.5	10.7
United Kingdom	12.9[6]	14.7	12.8	13.5	15.3	15.6	15.9			
United States	16.6	12.4	9.1	9.2	8.9	9.2	9.7	10.3	11.3	12.0

[1]Data from 1969
[2]Data from 1991
[3]Data from 1972
[4]Data from 1971
[5]Data from 1962
[6]Data from 1963

SOURCE: "Table 14: Total expenditure on pharmaceuticals and other medical durables. % total expenditure on health," in *OECD Health Data: A Comprehensive Analysis of 30 Countries: 2002 Edition (CD-ROM Windows/Single User),* Organisation for Economic Co-operation and Development, Paris, France, July 2002

as the availability of other health care providers, as well as accessibility and affordability of health care services also influence the quality of health care systems. Further, during the last two decades, research has shown that more medical care, in terms of numbers and concentration of providers, is not necessarily linked to better health status for the population. Researchers in the United States have found that an oversupply of providers may result in unnecessary treatment, procedures, and health care costs.

OVERVIEWS OF SELECTED HEALTH CARE SYSTEMS

In 2001 renowned political economist Uwe Reinhardt and his public health colleagues Peter Hussey and Gerard Anderson analyzed OECD data describing the health care systems in the 30 member countries. The researchers studied the economic development, spending, supply, population health status, service utilization, and technology, and issued a paper detailing key differences between the systems, "Cross-National Comparisons of Health Systems Using OECD Data, 1999," (*Health Affairs,* May/June 2002). An earlier report by Gerard Anderson of the Center for Hospital Finance and Man-

agement of Johns Hopkins University ("Multinational Comparisons of Health Care," the Commonwealth Fund, October 1998) provided a comprehensive examination of health care expenditures, coverage, and outcomes in eight OECD member countries. These overviews draw upon both publications' assessments of the strengths, weaknesses, and challenges faced by the various models of health service delivery.

United States

The U.S. health care financing system is based on the consumer sovereignty, or private insurance, model. There are more than 1,000 private insurance companies in the United States. Employer-based health insurance is tax-subsidized: health insurance premiums are a tax-deductible business expense and are not generally taxed as employee compensation. Individually purchased policies are partially tax-subsidized for self-employed Americans. Benefits, premiums, and provider reimbursement methods differ among private insurance plans, and among public programs as well.

Most physicians who provide both ambulatory care—hospital outpatient service and office visits—and inpatient

TABLE 7.7

Total hospital and other in-patient care beds in OECD countries per 1,000 population, 1960–2000

	1960	1970	1980	1990	1995	1996	1997	1998	1999	2000
Australia	11.4	11.7	12.3	9.8[1]	8.7	8.5	8.3	8.2	7.9	
Austria	10.8	10.8	11.2	10.1	9.3	9.2	9.1	8.9	8.8	8.6
Belgium		8.3	9.4	8.0	7.4	7.3	7.3			
Canada	6.2	7.0	6.8	6.3	4.8	4.5	4.4	4.1	3.9	
Czech Republic			11.3	11.3	9.5	9.2	9.0	8.9	8.7	8.8
Denmark	8.1[2]	8.1	8.1	5.6	4.9	4.7	4.6	4.5		
Finland	12.9[2]	15.1	15.6	12.5	9.3	9.2	7.9	7.8	7.6	7.5
France	9.6[3]	9.8[4]	11.1	9.7	8.9	8.8	8.6	8.5	8.4	8.2
Germany	10.5	11.3	11.5	10.4	9.7	9.6	9.4	9.3	9.2	9.1
Greece	5.8	6.2	6.2	5.1	5.0	5.0	5.0	5.0	4.9	
Hungary	6.9	7.9	9.1	10.1	8.9	8.9	8.1	8.2	8.3	8.2
Iceland	9.8	12.9	14.8	16.7	14.6					
Ireland			13.0	10.5	10.1	10.1	10.2	9.7		
Italy	8.9	10.6	9.6	7.2	6.2	6.5	5.8	5.5	4.9	
Japan	9.0	12.5	13.7	16.0	16.2	16.2	16.4	16.5	16.4	16.5
Korea			1.7	3.1	4.4	4.6	4.8	5.1	5.5	6.1
Luxembourg	11.8	12.6	12.8	11.7	8.2	8.2	8.1	8.0		
Mexico			0.7	0.8	1.2	1.2	1.1	1.1	1.1	1.1
Netherlands	11.0	11.4	12.3	11.5	11.3	11.2	11.2	11.2	11.1	10.8
New Zealand	11.7	10.8	10.2	8.5	6.2	6.1	6.1	6.2		
Norway			16.5	14.5[1]	15.1	15.0	14.7	14.5	14.4	14.6
Poland	4.6	5.2	5.6	5.7	5.5	5.5	5.4	5.3	5.1	4.9
Portugal	5.4	6.3	5.2	4.6	4.1	4.1	4.1	4.0	3.9	
Slovak Republic									8.1	
Spain	5.0[5]	4.7	5.4	4.3	3.9	3.9	3.8	4.2	4.1	4.1
Sweden	14.2	15.3	15.1	12.4	4.9	4.4	4.0	3.8	3.7	3.6
Switzerland				19.9[6]			20.0	18.9	18.3	17.9
Turkey	1.7	2.0	2.2	2.1	2.5	2.5	2.5	2.5	2.6	2.6
United Kingdom	10.7	9.6	8.1	5.9	4.7	4.5	4.4	4.2	4.1	4.1
United States	9.2	7.9	6.0	4.9	4.1	4.0	3.9	3.7	3.6	3.6

[1]Data from 1989
[2]Data from 1961
[3]Data from 1962
[4]Data from 1967
[5]Data from 1963
[6]Data from 1991

SOURCE: "Table 5: Total in-patient care beds. Per 1,000 population," in *OECD Health Data: A Comprehensive Analysis of 30 Countries: 2002 Edition (CD-ROM Windows/Single User),* Organisation for Economic Co-operation and Development, Paris, France, July 2002

hospital care are generally reimbursed on either a fee-for-service basis, per capita (literally, per head, but in managed care frequently per member per month, or PMPM) and payment rates vary among insurers. Increasing numbers of physicians are salaried; they are employees of the government, hospital and health care delivery systems, universities, and private industry.

The nation's more than 6,500 hospitals are paid on the basis of charges, costs, negotiated rates, or diagnosis-related groups (DRGs), depending on the patient's insurer. There are no overall global budgets or expenditure limits. Nevertheless, managed care (oversight by some group or authority to verify the medical necessity of treatments and to control the cost of health care) has assumed an expanding role. Health maintenance organizations (HMOs), preferred provider organizations (PPOs), and other managed care plans and payers (government and private health insurance) now exert greater control over the practices of individual health care providers, in an effort to control costs. To the extent that they govern reimbursement, managed care organizations are viewed by many physicians and other industry observers as dictating the methods, terms, and quality of health care delivery.

IS THE UNITED STATES SPENDING MORE AND GETTING LESS? A primary indicator of the quality of health care delivery in any nation is the health status of its people. Many factors can affect the health of individuals and populations: heredity, race/ethnicity, gender, income, education, geography, violent crime, environmental agents, and exposure to infectious diseases, as well as access to, and availability of, health care services.

Still, in the nation that spends the most on the health of its citizens, it seems reasonable to expect to see tangible benefits of expenditures for health care—measurable gains in health status. This section considers three health outcomes—measures used to assess the health of a population—including life expectancy at birth, infant mortality, and the incidence of cancer, to determine the extent to which Americans citizens benefit from record-high outlays for health care.

TABLE 7.8

Average length of stay in acute care health facilities in OECD countries, 1960–2000
Measured in days

	1960	1970	1980	1990	1995	1996	1997	1998	1999	2000
Australia	11.5	8.7	7.7	7.2[1]	6.5	6.4	6.3	6.2	6.2	
Austria			14.5	9.3	7.9	7.6	7.1	6.8	6.5	6.3
Belgium		15.6	10.0	8.7	9.4	9.2	8.8			
Canada			10.2	8.6	7.2	7.1	7.0	7.1	7.1	
Czech Republic	15.0	15.0	13.6	12.0	10.2	9.6	9.1	8.8	8.6	8.7
Denmark		12.5	8.5	6.4	5.7	5.6	5.4	5.3		
Finland	12.5	12.8	8.8	7.0	5.5	5.3	5.0	4.7	4.5	4.4
France	20.0[2]	16.0	9.9	7.0	5.9	5.8	5.6	5.6	5.5	
Germany	20.6	17.7	14.5	14.1	11.4	10.8	10.5	10.2	9.9	9.6
Greece			10.2	7.5	6.4	6.5	6.3	6.3		
Hungary	11.3	11.2	11.2	9.9	8.6	8.5	7.6	8.5	8.2	7.9
Iceland				7.0	5.9					
Ireland			8.5	6.7	6.6	6.5	6.5	6.5	6.5	6.4
Italy				9.5[3]	8.4	8.0	7.3	7.2		
Korea			10.0	12.0	11.0	11.0	11.0	11.0	10.0	11.0
Luxembourg			13.0	11.0	9.8	9.8				
Netherlands	20.1	18.8	14.0	11.2	9.9	9.8	9.6	9.5	9.2	9.0
Norway		14.8	10.9	7.8	6.5	6.3	6.4	6.2	6.1	6.0
Portugal	19.0[4]	15.3	11.4	8.4	7.9	7.9	7.5	7.3		
Spain				9.6	8.8	8.0	7.6			
Sweden		11.0	8.5	6.5	5.2	5.0	5.1	5.1	5.0	5.0
Switzerland			15.5	13.4	12.0	12.0	10.5	9.9	9.8	9.3
Turkey			6.3	6.0	5.7	5.6	5.5	5.4	5.4	5.4
United Kingdom			8.5	5.7	6.3	6.3	6.3	6.1	6.0	6.2
United States	7.6	8.2	7.6	7.3	6.5	6.2	6.1	6.0	5.9	

[1]Data from 1989
[2]Data from 1962
[3]Data from 1991
[4]Data from 1961

SOURCE: "Table 7: Average length of stay: acute care. Days," in *OECD Health Data: A Comprehensive Analysis of 30 Countries: 2002 Edition (CD-ROM Windows/Single User)*, Organisation for Economic Co-operation and Development, Paris, France, July 2002

Overall life expectancy at birth consistently increased in all 30 OECD member nations between 1960 and 1999; however, in every year including 1999, U.S. life expectancy was slightly below the OECD median (half were higher and half were lower) for males and females. (See Table 7.11.) Infant mortality also declined sharply during the same period but the United States fared far worse than the majority of OECD countries—in 1999 the United States had the 6th highest infant mortality rate. (See Table 7.12.) Finally, despite the well-funded U.S. "war on cancer," in 1997 the incidence rates of cancer per 100,000 were the highest of any OECD nation reporting (483.8 per 100,000) and they remained high throughout the remainder of the twentieth century. (See Table 7.13.)

Uwe Reinhardt and his colleagues suggest that part of the explanation of why exceedingly high U.S. health care expenditures do not produce better health outcomes is excessive spending on health care administration. The researchers note that financing a less complex and less costly administrative bureaucracy might enable the United States to focus more resources on direct provision of health care services.

Germany

The German health care system is based on the social insurance model. Statutory sickness funds and private insurance cover the entire population. Approximately 1,200 sickness funds cover about 92 percent of the population. Employees and employers finance these sickness funds through payroll contributions. Nearly all employers, including small businesses and low-wage industries, must participate.

During the late 1990s, Germany had the second highest per capita health care expenditures. Contributions to sickness funds averaged about 13 percent of a worker's salary and about 10 percent of sickness fund members purchased complementary private insurance. Another 8 percent of the population chose not to participate in the public system and were fully covered by private insurance. Nearly three quarters of all health expenditures were public, and about 11 percent were direct, out-of-pocket payments. Less than 1 percent of the population does not have health insurance. Unlike U.S. health insurance, which is often not "portable," under the sickness funds, losing or changing jobs does not affect health insurance protection. The German government does not require its wealthiest citizens to purchase health insurance, but almost all of them do so voluntarily.

Ambulatory (outpatient) and inpatient care operate completely separately in the German health care system. German hospitals are public and private, operate for profit

TABLE 7.9

Caesarean sections performed in OECD countries, 1960–2000

Procedures per 1,000 live births

	1960	1970	1980	1990	1995	1996	1997	1998	1999	2000
Australia		42.0	128.0	175.0	192.0	193.0	201.0	209.0	217.0	
Austria			65.0[1]		123.9	130.9	139.5	145.8	164.2	172.0
Belgium			74.0	104.5	134.5	136.7	137.7	144.1	159.2	
Canada					175.2	180.4	172.5	181.3	190.4	
Czech Republic		21.9	44.1	76.1	112.0	115.6	117.9	122.7	123.4	128.9
Denmark		57.0	104.0	125.8	125.5	128.8	129.8	137.8	142.9	152.7
Finland	42.0[2]	60.0	119.0[3]	142.0	155.1	155.2	154.4	152.8	154.7	157.3
France				139.4	149.8	153.7	159.7	157.2		
Germany				157.0	172.4	176.1	181.4	190.7	198.0	
Hungary					136.1		156.8	170.1	187.2	201.5
Iceland		31.0	74.0	118.1	141.1	151.5	162.6	159.2	173.2	176.8
Ireland				105.4	128.7[4]				179.1	187.4
Italy			112.0	207.9	260.7	264.3	271.2	290.9	311.1	
Luxembourg			132.0	165.0	164.0	164.0	169.0	181.0		
Mexico				235.3[5]	305.6	311.6	328.3	332.8	356.5	363.4
Netherlands				74.1	96.5	100.6	103.9	110.6	113.4	129.0
New Zealand				121.0	151.2	156.7	164.5	181.6	183.7	201.5
Norway			83.8	127.5	126.4	127.3	128.8	136.7		
Portugal				186.1	241.7	246.3	274.1	275.3		
Slovak Republic				87.1	116.0	122.4	129.7	132.9	138.5	146.4
Spain			87.0[6]	142.2	188.0	192.9				
Sweden		55.0[7]	118.4	107.9	120.0	117.3	131.6	137.6	144.0	
United Kingdom	28.0	43.0	88.0	124.0	158.0	160.0	170.0			
United States				227.0	208.0	207.0	208.0	212.0	220.0	229.0

[1]Data from 1981
[2]Data from 1961
[3]Data from 1979
[4]Data from 1993
[5]Data from 1991
[6]Data from 1983
[7]Data from 1973

SOURCE: "Table 8: Surgical procedures: Caesarean sections. Procedures per 1,000 live births," in *OECD Health Data: A Comprehensive Analysis of 30 Countries: 2002 Edition (CD-ROM Windows/Single User)*, Organisation for Economic Co-operation and Development, Paris, France, July 2002

and not-for-profit, and generally do not have outpatient departments. Ambulatory care physicians are paid on the basis of fee schedules negotiated between the organizations of sickness funds and organizations of physicians. A separate fee schedule for private patients uses a similar scale. Hospitals were previously paid on the basis of negotiated per diem (or length of stay) payments, but the 1993 Health Care Reform law instituted a sliding scale based on specific fees for specific procedures and per-admission payment schedules.

Public (federal, state, and local) hospitals account for about 50 percent of hospital beds; private voluntary hospitals, often run by religious organizations, account for 35 percent of beds; and private for-profit hospitals, generally owned by physicians, account for 15 percent. Ambulatory care physicians are generally self-employed professionals paid on a fee-for-service basis, while most hospital-based physicians are salaried employees of the hospital.

On January 1, 1993, Germany's Health Care Reform law went into effect. Among its many provisions, the law tied increases in physician, dental, and hospital expenditures to the income growth rate of members of the sickness funds. It also limited the licensing of new ambulatory

care physicians (based on the number of physicians already in an area) and set a cap for overall pharmaceutical outlays. Still, in 2000 Germany boasted 3.6 practicing physicians per 1,000 population, the third highest ratio reported by OECD countries. (See Table 7.10.) The 1993 legislation also changed the hospital compensation system from per diem payments to specific fees for individual procedures and conditions.

Health care reforms instituted in the 1990s also served to stimulate competition between sickness funds, and improved coordination of inpatient and ambulatory care. During the mid-1990s, the government also attempted to control health care costs by reducing health benefits, such as limiting how often patients could visit health spas to recuperate.

Canada

The Canadian system has been characterized as a provincial government health insurance model, in which each of the ten provinces operates its own health system under general federal rules and with a fixed federal contribution. All provinces are required to offer insurance coverage for "all medically necessary services," including hospital care and physician services. However, additional

TABLE 7.10

Number of practicing physicians per 1,000 population in OECD countries, 1960–2000

	1960	1970	1980	1990	1995	1996	1997	1998	1999	2000
Australia	1.1	1.2[1]	1.8[2]	2.3[3]	2.5	2.5	2.5	2.5		
Austria	1.4	1.4	1.6	2.2	2.7	2.8	2.9	3.0	3.0	3.1
Belgium	1.3	1.6[4]	2.3	3.3	3.5	3.6	3.7	3.7	3.8	3.9
Canada		1.5	1.8	2.1	2.1	2.1	2.1	2.1	2.1	2.1
Czech Republic		1.9	2.3	2.8	2.9	2.9	3.0	3.0	3.0	3.1
Denmark	1.2	1.4	2.2	3.1	3.3	3.3	3.3	3.3	3.4	
Finland	0.6	0.9	1.7	2.4	2.8	2.8	3.0	3.0	3.1	3.1
France	1.0	1.3	2.0	2.6	2.9	3.0	3.0	3.0		
Germany	1.4	1.6	2.3	3.1	3.4	3.4	3.4	3.5	3.5	3.6
Greece	1.3	1.6	2.4	3.4	3.9	4.0	4.1	4.3	4.4	
Hungary	1.5	2.0	2.3	2.9	3.0	3.1	3.1	3.1	3.2	
Iceland	1.2	1.4	2.1	2.8	3.0	3.1	3.3	3.3	3.4	
Ireland				1.6	2.1	2.1	2.1	2.2	2.3	
Italy	0.7	1.1	2.6	4.7	5.7	5.7	5.8	5.8	5.9	6.0
Japan	1.0	1.1	1.3	1.7	1.8[5]	1.8		1.9		1.9
Korea			0.5	0.8	1.1	1.2	1.2	1.3	1.3	1.3
Luxembourg	1.0	1.1	1.7	2.0	2.8	2.9	3.0	3.0	3.1	3.1
Mexico				1.1	1.6	1.6	1.6	1.6	1.7	1.8
Netherlands	1.1	1.2	1.9	2.5				2.9	3.1	3.2
New Zealand	1.1[6]	1.1[1]	1.6	1.9	2.1	2.1	2.2	2.2	2.3	2.2
Norway	1.2	1.4	2.0	2.6[3]	2.8	2.8	2.5	2.7	2.8	2.9
Poland	1.0	1.4	1.8	2.1	2.3	2.4	2.4	2.3	2.3	2.2
Portugal	0.8	0.9	2.0	2.8	3.0	3.0	3.1	3.1	3.2	3.2
Spain				2.3	2.5	2.9	2.9	2.9	3.1	3.3
Sweden	1.0	1.3	2.2	2.9	2.8	2.8	2.8	2.8	2.9	
Switzerland	1.4	1.5	2.4	3.0	3.2	3.2	3.3	3.3	3.4	3.5
Turkey	0.3	0.4	0.6	0.9	1.1	1.1	1.2	1.2	1.2	1.3
United Kingdom	0.8	0.9	1.3	1.4	1.6	1.7	1.7	1.8	1.8	1.8
United States	1.4	1.6	2.0	2.4	2.6	2.6	2.7	2.8	2.8	

[1] Data from 1971
[2] Data from 1981
[3] Data from 1991
[4] Data from 1969
[5] Data from 1994
[6] Data from 1961

SOURCE: "Table 4: Practising physicians. Density per 1,000 population," in *OECD Health Data: A Comprehensive Analysis of 30 Countries: 2002 Edition (CD-ROM Windows/Single User)*, Organisation for Economic Co-operation and Development, July 2002

services and benefits may be offered at the discretion of each province. Most provinces cover preventive services, routine dental care for children, and outpatient drugs for the elderly (with a copayment) and the poor. No restrictions are placed on a patient's choice of physicians.

Canadian citizens have equal access to medical care, regardless of their ability to pay. Entitlement to benefits is linked to residency, and the system is financed through general taxation. Private insurance is prohibited from covering the same benefits covered by the public system yet more than 60 percent of Canadians are covered by private supplemental insurance policies. These policies generally cover services such as adult dental care, cosmetic surgery, and private or semiprivate hospital rooms. Seventy-three percent of all health expenditures are public, and consumers pay less than 30 percent of health care expenditures out-of-pocket.

The majority of hospitals are not-for-profit and are funded on the basis of global institution-specific, or regional budgets. (A global budget allocates a lump sum of money to a large department or area. Then all the groups in that department or area must negotiate to see how much of the total money each group receives.) Physicians in both inpatient and outpatient settings are paid on a negotiated, fee-for-service basis. The systems vary somewhat from province to province, and certain provinces, such as Quebec, have also established global budgets for physician services. The federal government's contribution to Canada's health care bill has progressively declined in the past two decades. During the early 1980s, the federal government paid for a historic high of 50 percent of the total health care bill. This dropped in subsequent years, to 38 percent in 1990, 30 percent in 1993, and less than 20 percent in 1998. The resulting shift in costs has increased expenditures by the provinces and territories as well as out-of-pocket expenses paid by Canadians. The delivery system is composed largely of community hospitals and self-employed physicians. About 95 percent of Canadian hospital beds are public; private hospitals do not participate in the public insurance program.

FINANCIAL PROBLEMS. During the 1990s public revenues did not increase rapidly enough in Canada to cover

TABLE 7.11

Life expectancy at birth in years in OECD countries, 1960–99

	1960 Females at birth	1960 Males at birth	1970 Females at birth	1970 Males at birth	1980 Females at birth	1980 Males at birth	1990 Females at birth	1990 Males at birth	1995 Females at birth	1995 Males at birth	1996 Females at birth	1996 Males at birth	1997 Females at birth	1997 Males at birth	1998 Females at birth	1998 Males at birth	1999 Females at birth	1999 Males at birth
Australia	73.9	67.9	74.2	67.4	78.1	71.0	80.1	73.9	80.8	75.0	81.1	75.2	81.3	75.6	81.5	75.9	81.8	76.2
Austria	71.9	65.4	73.4	66.5	76.1	69.0	78.9	72.3	80.1	73.5	80.2	73.9	80.6	74.3	80.9	74.7	80.9	75.1
Belgium	73.5	67.7	74.2	67.8	76.8	70.0	79.4	72.7	80.2	73.4	80.5	73.8	80.6	74.1	80.5	74.3	80.8	74.4
Canada	74.3[1]	68.4[1]	76.4[2]	69.3[2]	78.9	71.7	80.8	74.4	81.1	75.1	81.2	75.5	81.3	75.8	81.5	76.0	81.7	76.3
Czech Republic	73.4	67.9	73.0	66.1	73.9	66.8	75.4	67.6	76.6	69.7	77.3	70.4	77.5	70.5	78.1	71.1	78.1	71.4
Denmark	74.4	70.4	75.9	70.7	77.3	71.2	77.7	72.0	77.8	72.7	78.2	73.1	78.4	73.6	78.8	73.9	79.0	74.2
Finland	72.5	65.5	75.0	66.5	77.6	69.2	78.9	70.9	80.2	72.8	80.5	73.0	80.5	73.4	80.8	73.5	81.0	73.8
France	73.6	67.0	75.9	68.4	78.4	70.2	81.0	72.7	81.9	73.9	82.1	74.1	82.3	74.6	82.4	74.8	82.5	75.0
Germany	72.4	66.9	73.6	67.2	76.1	69.6	78.4	72.0	79.7	73.3	79.9	73.6	80.3	74.0	80.6	74.5	80.7	74.7
Greece	72.4	67.3	73.8	70.1	76.8	72.2	79.5	74.6	80.3	75.0	80.4	75.1	80.8	75.6	80.6	75.5		
Hungary	70.1	65.9	72.1	66.3	72.7	65.5	73.7	65.1	74.5	65.3	74.7	66.6	75.1	66.4	75.2	66.1	75.1	66.3
Iceland	75.0	70.7	77.3	71.2	79.7	73.7	80.3	75.7	80.6	76.5	80.6	76.2	81.3	76.4	81.5	77.0	81.4	77.5
Ireland	71.9	68.1	73.5	68.8	75.6	70.1	77.6	72.1	78.4	72.9	78.6	73.1	78.6	73.4	79.1	73.5	79.1	73.9
Italy	72.3[1]	67.2[1]	74.9[2]	69.0[2]	77.4	70.6	80.0	73.5	81.0	74.6	81.3	75.0	81.6	75.3				
Japan	70.2	65.3	74.7	69.3	78.8	73.4	81.9	75.9	82.9	76.4	83.6	77.0	83.8	77.2	84.0	77.2	84.0	77.1
Korea	53.7	51.1	66.1[2]	59.0[2]	69.5[3]	61.3[3]	75.1[4]	66.8[4]	77.4	69.6			78.1	70.6			79.2	71.7
Luxembourg	72.2	66.5	73.4	67.1	75.9	69.1	78.5	72.3	80.2	73.0	79.9	73.3	79.8	74.1	80.5	73.7	81.2	74.7
Mexico	59.5	56.2	63.6	59.7	70.0	64.0	74.0	68.8	75.9	71.3	76.3	71.7	76.6	72.0	77.0	72.4	77.3	72.8
Netherlands	75.4	71.5	76.5	70.8	79.2	72.5	80.1	73.8	80.4	74.6	80.4	74.7	80.6	75.2	80.7	75.2	80.5	75.3
New Zealand	73.9	68.7	74.6	68.3	76.3	70.0	78.3	72.4	79.5	74.2	79.6	74.3	80.1	74.9	80.4	75.2	80.8	75.7
Norway	75.8	71.3	77.3	71.0	79.2	72.3	79.8	73.4	80.8	74.8	81.1	75.4	81.0	75.4	81.3	75.5	81.1	75.6
Poland	70.6	64.9	73.3	66.6	74.4	66.0	75.5	66.5	76.4	67.6	76.6	68.1	77.0	68.5	77.3	68.9	77.5	68.8
Portugal	66.8	61.2	70.8	64.2	75.2	67.7	77.4	70.4	78.6	71.2	78.6	71.1	78.8	71.6	78.9	71.7	79.1	72.0
Slovak Republic	72.7	68.4	72.9	66.7	74.3	66.8	75.4	66.6	76.3	68.4	76.8	68.9	76.7	68.9	76.7	68.6	77.0	69.0
Spain	72.2	67.4	74.8	69.2	78.6	72.5	80.4	73.3	81.5	74.3	81.7	74.4	81.9	74.9	82.2	74.8	82.4	74.9
Sweden	74.9	71.2	77.1	72.2	78.8	72.8	80.4	74.8	81.3	75.9	81.5	76.5	81.8	76.7	81.9	76.9	81.9	77.0
Switzerland	74.5	68.7	76.9	70.7	79.6	72.8	80.7	74.0	81.7	75.3	82.0	75.9	82.1	76.3	82.4	76.3	82.5	76.8
Turkey	50.3	46.3	56.3	52.0	60.3	55.8	68.3	63.8	69.8	65.2	70.0	65.5	70.3	65.7	70.5	65.9	70.7	66.1
United Kingdom	73.7	67.9	75.0	68.7	76.2	70.2	78.5	72.9	79.2	74.0	79.5	74.3	79.6	74.7	79.7	74.8	79.8	75.0
United States	73.1	66.6	74.7	67.1	77.4	70.0	78.8	71.8	78.9	72.5	79.1	73.1	79.4	73.6	79.5	73.8	79.4	73.9

[1]Data from 1961
[2]Data from 1971
[3]Data from 1979
[4]Data from 1989

SOURCE: "Table 1: Life expectancy at birth. Years," in *OECD Health Data: A Comprehensive Analysis of 30 Countries: 2002 Edition (CD-ROM Windows/Single User)*, Organisation for Economic Co-operation and Development, July 2002

TABLE 7.12

Infant mortality rates in OECD countries, 1960–2000
Deaths per 1,000 live births

	1960	1970	1980	1990	1995	1996	1997	1998	1999	2000
Australia	20.2	17.9	10.7	8.2	5.7	5.8	5.3	5.0	5.7	5.2
Austria	37.5	25.9	14.3	7.8	5.4	5.1	4.7	4.9	4.4	4.8
Belgium	31.2	21.1	12.1	8.0	6.1	5.6	6.1	5.6	4.9	5.2
Canada	27.3	18.8	10.4	6.8	6.0	5.6	5.5	5.3	5.3	
Czech Republic	20.0	20.2	16.9	10.8	7.7	6.0	5.9	5.2	4.6	4.1
Denmark	21.5	14.2	8.4	7.5	5.1	5.6	5.2	4.7	4.2	5.3
Finland	21.0	13.2	7.6	5.6	4.0	3.9	3.9	4.1	3.7	3.8
France	27.5	18.2	10.0	7.3	4.9	4.8	4.7	4.6	4.3	4.5
Germany	35.0	22.5	12.4	7.0	5.3	5.0	4.9	4.7	4.5	4.4
Greece	40.1	29.6	17.9	9.7	8.1	7.2	6.4	6.7	6.2	6.1
Hungary	47.6	35.9	23.2	14.8	10.7	10.9	9.9	9.7	8.4	9.2
Iceland	13.0	13.2	7.7	5.9	6.1	3.7	5.5	2.6	2.4	3.0
Ireland	29.3	19.5	11.1	8.2	6.3	6.0	6.1	6.2	5.5	5.9
Italy	43.9	29.6	14.6	8.2	6.2	6.2	5.6	5.4	5.1	5.1
Japan	30.7	13.1	7.5	4.6	4.3	3.8	3.7	3.6	3.4	3.2
Korea		45.0	17.0[1]	12.0[2]		7.7				
Luxembourg	31.5	24.9	11.5	7.3	5.5	4.9	4.2	5.0	4.6	5.1
Mexico		79.0	53.0	36.6	30.5	29.3	28.1	26.9	25.9	24.9
Netherlands	17.9	12.7	8.6	7.1	5.5	5.7	5.0	5.2	5.2	5.1
New Zealand	22.6	16.7	13.0	8.4	6.7	7.3	6.8	5.4		
Norway	18.9	12.7	8.1	7.0	4.1	4.1	4.1	4.0	3.9	3.8
Poland	54.8	36.7	25.5	19.3	13.6	12.2	10.2	9.5	8.9	8.1
Portugal	77.5	55.5	24.3	11.0	7.5	6.9	6.4	6.0	5.6	5.5
Slovak Republic	28.6	25.7	20.9	12.0	11.0	10.2	8.7	8.8	8.3	8.6
Spain	43.7	28.1	12.3	7.6	5.5	5.5	5.0	4.9	4.5	4.6
Sweden	16.6	11.0	6.9	6.0	4.1	4.0	3.6	3.5	3.4	3.4
Switzerland	21.1	15.1	9.1	6.8	5.0	4.7	4.8	4.8	4.6	4.9
Turkey	189.5	145.0	117.5	57.6	45.6	44.0	42.4	42.7	40.3	39.7
United Kingdom	22.5	18.5	12.1	7.9	6.2	6.1	5.9	5.7	5.8	5.6
United States	26.0	20.0	12.6	9.2	7.6	7.3	7.2	7.2	7.1	

[1] Data from 1971
[2] Data from 1989

SOURCE: "Table 2: Infant mortality. Deaths per 1,000 live births," in *OECD Health Data: A Comprehensive Analysis of 30 Countries: 2002 Edition (CD-ROM Windows/Single User),* Organisation for Economic Co-operation and Development, Paris, France, July 2002

rising health care costs. The Canadian government attributed many of the financial problems to lower revenue from taxes, higher prices for biomedical technology, and relatively lengthy hospital stays. In 1993, for the first time since Canada instituted universal health insurance 27 years earlier, Canadians were required to pay for common services such as throat cultures to test for streptococcal infections (the bacterial cause of strep throat).

As a result of cutbacks and inadequate equipment, waiting times for nonemergency surgery, such as hip replacement, and high-technology diagnostic tools, such as computerized tomography (CT scans), could amount to months, or even years. Although Canadians generally still support their present system, physicians and consumers have expressed growing dissatisfaction with the rising costs and long waiting periods for diagnostic tests and nonemergency treatment.

THE SAFETY VALVE TO THE SOUTH. Some Canadians cross the border to the United States to avoid the waiting lines in their hospitals, clinics, and physicians' offices. Canadian physicians have been known to refer seriously ill patients in need of immediate medical attention to U.S.

hospitals in such cities as nearby Buffalo, New York; Cleveland, Ohio; and Detroit, Michigan. In fact, many American hospitals market medical services, most notably cardiac care and addiction treatment, to the Canadian public. Overall, however, there has been very little border-crossing to seek health care services. Canadians accounted for less than 1 percent of total admissions in the nine border hospitals surveyed by the American Medical Association.

CUTTING COSTS. The general consensus is that no one wants to disassemble what has become Canada's most popular social program, but most agree that change is inevitable. The Ontario Health Insurance Plan insures 10 million people, or almost 40 percent of all Canadians. They have managed to cut costs in several ways, such as:

• Reducing fees to commercial laboratories and allowing them to bill patients directly for tests performed.

• Stopping payment for certain services connected with employment. For example, many Canadians must pay out of pocket for pre-employment physical examinations.

TABLE 7.13

Incidence of cancer in OECD countries, 1960–1999

Incidence per 100,000 population

	1960	1970	1980	1990	1995	1996	1997	1998	1999
Australia			246.3[1]	274.0	312.4	303.3	302.3	299.7	
Austria			242.5[2]	248.6	251.1	254.2	249.2	245.1	236.7
Belgium				189.8[3]	178.6	196.9	221.1		
Canada			355.4	395.5		401.5			415.4
Czech Republic		223.5[4]	243.9	286.9	326.2	337.5	340.4	338.8	
Denmark			288.3	318.9	322.2	319.4			
Finland	200.4	215.9	233.7	235.2	251.3	261.3	258.6	262.0	268.5
France					261.0				
Germany				409.1[5]	407.8		412.3	423.2	
Hungary			215.4	271.2	247.7	319.4			
Ireland					384.3	361.9	367.4		
Japan					205.4				
Luxembourg			278.7[6]	366.6	403.1	395.7	413.5	430.1	406.7
Netherlands			320.0	381.1	407.3	420.2	417.8		
New Zealand	155.4	203.1	253.9	272.4	329.6	323.6	309.4	311.9	
Norway	167.7	193.7	225.4	249.4	265.5	273.6	283.8	277.7	
Slovak Republic	178.0	271.6	281.4	340.8	377.6	385.3	389.0	399.8	
United Kingdom		194.0[7]	216.8	239.3	241.9	243.3	242.5		
United States		385.0[4]	417.5	482.6	476.2	477.6	483.8	482.6	476.1

[1]Data from 1982
[2]Data from 1983
[3]Data from 1993
[4]Data from 1973
[5]Data from 1991
[6]Data from 1981
[7]Data from 1971

SOURCE: "Table 3: Cancer. Malignant neoplasms. Incidence per 100,000 population," in *OECD Health Data: A Comprehensive Analysis of 30 Countries: 2002 Edition (CD-ROM Windows/Single User),* Organisation for Economic Co-operation and Development, Paris, France, July 2002

- Ending coverage of electrolysis (removal of unwanted hair) and reviewing coverage of services and procedures such as psychoanalysis, vasectomies, newborn circumcision, in vitro fertilization, as well as chiropractic, podiatric, and osteopathic services.

- Increasing copayments—the amounts patients must pay for prescriptions covered under the Ontario Drug Benefit Plan, which is used mainly by persons over age 65.

Similarly, in an effort to cut hospital costs, British Columbia has moved to shift some services away from hospitals to outpatient clinics, public health programs, and home care. Canadian officials hoped that cutbacks in covered services, caps on physicians' fees and hospital budgets, and controlling the use of expensive medical technology could keep the popular health care system afloat.

United Kingdom

The United Kingdom employs the National Health Service, or Beveridge, model to finance and deliver health care. The entire population is covered under a system that is financed mainly from general taxation. There is minimal cost sharing. About 12 percent of the population also purchases private insurance as a supplement to the public system. Eighty-eight percent of all health spending is from public funds, and in 1998, about 8 percent of health expenditures were out-of-pocket payments.

Services are organized and managed by regional and local public authorities. General practitioners serve as primary care physicians and are reimbursed on the basis of a combination of capitation payments (payments for each person served), fee-for-service, and other allowances. Hospitals receive overall budget allotments from district health authorities, and hospital-based physicians are salaried. Private insurance reimburses both physicians and hospitals on a fee-for-service basis.

Self-employed general practitioners are considered independent contractors, and salaried hospital-based physicians are public employees. Of the United Kingdom's hospital beds, 90 percent are public and generally owned by the National Health Service. As of 1991, it became possible for large physician practices to become "budget holders," and receive larger capitation payments. Similarly, individual hospitals may become "self-governing trust hospitals," enabling them to compete for patients and market their services. While emergency health service is immediate, persons needing elective surgery, such as hip replacement, may end up on a waiting list for years.

The NHS pioneered many cost-containment measures that are currently used by the United States and other countries seeking to slow escalating health care expenditures. These approaches to evaluating and managing health care costs include:

- Cost-effective analysis: Calculated as a ratio, and often expressed as the cost per year per life saved, the cost-effectiveness analysis of a drug or procedure relates the cost of the drug or procedure to the health benefits it produces. This analysis enables delivery of clinically efficient, cost-effective care.

- Cost-minimization analysis: Primarily applied to the pharmaceutical industry, this technique identifies the lowest cost among pharmaceuticals alternatives that provide clinically comparable health outcomes.

- Cost-utility analysis: This measures the costs of therapy or treatment. Economists use the term "utility" to describe the amount of satisfaction a consumer receives from a given product or service. This analysis measures outcomes in terms of patient preference and is generally expressed as quality-adjusted life years. For example, an analysis of cancer chemotherapy drugs considers the various adverse side effects of these drugs because some patients may prefer a shorter duration of symptom-free survival rather than a longer life span marked by pain, suffering, and dependence on others for care.

France

The French health care system is based on the social insurance, or Bismarck, model. Virtually the entire population is covered by a legislated, compulsory health insurance plan that is financed through the social security system. Three major programs, and several smaller ones, are quasi-autonomous, nongovernmental bodies. The system is financed through employee and employer payroll tax contributions. More than 80 percent of the population supplements their public benefits by purchasing insurance from private, nonprofit *mutuels,* and about 2 percent of the population has private commercial insurance.

The public share of total health spending is 74 percent, and about 17 percent of expenditures represent direct, out-of-pocket payments. Physicians practicing in municipal health centers and public hospitals are salaried, but physicians in private hospitals and in ambulatory care settings are typically paid on a negotiated, fee-for-service basis. Public hospitals are granted lump-sum budgets, and private hospitals are paid on the basis of negotiated per diem payment rates. About 65 percent of hospital beds are public, while the remaining 35 percent are private (and equally divided between profit and nonprofit).

In April 1996, the French government announced major reforms aimed at containing rising costs in the national health care system. The new system monitored each patient's total health costs and penalized physicians if they overran their budgets for specific types of care and prescriptions. In addition, French citizens were required to consult general practitioners before going to specialists. Initially, physicians—specialists, in particular—denounced the reforms and

warned that they could lead to rationing and compromise the quality of health care. However, over time these cost-containment efforts met with less resistance from physicians and consumers. By 2000 physicians and hospitals were generally accepting of moderate fee schedules, cost-sharing arrangements, and global budgeting to control costs.

Japan

Japan's health care financing is also based on the social insurance model and, in particular, on the German health care system. Three general programs cover the entire population: Employee Health Insurance, Community Health Insurance, and Health and Medical Services for the Aged. About 62 percent of the population obtains coverage through about 1,900 not-for-profit, nongovernmental, employer-sponsored plans. Small businesses, the self-employed, and farmers are covered through Community Health Insurance, which is administered by a conglomeration of local governmental and private bodies. The elderly are covered by a separate plan that largely pools funds from the other plans. The emphasis is on the government, as opposed to business, bearing the major financial burden for the nation's health care.

The system is financed through employer and employee income-related premiums. There are different levels of public subsidization of the three different programs. Limited private insurance exists for supplemental coverage, which is purchased by about one-third of the population and accounts for 7 percent of health expenditures. Public expenditures account for 72 percent of total health spending, while out-of-pocket expenses account for about 12 percent.

Physicians and hospitals are paid on the basis of national, negotiated fee schedules. Physicians practicing in public hospitals are salaried, while those practicing in physician-owned clinics and private hospitals are reimbursed on a fee-for-service basis. The amount paid for each medical procedure is rigidly controlled. Physicians not only diagnose, treat, and manage illnesses, they also prescribe and dispense pharmaceuticals, and a considerable portion of a physician's income is derived from dispensing prescription drugs.

A close physician–patient relationship is unusual in Japan; the typical physician endeavors to see as many patients as possible in a day in order to earn a living. A patient going to a clinic for treatment may have to wait many hours in a very crowded facility. As a result, health care is rarely a joint physician–patient effort. Instead, physicians tend to dictate treatment without fully informing patients about their conditions or the tests, drugs, and therapy that have been ordered or prescribed.

About 80 percent of Japan's hospitals are privately operated (and often physician-owned) and the remaining 20 percent are public. Hospitals are paid according to a uniform fee schedule and for-profit hospitals are prohibited. Hospital stays are typically far longer than in the United States, or any other developed member nation of OECD, allowing hospitals and physicians to overcome the limitations of the fee schedules.

Despite the limitations of Japan's health care system, Japanese men and women are among the longest lived in the world. In 1999 life expectancy was 84 years for women and 77.1 years for men. (See Table 7.11.) The Japanese infant mortality rate in 2000, at 3.2 per 1,000 live births, was almost the lowest in the world (Iceland's was 3 per 1,000 live births). (See Table 7.12.) These two statistics are usually considered reliable indicators of a successful health care system. It should be noted, though, that Japan does not have a large impoverished class, as does the United States, and its diet is considered to be among the healthiest in the world.

CHAPTER 8

CHANGE, CHALLENGES, AND INNOVATION
IN HEALTH CARE DELIVERY

Since the 1970s the U.S. health care system has experienced rapid and unprecedented change. The sites where health care is delivered have shifted from acute inpatient hospitals to outpatient settings such as ambulatory care and surgical centers, clinics, and physicians' offices as well as long-term care and rehabilitation facilities. Patterns of disease have changed from acute infectious diseases that require acute episodic care to chronic conditions that require ongoing care. Even threats to U.S. public health have changed—epidemics of infectious diseases have been replaced by epidemics of health risks such as obesity, substance abuse, and physical inactivity. At the end of 2001, the threat of bioterrorism became an urgent concern of health care planners, providers, policymakers, and the American public.

There are new health care providers—mid-level practitioners (advance practice nurses, certified nurse midwives, physician assistants, medical technologists) and new equipment for diagnosis such as magnetic resonance imaging (MRI) and genetic testing. Further, the rise of managed care, explosion of biotechnology, and availability of information on the Internet have dramatically changed how health care is delivered.

Some health care industry observers suggest that the speed at which these changes have occurred has further harmed an already complicated and uncoordinated health care system. There is concern that the present health care system cannot keep pace with scientific and technological advances. Many worry that the health care system is already unable to deliver quality care to all Americans and that it is so disorganized that it will be unable to meet the needs of the growing population of older Americans.

This chapter considers several of the most pressing challenges and opportunities faced by the U.S. health care system. These include:

• Safety: Ensuring safety by protecting patients from harm or injury inflicted by the health care system—

preventing medical errors, reducing hospital infections, and safeguarding consumers from medical fraud. In addition to actions to reduce problems caused by the health care system, safety and quality may be ensured by providers' use of clinical practice guidelines—standardized plans for diagnosis and treatment of disease and the effective application of technology to information and communication systems.

• Information Management: Information technology, including the Internet, has the potential to provide health care providers and consumers with timely access to medical data, patient information, and the clinical expertise of experts. Public sources of consumer and provider health information on the Internet include the National Institutes of Health (NIH), Centers for Disease Control and Prevention (CDC), and Medline. Using this technology effectively is a health system challenge, especially in terms of protecting patient privacy and confidentiality and ensuring that consumers have access to accurate and reliable health information.

• Innovation: Widespread use of innovations in health care delivery should be recommended only after objective analysis has demonstrated that the innovation will measurably benefit the safety, effectiveness, efficiency, or timeliness of health service delivery. Innovations should also be considered if they have the potential to reduce waste of equipment, supplies, or personnel time or if they have the capacity to allocate or distribute health care more equitably. Equitable distribution refers to care that does not vary in quality based on the characteristics, such as race, gender, ethnicity, or socioeconomic status of the population served.

SAFETY

Although the United States is generally viewed as providing quality health care services to its citizens, a

1999 report issued by the Institute of Medicine (IOM) *To Err Is Human: Building a Safer Health System* (Academy Press, Washington, DC), estimated that as many as 98,000 American deaths per year are the result of preventable medical errors. More than 7,000 of these deaths were estimated to be due to preventable medication errors.

The IOM calculated the cost of medical errors, in terms of lost income, disability, and health care costs, at about $29 billion per year. Other costs, such as pain, loss of loved ones, and human suffering are incalculable. However, they are important because unlike errors in other industries, medical errors often do more than merely inconvenience consumers—they may cause disability and death. According to the CDC, adverse events (bad outcomes) affecting medical care occur in about 3 to 4 percent of all patients. The IOM report found that most medical errors occurred as a result of system problems rather than mistakes made by individual health care providers.

Who Is Responsible for Patient Safety?

Many federal, state, and private sector organizations work together to reduce medical errors and improve patient safety. The CDC and Food and Drug Administration (FDA) are the leading federal agencies that conduct surveillance and collect information about adverse events resulting from treatment or the use of medical devices, drugs, or other products. The CDC directs the National Nosocomial Infections Surveillance (NNIS) system to track the hospital-acquired infections estimated to affect about 2 million patients per year. (Nosocomial infections are defined as infections that are not present or incubating at the time of admission to the hospital and as such, are considered hospital-acquired.)

Table 8.1 shows the decline in hospital-acquired infection rates in hospitals participating in the NNIS system. In the March 3, 2000 issue of *Morbidity and Mortality Weekly Report* (MMWR), the CDC reported that the voluntary infection monitoring performed by NNIS hospitals produced significant reductions in hospital-acquired infections, including a 31–43 percent drop in bloodstream infections in the intensive care units (ICUs). In fiscal year 2002 the CDC collaborated with state and local health departments, private sector groups, academic medical centers, and health care providers to develop and implement other programs to reduce errors and bad outcomes of care.

The Centers for Medicare and Medicaid Services (CMMS, formerly known as the Health Care Financing Administration) acts to reduce medical errors for the approximately 75 million Medicare, Medicaid, and State Children's Health Insurance Program (SCHIP) beneficiaries through its peer review organizations (PROs). The PROs concentrate on preventing delays in diagnosis and treatment that have adverse effects on health.

The Department of Defense (DoD) and Department of Veterans Affairs (VA), responsible for health care services for U.S. military personnel, their families, and veterans, have instituted computerized systems that have been demonstrated to reduce medical errors. The VA established Centers of Inquiry for Patient Safety, and its hospitals also use barcode technology and computerized medical records to prevent medical errors.

Safe medical care is also a top priority of the states and the private sector. Some of the nation's largest corporations, including General Motors and General Electric Company, have joined together to address health care safety and efficacy and to help direct their workers to health care providers—hospitals and physicians—with the best performance records. Called "The Leapfrog Group," as of 2001 more than 80 Fortune 500 companies were actively involved in promoting health care safety programs and advocating innovative solutions to existing problems, such as equipping physicians with handheld devices to record patient information and perform electronic prescribing.

HEALTH CARE PROVIDERS SEEK TO PREVENT MEDICAL ERRORS AND IMPROVE PATIENT SAFETY. Since medical errors occur with alarming frequency it is not surprising that nearly all physicians (95 percent) and the overwhelming majority of nurses (89 percent) and health care executives (82 percent) report having seen serious medical errors. (See Figure 8.1.)

Professional societies also are concerned with patient safety. More than 50 percent of all Joint Commission on Accreditation of Healthcare Organizations (JCAHO) hospital standards relate to patient safety. As of July 1, 2002 hospitals seeking accreditation from the JCAHO were required to adhere to stringent patient safety standards to prevent medical errors. The new JCAHO standards also require hospitals and individual health care providers to inform patients when they have been harmed in the course of treatment. The standards aim to prevent medical errors by identifying actions and systems likely to produce problems before they occur. An example of this type of preventive measure, which is called "prospective review," is close scrutiny of hospital pharmacies to be certain that ordering, preparation, and dispensing of medications is accurate. Similar standards have been developed for JCAHO-accredited nursing homes, outpatient clinics, laboratories, and managed care organizations.

Chief among the safety measures that concern professional societies are programs to prevent and report medication errors. Researchers estimate that about half of all medication errors are preventable. They suggest that when a medication error occurs, it is not the result of a single mistake, but rather a series of breakdowns in the health care delivery system. Research also supports the idea that

TABLE 8.1

Decrease in hospital-acquired infection rates, National Nosocomial Infections Surveillance (NNIS), 1990–99

Type of ICU	Bloodstream infection rate[1] (%)	Ventilator-associated pneumonia rate (%)	Urinary tract infection rate[2] (%)
Coronary	43	42	40
Medical	44	56	46
Surgical	31	38	30
Pediatric	32	26	59

[1]Central line associated.
[2]Catheter associated.

SOURCE: Robert Gaynes, et al, "Table 2. Decrease in hospital-acquired infection rates, NNIS, 1990–1999," in "Feeding Back Surveillance Data To Prevent Hospital-Acquired Infections," in *Emerging Infectious Diseases,* Centers for Disease Control and Prevention, Atlanta, GA, vol 7, no 2, March–April 2001

FIGURE 8.1

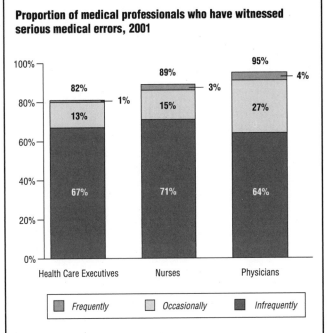

Proportion of medical professionals who have witnessed serious medical errors, 2001

Note: May not add to total due to rounding.

SOURCE: "Exhibit 7.8. Proportion of Medical Professionals Who Have Witnessed Serious Medical Errors, 2001," in *Trends And Indicators In The Changing Health Care Marketplace, 2002,* The Henry J. Kaiser Family Foundation, Menlo Park, CA [Online] http://www.kff.org/content/2002/3162/marketplace2002_finalc.pdf [accessed September 12, 2002]

the underreporting of medication errors stems from practitioners' concern that individuals will be punished rather than health system failures corrected. These researchers and many professional societies such as the Oncology (cancer) Nursing Society take the position that confidential voluntary reporting of medical errors will increase the frequency with which errors are reported and fully described, and thereby will better identify health system deficiencies that lead to errors.

Professional organizations for nurses have also expressed concern about the effects of understaffed health care facilities on patient safety. On July 9, 2001 the CDC Division of Healthcare Quality Promotion and National Center for Infectious Diseases held a meeting to discuss the impact of the nation's nursing shortage on quality of care and patient safety with particular emphasis on health care-associated infections. Studies cited at the meeting showed a relationship between nursing staffing patterns and adverse patient outcomes such as infection rates. The participants observed, however, that staffing problems were not problems with nurses that could be solved by actions targeting nurses, but rather system problems that could only be resolved by actions to change the system.

Additional Actions to Improve Safety

The landmark 1999 IOM report called for aggressive, national action to reduce the number of medical errors by 50 percent over 5 years. Representatives from 11 federal departments and agencies (Departments of Commerce, Defense, Health and Human Services, Labor, Veterans Affairs, the Federal Bureau of Prisons, Federal Trade Commission, National Highway Transportation and Safety Administration, Office of Personnel Management, Office of Management and Budget, and United States Coast Guard) formed the Quality Interagency Coordina-

tion Taskforce (QuIC). In February 2000 QuIC issued recommendations to the president for improving patient safety and a blueprint for implementing them.

The recommendations focused on education and technology and included:

• Enhancing public awareness of medical errors—A survey conducted during 2000 found that nearly half (47 percent) of consumers are concerned about the possibility of a medical error that causes an injury occurring when they receive health care services. (See Figure 8.2.) The taskforce asserted that well-informed consumers could act to avert at least some medical errors by questioning providers, rather than assuming their actions are always correct. Improving the public's understanding of patient safety and the risks involved in obtaining medical care would also enable consumers to be more vigilant about the care they receive.

• Building purchasers' awareness of medical errors—To assist employers in offering quality health care plans and providers to their workers, it is vital that they be informed about quality, as well as cost, of competing plans and practitioners. In December 1998 the U.S. Department of Labor launched a Health Benefits Education Campaign to teach employers how to make informed choices about health care plans and benefits.

FIGURE 8.2

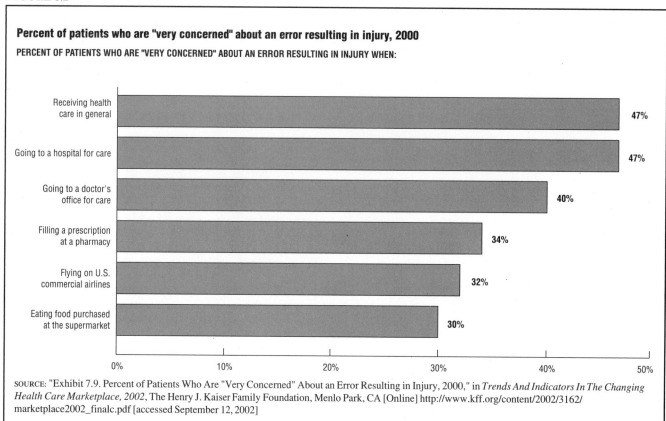

Percent of patients who are "very concerned" about an error resulting in injury, 2000

PERCENT OF PATIENTS WHO ARE "VERY CONCERNED" ABOUT AN ERROR RESULTING IN INJURY WHEN:

SOURCE: "Exhibit 7.9. Percent of Patients Who Are "Very Concerned" About an Error Resulting in Injury, 2000," in *Trends And Indicators In The Changing Health Care Marketplace, 2002*, The Henry J. Kaiser Family Foundation, Menlo Park, CA [Online] http://www.kff.org/content/2002/3162/marketplace2002_finalc.pdf [accessed September 12, 2002]

• Intensifying provider education—QuIC agencies resolved to work with professional societies and credentialing and accrediting organizations as well as with health care facilities to upgrade their overall safety knowledge with special emphasis on how to prevent medical errors.

• Applying information technology to health care delivery systems—Computerized medical records, computer reminder systems for laboratory testing, electronic prescribing, and test ordering should be widely adopted to reduce errors and enhance quality. Electronic patient records give health care providers immediate access to patient data such as recent diagnostic test results. Interactive decision-support tools can alert providers to allergies and potential drug interactions thereby preventing medication errors. An example of a decision support system's capacity to improve care is its ability to recommend the most appropriate antibiotic for a patient's diagnosed infection. Barcodes on medications and mechanical or robotic dispensing can help to ensure that the right patient receives the right prescription at the right time.

• Incorporating standardized procedures and checklists in medical devices—QuIC called for the FDA to intensify its premarket analyses of medical devices since some have been found to be substandard or defective after they have gone to market. This analysis also applied to human factors associated with misuse of medical devices—stringent testing of operating, maintenance, and user instructions, and labels with instructions intended to prevent errors.

The member agencies of QuIC resolved to seek documentation from independent accrediting organizations to find out how they are working to strengthen patient safety standards. QuIC also identified its ability to gather data from various member agencies to improve research and practice related to patient safety. For example, the FDA could use hospital and pharmaceutical company databases to identify the frequency of specific medication or prescribing errors.

PROPOSED LEGISLATION TO IMPROVE SAFETY. On June 5, 2002 the "Patient Safety and Quality Improvement Act (S. 2590)," a legislative response to the IOM report, was introduced by U.S. Senators Jim Jeffords of Vermont, Bill Frist of Tennessee, John Breaux of Louisiana, and Judd Gregg of New Hampshire. The following day a comparable bill (H.R. 4889) sponsored by Nancy Johnson of Connecticut was introduced in the U.S. House of Representatives. In addition to bipartisan support in the Senate, the legislation was widely hailed by hospital and health care practitioners' professional societies.

The legislation promotes the reporting, analysis, and prevention of medical errors by giving legal protection to health care providers who report patient safety data. The act protects this confidential information from being subpoenaed, disclosed under the Freedom of Information Act, or admitted as evidence in civil, criminal, or administrative proceedings. It also ensures that information reported may not be used to enforce personnel actions such as denying practitioners certain privileges (such as the ability to admit patients to the hospital) or credentials, such as licensure or recertification. Unlawful disclosure of patient safety data would be punishable by fines as high as $10,000 per violation.

The act does not change existing remedies available to injured patients or limit patient access to medical records. Is does stipulate that medical errors will be reported to "patient safety organizations," which may voluntarily submit the data they obtain to a national, non-identifiable patient safety database linked to the Agency for Healthcare Research and Quality. "Patient safety data" is an inclusive term and covers all reports, statements, and quality improvement information that is collected, developed, or reported by providers to patient safety organizations.

PROTECTING CONSUMERS FROM HEALTH CARE FRAUD

According to the FDA and the Federal Trade Commission (FTC), the lead agencies charged with protecting health care consumers from fraud, common health fraud targets are persons who are battling serious diseases, conditions with no known cure, and persons who are overweight. People who feel frightened or hopeless, or those suffering from chronic pain may be especially vulnerable. Officials at these federal agencies cite persons with diagnoses of cancer, diabetes, multiple sclerosis, Alzheimer's disease, HIV/AIDS, and arthritis as examples of consumers who may become victims of fraudulently marketed, frequently useless health care products, devices, and treatments.

Unproven and fraudulently marketed "miracle cures" are nearly always entirely ineffective, although most are harmless. They are dangerous, however, when consumers use them instead of seeking more effective, conventional medical care and treatment. Most victims of health fraud simply lose time and money but some lose their health, either by delaying needed treatment or by using a product or device that is harmful to their health.

The FTC and FDA urge consumers to exercise caution when purchasing medical or health care devices, products, and treatment. They encourage consumers to view claims of immediate cures or relief of chronic health problems with appropriate skepticism. Basically, the adage "if it sounds too good to be true, it probably isn't" holds true when evaluating the claims of health care products or services. Examples of such unbelievable and misleading claims are those for dietary supplements that promise, "You can eat all you like and still lose weight," or devices promising "instant relief from arthritis pain."

The Internet has provided a new arena for unscrupulous purveyors of prescription drugs as well as marketers of unproven health care products and services. It is often difficult for consumers to distinguish between legitimate Web sites that offer pharmaceutical drugs and irresponsible, unsafe sellers of prescription drugs. The FDA warns consumers that Web site purchases are risky—drugs may be counterfeit, doses may be incorrect, or the wrong drug may be delivered. The FDA also advises against filling prescriptions through a Web site that allows consumers to order prescription drugs after simply completing a health questionnaire. Both the FDA and AMA consider a completed health questionnaire as an insufficient, and potentially dangerous, basis for prescribing drugs. Additional FDA warnings include:

- Consumers should not purchase prescription drugs for the first time from sites that sell drugs without a prescription or a physical examination, or sites that sell drugs that are not FDA approved.

- It is unwise to purchase drugs from sites that do not have a registered pharmacist available to respond to questions.

- It is not advisable to order from sites that do not offer a U.S. address and phone number to contact in the event of problems with the drug, product, or device purchased.

- Purchases from foreign Web sites are especially risky because the U.S government cannot take any action if consumers are victims of fraud or receive otherwise unsatisfactory service.

CLINICAL PRACTICE GUIDELINES

Clinical practice guidelines (CPGs) are evidence-based protocols—documents that advise health care providers about how to diagnose and treat specific medical conditions and diseases. CPGs offer physicians, nurses, other health care practitioners, health plans, and institutions objective, detailed, condition- or disease-specific action plans.

Widespread dissemination and use of CPGs began during the 1990s in an effort to improve the quality of health care delivery by giving health care professionals access to current scientific information on which to base clinical decisions. The use of guidelines also aimed to enhance quality by standardizing care and treatment throughout a health care delivery system such as a managed care plan or hospital, and throughout the nation.

Early attempts to encourage physicians and other health professionals to use practice guidelines met resistance because many physicians rejected CPGs as formulaic "cookbook medicine," and believed that they interfered with physician-patient relationships. Over time physicians were educated about the quality problems resulting from variations in medical practice and opinions about CPGs gradually changed. Physician willingness to use practice guidelines also increased when they learned that adherence to CPGs offered some protection from medical malpractice and other liability. Nurses and other health professionals more readily adopted CPGs, presumably because their training and practice was oriented more toward following instructions than physicians' practices had been.

The National Guideline Clearinghouse (NGC) is a database of CPGs produced by the Agency for Healthcare Research and Quality in conjunction with the American Medical Association (AMA) and American Association of Health Plans. The NGC offers guideline summaries and comparisons of guidelines covering the same disease or condition prepared by different sources and serves as a resource for the exchange of guidelines between practitioners and health care organizations.

Clinical practice guidelines vary depending on their source, however, all detail recovery and treatment plans and are intended to generate the most favorable health outcomes. Federal agencies such as the U.S. Public Health Service and CDC, as well as professional societies, managed care plans, hospitals, academic medical centers, and health care consulting firms have produced their own versions of clinical practice guidelines.

Practically all guidelines assume that treatment and healing will occur without complications. Since CPGs represent an optimistic approach to treatment, they are not used as the sole resource for development or evaluation of treatment plans for specific patients. CPGs are intended for use in conjunction with evaluation by qualified health professionals able to determine the applicability of a specific CPG to the specific circumstances involved. Modification of the CPGs is often required and advisable to meet specific, organizational objectives of health care providers and payers.

It is unrealistic to expect that all patients will obtain ideal health outcomes as a result of health care providers' use of CPGs. Guidelines may have greater utility as quality indicators. Evaluating health care delivery against CPGs enables providers, payers, and policymakers to identify and evaluate care that deviates from CPGs as part of a concerted program of continuous improvement of health care quality.

INFORMATION AND COMMUNICATION TECHNOLOGY

The explosion of communication and information management technologies has already revolutionized

health care delivery and holds great promise for the future. Health care data are easily and securely collected, shared, stored, and used to promote research and development over great geographic distances and across traditionally isolated industries. Online distance learning programs for health professionals and the widespread availability of reliable consumer health information on the Internet have increased understanding and awareness of the causes and treatment of illness. This section describes several recent applications of technology to the health care system.

Telemedicine

Telemedicine is the term used to describe a variety of interactions that occur via telephone lines. Telemedicine may be as simple and commonplace as a conversation between a patient and a health professional in the same town or as sophisticated as surgery directed via satellite and video technology from one continent to another.

According to the Telemedicine Research Center (TRC), a non-profit public research organization based in Portland, Oregon, there are two types of technology used in most telemedicine applications. The first type stores and sends digital images taken with a digital camera from one location to another. The most common application of this kind of telemedicine is teleradiology—sending x-rays, CT scans, or MRIs from one facility to another. The same technology may be used to send slides or images from the pathology laboratory to another physician or laboratory for a second opinion. Another example of the use of digital image transfer is the rural primary care physician who, miles from the nearest dermatologist (physician specialist in skin diseases), can send a photograph of a patient's rash or lesion and receive an immediate, long-distance consultation from the dermatologist.

Another application of telemedicine that uses only the standard telephone line in a patient's home is transtelephonic pacemaker monitoring. (Cardiac pacemakers are battery-operated implanted devices that maintain normal heart rhythm.) Cardiac technicians at the other end of the telephone are able to check the implanted cardiac pacemaker's functions, including the status of its battery. Transtelephonic pacemaker monitoring is able to identify early signs of possible pacemaker failure and detect potential pacemaker system abnormalities, thereby reducing the number of emergency replacements. It can also send an ECG (electrocardiogram) rhythm strip to the patient's cardiologist.

The other type of technology described by the TRC is two-way interactive television (IATV), which uses video-teleconferencing equipment to create a "meeting" between a patient and primary care physician in one location and a physician specialist elsewhere when a face-to-face consultation is not feasible because of time or distance. Peripheral equipment even enables the consulting physician specialist to perform a "virtual physical examination" and hear the patient's heart sounds through a stethoscope. The availability of desktop videoconferencing has expanded this form of telemedicine from a novelty found exclusively in urban, university teaching hospitals to a valuable tool for patients and physicians in rural areas who were previously underserved and unable to access specialists readily.

Despite the promise of telemedicine, there are several obstacles that prevent Americans from realizing all of its potential benefits. As of October 2002, many states do not permit physicians who are not licensed in their states to practice telemedicine, and the Centers for Medicare and Medicaid Services will reimburse for interactive teleconference services but will not pay for digital image transfer. Many private insurers are reluctant to pay for telemedicine and some physicians fear additional liability (medical malpractice suits or other litigation) arising from telemedicine. Finally, some of the communities that would benefit most from telemedicine do not have the telecommunications equipment necessary to deliver the bandwidth for telemedicine.

WIRELESS TECHNOLOGY IN THE HOSPITAL. In *Hospitals Unplugged: The Wireless Revolution Reaches Healthcare* (California HealthCare Foundation, April 3, 2001), Glenn Wachter describes a hospital where nurses enter patient data at wireless mobile workstations, pagers deliver patients' ECGs and vital signs, a wireless scanning device verifies the correct medication and dosage for a patient, and physicians access instantly updated medical records on their wireless personal digital assistants (PDAs). Wachter asserts that mounting pressure to increase hospital and health service delivery efficiencies is driving interest and use of wireless technology but observes that its advocates maintain that along with saving money, it also will improve quality.

By improving communication of medical information, wireless technology can increase the accuracy of patient data, increase the efficiency of health care workers, deliver immediate access to medical and administrative information, and sharply reduce paperwork. Further, by linking wireless technology to pharmacy management systems, it can reduce prescribing and dispensing errors. Wachter also observed the application of wireless technology in pre-hospital care. Ambulances equipped with wireless devices can transmit video, audio, ECG, vital signs, and other images to the emergency department team awaiting arrival of the critically ill patient.

Online Patient-Physician Consultations

A report issued by the California Health Care Foundation in November 2001 called online exchanges between patients and health professionals "e-encounters" and defined them as "a two-way Web-based exchange of clinical information between a patient and his or her caregiver that involves a closed loop conversation around a particular clinical question or problem specific to the patient. It may be initiated by either the patient or the caregiver."

Although no one is absolutely certain about the frequency with which e-encounters occur, about 3.7 million Americans have communicated with their physicians via electronic mail (e-mail). Hence, with more than two-thirds of U.S. physicians and more than half of American adults online, the popularity of this practice is believed to be increasing. Some industry observers consider e-encounters simply as alternatives to telephone consultations, others think they may ultimately prove to be more time-efficient, affordable, and convenient than the "telephone tag" and frequent call-backs that commonly occur when physicians and patients attempt to talk by phone.

One advantage of e-encounters over telephone conversations is the patient's ability to communicate home monitoring results such as blood pressure or blood glucose levels in a format that is easily included as documentation in the patient's permanent (paper or electronic) medical record. Another advantage is that less time devoted to telephone calls improves the efficiency of the physician's office, boosting productivity, and potentially reducing practice expenses. Other electronic communications between patients and physicians' offices include appointment scheduling, reminders of follow-up visits, prescription renewal requests, and administrative functions such as billing, insurance verification, and changes of address.

Concerns about e-encounters center on privacy and security of patient information exchanged and physician reimbursement for the time spent in electronic correspondence with patients. In addition to legal and privacy issues, some industry observers suggest that guidelines should be developed for e-encounters to ensure that they are clinically appropriate and are not used as substitutes for needed, but more costly, face-to-face office visits.

Is Applied Technology the Solution to the Nursing Shortage?

According to surveys conducted in 2001, most U.S. hospitals, where nurses comprise up to 25 percent of the workforce, are facing a nursing shortage with estimates of between 10 to 15 percent vacancy rates for registered nurses, licensed practical nurses, and nursing assistants. The shortage is expected to increase. One study speculates that the nation will be short by half a million nurses needed to care for patients by 2020. Many industry observers attribute the shortage to the profession's diminished appeal since a wider range of career opportunities for women became available. Nurses themselves insist that working conditions such as caring for older, sicker patients, mounting paperwork as well as reduced nursing personnel and other workers are causing the exodus from hospitals.

While hospitals are intensifying recruitment efforts in order to fill nursing vacancies, they are also looking at ways to improve working conditions for nurses. One approach to improving working conditions is the application of technology systems to increase patient safety and clinical quality—key factors that contribute to nurses' job satisfaction. Automated workflow and clinical systems do not always increase nurses' efficiency. However, a report prepared by First Consulting Group for the California HealthCare Foundation in June 2002 found widespread support for a variety of technologies designed to safeguard patients and support nurses including:

- Scheduling nurses to shifts via the Internet

- Messaging, and automated documentation

- Mobile communication

- Patient education

- Medication administration systems—dispensing devices, bar-code technology, and "smart" IV (intravenous) pumps that check orders against a database to prevent errors

- Clinical decision support

- Computerized physician order entry and computerized patient record/data repository

The authors concluded that increasing adoption of technology, the urgent need for hospital nurses, and a generation of graduating nursing students that has been computer-literate since childhood should spur hospitals to consider integrating computer technology into nursing practices.

INNOVATION SUPPORTS QUALITY HEALTH CARE DELIVERY

The health care industry is awash in wave after wave of new technologies, models of service delivery, reimbursement formulae, legislative and regulatory changes, and increasingly specialized personnel. Creating change in hospitals and other health care organizations requires an understanding of diffusion—the process and channels by which new ideas are communicated, spread, and are adopted throughout institutions or organizations.

Diffusion of technology involves all of the stakeholders in the health care system. Policymakers and regulatory agencies establish safety and efficacy; government and private payers determine reimbursement; vendors of the technology are compared and one is selected; hospitals and health professionals adopt the technology and are trained in its use; and consumers are informed about the benefits of the new technology.

The decision to adopt new technology involves a five-stage process beginning with knowledge about the innovation. The second stage is persuasion, the period when decision makers form opinions based on experience and knowledge. Decision is the third phase, when commitment is made to a trial or pilot program, and is followed by implementation, the stage during which the new technology is put in place. The process concludes with the confirmation stage, the period during which the decision makers seek reinforcement for their decision to adopt and implement the new technology.

Communicating Quality

The IOM report on health care quality (*Crossing the Quality Chasm: A New Health System for the 21st Century,* Academy Press, Washington DC, 2001) set forth six aims for improvement and ten rules for redesign of the U.S. health care system. These ten rules are:

1. Care is based on continuous healing relationships.

2. Care is customized according to patient needs and values.

3. The patient is the source of control.

4. Knowledge is shared and information flows freely.

5. Decision-making is evidence-based.

6. Safety is a system priority.

7. Transparency is necessary.

8. Needs are anticipated.

9. Waste is continuously decreased.

10. Cooperation among clinicians is a priority.

This chapter has described some of the efforts currently underway to address and comply with these rules within the existing health care system, and concludes with a discussion of rule number seven, the need for transparency. Transparency refers to the need for public accountability for the quality of the health care system. Health care consumers should be given information that allows them to make thoughtful, informed choices and decisions about health insurance plans and providers. Although family, friends, and health care providers remain consumers' primary sources of information about quality of health services, a survey conducted during 2000 found 37 percent of consumers willing to contact a health plan representative or read materials to obtain quality information; 28 percent wanted to access information online. (See Figure 8.3.) The information provided must be understandable and should focus on performance measures of the plan or provider that show its commitment to safety, evidence-based practice, and patient satisfaction.

The requirement for transparency requires health care providers and plans to disclose information they previously did not share among themselves or with consumers. Further, many health care plans and providers have found that in order to compete successfully for health care consumers, they not only must demonstrate the ability to deliver health care services effectively but also to docu-

FIGURE 8.3

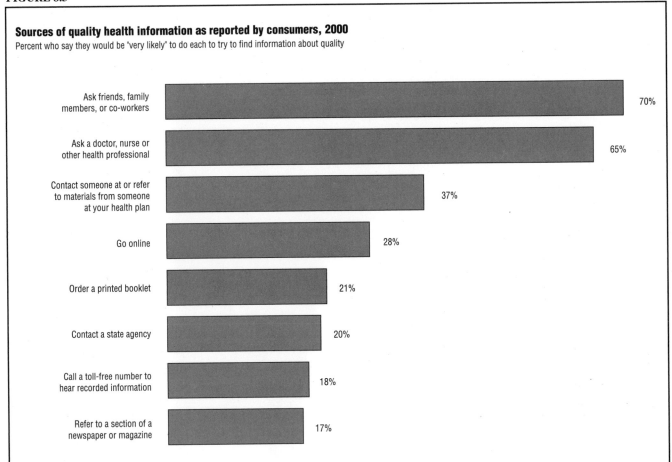

Sources of quality health information as reported by consumers, 2000

Percent who say they would be "very likely" to do each to try to find information about quality

Ask friends, family members, or co-workers	70%
Ask a doctor, nurse or other health professional	65%
Contact someone at or refer to materials from someone at your health plan	37%
Go online	28%
Order a printed booklet	21%
Contact a state agency	20%
Call a toll-free number to hear recorded information	18%
Refer to a section of a newspaper or magazine	17%

SOURCE: "Chart 13. Finding Quality Information," in *National Survey on Americans as Health Care Consumers: An Update on the Role of Quality Information*, The Henry J. Kaiser Family Foundation and the Agency for Healthcare Research and Quality, December 2000 [Online] http://www.kff.org/content/2000/3093/Survey%20Highlights.pdf [accessed October 4, 2002]

ment and communicate measures of clinical quality and fiscal accountability.

Publication of medical outcomes report cards and disease and procedure-specific morbidity and mortality rates has attracted widespread media attention and sparked controversy. Advocates of the public release of clinical outcomes and other performance measures contend that despite inherent limitations, these studies offer consumers, employers, and payers the means for comparing health care providers.

Some skeptics question the clinical credibility of scales such as surgical mortality as incomplete indicators of quality. Others cite problems with data collection or speculate that the data are readily manipulated by providers to enhance marketing opportunities sufficient to compromise the utility and validity of published reports. Long-term, the effect of published comparative evaluation of health care providers on network establishment, contracting, and exclusion from existing health plans is uncertain and in many instances may be punitive. Hospitals and medical groups may be forced to compete for network inclusion on the basis of standardized performance measures.

Despite legitimate concern about the reliability, validity, and interpretation of data, there is consensus that scrutiny and dissemination of quality data will escalate. To date, consumer interest has focused on individual providers—local hospitals and physicians. Employers, choosing between health plans involving the same group of participating hospitals and physicians, are requesting plan-specific information to guide their decisions. Companies and employer-driven health care coalitions seeking to assemble their own provider networks rely on physician and hospital-specific data during the selection process. By June 2002, the Leapfrog Group, an employer-based coalition with strong interest in health care quality, was composed of more than 100 member companies that purchase coverage for about 31 million people.

The most beneficial use of the data is not punitive, but as inspiration and incentive to improve health care delivery systematically. When evidence of quality problems is identified, health plans and providers must be prepared to launch a variety of interventions to address and promptly resolve problems.

CHAPTER 9

PUBLIC OPINION ABOUT HEALTH CARE

As with many other social issues, public opinion about health care systems, providers, plans, coverage, and benefits varies in response to a variety of personal, political, and economic forces. Personal experience, and the experience of friends, family, and community opinion leaders—trusted sources of information such as members of the clergy, prominent physicians, and local business and civic leaders—exert powerful influences on public opinion. Health care marketing executives have known for years that the most potent advertising any hospital, medical group, or managed care plan can have is not a full page newspaper advertisement or primetime television ad campaign. It is positive word-of-mouth publicity.

Political events and election campaigns can focus public attention on a particular health care concern, supplant one health-related issue with another, or eclipse health care from public view altogether. Health care reform and a strong push for national health insurance were hallmarks of former U.S. President Bill Clinton's campaigns in the 1990s, but by 2000 were all but forgotten in favor of debates about Medicare reform, prescription drug benefits, and passage of a patients' bill of rights. The events of September 11, 2001 also realigned health concerns as much as they affected other national priorities. In the final months of 2001, several public opinion surveys reported preventing bioterrorism as Americans' number one health concern. During September 2002, the media were focused on U.S. preparations to take military action in Iraq. As a result, there were far fewer news stories about the upcoming open-enrollment period (when employees can switch health plans) than usual.

The national economy and the rate of increase of health care costs, especially out-of-pocket expenses, play important roles in shaping public opinions. When unemployment rates are high, the proportion of persons without insurance increases, workers fear losing their jobs and their health care coverage, and dissatisfaction with the present health care system grows. Multiple surveys have shown a direct relationship between rising out-of-pocket expenses and dissatisfaction with the health care system. The recent spike in health care costs coupled with survey findings that employers intend to pass off some of the increasing costs to their employees will likely inspire renewed interest in health care reform.

Demographic changes, particularly the aging of the "baby boomer" generation into Medicare eligibility, may also fuel dissatisfaction with the health care system. If the health care futurists who have projected glaring deficiencies in the current system's capacity to meet the needs of the aging population are correct, this generation may become the largest and most vocal advocates for health care reform.

Finally, the influence of the news media, advertising, and other attempts to sway health care consumers' attitudes and purchasing behaviors cannot be overlooked. A single story about a miraculous medical breakthrough or lifesaving procedure can reflect favorably on an entire hospital or health care delivery system. Similarly, a lone mistake or misstep by a single health care practitioner can impugn a hospital or managed care plan for months or even years, prompting intense media scrutiny of every action taken by the facility or organization.

Some industry observers believe that health care providers, policymakers, biomedical technology and research firms, and academic medical centers have fanned the flames of consumer dissatisfaction with the health care system by "overselling" the promise and the progress of modern medicine and the U.S. health care system. They fear that overzealous promotion of every scientific discovery with a potential clinical application has created unrealistic expectations of modern medicine. Health care consumers who believe there should be "one pill for every ill" or feel that all technology should be made widely available even before its efficacy has been demonstrated

FIGURE 9.1

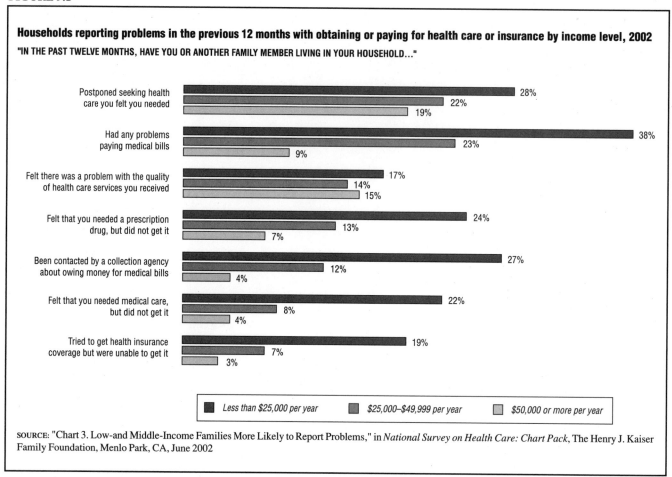

Households reporting problems in the previous 12 months with obtaining or paying for health care or insurance by income level, 2002

"IN THE PAST TWELVE MONTHS, HAVE YOU OR ANOTHER FAMILY MEMBER LIVING IN YOUR HOUSEHOLD..."

Postponed seeking health care you felt you needed
- 28%
- 22%
- 19%

Had any problems paying medical bills
- 38%
- 23%
- 9%

Felt there was a problem with the quality of health care services you received
- 17%
- 14%
- 15%

Felt that you needed a prescription drug, but did not get it
- 24%
- 13%
- 7%

Been contacted by a collection agency about owing money for medical bills
- 27%
- 12%
- 4%

Felt that you needed medical care, but did not get it
- 22%
- 8%
- 4%

Tried to get health insurance coverage but were unable to get it
- 19%
- 7%
- 3%

■ Less than $25,000 per year   ■ $25,000–$49,999 per year   □ $50,000 or more per year

SOURCE: "Chart 3. Low-and Middle-Income Families More Likely to Report Problems," in *National Survey on Health Care: Chart Pack,* The Henry J. Kaiser Family Foundation, Menlo Park, CA, June 2002

are more likely to be dissatisfied with the present health care system.

MANY AMERICANS ARE CONCERNED ABOUT ACCESS AND ABILITY TO PAY FOR HEALTH CARE

A survey conducted from March 28 to May 1, 2002 found public opinions and experience with the U.S. health care system depended largely on economic status. Americans with higher incomes generally had few or no problems gaining access to medical care or paying for the care they need. Those with lower incomes, and even many middle income families, reported problems with both access and ability to pay for care. Less than 10 percent of persons with incomes in excess of $50,000 per year reported difficulty paying medical bills during the previous year. (See Figure 9.1.) In contrast almost four out of ten (38 percent) families with incomes less than $25,000 per year and 23 percent of those with annual incomes ranging from $25,000 to $50,000 had problems paying medical bills. The analysis of the results of a nationwide telephone survey of a random sample of about 1,200 adults is part of an ongoing research project conducted by National Public Radio (NPR), the Henry J. Kaiser Family Foundation, and Harvard University's John F. Kennedy School of Government.

MOST WORRY ABOUT THE HEALTH CARE SYSTEM

The NPR/Kaiser Family Foundation/Kennedy School of Government survey also described Americans' concerns about the health care system and their personal worries about their own continuing ability to obtain needed health care services. While 20 percent of Americans feel the present health care system works well, a comparable proportion (23 percent) think it is so unworkable that it needs to be completely rebuilt. (See Figure 9.2.) The majority of survey respondents (57 percent) think the present system has merit but needs some major changes in order for it to function optimally.

Almost half of all those surveyed were somewhat or very worried (46 percent) that they would be unable to pay for needed care and 42 percent feared they would be unable to afford prescription drugs. (See Figure 9.3.) Even people with health insurance have immediate concerns about health care costs and access. More than half (51 percent) of insured respondents were concerned that insurance would become so costly that they would be unable to pay for it and exactly half fear that their benefits will be sharply reduced. Thirty-four percent of Americans with health insurance worried that they might lose their coverage in the coming year.

The Causes of Rising Health Care Costs

Survey respondents named pharmaceutical companies, system-wide greed and waste, and medical malpractice lawsuits as the top three factors driving escalating health care costs. (See Figure 9.4.) Almost 90 percent of respondents also felt that the aging population was a very important or somewhat important cause of higher health care costs. Nearly half considered the use of expensive new medical equipment (48 percent) or expensive new drugs (47 percent) as very important contributors to health care costs.

EMPLOYER-SPONSORED HEALTH PLANS GET HIGH MARKS

A Harris Interactive telephone survey of adults with health insurance conducted in December 2001 found that the majority of adults with employer-sponsored health plans (69 percent) were relatively happy with their plans, giving them grades of A or B. (See Table 9.1.) More than three-quarters of survey respondents said they would recommend their plans to friends who were healthy and 74 percent said they would recommend their plans to friends with serious or chronic illnesses.

Medicare beneficiaries were more satisfied with their health care plans than persons with employer-sponsored plans or Medicaid recipients. Higher percentages of

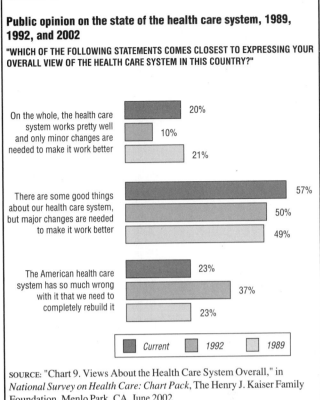

FIGURE 9.2

Public opinion on the state of the health care system, 1989, 1992, and 2002

"WHICH OF THE FOLLOWING STATEMENTS COMES CLOSEST TO EXPRESSING YOUR OVERALL VIEW OF THE HEALTH CARE SYSTEM IN THIS COUNTRY?"

On the whole, the health care system works pretty well and only minor changes are needed to make it work better — 20%, 10%, 21%

There are some good things about our health care system, but major changes are needed to make it work better — 57%, 50%, 49%

The American health care system has so much wrong with it that we need to completely rebuild it — 23%, 37%, 23%

Current / 1992 / 1989

SOURCE: "Chart 9. Views About the Health Care System Overall," in *National Survey on Health Care: Chart Pack*, The Henry J. Kaiser Family Foundation, Menlo Park, CA, June 2002

FIGURE 9.3

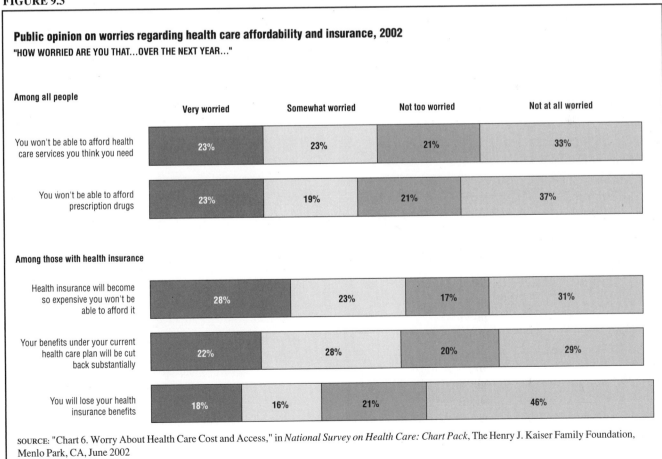

Public opinion on worries regarding health care affordability and insurance, 2002

"HOW WORRIED ARE YOU THAT...OVER THE NEXT YEAR..."

Among all people

	Very worried	Somewhat worried	Not too worried	Not at all worried
You won't be able to afford health care services you think you need	23%	23%	21%	33%
You won't be able to afford prescription drugs	23%	19%	21%	37%

Among those with health insurance

	Very worried	Somewhat worried	Not too worried	Not at all worried
Health insurance will become so expensive you won't be able to afford it	28%	23%	17%	31%
Your benefits under your current health care plan will be cut back substantially	22%	28%	20%	29%
You will lose your health insurance benefits	18%	16%	21%	46%

SOURCE: "Chart 6. Worry About Health Care Cost and Access," in *National Survey on Health Care: Chart Pack*, The Henry J. Kaiser Family Foundation, Menlo Park, CA, June 2002

FIGURE 9.4

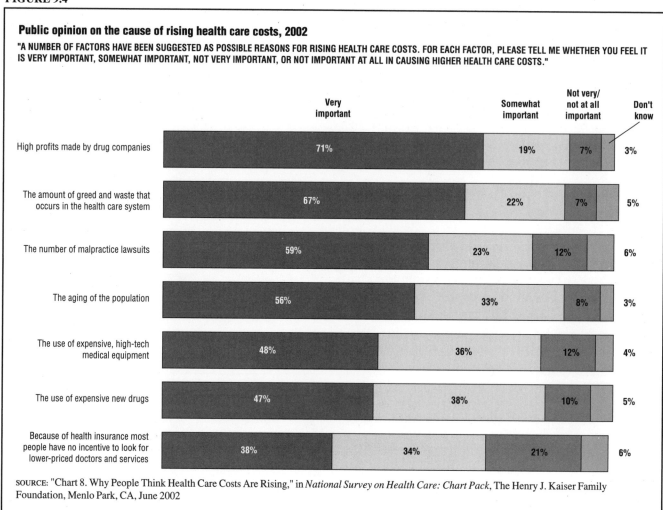

Public opinion on the cause of rising health care costs, 2002

"A NUMBER OF FACTORS HAVE BEEN SUGGESTED AS POSSIBLE REASONS FOR RISING HEALTH CARE COSTS. FOR EACH FACTOR, PLEASE TELL ME WHETHER YOU FEEL IT IS VERY IMPORTANT, SOMEWHAT IMPORTANT, NOT VERY IMPORTANT, OR NOT IMPORTANT AT ALL IN CAUSING HIGHER HEALTH CARE COSTS."

	Very important	Somewhat important	Not very/ not at all important	Don't know
High profits made by drug companies	71%	19%	7%	3%
The amount of greed and waste that occurs in the health care system	67%	22%	7%	5%
The number of malpractice lawsuits	59%	23%	12%	6%
The aging of the population	56%	33%	8%	3%
The use of expensive, high-tech medical equipment	48%	36%	12%	4%
The use of expensive new drugs	47%	38%	10%	5%
Because of health insurance most people have no incentive to look for lower-priced doctors and services	38%	34%	21%	6%

SOURCE: "Chart 8. Why People Think Health Care Costs Are Rising," in *National Survey on Health Care: Chart Pack*, The Henry J. Kaiser Family Foundation, Menlo Park, CA, June 2002

members of employer-sponsored plans and Medicaid recipients were unhappy with their health plans (31 percent of each group gave their plans grades of C, D, or F) than Medicare beneficiaries (24 percent gave their plans bad grades). (See Table 9.2.) Other health plan consumer satisfaction studies have found Medicare members generally more satisfied than other, generally younger members. Some industry observers speculate that Medicare members, who generally utilize services more often than younger adults, have more frequent contact with health plan providers and greater opportunities to establish satisfactory provider-patient relationships. Others feel that because many Medicare beneficiaries are retirees, they may be more patient and accepting of some aspects of health service delivery, such as long waits to schedule appointments and see their physicians, than younger, more harried working adults.

Rising Premiums and Reduced Benefits May Reduce Satisfaction with Employer-Sponsored Plans

An annual survey of employer health benefit plans conducted by the Henry J. Kaiser Family Foundation and the Health research and Educational Trust found that between May 2001 and May 2002 employer health insurance premiums rose 12.7 percent, the sharpest increase since 1990. Employees' share of the insurance premium jumped 27 percent for individuals and 16 percent for families. Preferred Provider Plan (PPO) deductibles rose 37 percent and workers with tiered benefit prescription drug coverage (there are different copayments for generic drugs, brand name drugs, and brand name drugs with generic substitutes) pay from 29 to 57 percent more per prescription.

The survey also found retiree benefits dwindling—just 34 percent of large employers offer retiree benefits compared to 66 percent in 1988. Nearly 10 percent of large employers eliminated retiree benefits altogether for new hires, 40 percent increased retirees' premiums, and 26 percent increased the amounts employees pay for prescriptions. Reduced benefits, higher costs, and fewer small employers offering coverage may combine to sharply reduce employee satisfaction with employer-sponsored health plans.

MOUNTING FRUSTRATION WITH MANAGED CARE PLANS

Despite relatively unchanged satisfaction ratings from 1998 to 2001 with employer-sponsored health plans and

TABLE 9.1

Trends among adults who are unhappy with their employer-provided health insurance plans, 1999–2001

	1999 %	2000 %	2001 %
Adults who gave their employer-provided health plans a grade of C, D, or F	29	26	31
Adults who would not recommend their employer-provided health plans to friends who are healthy	20	15	22
Adults who would not recommend their employer-provided health plans to friends who have serious or chronic illnesses	28	25	26

SOURCE: Humphrey Taylor, "Summary A. Those Unhappy with Employer-Provided Plans—Key Trends," in *Most People Continue to Think Well of Their Health Care Plans,* The Harris Poll #3, Harris Interactive, Rochester, NY, January 16, 2002 [Online] http://www.harrisinteractive.com/harris_poll/index.asp?PID=279 [accessed September 12, 2002]

TABLE 9.2

People who are unhappy with their health insurance plan, by type of plan, 2001

	Covered by:		
	Employer-provided plans %	Medicare %	Medicaid %
Give their health plans a low rating (C, D, or F)	31	24	31
Would not recommend their plans to friends who are healthy	22	18	31
Would not recommend their plans to friends who have serious or chronic illnesses	26	21	24

SOURCE: Humphrey Taylor, "Summary B. Those Unhappy with Different Types of Plans [2001]," in *Most People Continue to Think Well of Their Health Care Plans,* The Harris Poll #3, Harris Interactive, Rochester, NY, January 16, 2002 [Online] http://www.harrisinteractive.com/harris_poll/index.asp?PID=279 [accessed September 12, 2002]

TABLE 9.3

Consumer worries about health plans, by type of plan, 2001

PERCENT OF PRIVATELY INSURED ADULTS, BY TYPE OF HEALTH PLAN, WHO SAY THEY ARE WORRIED THAT IF THEY BECOME SICK, THEIR HEALTH PLAN WOULD BE MORE CONCERNED ABOUT SAVING MONEY THAN PROVIDING THE BEST TREATMENT:

	"Very" Worried	"Somewhat" Worried	"Not Too" Worried	"Not at All" Worried
Total for All Plans	24%	32%	25%	18%
Total for Managed Care	25%	34%	25%	16%
"Strict" Managed Care	31%	36%	21%	11%
"Loose" Managed Care	21%	32%	28%	19%

SOURCE: "Exhibit 7.7. Consumer Worries About Health Plans, by Type of Plan, 2001," in *Trends And Indicators In The Changing Health Care Marketplace, 2002,* The Henry J. Kaiser Family Foundation, Menlo Park, CA [Online] http://www.kff.org/content/2002/3162/marketplace2002_finalc.pdf [accessed September 12, 2002]

continued enrollment gains by managed care plans, Harris Interactive and other researchers report increasingly negative public attitudes about managed care. In fact, a May 2002 Harris Poll that asked Americans how well they thought different industries were serving their customers found managed care plans at the bottom of the list, with just 33 percent of respondents crediting them with a job well done. The Harris Poll researchers distinguish the growing dissatisfaction with the concept of managed care from how consumers feel personally about their own plans. The researchers contend that the personal experiences of most Americans are not as awful as the accounts described in the media.

The Henry J. Kaiser Family Foundation researches and analyzes trends in the health care industry through its *Changing Health Care Marketplace Project.* The project's most recent report, *Trends and Indicators in the Changing Healthcare Marketplace, 2002* (Washington, DC, May 2002), noted some significant changes since the prior report published in August 1998. The researchers found that while most people who obtain health care coverage through their employers are still enrolled in managed care plans, membership in health maintenance organizations (HMOs) declined and more people opted to enroll in preferred provider organizations (PPOs). (See Figure 9.5.)

Of those Americans under age 65 who have private health insurance, the majority (56 percent) believe that their health care plan "would be more concerned about saving money than providing the best treatment" if they became sick. (See Table 9.3.) For those in managed care plans, more adults, especially those in "strict" managed care plans (67 percent), were likely to believe this. PPOs offer members greater choice of providers and fewer restrictions than HMOs, and their popularity grew in response to anti-HMO sentiments expressed by con-

sumers, health professionals, and the media. PPO members surveyed expressed less concern that their health plans' would compromise care to save money than HMO members.

Figure 9.6 reveals that consumer dissatisfaction—persons who said managed care plans were doing a bad job serving consumers—nearly doubled from 21 percent in 1997 to 39 percent in 2000. More than half of consumers surveyed said managed care had decreased the quality of care for the sick, and two-thirds felt that managed care decreased the time physicians spent with patients. (See Table 9.4.) Frustration with managed care plans, especially HMOs, prompted state legislatures to enact record numbers of consumer protection laws. Figure 9.7 shows both the growing number of states with managed care and consumer protection laws and that all but seven states have mandated external review of health plan decisions.

FIGURE 9.5

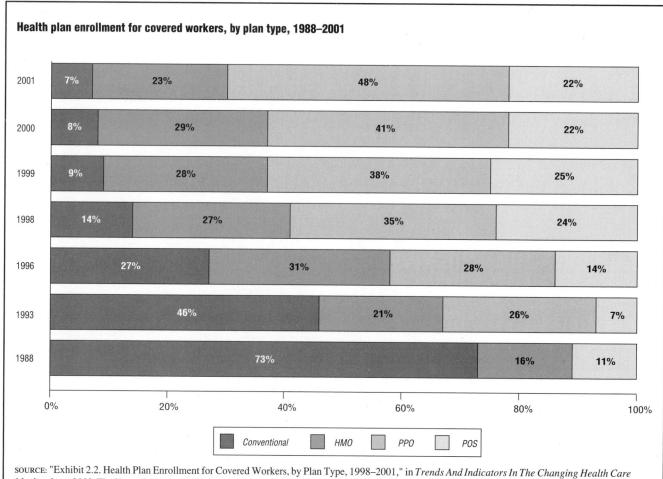

Health plan enrollment for covered workers, by plan type, 1988–2001

SOURCE: "Exhibit 2.2. Health Plan Enrollment for Covered Workers, by Plan Type, 1998–2001," in *Trends And Indicators In The Changing Health Care Marketplace, 2002*, The Henry J. Kaiser Family Foundation, Menlo Park, CA [Online] http://www.kff.org/content/2002/3162/marketplace2002_finalc.pdf [accessed September 12, 2002]

Are Members of For-Profit HMOs Less Satisfied with Care than Members of Nonprofit HMOs?

During the 1980s, about one quarter of all HMO members were enrolled in for-profit HMOs. However, conversion of many not-for-profit plans resulted in a dramatic shift, and by the late 1990s nearly two thirds of HMO members were enrolled in for-profit plans. Some industry observers worried that large, for-profit health plan owners might jeopardize the quality of care delivered by denying members needed services to save money. Investigators Ha Tu and James Reschovsky at the Center for Studying Health System Change in Washington, D.C., looked at the relationship between members' assessments of their care and the profit status of their HMOs to find out if profit status affected members' perceptions of the quality of health care they received.

The investigators examined data from more than 13,000 HMO members and published the results of their analysis in *The New England Journal of Medicine* (vol. 346, no. 17, April 25, 2002). They found that slightly more members of nonprofit HMOs were very satisfied with their care (64 percent) than members of for-profit plans (58.1

percent). In the for-profit HMOs, sick members reported greater dissatisfaction than healthy members, with sick members reporting more delays in receiving care, unmet needs, organizational or administrative obstacles to receiving treatment, and higher out-of-pocket expenses. In nonprofit HMOs, the only difference between sick and healthy members was that sick members expressed greater confidence that they would be referred for care when necessary.

The investigators speculated that while there may have been significant differences in the operation of for-profit and nonprofit plans in the past, in recent years all plans have been subjected to comparable market pressures and economic constraints, rendering the plans nearly indistinguishable from one another in terms of quality and health service delivery.

AMERICANS STILL TRUST HOSPITALS AND THEIR PERSONAL PHYSICIANS

The same May 2002 Harris Poll survey in which Americans condemned managed care plans for failing to meet adequately the needs of consumers, found hospitals high on the list of companies that consumers credited with

FIGURE 9.6

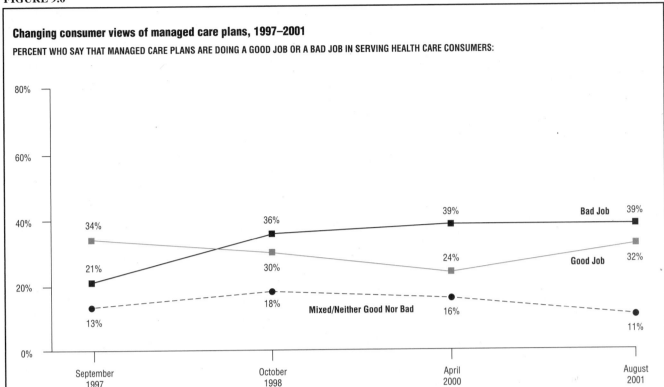

Changing consumer views of managed care plans, 1997–2001

PERCENT WHO SAY THAT MANAGED CARE PLANS ARE DOING A GOOD JOB OR A BAD JOB IN SERVING HEALTH CARE CONSUMERS:

Note: "Don't Know" not shown.

SOURCE: "Exhibit 7.4. Changing Consumer Views of Managed Care Plans, 1997–2001," in *Trends And Indicators In The Changing Health Care Marketplace, 2002*, The Henry J. Kaiser Family Foundation, Menlo Park, CA [Online] http://www.kff.org/content/2002/3162/marketplace2002_finalc.pdf [accessed September 12, 2002]

TABLE 9.4

Consumer views of the impact of managed care, 1997–2001

PERCENT WHO SAY THAT, DURING THE PAST FEW YEARS, HMOs AND OTHER MANAGED CARE PLANS HAVE:

	September 1997	August 1998	April 1999	August 2001
Decreased time doctors spend with patients	61%	64%	61%	67%
Made it harder for sick to see specialists	59%	62%	63%	59%
Not made much difference to health care costs	55%	59%	55%	59%
Decreased quality of health care for sick	51%	50%	50%	54%
Made it easier to get preventive services such as immunizations and health screenings	46%	40%	38%	39%

SOURCE: "Exhibit 7.5. Consumer Views of the Impact of Managed Care, 1997–2001," in *Trends And Indicators In The Changing Health Care Marketplace, 2002*, The Henry J. Kaiser Family Foundation, Menlo Park, CA [Online] http://www.kff.org/content/2002/3162/marketplace2002_finalc.pdf [accessed September 12, 2002]

FIGURE 9.7

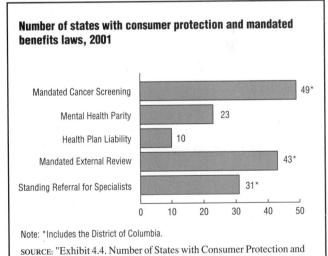

Number of states with consumer protection and mandated benefits laws, 2001

Note: *Includes the District of Columbia.

SOURCE: "Exhibit 4.4. Number of States with Consumer Protection and Mandated Benefit Laws, 2001," in *Trends And Indicators In The Changing Health Care Marketplace, 2002*, The Henry J. Kaiser Family Foundation, Menlo Park, CA [Online] http://www.kff.org/content/2002/3162/marketplace2002_finalc.pdf [accessed September 12, 2002]

good performance records. Nearly three-quarters of survey respondents said they felt hospitals were doing a good job of serving consumers.

While physicians may not enjoy the preeminence and reputations for infallibility they held in the past, most Americans still have confidence in their personal physi-

cians. More than 80 percent of respondents to a 2002 survey conducted by the Kaiser Family Foundation, Harvard University's Kennedy School of Government, and National

TABLE 9.5

Confidence in doctor's ability to do the right thing for patient's care, 2000

"HOW OFTEN DO YOU TRUST THE DOCTOR YOU USUALLY SEE TO DO THE RIGHT THING FOR YOUR CARE? WOULD YOU SAY JUST ABOUT ALWAYS, MOST OF THE TIME, OR ONLY SOME OF THE TIME?"

48%	Just about always
33	Most of the time
16	Only some of the time
2	Do not have a regular doctor (vol.)
*	Don't know

Note: *= less than .5 percent; "vol." = volunteered response

SOURCE: "28. How often do you trust the doctor you usually see to do the right thing for your care? Would you say just about always, most of the time, or only some of the time?," in *National Survey on Health Care: Toplines,* The Henry J. Kaiser Family Foundation, Menlo Park, CA, June 2002

TABLE 9.6

Trust that doctor would inform patient of a mistake in treatment, 2002

"IF A MISTAKE WERE MADE IN YOUR TREATMENT, DO YOU TRUST THE DOCTOR YOU USUALLY SEE TO TELL YOU ABOUT IT, OR NOT?"

77%	Yes, trust the doctor to tell you
20	No, do not trust the doctor to tell you
3	Don't know

Note: Asked of those who have a regular doctor

SOURCE: "29. If a mistake were made in your treatment, do you trust the doctor you usually see to tell you about it, or not?," in *National Survey on Health Care: Toplines,* The Henry J. Kaiser Family Foundation, Menlo Park, CA, June 2002

Public Radio said they trusted their doctor to take correct action "just about always" (48 percent) or "most of the time" (33 percent). (See Table 9.5.) The majority of respondents (77 percent) even expressed confidence that their physicians would inform them if a mistake were made in their care. (See Table 9.6.)

REPORT CARDS MAY HELP CONSUMERS MAKE INFORMED CHOICES

Report cards that grade health plans, hospitals, and other providers offer consumers a way to make accurate comparisons and informed choices. Since the early 1990s the number of agencies, organizations, and employer coalitions issuing report cards has grown. In 1995 the federal government initiated the Consumer Assessment of Health Plans Study (CAHPS) to develop a consumer information project. By 1999, 9 million federal employees had access to CAHPS data about available health plans. In 2002 Medicare beneficiaries also gained access to CAHPS data about Medicare managed care plans. CAHPS data are available to the public in print and on the Internet.

Many federal and state employees as well as workers employed in large corporations have become accustomed to comparing health plans using report cards, but report cards examining the quality of health care systems are relatively new additions to quality improvement and consumer education programs. Researchers from the Health Research Center, Park Nicollet Institute and Minnesota Health Data Institute studied consumer response to report cards that compared health care systems that deliver care rather than health plans that provide insurance coverage. Barbara Braun and her colleagues published their findings in *American Journal of Managed Care* (vol. 8, no. 6, June 2002).

The report cards that the study participants were given measured 7 aspects of care:

• Obtaining care without long waits

• Physician-patient communication

• Courtesy of office staff

• Ease of obtaining needed medical care

• Overall rating of the clinic experience

• Rating of health care provided

• Rating of the health care provider

The investigators found that most study participants had been unaware of the widespread use of report cards to compare health plans and the more recent use of them to measure and compare health service delivery. Nonetheless, the survey participants were very interested in quality measurement and considered report cards to be most valuable in two different circumstances—when they were faced with the personal choice of health care delivery system and as a way to direct system-wide quality improvement efforts. Participants felt they would be most likely to consider report card data if they were dissatisfied with their current providers of medical care. Many said their own personal experiences and the opinions of friends and family would remain their primary and most trusted means of evaluating health care quality.

A Growing Number Look for Health Information Online

Although trust in personal physicians remains high, and many people receive health education from physicians, nurses, and other health professionals, a growing number of Americans are seeking health information online. Harris Poll researchers have dubbed the more than 100 million adults who seek information about specific diseases or tips about how to maintain health on the Internet "cyberchondriacs."

A March 2002 nationwide survey found a steady increase in the percentage of adults seeking health information online between 1998 and 2002. From mid-1998 to March 2002 the number of adults who had looked for health

TABLE 9.7

TABLE 9.8

Frequency of accessing health care information online, 1998–2002

"HOW OFTEN DO YOU LOOK FOR INFORMATION ONLINE ABOUT HEALTH TOPICS—OFTEN, SOMETIMES, HARDLY EVER OR NEVER?"

Base: Have access to Internet

	June/July 1998 %	June 1999 %	March 2001 %	March 2002 %
Often	12	13	16	18
Sometimes	30	30	30	35
Hardly ever	29	31	30	27
Never	29	26	25	20
Total who have ever looked for health or medical information	71	74	75	80
% of all adults who are online*	38	46	63	66
% of all those online who have looked for health information	71	74	75	80
% of all adults who have looked for health information online	27	34	47	53
Numbers of adults who have looked for health information online	54 million	69 million	97 million	110 miilion

*Includes those online from home, office, school, library or other location.

SOURCE: "Table 1: Frequency of Accessing Health Care Information Online: 1998–2002" and "Table 2: Cyberchondriacs: Trends," in *Cyberchondriacs Update,* The Harris Poll #21, Harris Interactive, Rochester, NY, May 1, 2002 [Online] http://www.harrisinteractive.com/harris_poll/index.asp?PID=299 [accessed September 13, 2002]

People who have looked for health information online by demographic characteristics, 2002

	%
% of all adults who have looked for health information online	53
Age	
18–29	82
30–39	68
40–49	63
50–64	49
65 +	26
Sex	
Male	59
Female	60
Education	
High school or less	49
Some College	63
College graduate	75
Post graduate	84
Income	
Less than $15,000	50
$15,000 to $24,999	45
$25,000 to $34,999	55
$35,000 to $49,999	53
$50,000 to $74,999	67
$75,000 and over	77

SOURCE: Humphrey Taylor, "Table 5. Cyberchondriacs Penetration: Demographic profile of people who have looked for health information online," *Cyberchondriacs Update,* The Harris Poll, Harris Interactive, Rochester, NY, May 1, 2002 [Online] http://www.harrisinteractive.com/harris_poll/index.asp?PID=299 [accessed September 13, 2002]

information online more than doubled from 54 million to 110 million. (See Table 9.7.) As of March 2002, about 80 percent of all adults who were online said they sometimes seek health care information on the Internet and, on average, they look for health information three times per month.

Like the most frequent users of the Internet, cyberchondriacs tend to be young adults—82 of those between the ages of 18 and 29 had looked for health information online. Cyberchondriacs also were more likely to have had post-graduate education (84 percent of those adults looking for information online) and were more likely to be wealthier (77 percent of those reporting incomes in excess of $75,000 had looked for information online). (See Table 9.8.)

MARKETING PRESCRIPTION DRUGS TO CONSUMERS

Although health care consumers continue to receive much of their information from physicians, nurses, other health professionals, and the Internet, many also learn about health care services and products from reports in the news media and from advertising. Media advertising—promotion of hospitals, health insurance and managed care plans, medical groups, and related health services and products—has been a mainstay of health care marketing efforts since the 1970s. During the early 1990s, pharmaceutical companies made their first forays into

advertising of prescription drugs directly to consumers. Prior to the 1990s, pharmaceutical companies' promotion efforts had focused almost exclusively on physicians, the health professionals who prescribe their products.

Since the mid 1990s, spending on prescription drugs has escalated and has become the fastest growing segment of U.S. health care expenditures. In 1997 the Food and Drug Administration (FDA) released guidelines governing direct-to-consumer advertising and seemingly opened a floodgate of print, radio, and television advertisements promoting prescription drugs. Industry observers wondered if this upsurge of direct-to-consumer advertising had resulted in more, and possibly inappropriate, prescribing and higher costs.

Researchers from the Harvard School of Public Health and the Sloan School of Management at the Massachusetts Institute of Technology (MIT) examined the relationship between spending for promotional purposes and prescription drug sales and published their findings in the *New England Journal of Medicine* (vol. 346, no. 7, February 14, 2002). The researchers observed that pharmaceutical companies' budgets for promotion increased from $266 million in 1994 to almost $2.5 billion in 2000 and that television advertising, which accounted for 13 percent of direct-to-consumer promotions in 1994 and 64 percent in 2000, contributed to this growth. They found that direct-to-consumer

FIGURE 9.8

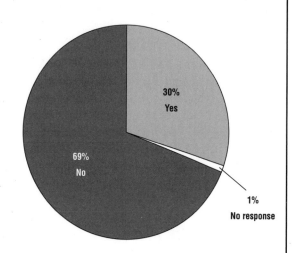

Patient requests for medicines advertised directly to consumers, 2001

"AS A RESULT OF SEEING ANY AD FOR A PRESCRIPTION MEDICINE, HAVE YOU EVER TALKED WITH A DOCTOR ABOUT THE SPECIFIC MEDICINE YOU SAW ADVERTISED?"

30% Yes

69% No

1% No response

AMONG THE 30% WHO TALKED TO THEIR DOCTOR ABOUT ANY MEDICINE THEY SAW ADVERTISED... "DID YOUR DOCTOR..."

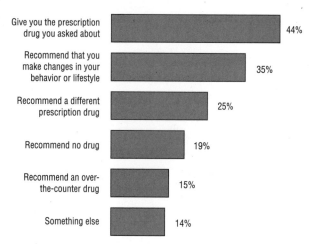

Give you the prescription drug you asked about — 44%

Recommend that you make changes in your behavior or lifestyle — 35%

Recommend a different prescription drug — 25%

Recommend no drug — 19%

Recommend an over-the-counter drug — 15%

Something else — 14%

Note: Multiple responses accepted.

SOURCE: Mollyann Brodie, "Chart 1. Talking with a Doctor about an Advertised Medicine" and "Chart 2. What did your doctor do?," in *Understanding the Effects of Direct-to-Consumer Prescription Drug Advertising,* The Henry J. Kaiser Family Foundation, Menlo Park, CA, November 2001 [Online] http://www.kff.org/content/2001/20011129a/ mollyfinalchartpack.pdf [accessed September 13, 2002]

TABLE 9.9

Recall among viewers of the potential side effects of three advertised drugs, 2001

PERCENT WHO *CORRECTLY* IDENTIFIED POTENTIAL SIDE EFFECTS NAMED IN THE AD...

Lipitor	
Liver problems	74%
Muscle pain/weakness	42%
Nexium	
Diarrhea	54%
Abdominal pain	53%
Headache	47%
Singulair	
Headache	51%
Flu	29%
Runny nose	29%
Ear infection	28%

SOURCE: Mollyann Brodie, "Chart 8. Recall Among Viewers: Potential Side Effects," in *Understanding the Effects of Direct-to-Consumer Prescription Drug Advertising,* The Henry J. Kaiser Family Foundation, Menlo Park, CA, November 2001 [Online] http://www.kff.org/content/2001/20011129a/ mollyfinalchartpack.pdf [accessed September 13, 2002]

consumer advertising investments in order to justify increasing budgets for consumer advertising, but it is difficult to measure the precise impact of consumer advertising on drug sales. The Harvard and MIT researchers observed that consumer awareness of prescription drug ads, in terms of adults surveyed who reported having seen drug ads, has more than doubled from nearly 40 percent in 1993 to more than 90 percent of consumers surveyed in 2000.

Mollyann Brodie evaluated consumers' reactions to drug ads by showing research participants actual prescription drug ads and recording their responses. In *Understanding the Effects of Direct-to-Consumer Prescription Drug Advertising* (Henry J. Kaiser Family Foundation, Washington, DC, November 2001), Brodie reported that one in three adults said they talked with their doctor after seeing an ad for a prescription drug and nearly half of those who spoke with their physicians about the drug (44 percent) received a prescription for that drug. (See Figure 9.8.) Brodie also found that two-thirds of consumers who viewed prescription drug ads trusted the information they received in the ads and 84 percent said the ads did an excellent or good job informing them about the condition that the advertised drug was intended to treat. Despite the ad viewers' perception that they were well informed, Brodie found that recall about potential drug side effects, and viewer knowledge about where they could find more information about the advertised medication, varied widely. (See Table 9.9.) In view of the speed with which some television drug ads announce potential side effects and adverse reactions, it was not surprising that as many as 75 percent of viewers could not accurately identify many of the advertised drug's side effects.

advertising was generally used to promote long-term-use drugs prescribed for chronic conditions such as allergies, elevated blood cholesterol, and ulcers.

Is Direct-to-Consumer Advertising Effective?

It stands to reason that pharmaceutical companies must be receiving significant returns on their direct-to-

IMPORTANT NAMES AND ADDRESSES

Accreditation Association for Ambulatory Health Care, Inc.
3201 Old Glenview Rd., Suite 300
Wilmette, IL 60091-2992
(847) 853-6060
FAX: (847) 853-9028
E-mail: info@aaahc.org
URL: http://www.aaahc.org

American Academy of Physician Assistants
950 North Washington St.
Alexandria, VA 22314-1552
(703) 836-2272
FAX: (703) 684-1924
E-mail: aapa@aapa.org
URL: http://www.aapa.org

American Cancer Society
1599 Clifton Rd. NE
Atlanta, GA 30329-4251
(404) 320-3333
Toll-free: (800) ACS-2345
URL: http://www.cancer.org

American Chiropractic Association
1701 Clarendon Blvd.
Arlington, VA 22209
FAX: (703) 243-2593
Toll-free: (800) 986-4636
E-mail: memberinfor@amerchiro.org
URL: http://www.amerchiro.org

American Dental Association
211 E. Chicago Ave.
Chicago, IL 60611
(312) 440-2500
FAX: (312) 440-2800
URL: http://www.ada.org

American Diabetes Association
1701 N. Beauregard St.
Alexandria, VA 22311
(703) 549-1500
FAX: (703) 836-7439
Toll-free: (800) DIABETES

E-mail: askADA@diabetes.org
URL: http://www.diabetes.org

American Heart Association
7272 Greenville Ave.
Dallas, TX 75231
(214) 373-6300
FAX: (214) 706-1341
Toll-free: (800) AHA-USA1
URL: http://www.americanheart.org

American Hospital Association
1 N. Franklin
Chicago, IL 60606
(312) 422-3000
FAX: (312) 422-4796
Toll-free: (800) 424-4301
URL: http://www.aha.org

American Medical Association
515 N. State St.
Chicago, IL 60610
(312) 464-5000
FAX: (312) 464-4184
URL: http://www.ama-assn.org

American Osteopathic Association
142 East Ontario St.
Chicago, IL 60611
(312) 202-8000
FAX: (312) 202-8200
Toll-free: (800) 621-1773
E-mail: info@aoa-net.org
URL: http://www.aoa-net.org

American Physical Therapy Association
1111 North Fairfax St.
Alexandria, VA 22314-1488
(703) 684-2782
FAX: (703) 683-7343
Toll-free: (800) 999-2782
E-mail: public-relations@apta.org
URL: http://www.apta.org

Association of American Medical Colleges
2450 N St. NW
Washington, DC 20037-1126
(202) 828-0400
FAX: (202) 828-1125
URL: http://www.aamc.org

Centers for Disease Control and Prevention
1600 Clifton Rd.
Atlanta, GA 30333
(404) 639-3311
Toll-frree: (800) 311-3435
URL: http://www.cdc.gov

Centers for Medicare & Medicaid Services (CMS)
7500 Security Blvd.
Baltimore, MD 21244-1850
(410) 786-3000
Toll-free: (877) 267-2323
URL: http://www.cms.gov

Children's Defense Fund
25 E St. NW
Washington, DC 20001
(202) 628-8787
FAX: (202) 662-3510
E-mail: cdfinfo@childrensdefense.org
URL: http://www.childrensdefense.org

Families USA
1334 G St. NW
Washington, DC 20005
(202) 628-3030
FAX: (202) 347-2417
E-mail: info@familiesusa.org
URL: http://www.familiesusa.org

Hospice Association of America
228 7th St. SE
Washington, DC 20003
(202) 546-4759
FAX: (202) 547-9559
URL: http://www.nahc.org/HAA

Joint Commission on Accreditation of Healthcare Organizations (JCAHO)
1 Rennissance Blvd.
Oakbrook Terrace, IL 60181
(630) 792-5000
FAX: (630) 792-5005
Toll-free: (800) 994-6610
URL: http://www.jcaho.org

March of Dimes Birth Defects Foundation, National Office
1275 Mamaroneck Ave.
White Plains, NY 10605
(914) 997-4525
Toll-free: 888 MODIMES (663-4637)
URL: http://www.modimes.org

National Association of Public Hospitals and Health Systems
1301 Pennsylvania Ave. NW, Suite 950
Washington, DC 20004
(202) 585-0100
FAX: (202) 585-0101
E-mail: NAPH@naph.org
URL: http://www.naph.org

National Center for Health Statistics U.S. Department of Health and Human Services
6525 Belcrest Rd.
Hyattsville, MD 20782-2003
(301) 458-4636
FAX: (301) 436-4258
URL: http://www.cdc.gov/nchs

United Network for Organ Sharing
1100 Boulders Pkwy., Suite 500
P.O. Box 13770
Richmond, VA 23225-8770
(804) 330-8500
FAX: (804) 330-8507
Toll-free: (888) TXINFO1
URL: http://www.unos.org

RESOURCES

Agencies of the U.S. Department of Health and Human Services (HHS) collect, analyze, and publish a wide variety of health statistics that describe and measure the operation and effectiveness of the American health care system. The Centers for Disease Control and Prevention (CDC) in Atlanta, Georgia, tracks nationwide health trends and reports its findings in several periodicals, especially its *Advance Data* series, *National Ambulatory Medical Care Survey, HIV/AIDS Surveillance Reports,* and *Morbidity and Mortality Weekly Reports.* The National Center for Health Statistics (NCHS) provides a complete statistical overview of the nation's health in its annual *Health, United States.*

The National Institutes of Health (NIH) provide definitions, epidemiological data, and research findings about a comprehensive range of medical and public health subjects. The Centers for Medicare and Medicaid Services (CMMS) monitor the nation's health spending. The agency's quarterly *Health Care Financing Review* and annual *Data Compendium* provide complete information on health care spending, particularly allocations for Medicare and Medicaid. The Administration on Aging (AoA) provides information about the health, welfare, and services available for older Americans.

The Agency for Healthcare Research and Quality (AHRQ) researches and documents access to health care, quality of care, and efforts to control health care costs. It also examines the safety of health care services and ways to prevent medical errors. The Joint Commission on Accreditation of Healthcare Organizations (JCAHO) and the National Committee for Quality Assurance (NCQA) are accrediting organizations that focus attention on institutional health care providers including the managed care industry.

The Bureau of the Census, in its *Current Population Reports* series, details the status of insurance among selected American households.

Medical, public health, and nursing journals offer a wealth of health care system information and research findings. The studies cited in this edition are drawn from a range of professional publications including the *Journal of the American Medical Association, Annals of Internal Medicine, New England Journal of Medicine, Health Affairs, The American Journal of Managed Care,* and *Journal of Nursing Administration.*

The Harris Interactive/The Harris Poll were used as sources of public opinion research about employer-sponsored health plans and accessing health information online. Also helpful was the Organisation for Economic Cooperation and Development's information from its *Comprehensive Analysis of 30 Countries: 2002 Edition.* Families USA data from *Profiting from Pain: Where Prescription Drug Dollars Go,* Washington DC, 2002 was used for information about prescription drugs. Also of use was the Henry J. Kaiser Family Foundation's information from its many reports, including *Seniors and Prescription Drugs Findings from a 2001 Survey of Seniors in Eight States, Employer Health Benefits, 2001 Annual Survey, Trends and Indicators in the Changing Health Care Marketplace, 2002, National Survey on Health Care,* and *Understanding the Effects of Direct-to-Consumer Prescription Drug Advertising.* Our thanks also go to the many professional associations, voluntary medical organizations, and foundations dedicated to research, education, and advocacy about efforts to reform and improve the health care system that were included in this edition.

INDEX

A

AAAHC (Accreditation Association for Ambulatory Health Care, Inc.), 75–76

Access to care
children's, 6–9, 8t–9t, 10t–11t, 12(f1.7), 13t–14t, 15t
community needs, 3
financial barriers, 5f, 6(f1.4), 7f, 15(t1.6)
insurance, 3–4, 4t, 8t–9t, 9, 15t
providers' roles, 2–3
public opinion, 146, 146f
race/ethnicity, 4–5, 7–8, 7(f1.6), 13t–14t
regular sources of care, 3–4, 4t, 6(f1.3), 10t–11t
right to, 9
See also Consumers; Patients

Accountability and transparency, 142–143

Accreditation, 74–76
See also Oversight

Accreditation Association for Ambulatory Health Care, Inc. (AAAHC), 75–76

ACF (Administration for Children and Families), 66

ACS (American Cancer Society), 76–77

Acupuncture, 36

Administration for Children and Families (ACF), 66

Administration on Aging (AoA), 66

Advertising, prescription drug, 153–154, 154f, 154t

African Americans. *See* Race/ethnicity

Agency for Healthcare Research and Quality (AHRQ), 4–5, 66

Agency for Toxic Substances and Disease Registry (ATSDR), 66

AHA (American Hospital Association), 76

AHRQ (Agency for Healthcare Research and Quality), 4–5, 66

AIDS. *See* HIV/AIDS

Allied health care providers, 30–32, 33(t2.8)

Alternative medicine, 34–37

AMA (American Medical Association), 76

Ambulatory care facilities
accreditation, 75–76
Germany, 126–127
surgery centers, 52

American Cancer Society (ACS), 76–77

American Heart Association, 76

American Hospital Association (AHA), 76

American Medical Association (AMA), 76

American Nurses Association (ANA), 76

AoA (Administration on Aging), 66

Applications, medical school, 19

ATSDR (Agency for Toxic Substances and Disease Registry), 66

B

Balanced Budget Act of 1977, 58

Behavioral Risk Factor Surveillance System (BRFSS) surveys, 3–4

Bigby, Judy Ann, 8

Birth defects, 77

BRFSS (Behavioral Risk Factor Surveillance System) surveys, 3–4

Brodie, Mollyann, 154

Byock, Ira, 59

C

Caesarean sections, 127t

Canada, 127–128, 130–131

Cancer
American Cancer Society (ACS), 76–77
rates, international comparison of, 131t

Centers for Disease Control and Prevention (CDC)
Behavioral Risk Factor Surveillance System (BRFSS) surveys, 3–4
overview, 69–71
patient safety, 136–137

Centers for Medicare and Medicaid Services (CMMS), 66, 136

Children
access to care, 6–9, 8t–9t, 10t–11t, 12(f1.7), 13t–14t, 15t
emergency room visits, 41t–43t
health insurance, 8t–9t, 10t–11t, 13t–14t, 15t, 110–112, 117f

Chinese medicine, traditional, 36

Chiropractors, 36–37

Clinical practice guidelines (CPGs), 139–140

Clinics, medical, 1

CMMS (Centers for Medicare and Medicaid Services), 66, 136

Commissioned Corps, U.S. Public Health Service, 67, 69

Communication
innovations, 142–143
online physician-patient, 141

Community hospitals, 39–40

Community needs, 3

Compensation, physicians', 21–22

Complementary and alternative medicine, 34–37

Components of the health care system, 2

Consumer Price Index (CPI), 79, 82t

Consumers
access to health quality information, 142–143, 152–153, 153t
characteristics, 2
complementary and alternative medicine, 34–35, 37
factors affecting attitudes, 145–146
Families USA, 97–98
health care fraud, 139
health industry report cards, 152
health insurance satisfaction, 147–150, 149t
hospital satisfaction, 150–151
medical error, 137–138, 138f
online information for, 152–153, 153t
physician satisfaction, 151–152, 152t
prescription drug advertising, 153–154, 154f, 154t
protection laws, 151(f9.7)
See also Access to care; Patients; Public opinion

Costs
access to care, 5f, 6(f1.4), 7f, 15(t1.6)
affect on consumer attitudes, 145
affordability of care and insurance, 146–147, 147(f9.3)
as percent of gross domestic product (GDP), 79, 119–120
Canada, 128, 130
consumer groups, 97–98
controlling, 86–90, 130–132
Families USA, 97–98